RULING BY CHEATING

There is widespread agreement that democracy today faces unprecedented challenges. Populism has pushed governments in new and surprising constitutional directions. Analyzing the constitutional system of illiberal democracies (from Venezuela to Poland) and illiberal phenomena in "mature democracies" that are justified in the name of "the will of the people," this book explains that this drift to mild despotism is not authoritarianism, but an abuse of constitutionalism. Illiberal governments claim that they are as democratic and constitutional as any other. They also claim that they are more popular and therefore more genuine because their rule is based on traditional, plebeian, and "patriotic" constitutional and rule of law values rather than the values liberals espouse. However, this book shows that these claims are deeply deceptive – and constitute an abuse of constitutionalism and the rule of law, not a different conception of these ideas.

ANDRÁS SAJÓ is University Professor at Central European University and a former Vice-President-Judge at the European Court of Human Rights. He holds an honorary doctorate from the European University Institute and visiting professorships at Cardozo Law School, University of Chicago Law School, NYU Law School, and Harvard Law School. His recent publications include *Constitutional Sentiments* (2011) and, with Renáta Uitz, *The Constitution of Freedom* (2017).

CAMBRIDGE STUDIES IN CONSTITUTIONAL LAW

The aim of this series is to produce leading monographs in constitutional law. All areas of constitutional law and public law fall within the ambit of the series, including human rights and civil liberties law, administrative law, as well as constitutional theory and the history of constitutional law. A wide variety of scholarly approaches is encouraged, with the governing criterion being simply that the work is of interest to an international audience. Thus, works concerned with only one jurisdiction will be included in the series as appropriate, while, at the same time, the series will include works which are explicitly comparative or theoretical – or both. The series editor likewise welcomes proposals that work at the intersection of constitutional and international law, or that seek to bridge the gaps between civil law systems, the USA, and the common law jurisdictions of the Commonwealth.

Series Editors
David Dyzenhaus
Professor of Law and Philosophy, University of Toronto, Canada
Thomas Poole
Professor of Law, London School of Economics and Political Science

Editorial Advisory Board
T.R.S. Allan, Cambridge, UK
Damian Chalmers, LSE, UK
Sujit Choudhry, Berkeley, USA
Monica Claes, Maastricht, Netherlands
David Cole, Georgetown, USA
K.D. Ewing, King's College London, UK
David Feldman, Cambridge, UK
Cora Hoexter, Witwatersrand, South Africa
Christoph Moellers, Humboldt, Germany
Adrienne Stone, Melbourne, Australia
Adam Tomkins, Glasgow, UK
Adrian Vermeule, Harvard, USA

Books in the series

Ruling by Cheating: Governance in Illiberal Democracy
András Sajó

Local Meanings of Proportionality
Afroditi Marketou

Property Rights and Social Justice: Progressive Property in Action
Rachael Walsh

RULING BY CHEATING

Governance in Illiberal Democracy

ANDRÁS SAJÓ

Central European University, Budapest

CAMBRIDGE
UNIVERSITY PRESS

CAMBRIDGE
UNIVERSITY PRESS

University Printing House, Cambridge CB2 8BS, United Kingdom

One Liberty Plaza, 20th Floor, New York, NY 10006, USA

477 Williamstown Road, Port Melbourne, VIC 3207, Australia

314–321, 3rd Floor, Plot 3, Splendor Forum, Jasola District Centre,
New Delhi – 110025, India

79 Anson Road, #06–04/06, Singapore 079906

Cambridge University Press is part of the University of Cambridge.

It furthers the University's mission by disseminating knowledge in the pursuit of
education, learning, and research at the highest international levels of excellence.

www.cambridge.org
Information on this title: www.cambridge.org/9781108844635
DOI: 10.1017/9781108952996

© András Sajó 2021

First published 2021

An earlier version of Chapter 6 was originally published in *Critical Essays on Human Rights
Criticism*, edited by András Sajó and Renáta Uitz, and has been reproduced with the
permission of Eleven International Publishing.

A catalogue record for this publication is available from the British Library.

Library of Congress Cataloging-in-Publication Data
Names: Sajó, András, author.
Title: Ruling by cheating : governance in illiberal democracy / András Sajó, Central
European University, Budapest.
Description: Cambridge, United Kingdom ; New York, NY : Cambridge University Press,
2021. | Series: Cambridge studies in constitutional law | Includes index.
Identifiers: LCCN 2021014742 | ISBN 9781108844635 (hardback) | ISBN 9781108948630
(paperback) | ISBN 9781108952996 (ebook)
Subjects: LCSH: Abuse of administrative power. | Legitimacy of governments. |
Constitutional law. | People (Constitutional law) | Rule of law. | Human rights. |
Totalitarianism. | Democracy.
Classification: LCC K3416 .S25 2021 | DDC 342–dc23
LC record available at https://lccn.loc.gov/2021014742

ISBN 978-1-108-84463-5 Hardback
ISBN 978-1-108-94863-0 Paperback

CONTENTS

vii

ACKNOWLEDGMENTS

This book was inspired by discussions with my late friend, Professor Tamás Sárközy, a brilliant observer of the techniques of illiberal governance. Many people helped me to develop this manuscript. Martin Krygier and Gianluigi Palombella convinced me about the virtues of the ideal of the rule of law, which were hard to see amidst its systematic abuse. Martin Krygier, Monroe Price and Renáta Uitz provided important comments. Dorjana Bojanovska and Kylia Cassone, my students at Central European University, provided editorial help, and Joseph Shaw edited the text with extreme care on behalf of the Publisher. I am grateful to Eleven International Publishing (Boom Uitgevers) for allowing me to use an earlier version of Chapter 6 ("The Fate of Human Rights in Indifferent Societies – (i.e. More and More Constitutional Democracies)," in A. Sajó and R. Uitz, [eds.], *Critical Essays on Human Rights Criticism* [2019]). The ideas on plebiscitarian leader democracy and neopatrimonial domination in illiberal democracy were presented at my Illiberal Democracy courses held at Central European University, NYU Law School and Harvard Law School (2017–19) and in a lecture held in honor of Grazyna Skapska in Krakow in June 2018 (A. Sajó, "The Constitution of Illiberal Democracy as a Theory About Society," *Polish Sociological Review,* 208:4 (2019), pp. 395–412).

Special thanks go to Cara Stern for her most generous support improving the text. I would like to express my gratitude to Central European University (still in Budapest at the time of writing this book) and its Democracy Institute for generous spiritual and financial support. This book was written in memory of and inspired by CEU, Budapest. May it rise from the ashes!

ABBREVIATIONS

AKP	Turkish Justice and Development Party (*Adalet ve Kalkınma Partisi*)
CJEU	Court of Justice of the European Union
ECHR	European Convention on Human Rights
ECtHR	European Court of Human Rights
GFCC	German Federal Constitutional Court
HCC	Hungarian Constitutional Court
HFL	Fundamental Law of Hungary
HPM	Hungarian Prime Minister (Viktor Orbán)
IACtHR	Inter-American Court of Human Rights
PCT	Polish Constitutional Tribunal
PiS	Polish Law and Justice Party (*Prawo i Sprawiedliwość*)
PLD	Plebiscitarian leader democracy
RoL	Rule of law
SCOTUS	Supreme Court of the United States
TCC	Turkish Constitutional Court
TSJ	Venezuelan Supreme Tribunal of Justice (*Tribunal Supremo de Justicia*)

~

Introduction

> ... commencing demagogues and ending tyrants.
>
> Alexander Hamilton[1]

In the last twenty years populist movements have given birth to a growing number of illiberal democracies, including Hungary, Poland, Turkey, and Venezuela, and so-called "mature democracies" are increasingly tempted by these examples. Antiliberal popular sentiment is challenging the hegemony of the liberal institutions that saw themselves as the only legitimate and possible political organization of modernity. When democratic regimes reject concerns about liberalism, what is the impact on constitutional discourse? What lies beneath these developments? Have power-hungry demagogues hijacked democracy? Have desperate citizens simply been manipulated?

Scholarly opinion in the United States and Western Europe too often believed that illiberal darkness reigns only in faraway forests: "it can't happen here."[2] The history of fascism shows otherwise. Overly confident democracies have paid an immense price for their careless shortsightedness. The prevailing understanding of illiberal regimes,[3] particularly those that emerge from populist movements, is that we are facing a *general* "democratic backlash."[4] Increasingly, contemporary political

---

[1] A. Hamilton, J. Madison, and J. Jay, *The Federalist Papers. No. 1* (Mentor Book, 1961), p. 35.

[2] See, for example, E. Posner and A. Vermeule, *The Executive Unbound* (Oxford University Press, 2010), p. 176.

[3] "Regime" refers to a political arrangement where the probability that the ruling force will lose power in the foreseeable future is very low. However, because of the democratic nature of the illiberal regime, the leader and his party, aspiring to have continuous popular support forever, may lose (see the fate of Evo Morales).

[4] The allegory of a backlash is intuitively attractive as it presupposes a pre-existing state of affairs that is related to a self-perfecting democracy. See J. M. Balkin and S. V. Levinson "The Processes of Constitutional Change: From Partisan Entrenchment to the National Surveillance State," *Fordham Law Review*, 75:2 (2006), pp. 489–535. General democratic

1

science (and, to a lesser degree, constitutional theory) agrees that the phenomena that undermine democracy are not limited to so-called "new democracies," where democracy is not historically and culturally rooted.

Today, the international community considers democracy as the only form of legitimate government. Populist leaders understand its continuing pull, and all emerging illiberal democracies are eager to present themselves as democratic: more democratic than the predecessor system, which betrayed democracy and the people. In the struggle between the people and the elite, the people's will, as molded by the political orientation of the populist leader, must win at any cost. At the same time, with pride and anti-elitist arrogance, these regimes declare themselves to be illiberal in line with the dreams of their "authentic" people. With illiberalism unleashed, populism in power turns its actions against constitutionalism. Democracy here takes the shape of a plebiscitarian leader democracy (PLD), a concept used by Max Weber, who proposed it for Germany after the collapse of the German Empire in 1918. "PLD . . . is an authority and regime type with authoritarian traits, like charismatic leadership, generated by the internal logic of modern mass democracy per se."[5]

PLD, née *Führer-Demokratie*, has an understandably bad reputation within academia, which excommunicates contemporary plebiscitarian regimes from the temple of democracy and labels illiberal democracies as kinds of authoritarian regime.[6] However, one should not confuse the "inherent tendency to authoritarian rule," which originates from "[t]he irresistible presidentialization of democracy,"[7] with actual authoritarian

backlash is defined as a large-scale democratic change in institutional arrangements that lead to democratic erosion. When presidents can appoint enough judges and justices, constitutional doctrines start to change, and democracies turn into illiberal surveillance states.

Undeniably, populism-generated changes rely on erosion techniques, but in a concentrated way. The ongoing erosion and related value shifts in dominant democracies facilitate illiberal institution building. See, for example, the "liberating" impact of the global human rights erosion on Eastern European rights restrictions, in Chapter 6.

[5] A. Körösényi, "The Theory and Practice of Plebiscitary Leadership: Weber and the Orbán regime," *East European Politics and Societies and Cultures*, 33:2 (2019), p. 283. Contrary to Max Weber, Körösényi claims that "PLD, unlike competitive authoritarianism, is not a combination of democratic and authoritarian elements, but it is democratic (formally) and authoritarian (substantively) simultaneously."

[6] A characteristic term used to indicate that regimes are no longer democratic is "competitive authoritarianism." S. Levitsky and L. Way, *Competitive Authoritarianism: Hybrid Regimes after the Cold War* (Cambridge University Press, 2010).

[7] P. Rosanvallon, *Good Government: Democracy Beyond Elections* (Harvard University Press, 2018), p. 114.

rule. An illiberal PLD has a destructive potential and can turn into despotism: not the despotism of the multitude (as citizens will be prevented from decision-making), but despotism in the name of the people. The democratic ideal of popular participation in decision-making (popular self-government) is transformed into support for the leader in imperfect elections, where the leader caters only to his people, and where only the "real" people (often construed as an ethnic, tribal community) is relevant. While the government may be formed through imperfect elections, (often sizable) majorities stand behind legislation that does not depart from the preferences of the majority.

In view of this contradiction, the working hypothesis of this book is that illiberal democracies belong to the democratic family in the original Rousseauist understanding of democracy. Democracy, as understood by Rousseau, has a totalitarian *potential*. The totalitarian potential of democracy is not to be confused with the standard meaning of totalitarianism provided by Arendt. Democracy is potentially totalitarian, not in the sense of being all-encompassing but for having the potential to become a single-voice regime. Illiberal democracies unfold the already existing oppressive potential of democracies not by silencing and extirpating opposition but by making opposition completely irrelevant. But illiberal democracies in which the totalitarian potential of democracy unfolds remain concerned of the electorate, or at least its majority, and respond to their private needs and desires, contrary to actual totalitarian regimes, which insist on imposing their single, messianistic world view on all subjects. "The authoritarian traits of PLD are endogenous to democracy, which is quite an unconventional result for democratic theory."[8] The plebiscitarianism of leader democracy, with its emphasis on the people's sovereign (i.e. unlimited) power, extracts totalitarianism. Populism in power often enhances democracy with its inclusionary policies; however, this often leads to concentrated power in the executive and growing totalitarianism. This is what happened under Juan Perón and Hugo Chávez; they both used laws instrumentally to repress dissent and "made use of the state apparatus to colonise the public sphere and civil society."[9]

The regimes that originate in populist movements, and are conceived in populist terms, should be understood "as an internal periphery of

---

[8] Körösényi, "The Theory," p. 283.
[9] C. de la Torre, "Populism and Nationalism in Latin America," *Javnost – The Public*, 24:4 (2017), p. 375.

democratic politics," consisting in "a region where the distinction between inside and outside is a matter of dispute and cannot be thought outside a polemic."[10]

The study of the illiberal order helps to identify the shortcomings of the democratic constitutional system and fight the self-destructive complacency of the "it can't happen here" attitude. Authoritarianism is not a foreign country. The mirror of illiberalism reflects the weaknesses of the liberal. A resilient democracy must look into this mirror – before it is too late.[11] Populism and illiberal democracy do not just challenge normative theories; they expose the totalitarian and authoritarian in liberal constitutionalism, as well as the technical shortcomings of constitutional democracies. Illiberal democracies rely upon and expose the *inherent contradictions* of democracy and the rule of law (RoL), namely that democracy has an inherently totalitarian potential. Plebiscitarian democracies are the manifestation of this potential, enabled by the illiberal and even authoritarian elements of an intellectually and politically enfeebled constitutionalism and the local imperfections of the constitutional order. The discussion of illiberal PLD within the framework of democracy offers an opportunity to understand democracy and constitutional democracy in their deepest and most troubling contradictions and weaknesses. This applies just as much to building theory as it does to the practical reinforcement of constitutional democracy.

This book discusses the constitutional (public law) order of illiberal democracy as a regime[12] that continues to take the twisted form of democracy while pursuing its leader's decisive interest in holding on to power. It does not aim to reconstruct a constitutional theory out of the fragments of populist illiberal constitutional rhetoric and action,

---

[10] B. Arditi, *Politics on the Edges of Liberalism* (Edinburgh University Press, 2007), p. 2. See also P.-A. Taguieff, *L'illusion populiste* (Flammarion, 2007); E. Laclau, *On Populist Reason* (Verso, 2005); and C. Pinelli, "The Rise of Populism in Europe and the Malaise of Constitutional Democracies," in S. Garben, I. Govaere, and P. Nemitz (eds.), *Critical Reflections on Constitutional Democracy in the European Union* (Hart, 2019). Pinelli argues that constitutional democracies have a built-in flexibility that has absorbed de-structuring tensions, but that now face challenges through their own institutions.

[11] K. L. Scheppele, "The Opportunism of Populists and the Defense of Constitutional Liberalism," *German Law Journal*, 20:3 (2019), p. 315. "Populists expose the vulnerabilities in the theories that our profession has taken for granted ... [and] are also a challenge to ... the normative defensibility of liberal constitutionalism." See in a similar sense D. Landau, "Populist Constitutions," *University of Chicago Law Review*, 85 (2018), pp. 521–43.

[12] This book uses the terms illiberal democracy, illiberal regime, plebiscitarianism and regime interchangeably.

although a "theory of cheating" (including lies, deceit, fraud, spin, tricks, etc.) in constitutional law will inevitably emerge. The plebiscitarian leader democracies that emerge from populism are ruled by all efforts to conceal the truth in order to mislead. "Cheating" is pretending to observe a rule in order to depart from it, often reaping undeserved benefits from those cheated; "in violating a rule that others follow, and thereby breaching an obligation to restrict his liberty in a manner agreed, the cheater gains an unfair advantage."[13] In the act of cheating, the cheater – the plebiscitarian leader – (mis)represents himself as norm-observant.[14] The illiberal regimes relying on systemic cheating pretend to satisfy the requirements of the RoL by following specific rules that seem applicable, but they do so in disregard of the relevant standards or principles of the RoL. A regime that cheats in its use of the law breaches a promise of "truth" or authenticity that the underlying norms of the game will be observed.

To conceive PLD as a member of the democracy family is troubling, or even an offensive sacrilege, to many constitutional scholars (and committed democrats). It compromises the impeccability of the democratic ideal and the noble character of the people, a cornerstone of Jacobin thinking: "Any institution which does not suppose the people good, and the magistrate corruptible, is evil."[15] Most scholars of populism and illiberal democracy nurture strong emotions and have intellectual or moral reservations regarding the subject of their study. This is a problem: passionate analysis is self-blinding. Feeling sympathy or antipathy toward the source of their livelihood would seem unprofessional to forensic scientists interpreting the results of an autopsy. Academia's common and well-deserved contempt toward illiberal democracy and populism only helps populism. Populists thrive on scorn by

---

[13] S. P. Green, *Lying, Cheating, and Stealing: A Moral Theory of White-Collar Crime* (Oxford University Press, 2007), p. 55. See further M. S. Quinn, "Practice-Defining Rules," *Ethics*, 86:1 (1975), pp. 76–86.

[14] I will refer to the "leader," "cheater," and "ruler" throughout this book using male pronouns since there have been no women PLD leaders to date (Isabel Perón and Cristina Kirchner come close but they both inherited their position from their late husbands). The leaders this book focuses on (of Hungary, Poland, Turkey, and Venezuela) are all men. Male dominance is part and parcel of macho populist leadership: illiberal policies regarding the family emphasize traditional female roles and the leaders' rhetoric is quite macho.

[15] M. Robespierre, *Déclaration des droits de l'homme et du citoyen, présentée par Maximilien Robespierre* [in French] (de l'Impr. Patriotique et Républicaine, 1793), art. xxx, p. 10, www.gallica.bnf.fr/ark:/12148/bpt6k62625013/f14.image. English translation listed in *The Concise Dictionary of Foreign Quotations* (Fitzroy Dearborn Publishers, 2001), p. 117.

"dominant elite forces."[16] After the initial excommunication from the realm of respectable politics, the strategy of quarantine backfires: successful populist leaders have learned how to neutralize the labels of populism and illiberalism by proudly declaring them a badge of honor.[17]

Whatever moral and political assumptions they may have about the people and democracy, scholars must learn to live with ambiguous concepts and phenomena, rather than pursuing politically driven research agendas or counterproductive excommunication strategies. Democracy is ambiguous: "an understanding of democracy cannot be separated from an understanding of its perversions."[18] Those who imagine democracy (even its ideal) as being without inner contradictions and inherently troubling traits (like the emotionalism of the masses) mimic populist simplifications. Populism, and its victorious version in illiberal democracy, is not simply the plot of another, demagogic elite or a manipulative imposition of a false identity on a victimized population: populism remains democracy, but one that is plagued by an illiberalism that undermines constitutionalism. The conviction that illiberal regimes are not democratic, and that their support is illegitimate because elections are manipulated, results in a methodological error that cannot see the genuine popular embrace of plebiscitarian leaders. Such regimes derive legitimacy from their democratic credentials: the system, manipulative as it is, enables citizens to express their support (and even rejection). Academics cannot underestimate the importance, sincerity, and legitimacy of popular support for the leader and his regime, even if this support is based on xenophobic and authoritarian predispositions, or conservative patriotism in search of recognition. These regimes may or may not be democracies in an ideal sense of the term, but they *operate* democratically: their political organs are the same as those in "respected" democracies and are construed by the same democratic (electoral) processes. This gives legitimacy (power) to the regime, and to disregard it on the basis of an abstract and sterile ideal of democracy only serves the populists. In their propaganda, such positions represent another act of external disrespect of the Nation, based on obvious factual errors, deliberately spread by foreign conspirators.

---

[16] For an example, see J. Rancière, *Hatred of Democracy* (Verso, 2006).

[17] J. P. Zúquete, "From Left to Right and Beyond," in C. de la Torre (ed.), *Routledge Handbook of Global Populism* (Routledge, 2018), p. 417. Zúquete provides a review of "anti-populist demagoguery" and its dangers.

[18] P. Rosanvallon, "A Reflection on Populism," Books & Ideas (November 10, 2011), www.booksandideas.net/A-Reflection-on-Populism.html.

In an oft-quoted self-description of his regime, Hungarian Prime Minister Viktor Orbán (hereinafter the HPM), insisted that Hungary is democratic and respects democracy. Contrary to Chávez, he did not aspire to offer a more authentic democracy, as most populists do, only a more patriotic one, a democracy for the ethnos. The specificity of the PLD regime is that constitutional institutions are not called on to limit power, and that substantive liberal values are of no importance. In other words, populism (right and left! – let's be under no political illusions) and its resulting system of governance deny *constitutional* democracy. Plebiscitarian democracy disregards liberal constitutionalism and its institutions in the name of majority rule. It is illiberalism and the leader's lust for power that unleashes democracy's self-destructive tendencies, which in the end turn it into despotism through unconstrained government in the name of the people. "Illiberal" means both a lack of the liberal constitutional instruments that limit power, enabling arbitrary personal rule, and substantive illiberal values, like the imposition of a single world view on society. Illiberal democracies are the democracy of, and for, illiberals.

*

How does the illiberalism of the PLD regime affect democracy? In a growing number of countries, democracy first killed liberalism and then, dancing on its corpse, committed suicide.

Illiberal democracies thrive on the inherent shortcomings, uncertainties, and inconsistencies of constitutionalism. These weaknesses were always known or at least sensed in constitutional theory, if not always admitted, and important measures are occasionally taken in constitutions to counter them by setting constitutional limits to the totalitarian and self-destructive tendencies of democracy as self-government. The uncertainties of constitutionalism facilitate raw democracy. Where constitutionalism demands homogeneity,[19] it enables populism and illiberal democracy to represent themselves as a solution to the pluralism and diversity that undermine them. Populism claims that by undoing diversity it offers a more solid constitutional foundation.

Illiberal democracies assert deeply illiberal values, some of them bordering on authoritarian. Populists mobilize communitarianism and/or nationalism: it is therefore not surprising that the illiberal regime prefers

---

[19] "The nation exists prior to everything; it is the origin of everything. ... It would be ridiculous to suppose that the nation itself was bound by the formalities of the constitution." E. Sieyès, *Political Writings*, ed. M. Sonenscher (Hackett Publishing Company, 2003), p. 136.

collectivist fictions. However, in one of their many acts of pragmatism, such rulers accept a *consumerist* concept of individualism as privacy and personal (bodily) freedom. The ruler knows the secret of the postmaterial world, where the active electorate takes the satisfaction of primary needs for granted: "Wellness is a daily, active pursuit."[20] The regime does not interfere into private life directly, although it promotes traditional roles for women and family at the symbolic level.[21] It stands for traditional marriage but does not discriminate openly against sexual minorities (which it prefers remain invisible). It favors traditional religions and promotes traditional churches and their values (in countries where right-wing populism is in power), but without the formal oppression of those who fall outside these traditions. In areas like education and culture, it tries diligently to make its illiberal (nationalist, authority-respecting) preferences prevail. It even protects freedom of expression, including harsh criticism of the government, though it conceives of the role of the state in communication in an illiberal way: there is freedom of speech for all, but the means of socially effective speech (what can be heard) are increasingly monopolized by the state. This strange mixture, which falsely claims respect for fundamental rights, renders illiberal democracies a class of their own.

The popular support of illiberal democracy, and its social success, tests the resilience and even legitimacy of liberalism's constitutional institutions. Particularly troublingly, many people willingly approve of illiberalism: the orgy of irrationality masquerading as common sense challenges – not the first time in history – fundamental assumptions of equal respect for all.

The cunning genius of constitutionalism has invented institutions and beliefs that can contain the totalitarian potential of democracy. But constitutionalism often fails, and these current failures expose the unfinished nature of liberal constitutions. Constitutions, as liberal as they can be, are political creatures and reflect existing social and cultural values, and therefore become containers for the survival of illiberal, authoritarian solutions. Their unfinished nature not only captures historical contingencies, an inevitable inconvenience in constitutional design and constitutional development, but it also embodies the inherent contradictions of the *politically determined* constitutional order.

[20] "Millennials," Goldman Sachs (website), accessed January 6, 2021, www.goldmansachs.com /insights/archive/millennials.

[21] The plebiscitarian leader accepts popular values and changes them carefully: Jarosław Kaczyński did not push ahead with an absolute ban on abortion when in 2016 he ran into mass demonstrations; according to urban legend, the HPM refused to amend a relatively liberal Hungarian abortion law because he had no intention of losing the next election.

Populist illiberal democracy relies upon and brings to light the authoritarian elements of Western constitutional systems. Many of these elements relate to the dictates of market capitalism or distortions of the market.[22] Other features simply reflect "normal" political power. Political power, including such power in constitutional democracies, relies on the oppressive and discretionary logic of the public bureaucracy. At the level of constitutional law, here too the illiberal regime can rely on the illiberal values that were built into the constitutions of many countries that claim to be liberal.

The liberal institutional order has been further debilitated in the name of popular, republican democracy. Academia and public intellectuals bear a certain responsibility here. Self-proclaimed prophets of popular democracy have promoted the ideas of political constitutionalism and weak courts,[23] while the liberal component of constitutional democracies was shoved in the backroom, a dirty little secret of democracy – as if liberalism were a matter of shame for a progressive democrat or human progress.[24] An influential stream in academia blames liberal democracy for the backlash or crisis of democracy, as if the confrontation with and even partial imposition of liberal values had caused the populist-authoritarian counterrevolution.[25] As the accusation goes: "Populism has essentially become an illiberal democratic response to undemocratic liberalism."[26] Though liberalism (defined here as individual rights and the separation of powers) had very little to do with the lack of responsiveness by politicians or the corruption among them, "liberal" became a badge of shame (and, perhaps unrelated, an anti-Semitic dog whistle), and not just in Eastern

---

[22] G. Frankenberg, "Authoritarian Constitutionalism: Coming to Terms with Modernity's Nightmares," in H. A. García and G. Frankenberg (eds.), *Authoritarian Constitutionalism* (Edward Elgar, 2019).

[23] For a summary of the position that these republican ideas are not related to populism, see G. Halmai, "Populism, Authoritarianism and Constitutionalism," *German Law Journal*, 20:3 (2019), pp. 296–313.

[24] On top of this leftist scorn of (classic) liberalism, "liberal" in the United States became confused with social democracy and a strawman for conservatives as well. Yet left-oriented politicians and associated academics and intellectuals considered liberalism a historical malefactor responsible for both past injustice and the present democratic backlash (originating in liberalism's latest reincarnation, neoliberalism).

[25] See J. C. Isaac, "Is there Illiberal Democracy? A Problem with no Semantic Solution," *Eurozine* (August 9, 2017). http://www.eurozine.com/is-there-illiberal-democracy; I. Krastev, "What's Wrong with East-Central Europe: Liberalism's Failure to Deliver," *Journal of Democracy*, 27:1 (2016), pp. 35–39. It is telling that Farid Zakaria's emphasis on the centrality of the lack of liberalism was received with indifference.

[26] C. Mudde and C. R. Kaltwasser, *Populism. A Very Short Introduction* (Oxford University Press, 2017), p. 116.

Europe. "Between the pressures of post-modern deconstruction on the one side and pre-modernist fundamentalism on the other, the liberal project is now being squeezed as it has never been squeezed before."[27] These words were written in 1989 but they remain as accurate as ever.

*

This book addresses the constitutional structures and operations of illiberal democracies, and yet it looks odd to center the analysis on (public) law. After all, the success of populism and the domination of PLD depends primarily on nonlegal factors. Indeed, the whole PLD regime is an emotionally manipulated patronage system that maneuvers *around* the law. Illiberal democracy cannot be understood merely as a legal phenomenon or pure governance concern: it is embedded in the ability of a centralized executive to dominate a society of dependent people. Nevertheless, the constitutional system remains central as the actual power of the plebiscitarian leader relies on his control over the state, and this control is achieved through constitutional measures. The state as an administrative apparatus is managed through formal law, which requires the observance of legal formalities. The principal technique to control the state, and to influence society through the state, is a legal one. Illiberal democracies are state centered: the ruler reigns over society through the strict, centralized legal control over administrative and ideological resources. This is not to deny or dismiss the centrality of material factors in the domination and maintenance of legitimacy. Chávez owed his success to the services he provided to his constituency (the "Bolivarian mission" social programs, personally overseen by the President); legalized persecution was secondary.

In most countries where illiberal democracy has been victorious, the society remains fragmented, lacking comprehensive tools for social cohesion. The distorted market is a poor coordinator. In the absence of common bonds[28] or other forms of social coordination, law becomes an important cementer of society. In this system of rule by law, the powerholders cheat through law: both on law and the recipients of law.

Over the last seventy or so years, the concept of a constitution has been increasingly understood in the spirit of *Marbury* v. *Madison*, as the supreme *legal* norm of the country. Today, most societies imagine their

---

[27] R. K. Sherwin, "Law, Violence, and Illiberal Belief," *The Georgetown Law Journal*, 78 (1990), p. 1785.

[28] In Hungary, only family relations are considered trustworthy, while in Poland the Church is added.

political system to be legally prescribed. This book understands "constitution" in a broader sense that goes beyond the written document. It acknowledges that many constitutional functions are left or delegated to subconstitutional norms, including other public laws, institutions, and institutional practices that determine the use of and access to political power exercised by or in the name of the state. Constitutions do reflect social facts beyond the normative, and impact behavior beyond what is legally prescribed. The legal constitution is a social phenomenon, which at the same time provides a theory of society.[29]

The constitution is relevant beyond law "at the political level, for it is there that social relations take shape and are symbolically ordered."[30] This symbolic order offers a theory of society; it is an odd theory as it has both explanatory (justificatory) and regulatory (normative) effects. Moreover, the constitution provides a theory of society in determining its own subject, the people. All democratic constitutional orders cultivate a mythology regarding their people, laying the foundation for their constitutional theory. The theory of the people singles out those who are "real," and the theory lies and cheats when it comes to their actual political role, which is limited to praise and acclamation.

The constitution, with its representation of society, creates new social facts. Indeed, it is a social fact: "the view men have of themselves forms part of the reality for which such theories provide an account."[31] The constitutional self-presentation of political power influences the operations of the state in both liberal and illiberal democracies. Illiberal democracies do not provide a specific constitutional theory as they pretend to be ordinary constitutional democracies:[32] it is the pretension, the hypocrisy itself, that depicts and structures society. The pretension that society is organized in a democratic constitutional structure influences social action: citizens will act based on these presuppositions. (If they believe that the state does not overly lie about its debt, and trust the statutory promise that such debt will be honored, they will buy

---

[29] G. Skapska, "The Constitution as a Theory of Society in the Society: A Reflection after Twenty Years of Democratic Changes in East Central Europe," in A. Sajó (ed.), *Constitutional Topography. Values and Constitutions* (Eleven International, 2010); C. Thornhill, *A Sociology of Constitutions and State Legitimacy in Historical-Sociological Perspective* (Cambridge University Press, 2012).

[30] C. Mouffe, *The Return of the Political* (Verso, 1993), p. 11.

[31] R. M. Unger, *Knowledge and Politics* (The Free Press, 1975), p. 24.

[32] However, the Preamble of the Fundamental Law of Hungary (HFL) offers an ideology-heavy description of Hungarian society. Technically, this "National Avowal" is applicable in the interpretation of the constitution.

government bonds.) For the purposes of domination, however, the constitutional system that has overcommitted itself to classic democratic and liberal values must lie about the government's actions and intent. This will structure social relations as relations of cheating and corruption. The constitutional system becomes one of duplicity and immorality. The real constitution demonstrates how power disregards the constitutional formalities it has accepted, while pretending to be constitutionally faithful. The liberal constitution does not preclude the concentration of power, but given democratic presuppositions, the leader cannot formally perpetuate his rule. Only Central Asian democracies dare to resemble hereditary monarchy, but succession undergoes constitutional and pseudo-democratic processes even there. The perpetuation of power, and the effective domination of society, needs a lot of *circumvention*.

All in all, what we have in illiberal democracies is *usurpation*. In Benjamin Constant's classic formulation: "Despotism banishes all forms of liberty; usurpation needs these forms in order to justify the overturning of what it replaces; but in appropriating them it profanes them."[33] Illiberal democracy is the usurpation of constitutional democracy. However, as this term refers to the legitimacy of a monarch who is not qualified to rule according to the rules of succession and yet still exercises royal power, I will refrain from its use. Yet as Constant identifies, the problem of the leaders of plebiscitarian democracies is that it is "a force that nothing ... softens. It is necessarily stamped with the individuality of the usurper, and such individuality ... must be in a state of permanent defiance and hostility."[34] If you have met Napoleon, you have seen all such leaders, minus the genius.

*

While illiberal plebiscitarian rule is neither autocratic nor authoritarian per se,[35] the pressure of its own sins, and consequential occasional

---

[33] B. Constant, *Political Writings* (Cambridge University Press, 1993), p. 95.

[34] Ibid., p. 88.

[35] There is confusion in the use of autocracy, despotism and authoritarianism. Autocracy is often used "as a generic term for a rule free of legal constraints. Thus understood, the term covers different regime types: despotism, tyranny, dictatorship, absolutist monarchy, and totalitarianism. Carl Friedrich and Zbigniew Brzezinski emphasize the contrast between 'older autocracies' ('tyrannies, despotisms, and absolutisms') and contemporary totalitarian dictatorship. C. J. Friedrich and Z. Brzezinski, *Totalitarian Dictatorship and Autocracy* (Harvard University Press, 1965), p. 4.

  The distinguishing feature of an autocratic regime is the ruler's lack of legal and political accountability. Legally, the ruler is bound neither by any pre-existing law, nor by the laws

resistance lead the PLD regime to drift toward "mild," and less and less mild despotism.[36] However, contrary to the views of the morally (rightly) outraged, illiberal democracy is *not yet* despotic, nor despotism (nor "authoritarianism," as it is called provocatively, in the hope that the headline will shock the world). The difference between illiberal democracy and despotism remains crucial.[37]

Despots may accept the law as binding on all, including (within limits) themselves, but they also are ready to change the law unilaterally, at will and whim, irrespective of any commitments. Plebiscitarian leaders will follow their pleasure but with moderation: they are not modern Neros. Their rule is not a matter of personal caprice; they are bound by law, but the system is not bound by inhibitions when it comes to changing the meaning of the constitution. As to legitimacy, despots can be democratically endorsed by elections, or may rely on some other source of culturally legitimate power. The Tsar as autocrat could rule out of his own will (force); others rule by the grace of some suprahuman source.

"The main characteristics of despotism are lawlessness, suppression of conflicts, destruction of intermediate institutions, unconditional obedience of the sovereign, and imposed tranquility."[38] Despotism is the accurate term for the *potential* of illiberal democracy, which is short on constitutionalism. Constitutionalism was invented as a denial or negation of despotism, an institutional tool to prevent it.[39] Illiberal democracies are not yet despotic; the plebiscitarian leader is not a despot, not even necessarily a despot in the making. From the perspective of liberal constitutionalism, the vague term of despotism anticipates the terminus of the journey the new Caesar invites his people to enjoy; a terminus that liberals fear so much that they often claim we are already there.

---

they enacted. Politically, the ruler is not accountable to any other governmental institution or to the subjects (Ibid., p. 5). "Autocracy combines the rejection of democracy (the ruler is not elected) with the rejection of the rule of law (the ruler is not subject to law and institutional checks and balances)." N. Dimitrijevic, *"Illiberal Regime Types,"* (Routledge, in press) in A. Sajó, R. Uitz and S. Holmes (eds.), *Routledge Handbook of Illiberalism* (Routledge, in press).

[36] A. de Tocqueville, *Democracy in America*, vol. 4, (Liberty Fund, 2010), p. 1247.

[37] On the appropriateness of the term despotism in the context of illiberal democracy, see A. Sajó, "The Constitution of Illiberal Democracy as a Theory About Society," *Polish Sociological Review*, 208:4 (2019), pp. 395–412.

[38] M. Richter, "Despotism," in P. Wiener (ed.), *Dictionary of the History of Ideas. Study of Selected Pivotal Ideas* (Charles Scribner's Sons, 1973), p. 13.

[39] Chapter 1 explains why calling illiberal democracies authoritarian is a mistake. Authoritarianism in this book refers to a sociocultural, as well as individual, predisposition to be subordinate to the authorities.

Illiberal regimes exist in a precarious balance on the fringes of democracy. This is a key characteristic of the regime. That they may turn into despotism is a viable threat, and the leader reminds his subjects of this possibility with sufficient frequency. This forms part of his strategy of governance: he rules by chilling effect. However, the regime does not intend to become despotic. The pragmatic plebiscitarian leader sticks to the perpetuation of power. Plebiscitarian, patronage-based rule is more efficient than autocratic, coercion-based missionary rule, and even in an imperfect world, is better than risking resistance and the return of a revengeful enemy. Even zealous leaders like Kaczyński have learned that.

Illiberal democracies exist in a precarious equilibrium on the edge of democracy, with a penchant for despotism but still with a chance of readjusting constitutional democracy (in an orderly, nonviolent, nonexternal, and disaster-related manner). The regimes emerging from victorious populist movements never fully enable popular will to prevail. The leader will control the plebiscitarian structures that provide their legitimacy by strictly manipulating acclamation. He will even rely on traditional constitutional institutions, the RoL, and the respect for human rights, but without genuine commitment, and only instrumentally. It is for this reason that the state will "cheat" on its very normative foundations.

Chapter 1 presents the key concepts of illiberal democracy, namely "totalitarian democracy" and "authoritarianism in constitutionalism," and it explains why the term "illiberal democracy" is not an oxymoron. It asserts that illiberal democracy is a PLD-type regime led by a modern Caesar, as understood by Max Weber. This necessitates a short excursus into the concept of PLD as advanced by Weber, who held somewhat contradictory but always inspiring views on this matter (too).

Chapter 2 describes the constitutional takeover by victorious populists, concentrating on the legal techniques used in the formation of the new illiberal constitutional order. Chapter 3 deals with the social, cultural, economic, and psychological conditions that form the domination that sustains plebiscitarian rule: feudalistic dependencies maintain the regime and help the plebiscitarian perpetuation of power. These relations were created partly with the help of legal institutions.

The analysis of the new constitutional order starts in Chapter 4 with the review of the populist understanding of the people as sovereign. While the people, beyond plebiscitary acclamation, plays a very limited role in the actual structure of constitutional power in these regimes, it remains the foundational element of constitutional power and becomes a political force of its own as envisioned by the leader.

An obligatory review of actual constitutional texts and arrangements offers relatively little of interest, except that they very much resemble those in established democracies (Chapter 5). Of course, formal institutions are designed or used instrumentally, and loyalty to the leader replaces the spirit of constitutionalism, thanks to the change in the personnel described in Chapter 2. A similar ambiguity characterizes the human rights record of illiberal democracies (Chapter 6), which do not deny human rights. The actual level of human rights violation is not excessive, though backlash is undeniable. Disrespecting fundamental rights fits into a more general, worldwide trend where human rights are losing their authority. The chapter offers a review of the intellectual causes of this decline.

Chapter 7 considers a new "spirit" of the laws: it will indicate how a botched RoL is sustained to serve the authorities' contradictory interests, and how it becomes compromised in this (ab)use. Chapter 8 discusses how such instrumentalism, along with a lack of principled commitment and pervasive duplicity, leads to the conclusion that the constitutional order of illiberal democracy is one of cheating and deceit. Clearly, mistakes in law are normal, cheating is inherent, and laws are full of misrepresentations (legal fictions and reductive legal frames, as admissible evidence), but legal cheating in illiberal democracy became the amoral norm. The chapter reviews the techniques of legal cheating in illiberal democracy and the moral consequences of living in a lie.

The analysis of illiberal democracy concentrates on Venezuela, Hungary, Poland, and Turkey, the four governments of populist origin with the most elaborate illiberal constitutional structure.[40] It more

---

[40] In the EU, contemporary Romanian and Bulgarian experiences are relevant too, though the political systems are not sufficiently stable to have had crystallized into an illiberal regime. However, "the literature has documented the extreme permeability of the Romanian political arena to populism since the early 1990s ... [and] the mainstreaming of populism in the Romanian arena equates to the diffusion of the communication repertoires of the radical-right populist parties into mainstream political fare and the media in general." S. Soare and C. D. Tufiş, "Phoenix Populism," *Problems of Post-Communism*, 66:1 (2019), p. 9. See further D. Dragoman and C. Ungureanu, "The Faces of Populism in Post-Communist Romania," in *Populism in Europe: From Symptom to Alternative?*, CIDOB Report # 01–2017.

Some observers believe that the Czech Republic, under the coalition government of Prime Minister Babiš is at the early stage of the path taken by the HPM. See S. Hanley and

frequently relies on Hungarian examples due to its avatar status in modeling illiberal democracy. The parochial pride in the felicitous circumstance of living in an illiberal democracy should not make the author blind to the fact that illiberal democracy is not a recent or Western phenomenon: its autocratic constitutional version in Singapore has become a hard-to-imitate model for future strongmen and development economists over the last several decades.[41] Furthermore, there are other schools for beginners in populist regime-building. Populist rule was well known in Latin America for nearly three-quarters of a century, but the kind of victorious populism that enabled illiberal democracy was less known in the EU until recently.

Populism has been continuously present in the political systems of some Western states, such as Greece.[42] According to Ruth Wodak, in Austria, the coalition between two right-wing parties (the Austrian People's Party and the Freedom Party of Austria) has allowed a "potentially Orbanesque illiberal democracy" to become a reality there.[43] Contemporary illiberal trends and developments in so-called mature European democracies (e.g. Italy, France, and the United Kingdom) are also taken into consideration. Populism has political system–changing effects in other parts of the world,[44] notably in Brazil

M. A. Vachudova, "Understanding the Illiberal Turn: Democratic Backsliding in the Czech Republic," *East European Politics*, 34:3 (2018), pp. 276–96.

Russia is relevant for inventing many of the techniques of illiberal government, although it became despotic early, leapfrogging the illiberal democracy stage.

[41] Notwithstanding important historical, economic, and cultural differences, there are significant similarities. In the Economist Intelligence Unit's Democracy Index, Singapore is comparable to Hungary and Poland, and Venezuela was at least as democratic in 1999 as the Central European states, etc.

[42] T. S. Pappas, *Populism and Liberal Democracy. A Comparative and Theoretical Analysis* (Oxford University Press, 2019).

[43] R. Wodak, "Entering the 'Post-Shame Era': The Rise of Illiberal Democracy, Populism and Neo-authoritarianism in Europe," *Global Discourse*, 9:1 (2019), p. 197. This now defunct coalition started with a raid on the Constitution Protection Office, carried out by the Freedom Party–controlled municipal traffic police and resulting in the confiscation of the files of extremists, including Freedom Party members. The collapse of this alliance did not originate in some democratic sobering or institutional resistance. It was due to hubris combined with parochial stupidity, an action of the deep state, personal greed, or a desperate last-minute effort of a fourth estate that was not yet fully domesticated.

[44] See the Philippines under Duterte (although so far, he refuses constitutional change to abolish the term limit, which contradicts expectations of power perpetuation). Scholarly literature also describes Indonesia in terms of illiberal democracy. D. Bourchier, *Illiberal Democracy in Indonesia: The Ideology of the Family State* (Routledge, 2016); V. R. Hadiz, "The Rise of Neo-Third Worldism? The Indonesian Trajectory and the Consolidation of Illiberal Democracy," *Third World Quarterly*, 25:1 (2004), pp. 55–71.

and in the United States, where North Carolina and Wisconsin offer textbook examples of anticonstitutionalist majoritarianism, to the detriment of the separation of powers and in disregard of constitutional decency.[45] The success of plebiscitarianism reveals the vulnerability of constitutional democracy: the lasting success of constitutionalism in a few enduring countries remains in desperate need of explanation because of the implausibility of constitutionalism, a miracle of counterintuitive answers and beliefs. After all, constitutions are only sets of vague words proposing solutions that defy the natural tendencies of power aggrandizement.

Unfinished constitutions could be improved by design, and with the tools of militant constitutionalism, but they cannot overcome the popular dislike of neutrality, tolerance, and checks on power. The more popular the power is thought to be, the less likely people would like to see it curtailed. Nevertheless, the study of illiberal democracy demonstrates the opportunities for resistance. Structural injustices may one day convince even bigots that they were cheated in the illiberal regime. Illiberal democracies may end thanks to the disillusionment of the same authoritarian electorate that brought such leaders to power. When money runs out, democracy gets a chance. The plebiscitarian system is unstable: unsurprisingly, smart leaders try systematically to build their own loyal institutions, and through these a social dependency that can replace devotion on a rainy day.

Resentment is the mother of illiberal democracy, and resentment can destroy its child.

---

[45] It is still too early to discern the impact of Trump's populist presidency on US government and constitutional culture. He never elicited the full potential of illiberal power that exists in executive aggrandizement, and even his less liberal actions (allowed by the courts) remain within the limits of constitutional democracy. What he did in terms of manipulating public anger is a different matter.

1

Placing Illiberal Democracy

Caesarism, Totalitarian Democracy, and Unfinished Constitutionalism

If we were asked to divide the objects we know into mountains and non-mountains, then we should certainly put Ayers Rock in the first category. . . . Nevertheless, from a scientific point of view, Ayers Rock is not a mountain, it is a *stone*.

Umberto Eco[1]

1.1 Introduction

Constitutional theory, replicating an age-old confusion in political science, desperately endeavors to comprehend the current democratic backlash. Theoreticians sit uneasily with the unpleasant but popular regimes that emerge from populism and cannot be easily squeezed into comfortable categories of evil.[2] It is always frustrating, even intellectually scandalous, when new phenomena do not fit into existing boxes. "[W]here empirical reality is fuzzy, no amount of conceptual sophistication will allow us to draw clear and consensual lines between regime types."[3] Unease breeds confusion, which predictably ends in a war of typologies and fifty shades of in-between (gray).[4] *Faute de mieux*, these

---

[1] U. Eco, *Kant and the Platypus: Essays on Language and Cognition* (Mariner Books, 2000), p. 225.

[2] "Populism" is used here to refer to a set of beliefs about society, politics, and a political movement (see Section 1.3).

[3] A. Schedler, "Elections Without Democracy: The Menu of Manipulation," *Journal of Democracy*, 13:2 (2002), p. 38.

[4] Bugarič characterizes both Hungary and Poland as "a new version of semi-authoritarian regime, which is halfway between 'diminished democracy' and 'competitive authoritarianism.'" B. Bugarič, "Could Populism Be Good for Constitutional Democracy?," *Annual Review of Law and Social Science*, 15:1 (2019), p. 48. Elsewhere, constitutional systems are seen to exist on a continuum from authoritarian constitutionalism to liberal.

types of regimes are forced into the terminological prison of authoritarianism.[5] This is not the place to challenge the importance of classification debates, reciting other scholars. Such debates are normal in scholarship, but currently they unfortunately preempt the collection and analysis of empirical information on how illiberal democracies *actually work*. We have not even reached the level of Kremlinology, which was able to explain whose appointment depended on whom.

The standard wisdom holds that emerging illiberal democracies are authoritarian regimes. One should thus clarify what the populist shift does *not* entail. The democratic power-grab has not centered on taking over the armed forces or secret service as tools of violent oppression or total domination; changes in these domains have been more or less within the standard of controlling personnel, although with stronger

G. Frankenberg, "Authoritarian Constitutionalism: Coming to Terms with Modernity's Nightmares," in H. A. García and G. Frankenberg, *Authoritarian Constitutionalism*. Halmai sees constitutionalism as liberal by definition. G. Halmai, "The Rise and Fall of Constitutionalism in Hungary," in P. Blokker (ed.), *Constitutional Acceleration within the European Union and Beyond* (Taylor and Francis, 2017). For a minimalist liberal constitutional democracy (distinct from other constitutional democracies) see T. Ginsburg and A. Z. Huq, *How to Save a Constitutional Democracy* (University of Chicago Press, 2008), pp. 10–11.

5 Using Singapore as the country of reference, Tushnet wrote about "authoritarian constitutionalism." M. Tushnet, "Authoritarian Constitutionalism," *Cornell Law Review*, 100 (2015), pp. 391–462. Somek uses the same expression for a different kind of regime (Austria after 1934). A. Somek, "Authoritarian Constitutionalism: Austrian Constitutional Doctrine 1933 to 1938 and Its Legacy," in C. Joerges and N. S. Ghaleigh (eds.), *Darker Legacies of Law in Europe: The Shadow of National Socialism and Fascism Over Europe and its Legal Traditions* (Hart, 2003), pp. 361–62.

Other authors place the populist backlash governments in the authoritarian camp. O. O. Varol, "Stealth Authoritarianism," *Iowa Law Review*, 100 (2015), pp. 1673–742; J. Corrales, "The Authoritarian Resurgence: Autocratic Legalism in Venezuela," *Journal of Democracy*, 26:2 (2015), pp. 37–51. Sadurski discusses the "slide towards authoritarianism." W. Sadurski, *Poland's Constitutional Breakdown* (Oxford University Press, 2019), p. 228. He refers to an "authoritarian type of populism." Ibid., p. 313. Bonikowski considers Hungary and Poland to be authoritarian for having a "style of governance that attempts to circumvent the rule of law and democratic norms in favor of centralized authority and limited political freedom." B. Bonikowski, "Ethno-Nationalist Populism and the Mobilization of Collective Resentment," *The British Journal of Sociology*, 68:1 (2017), pp. 181–213. See further B. Bugarič, "Central Europe's Descent into Autocracy: A Constitutional Analysis of Authoritarian Populism," *International Journal of Constitutional Law*, 17:2 (2019), pp. 597–616.

Other authors are satisfied with noting a democratic or constitutional backlash or use imports from political science (hybrid regime, electoral democracy, etc.). For the dozen or more theories of hybrid formations, see T. G. Daly, "Democratic Decay: Conceptualising an Emerging Research Field," *Hague Journal on the Rule of Law*, 11 (2019), pp. 9–36.

emphasis on authoritarian virtue.[6] The forces of order remain subordinated to other branches.[7] Of course, illiberal democracies may drift toward despotism, and as they do so, their authoritarian (illiberal) elements become increasingly obvious. But to call them authoritarian does not render justice to the brutality of the oppression that characterizes authoritarian regimes. Violence and repression are not the primary tools of the plebiscitarian leader. The regime is upheld by the existential dependence and emotional commitment of its subjects. As discussed below, illiberal democracies drift toward a rule that relies increasingly on coercion and the restriction of rights, insisting on the perpetual rule of a single person. Many scholars describe this stage as authoritarian, and the stage leading to it as some kind of hybrid authoritarianism.

The current terminological uncertainties in the classification of illiberal democracies indicate that the prevailing political science models do not properly capture the nature of these plebiscitarian leader democracies, which rely heavily on democratic forms. Following Tocqueville and Benjamin Constant, it is useful to apply the less loaded term "despotism."[8] The illiberal regimes exist as welfare states and show the characteristics of Tocqueville's "mild despotism." In its historical uncertainty despotism is a good alternative term to authoritarianism. John Keane, motivated by a correct dislike of a Manichean division of good democracy versus bad authoritarianism, came to the same conclusion, namely that "the language of authoritarianism wrongly supposes that the new despotisms are devoid of democracy, which is the supposed opposite of an authoritarian regime."[9] However, despotism in the present context

---

[6] Turkey represents a special case. Notwithstanding the electoral victories of the Justice and Development Party (AKP), toppling the almighty military took time. See M. Somer, "Understanding Turkey's Democratic Breakdown: Old vs. New and Indigenous vs. Global Authoritarianism," *Southeast European and Black Sea Studies*, 16:4 (2016), pp. 481–503; C. B. Tansel, "Authoritarian Neoliberalism and Democratic Backsliding in Turkey: Beyond the Narratives of Progress," *South European Society and Politics*, 23:2 (2018), pp. 197–217.

[7] For example, the police remain under the control and supervision of the prosecutor (in their ability to conduct searches, etc.). The judiciary at least maintains powers in investigative matters. What matters is who controls these public bodies and for what purposes.

[8] For Constant, despotism is a form of government that oppresses liberty. In his view, democracy based on universal suffrage can be despotic as the majority will deprive the minority of their liberty. Majoritarianism in illiberal democracy undeniably shows similar traits.

[9] J. Keane, *The New Despotism* (Harvard University Press, 2020), p. 212. The despotism emerging from illiberal democracy, as the examples of Venezuela and Turkey indicate, is an oppressive arbitrary personal regime, combined with the care provided by a benevolent

refers to the end-station of the journey of illiberal democracies only and is not a prophecy on the general demise of democracy, though the populism-based democratic undoing of liberal democracy is likely to take the road of illiberal democracy. (The alternative is the absorption of populism, shifting existing democracy toward illiberalism and potentially despotism.)

Academics commonly treat constitutional and illiberal democracies as incompatible. Such Manichean contrast is understandable. Scholars of democracy are generally outraged by illiberal democracies and attempt to mobilize public opinion against their abuses by expelling these regimes from the hallowed categories of veneration.[10] Categorization comes at a price, as its scope determines the applicable characteristics. "As we gradually categorize, we await the identification of new properties; ... But every hypothesis regarding the categorical framework to be assumed influences the way we make observation sentences."[11] If one uses the frame of authoritarianism in the study of illiberal democracies, one will be less likely to note what actually happens. As to those who are satisfied with a *tertium datur*–like "hybrid regime", they will see nothing, or only the mirage of their obsession. Those who insist that the beauties of populism provide real democracy will end by praising Hugo Chávez.[12]

At this point a clarification is needed. "Liberalism" here means a social order serving individual liberty where the citizens have equal fundamental rights. In McIlwain's classic reconstruction, constitutionalism "still remains what it has been almost from the beginning, the limitation of government by law."[13] The liberal element (individual rights in a free

---

administration and not just "a hard government in soft velvet form." Ibid., p. 215. (The administration provides services for the regime's supporters, or at least it pretends to.)

[10] The following either/or question illustrates this state of mind: "[I]s Singapore a seriously flawed liberal constitutionalist nation, or an authoritarian constitutionalist one?" Tushnet, "Authoritarian Constitutionalism," p. 413.

[11] Eco, *Kant*, p. 249.

[12] An empirical analysis was "not able to corroborate any positive relationship of populist-led governments with respect to egalitarian or participatory aspects of democracy," finding instead that under some populist governments there was "a decline of liberalism, deliberation and the electoral core of democracy." S. P. Ruth-Lovell, A. Lührmann and S. Grahn, *Democracy and Populism: Testing a Contentious Relationship*, V-Dem Working Paper 2019:91 (2019), p. 24. Cross-national data on up to ninety-one countries indicates that populist rule is associated with a decline in most measures of media freedom. However, this effect is lessened for right-leaning populist governments. P. D. Kenny, "'The Enemy of the People': Populists and Press Freedom," *Political Research Quarterly*, 73:2 (2020), pp. 261–75.

[13] C. H. McIlwain, *Constitutionalism Ancient and Modern* (Cornell University Press, 1940), pp. 21–22.

society) is absent from this definition. Carl J. Friedrich added "the rights of free man" only later, in view of totalitarian barbarism.[14] In principle McIlwain's description of nonliberal constitutionalism as an institutional-legal limitation of state power remains a legitimate constitutional arrangement. Distinguishing between various types of constitutionalism requires adding the adjective "liberal," even if today liberal minimalism (a minimum of individual rights) is incorporated into all forms of constitutionalism.[15] This holds true in nonliberal constitutional states as well (including illiberal democracies). Illiberal democracies, however, cannot sustain this minimum in the long run, because they cannot accept being bound by (higher) law. Although liberal constitutionalism without democracy has been historically possible, today democracy forms an inherent element of constitutionalism, as a limitation of power (by allowing the people to generate it).

"Constitutionalism" here refers to an arrangement limiting state power through checks and balances, and law-bound authorities, with a minimum of personal freedom (the liberal minimum).[16] *Liberal* constitutionalism presupposes that the government will not impose adherence to an orthodoxy. Laws pursue only secular goals that can be enjoyed by all persons irrespective of moral outlook, pursuing happiness on the terms of their individual choosing.[17] One can envision a constitutional order that satisfies constitutionalism and endorses (but does not prescribe) conservative values (without prioritizing individual freedom) but only under three conditions: that these conservative preferences are not perpetual (i.e. subject to ordinary democratic change); that they are not oppressive (i.e. they respect minorities that do not share these values); and finally, that the nonliberal constitutional regime respects the equal freedom of all citizens.[18]

A nonliberal constitutional system (e.g. populism-inspired illiberal democracy) remains a risky venture for constitutionalism and democracy, even if it guarantees the minimal recognition of fundamental freedoms. Once the nonliberal component is built into the existing

---

[14] G. Walker, "The Idea of Nonliberal Constitutionalism," *Nomos*, 39 (1997), p. 162.

[15] "Liberal" is used here in the classic nineteenth century sense.

[16] M. Rosenfeld, "The Rule of Law and the Legitimacy of Constitutional Democracy," *Southern California Law Review*, 74 (2001), pp. 1307–52.

[17] J. Rawls, *Political Liberalism* (Columbia University Press, 1993), pp. 134–35.

[18] The conservative value choices in Poland and Hungary, or the social justice preferences in Venezuela, were clearly not liberal, but in principle these choices do not rule out per se that the regimes remain constitutional (minimally liberal).

constitutional system, it catalyzes a process that will undermine the institutional limits to overwhelming state power and transforms democracy from a force countering the egoism of powerholders and their wish to perpetuate power into an unbound majoritarianism. The same applies to an ethnocentric, tribal regime that officially claims only the primacy of patriotism.

Illiberal democracies are not known for special constitutional theories of their own. Illiberal governments claim that their regimes are simply constitutional and democratic – period. In their line of offense/defense, they

- are as democratic and constitutional as any other state, only more popular and therefore more genuine;
- present merely a variation within the family of possible constitutional democracies, even if the constitutional values they cherish may be more tradition-bound, plebeian, and patriotic than liberal-universalists would like; and
- observe the RoL.

This chapter reviews the authenticity of these claims. After a discussion in Section 1.2 on the appropriateness of the term "illiberal democracy," Section 1.3 suggests that these types of regime are indeed democracies, but in the plebiscitarian leader democracy sense (with clear despotic potential). Section 1.4 proposes that illiberal democracies are democracies of a troubling sort, mobilizing the totalitarian potential inherent in mass democracy. Section 1.5 deals with the authoritarian elements in liberal constitutions, which are historically unfinished and internally vulnerable. The illiberal (authoritarian) elements (enclaves) that inevitably exist in constitutional systems are unleashed in the constitutional order of the plebiscitarian regimes. Section 1.6 focuses on the authoritarianism inherent in the constitutional order of established democracies and the populist mobilization of authoritarian predispositions in the citizenry, which facilitate the unfolding of the totalitarian potential of democracy, and the illiberal transformation of constitutionalism.

1.2 "Illiberal Democracy" Is an Appropriate Term

The constitutional structures of the regimes that came to power in populist victories are rightly called illiberal democracies, and not only because this is how Orbán, the father of the most characteristic and successful example of democratic backlash, called his creature.[19] It comes from the horse's mouth; he should know. More importantly, the expression grasps the reality of the regime. As an electoral democracy undermined by its populist illiberalism, the regime is illiberal in two senses of the word: in terms of officially preferred values and in its disregard of limits to power. At the same time, it is democratic in a plebiscitarian sense. According to Max Weber, leader democracy counts as democracy but like every mass democracy it tends toward Caesarism.[20]

The appearance of the word "democracy" in the context of the plebiscitarian regime is abhorrent to many democrats. "Liberal orthodoxy treats authoritarian constitutionalism not just as a contested concept, but as a mere travesty or deceitful rendition of the rules and principles, values, and institutions of what is innocently referred to as 'Western constitutionalism.'"[21] According to critiques, to claim that election-based illiberal regimes belong to the family of democratic states is a regime-friendly mistake at best, or more likely apologia.[22] Claiming that plebiscitarian regimes are democracies is in itself a *denunciation of liberal democracy*. The possibility that such a "rudely stamp'd" creature can exist insults the prevailing democratic theodicy. That illiberal democracies with their power-domesticated populism can be placed (uncomfortably) in the democracy family indicates that constitutional democracy (liberal or otherwise) remains far from the idealized and even apologetic description originating in normative (and political) considerations.

Recognizing the democratic nature of plebiscitarian regimes is not an endorsement of relativism. Constitutional democracy is a normative concept that provides justifications for its sustenance. Further, it provides standards to evaluate regimes, enabling transgressions to be identified, albeit at the price that a compromising continuity with real, existing unprincipled and illiberal democracies may come to light. Currently the Hungarian and Polish governments argue that other EU member states are afraid to come up with a common standard of the RoL, as they themselves will be found wanting. However, this complicit continuity

---

[19] V. Orbán, "Prime Minister Viktor Orbán's speech at the 30th Bálványos Summer Open University and Student Camp" (speech, Băile Tuşnad, July 29, 2019), *About Hungary*, www.abouthungary.hu/speeches-and-remarks/prime-minister-viktor-orbans-speech-at-the-30th-balvanyos-summer-open-university-and-student-camp.

[20] M. Weber, *Economy and Society*, eds. G. Roth and C. Wittich (University of California Press, 1978), p. 1451. Based on his experience with President Jackson's patronage-democracy, Tocqueville came to the same conclusion.

[21] Frankenberg, *Authoritarian Constitutionalism*, p. 7.

[22] A. Schedler, "The Menu of Manipulation," *Journal of Democracy*, 13 (2002), pp. 37–50.

does not prevent the observation of important differences.[23] Illiberal political regimes, after traversing a gray area, reach a point when they can rightly be called antidemocratic, or despotic (and after a while, deeper in the marsh, even authoritarian).

Some argue that the term "illiberal democracy" is an oxymoron, like an "atheist pope."[24] However, it is not his professed dogma that makes a pope the Pope. His legitimacy and authority comes from being properly elected (with the help of the Holy Spirit). Inconvenient and troubling as they may be, oxymorons do exist, just like the platypus: an egg-laying mammal, a scandal of zoological classification. The plebiscitarian regime's vitality stems from the combination of illiberalism, electoral democracy, and a charismatic leader. It does not help analytical clarity and political action to uncritically adore and adulate democracy. It is more fruitful to follow Pierre Rosanvallon's advice: "Behind a facade of clarity, the word 'democracy' conveys modern society's perplexities concerning its ultimate political foundations."[25] Of course, fuzzy realities are hardly compatible with most expectations of democracy, namely "popular political self-government," where people themselves (i.e. not "the people" but the citizens in their empirical majoritarian reality) decide "the contents ... of the laws that organize and regulate their political association."[26] The admission of illiberal democracy into this sacred hall of popular self-government (a Holy Grail that serves normative and apologetic purposes) is understandably disconcerting: The possibility that illiberal democracy is a *mirror image* of the potential pitfalls and Rousseauist totalitarianism of democracy is difficult to stomach.

---

[23] Complicit continuity means that illiberal democracies rely on the shortcomings of respected democracies, which tolerate and support these regimes.

[24] Z. Farkas, "Vulnerable Democracies – An Interview with János Kornai," *Heti Világgazdaság*, 2016/41 (October 13, 2016), pp. 10–13.

Müller claims that the term undermines efforts to rein in would-be autocrats. J.-W. Müller, "The Problem with 'Illiberal Democracy,'" *Project Syndicate* (January 21, 2016), www.project-syndicate.org/commentary/the-problem-with-illiberal-democracy-by-jan-werner-mueller-2016–01?barrier=accesspaylog.

Isaac finds the label applicable but with qualifications. "To claim that these bad things are not 'really' democracy at all is to play an essentialist semantic game." J. C. Isaac, "Is There Illiberal Democracy? A Problem with No Semantic Solution," *Eurozine* (August 9, 2017), www.eurozine.com/is-there-illiberal-democracy.

[25] P. Rosanvallon, "The Political Theory of Democracy," in O. Flügel-Martinsen, F. Martinsen, S. W. Sawyer and D. Schulz (eds.), *Pierre Rosanvallon's Political Thought. Interdisciplinary Approaches* (Bielefeld University Press, 2019), p. 27.

[26] F. Michelman, *Brennan and Democracy* (Princeton University Press, 1999), pp. 5–6.

"One man's populism is another man's democracy, and vice versa."[27]
The uncertainties surrounding populism, and its easy use in the analysis
of unpleasant political movements and regimes, reflect the shortcomings
of democratic theory and democracy. Under the spell of emotions liberated by populist leaders, democracy enables the vices of the "real existing"
people to overrun the public space.[28] Bad money tends to drive good
money out.

Democracy is fuzzy and illiberal democracy is even more so. As Svolik
has stated, "the ... changes [occurring in illiberal regimes] – especially
when considered in isolation – rarely amount to an outright violation of
core democratic principles."[29] The regimes hold legitimacy in the eyes of
many people not only because they stand for nationalist values or generous welfare. A lot of local people see the regime as democratic.[30] "What
happened in Hungary is certainly less than a total breakdown of constitutional democracy, but also more than just a transformation of the way
that liberal democracy is functioning."[31] Is Hungary fundamentally still
a democracy as of today (August 2020 – days can make all the difference)? It is not proven that the incumbent will not accept electoral loss,
and the transfer of political power is what makes democracy.[32] After all,
elections are regular, free, even if not fair.[33] But again, electoral fairness is
a matter of degree: gerrymandering is less important in Hungary than in

---

[27] R. Dahrendorf, "Acht Anmerkungen zum Populismus," *Transit*, 156 (2003), p. 25.

[28] "Contemporary populism is not the product of some malevolent force but of the very
model of democracy, representative and constitutional, that stabilized our societies after
World War II." N. Urbinati, "Political Theory of Populism," *Annual Review of Political
Science*, 22 (2019), p. 124. See further, P. Rosanvallon, *Counter-Democracy: Politics in an
Age of Distrust* (Cambridge University Press, 2008), p. 265. For earlier authorities, see Karl
Mannheim: "Dictatorship is not the antithesis of democracy; it represents one of the
possible ways in which a democratic society may try to solve its problems." He also stated
that "a plebiscitarian democracy may be characterized as the self-neutralization of polit-
ical democracy." K. Mannheim, "The Democratization of Culture," in K. H. Wolff (ed.),
From Karl Mannheim (Routledge, 1971), pp. 447–48.

[29] M. W. Svolik, "Polarization versus Democracy," *Journal of Democracy*, 30:3 (2019), p. 22.

[30] For example, "In 2011, when a Latinobarometer survey asked Venezuelans to rate their
own country from 1 ('not at all democratic') to 10 ('completely democratic'), 51 percent of
respondents gave their country a score of 8 or higher." S. Levitsky and D. Ziblatt, *How
Democracies Die: What History Reveals About Our Future* (Crown, 2018).

[31] Halmai, "The Rise and Fall," p. 225.

[32] Municipal election losses in large cities are accepted but revenge is swift: powers and
financial resources are rescinded (and loyal cities compensated through fiscal
redistribution).

[33] Schedler claims that elections are relevant in hybrid regimes, and not purely for legitimation, because the political fight is not fully determined. A. Schedler, *The Politics of
Uncertainty* (Oxford University Press, 2013).

the United States (since 1901) and voter suppression is rare. By many formal criteria democratic elections are more problematic in the United States than in Hungary, where fairness is undermined by the use of state resources.

Illiberal democracies remain popularly endorsed, though in a problematic and illiberal plebiscitarian way, with no guarantee that they will satisfy the criteria of even a minimal Schumpeterian democracy (choice of leader accountability). Democracy, in a substantive sense, is certainly absent: the illiberal regime fails to recognize the legitimacy of compromise because it denies the legitimacy of the opposition, although in the usual twilight zone of the plebiscitarian regime, the opposition remains legal.

More than the shallowness of electoral democracy, it is the nature of the policy deliberation that is troublesome. "Outcomes are democratically legitimate only if they could be the object of a free and reasoned agreement among equals."[34] This legitimacy is missing as the outcomes are preset. Government decisions in illiberal democracy regularly reflect agreements that supposedly exist (or could have been achieved) among a sizable majority (e.g. "keep 'migrants' out!," "alleviate bank creditors' mortgage burden!," "provide benefits to families with many children!," etc.). However, such agreements are not "free and reasoned." Citizens who do not count as "authentic people" do not participate as equals in the "agreement" process and are not even considered in the "imaginary" agreement the leader envisions in the blueprint that he imposes as coming from his people (see Chapter 4).

1.3 Caesarism and Plebiscitarian Leader Democracy

The legitimacy of illiberal democracy originates partly from its popular endorsement: power emanates from the people, and the people chooses who will carry out its will. While this is as legitimate as popular self-determination, it results in personal rule. Movement populism needs a leader, a hero of the people's cause, who senses and articulates the distress of ordinary people. He is accepted because he can articulate popular resentment. He advocates government takeover and, once victorious, turns into a Bonaparte, who uses sovereign power for personal, Caesaristic rule. A modern scholar describes Julius Caesar's rule in the

---

[34] J. Cohen, "The Economic Basis of Deliberative Democracy," *Social Philosophy and Policy*, 6:2 (1989), p. 22.

following terms (offering obvious parallels with contemporary plebiscitarian rule):

> Though Caesar effectively controlled Rome, the Republic still operated in a legal sense. Elections for offices continued, Roman law continued to govern commercial and personal transactions . . . Caesar in fact exercised power as a dictator, a formally defined Republican office whose term he had extended. The extensions defied true Republican precedents, but they had been done using legal means and with apparent popular support.[35]

The illiberal plebiscitarian turn of democracy is quintessential for populism but in many respects it only continues existing democratic practices: "even in the stable democratic countries, the collapse of the traditional political parties turns elections into a vote of approbation."[36] In the plebiscitarian regime, elections are about endorsing the person of the leader. Both in presidential and parliamentary systems, plebiscitarian democracy means citizens can make this choice without the inconveniences of representative democracy which, as citizens are told, only favors elites. The people's role is acclamation, the voicing of support. And if even voice is too demanding (or risky), the supportive gaze of the spectator citizen will do.[37] Parliamentary elections also form part of the acclamation: the (re)election affirms the leader, expressing agreement with, and trust in, Caesar.[38] The citizens vote for or against him, as the only issue on the agenda; there is nothing to represent, only *who* will represent this nothingness.

Plebiscitarian leader democracy owes its scholarly reputation to Max Weber.[39] According to Weber, the plebiscite primarily selects and

---

[35] E. J. Watts, *Mortal Republic. How Rome Fell into Tyranny* (Basic Books, 2018), pp. 238–39.

[36] S. Issacharoff and J. C. Bradley, "The Plebiscite in Modern Democracy," in A. Sajó, R. Uitz and S. Holmes (eds.), *Routledge Handbook of Illiberalism* (Routledge, in press). Latin American populist leaders continue to apply personal rule, which is characteristic of *caudillismo*. See J. Lynch, *Caudillos in Spanish America 1800–1850* (Oxford University Press, 2002).

[37] See J. E. Green, *The Eyes of the People: Democracy in an Age of Spectatorship* (Oxford University Press, 2010).

[38] M. Weber, "Parliament and Government in Germany," in P. Lassman and R. Speirs (eds.), *Weber: Political Writings* (Cambridge University Press, 1994), pp. 226–27. The prime minister in a parliamentary system can be a Caesaristic leader supported by acclamation whereby "Parliament acquiesces (with considerable inner reluctance)." Weber, *Economy and Society*, p. 1452.

[39] Weber's scholarly and political writings use diverging concepts of leader (plebiscitarian) democracy. See P. Baehr, *Caesarism, Charisma, and Fate – Historical Sources and Modern Resonances in the Work of Max Weber* (Transaction, 2008).

confirms the leader, whose personal rule is legitimized by permanent popular support. This popular affirmation is irrational, as opposed to institutional affirmation in a democracy, which is rational.[40] "Plebiscitary democracy – the most important type of *Führer-Demokratie* – is a variant of charismatic authority, which hides behind a legitimacy that is formally derived from the will of the governed. The leader (demagogue) rules by virtue of the devotion and trust which his political followers have in him personally."[41] The leader "responds to his electorate's psychic, physical, economic, ethical, religious, or political needs; he knows no supervisory or appeals body, no technical jurisdiction."[42] Charisma is routinized and serves as the basis of legitimate rule in mass democracy.[43]

Weber referred to Caesarism as a historical form of PLD government.[44] Illiberal democracies operate as Caesaristic regimes. According to Weber, Caesarism is a historical form of PLD, and Bonapartism is its "modern" example. "PLD ... is an authority and regime type with authoritarian traits, like charismatic leadership, generated by the internal logic of modern mass democracy per se. ... PLD, unlike competitive authoritarianism,

---

[40] F. Panizza, "Introduction," in F. Panizza (ed.), *Populism and the Mirror of Democracy* (Verso, 2005), p. 18 (with reference to Juan Pablo Lichtmajer).

[41] Weber, *Economy and Society*, p. 268.

Führer (leader) democracy is not to be confused with Hitler's *Führerstaat*, as the mainstream press misleadingly called the HPM's rule as early as 2010. V. M. Stürmer, "Führerstaat Ungarn," *Die Welt* (December 22, 2010), www.welt.de/print/die_welt/poli tik/article11776564/Fuehrerstaat-Ungarn.html.

Leader democracy is criticized today as elitist and a "denigration of the masses," with dictatorial potential. See J. E. Green, "Max Weber and the Reinvention of Popular Power," *Max Weber Studies*, 8:2 (2008), pp. 187–224. See further A. Scott, "(Plebiscitary) Leader Democracy: The Return of an Illusion?," *Thesis Eleven*, 148:1 (2018), pp. 3–20.

[42] G. Casper, "Caesarism in Democratic Politics: Reflections on Max Weber," *SSRN* (March 22, 2007), p. 15. Kurt Weyland uses a similar definition to describe populism as a political strategy. K. Weyland, "Clarifying a Contested Concept: Populism in the Study of Latin American Politics," *Comparative Politics*, 34:1 (2001), p. 12.

[43] Weber, *Economy and Society*, p. 1455.

[44] András Körösényi, who praised the advantages of a personalistic leadership democracy even before Orbán came to power, concluded later that here "the electoral contest is bordering on a 'plebiscitary' 'pledge of allegiance.'" J. Pakulski and A. Körösényi, *Toward Leader Democracy* (Anthem Press, 2012) p. 106. By 2019 Körösényi admitted that Orbán's voluntarism "has resulted in a wielding of power that is in many ways authoritarian." A. Körösényi, "The Theory and Practice of Plebiscitary Leadership: Weber and the Orbán regime," *East European Politics and Societies*, 33:2 (2019), p. 295.

On the intellectual foundations of the Orbán regime, see A. Buzogány and M. Varga, "Against 'Post-communism.' The Conservative Dawn in Hungary," in K. Bluhm and M. Varga (eds.), *New Conservatives in Russia and East Central Europe* (Routledge, 2019).

is not a combination of democratic and authoritarian elements, but it is democratic (formally) and authoritarian (substantively) simultaneously."[45]

Caesarism is not an exceptional phenomenon limited to a few instances of the nineteenth century, then known as Bonapartism. For Max Weber, it applied to not only the two Napoleons but also to Bismarck and Lloyd George. In Latin America, it took the form of Simón Bolívar and the *caudillos*. In the United States, at least by 1972, "the election process had been transformed into what is essentially a plebiscitary system."[46]

The normalization of personalized leadership and leader democracy continued after World War ii. "[T]he 'presidentialisation' of democracy began in earnest with de Gaulle. . . . Presidentialisation means personalisation: elections are less about parties and more about endorsing the individual character of the person at its head."[47] Parliamentary systems do not differ; they produce prime ministerial dictatorship, which easily ends in personal rule, although such rule is more fragile, as it can be institutionally ended by parliamentary vote. The personal rule that defines illiberal democracies features all the characteristics of PLD.[48]

Caesarism is a common, though rather extreme form of leader democracy. This extremism makes the totalitarian potential of democracy manifest, since "a directly elected president can claim uniquely to incarnate the 'will of the people'; as a result, a president is prone to assume a 'superlegitimacy' which he or she will be tempted to deploy against any countervailing institution, including the courts and the press."[49] Rosanvallon adds that presidentialism carries with it the danger of all-out majoritarianism. Though Weber backed PLD for German democracy after the collapse of the Empire, he remained aware of its dangers and advocated precautionary measures: "Let us ensure that the president of

---

[45] Körösényi, "The Theory," p. 283.

[46] J. W. Caeser, *Presidential Selection: Theory and Development* (Princeton University Press, 1979), p. 215.

[47] J.-W. Müller, "Le Roi-machine," *London Review of Books*, 42:6 (2020), summarizing P. Rosanvallon, *Good Government: Democracy beyond Elections* (Harvard University Press, 2018).

[48] A Sajó, "The Constitution of Illiberal Democracy as a Theory about Society," *Polish Sociological Review*, 208:4 (2019), pp. 395–412 (from a lecture held in honor of Grazyna Skapska, Krakow, June 2018); R. Sata and I. P. Karolewski, "Caesarean Politics in Hungary and Poland," *East European Politics*, 36:2 (2019), pp. 206–25.

Sadurski speaks of "plebiscitary autocracy." See W. Sadurski, "Constitutional Crisis in Poland," in M. A. Graber, S. Levinson and M. Tushnet (eds.), *Constitutional Democracy in Crisis?* (Oxford University Press, 2018).

[49] Müller, "Le Roi-machine."

the Reich [Weber's institutional incarnation of the leader] sees the prospect of the gallows as the reward awaiting any attempt to interfere with the laws to govern autocratically."[50] The personalism in illiberal democracy is only the logical conclusion of the Bonapartist and plebiscitarian traditions of "established" democracies. (For details regarding domination, see Chapter 3.)

1.4 Illiberal Mass Democracy and Its Totalitarian Potential

"Populists understand politics as the expression of the general will (*volonté générale*) of the people."[51] For the populist imagination, this general will is that of the pure people, in a world where "two antagonistic and homogeneous groups, the 'pure people' and the 'corrupt elite'" conflict.[52] The general will of the pure ("real" and "authentic") people remains sovereign and shall always prevail. Populism challenges the existing institutional system of democracy, which operates as an obstacle to people's will and instead protects the elite and its privileges. Populism insists on genuine, enhanced democracy; such genuineness knows no limits as the people is sovereign, and the emerging populist democracy drifts toward a totalitarian version of democracy. This drifting is due partly to limitless majoritarianism, and partly to the difficulties of the underlying system, especially if patronage and the increasing costs of the biased redistribution will force the leader to apply more and more coercive means in the name of popular will (the will of *his* people), ready to endorse increasing disregard of others. This difficulty was described in the Turkish context as follows: "The causal mechanism behind democratic collapse is the 'partisan redistribution' of resources ... Incumbents' fear of retribution and prosecution increases their cost of losing power through free and fair elections. Their clients also fear change of government because they receive favors via partisan

---

[50] Weber, *Economy and Society*, pp. 305 and 307. He expected the parliamentary system (with budgetary control and compromises among parties) to function as "a check upon 'Caesarist' leaders" and assumed that the ruler leaves his post once he has lost popular support. Weber, *Economy and Society*, p. 1456. See further W.J. Mommsen, *Max Weber and German Politics, 1890–1920* (University of Chicago Press, 1990), p. 411, with a summary on the debate how PLD leads to authoritarian rule.

[51] C. Mudde, "The Populist Zeitgeist," *Government and Opposition*, 39:4 (2004), p. 543.
    The populist leader remains (at least to some extent) captive of the populist ideology that served as his "political strategy" to obtain power. Weyland, "Clarifying a Contested Concept," p. 12.

[52] Mudde, "Zeitgeist," p. 543.

redistribution, and they presume that government change could result in loss of such resources to other social groups. Hence, their 'fear of future redistribution' of their current benefits under the AKP government drives their cost of toleration up."[53] Secondly, the drift toward authoritarianism is inherent in the totalitarian potential of democracy. PLD accepts majoritarianism enthusiastically, disregards moderating institutions, pursues homogeneity instead of pluralism, and claims a moral mission. This is a recipe to unfold the totalitarian in democracy. At the practical level, totalitarianism manifests in the majority's relationship to political opposition. As opposition is outside the people, it has no moral mandate; as such, it is illegitimate and does not count. There is no need to enter into dialogue with "them," and therefore there is neither dialogue nor deliberation.

Democracy as the rule of the people can be totalitarian, not so much because the multitude inclines toward totalitarianism, but simply because democracy has totalitarian potential. This totalitarianism originates from the desire for perfect democracy, where the people is sovereign and unified and the general will emerges from them. This potential emerges is realised when raw popular self-rule prevails in democracy. Raw self-rule knows no limits, and this is (ab)used by the populist leader, who succeeds to control government power. The leader who hijacks the people endorses the idea of unlimited (i.e. total) power that he can exercise for his benefit on behalf of the people. This was the perspective of Robespierre & Co. in 1794. The Jacobins needed the love of the people, as without it there remains only one method to rule, the terrible *Terreur*. If terror, deprived of popular support, fails, the government of the people will also fail, which is, of course, impermissible. The plebiscitarian populist leader ruling in his illiberal democracy encounters a similar dilemma. He faces the possibility of losing popular support in a plebiscite. His alternative is to unleash the totalitarian potential of the democracy that he controls. For this reason, the population must support the leader to avoid its own totalitarian rule. Plebiscitarian leader democracy aims to undo institutions that limit power. Neither the people nor its leader needs intermediaries in their happy union. In this logic, a single, mandatory position shall apply to all relations. The search for the select, unified people characterizes illiberal plebiscitarian regimes, increasing the potential of totalitarianism.

---

[53] B. Esen and S. Gumuscu, "Why Did Turkish Democracy Collapse? A Political Economy Account of AKP's Authoritarianism," *Party Politics*, 20:10 (2020), p. 2.

In his classic work *The Origins of Totalitarian Democracy*, Talmon claimed that there are two kinds of democracy, which were not separated in the early Enlightenment stage: liberal and totalitarian.[54] The former "finds the essence of freedom in spontaneity and the absence of coercion," while the latter is "in the pursuit and attainment of an absolute collective purpose" and assumes "a sole and exclusive truth in politics."[55] Contrary to Talmon, though, these can be seen as theoretical endpoints; in the real life of democracies there are only mixtures unfolding one or the other's potential. Talmon did not provide a pedantic definition of "totalitarian." His term stands for an all-encompassing single solution for all social problems: a totalitarian rule reached in a democratic process. It imposes a single set of values and invalidates pluralism, plurality, and ambiguity. Recall Rousseau describing assemblies engaged in forming the general will. They oppose disagreement and debate and instead celebrate consensus: however, "if unanimity is what is desired, it must be engineered through intimidation, election tricks, or the organization of the spontaneous popular expression."[56] Unanimity is inevitable, because there is only one common good, and those who do not accept it in the exercise of constituent power (the "social compact") remain alien. "If then there are opponents when the social compact is made, their opposition does not invalidate the contract, but merely prevents them from being included in it. They are foreigners among citizens. When the State is instituted, residence constitutes consent; to dwell within its territory is to submit to the Sovereign."[57] This submission is total. Whatever the general will decides must be obeyed; no sphere of life, no action is exempt

---

[54] J. L. Talmon, *The Origins of Totalitarian Democracy* (W. W. Norton & Co, 1970), p. 1. Raymond Aron (who published the French translation of Talmon's *chef d'oeuvre*) was also aware of the relationship between totalitarianism and democracy, where totalitarianism results from undivided popular will. See I. Stewart, "Antitotalitarianism," in *Raymond Aron and Liberal Thought in the Twentieth Century* (Cambridge University Press, 2019), chap. 3. According to Pappas, "democracy has two opposite faces, one liberal, the other populist." T. S. Pappas, *Populism and Liberal Democracy. A Comparative and Theoretical Analysis* (Oxford University Press, 2019), p. 216.
   See B. Constant, *Political Writings* (Cambridge University Press, 1993), p. 106: "[T]he subtle metaphysics of the *Social Contract* can only serve today to supply weapons and pretexts to all kinds of tyranny."

[55] Talmon, *Origins*, pp. 1–2. The totalitarian potential does not presuppose the level of coercion and violence that is characteristic of the totalitarian regimes as described by Arendt or Friedrich and Brezinski. But the development of the idea of democracy already in the writings of Rousseau indicate that a single truth based democracy entails coercion.

[56] Ibid., p. 48.

[57] J.-J. Rousseau, *The Social Contract & Discourses* (J.M. Dent & Sons, 1920), p. 93.

from this rule. Unity means that there is no separation of powers nor any control or accountability. The totalitarian popular sovereignty relates to its illiberal tendency: the aim is to train men to "bear with docility the yoke of public happiness."[58]

In Talmon's view, "liberty is safer in countries where politics are not considered all important and where there are numerous levels of non-political private and collective activity . . . than in countries where politics take everything in their stride."[59] The more politicized the country, particularly where social issues are decided to be political at a centralized political level (as is the case of illiberal plebiscitarian regimes), the more totalitarian the regime will be, and the more likely that the totalitarian temptation will grow. For Talmon, messianic ideology turns democracy totalitarian. Such ideologies tend toward a single, imposed social order; if necessary, by compulsion. Illiberal plebiscitarian regimes may be led by leaders and parties with strong ideological commitment (e.g. Poland and Venezuela), but even with this, the compulsion remains limited, intending to obtain hegemony in specific public spheres only. Populism as democracy tends to fall into the totalitarian camp, but without the messianic element (which of course remains tempting, for example, where it is argued that a nation has a special mission on earth).

Democracy's totalitarian tendency appears in the state's suspicion of all intermediaries (groups) that endanger the direct relation between the individual and the state (general will). A radical (totalitarian) democracy that maximizes the individuals' personal contribution to the general will shall exclude all intermediaries that may follow an agenda contrary to it – and intermediaries do follow such agendas.[60] The Le Chapelier Act of 1791, which prohibited all intermediary associations, provides a famous early example. While the Act is rightly considered pure class legislation (it aimed to preclude the self-organization of French workers), its general justification expressed mistrust toward all organizations that represented potential hotbeds of anti-revolutionary activity. Liberal constitutionalism satisfactorily relegated associations to the private sphere, without distorting, in principle, the political relation between the individual and the general will.[61]

---

[58] Ibid., p. 37. However, Rousseau found it impermissible to "put the legislative authority and the sovereign power into the same hands." Ibid., p. 36.

[59] Talmon, *Origins,* p. 47.

[60] For the importance of direct leader–people relations in PLDs, see Chapter 4.

[61] The Le Chapelier law was repealed in 1864 by the *loi Ollivier,* a *liberal* law enacted under the *plebiscitarian* rule of Napoleon III.

Populism is (at) the heart of raw democracy and enables the unfolding of the totalitarian in democracy. This holds true in the first glorious and glorified example of democracy: Athens under Pericles. "[Pericles] specifically appealed to the ordinary folk, expanded democracy at the expense of the oligarchic elites, knew how to speak to the hearts of citizens, and ... even allowed authoritarian tendencies ... to develop. Thucydides highlights the point lucidly: Athens was in name a democracy but, in fact, governed by its first citizen, Pericles."[62] This duality characterizes illiberal democracies. "Populists are hyperpersonalist, often viewing power as their individual possession ... Yet this antidemocratic view of the leader as an unbounded messiah coexists with the democratic conviction that elections are the only legitimate route to office."[63]

Illiberal democracy is viable because it can rely on the totalitarian potential of democracy. Democracy presupposes that citizens participate in decisions affecting their communities, at least by electing their rulers. This element of choice does not conflict with the totalitarian potential: "modern authoritarianism ... does not reduce individuals to passive subjects; ... it wants them to be citizens ... . The citizens ... must exercise choice ... but its content must correspond to the official ideology."[64] The manifestation of the totalitarian potential inherent in democracy more commonly occurs in polarized societies. In the 1950s, Seymour Martin Lipset observed that "inherent in all democratic systems is the constant threat that the group conflicts which are democracy's lifeblood may solidify to the point where they threaten to disintegrate society."[65]

The manifestation of the totalitarian potential is likely in *"enfeebled democracies,"* in this "antechamber of populism that is the current status of most contemporary 'old democracies.'" Here, the "actors no longer relate to one another as fellow inhabitants of a 'space of reasons' who deliberate about ... any issue of common interest. They relate to one another as members of opposite fan clubs. They exchange insults and derogatory terms of address and hardly exchange anything that resembles a reason. ... [It is] like a stadium ... where publics only cheer their

[62] A. Koutsoukis, "Democracy in Virulent Times: Symbols and the Future of National Populism," *E-International Relations* (March 31, 2020), p. 1.

[63] F. B. de Lara and C. de la Torre, "The Pushback Against Populism: Why Ecuador's Referendums Backfired," *Journal of Democracy*, 31:2 (2020), p. 78.

[64] G. Germani, *Authoritarianism, Fascism, and National Populism* (Transaction Books, 1978), p. 10.

[65] S. M. Lipset, *Political Man: The Social Bases of Politics* (Doubleday, 1959), p. 83.

favorite teams and never cross their divides."[66] These features extend into illiberal democracy.

It is in "enfeebled" or socially non-responsive democracies that populism emerges. In continental European and Latin American societies, "it was a 'charismatic nationalist outburst' that has brought in a 'Caesaristic' breakthrough."[67] In this 1956 paper, Almond prophetically described the totalitarian potential of the non-Anglo-American European continent with a preindustrial, predominantly Catholic tradition. Seventy years later, this description well suits East Central Europe, although important pockets of this tradition exist in Western Europe as well. Here, the nationalist (populist) outburst helps the leader sustain a mild social authoritarianism in and by plebiscitarian democracy.

Caesarism's shift toward illiberal democracy, and from there possibly to despotism, lies inherently in the charismatic and unmediated power of the plebiscitarian leader, who rules in the name of popular sovereignty. It is in the shifts toward plebiscitarian power concentration that the totalitarian potential of democracy unfolds. Apologists of illiberal regimes argue that assumptions about despotic tendencies are baseless: the institutional solutions and practices upon which the government relies are normal in model democracies and do not demonstrably differ from the expectations of democratic theory and principles. Without convincing refutation, the apologists of illiberal democracy have a strong point, but the need to sustain power in illiberal democracy follows the logic of Richard III. Either you proceed with the treacherous plan or you perish. Once a party regards all nonsupporters as enemies and treats them accordingly, it cannot hope that the other party, once it gets into power, will be magnanimous. Hence the reasonableness of the increasing paranoia of the leader. Empire building is not softball.

The Caesar came to power thanks to his will to it, his daring, unscrupulous "heroism," and he remains motivated by ambition and thirst of power. Kant foresaw it all: passion leads both to the instrumentalization of reason and the demoralization of the whole regime. The plebiscitarian ruler follows his lust of power, such lust is "an inclination, which hinders the use of reason to compare, at a particular moment of choice, a specific inclination against the sum of all inclinations." This passion is not necessarily self-destructive. It is powerful as it is "able to coexist with

---

[66] A. Ferrara, "Can Political Liberalism Help us Rescue 'the people' from Populism?," *Philosophy & Social Criticism*, 44:4 (2018), p. 471.

[67] G. A. Almond, "Comparative Political Systems," *The Journal of Politics*, 18:3 (1956), pp. 406 and 408.

reason. One can also easily see that passions do the greatest harm to freedom ... passion is an enchantment which also rejects improvement."[68] Servicing lust for power is immoral as it uses humans as objects in the ambition to obtain and maintain power. For Kant passions are the cause of true evil.[69]

1.5 Illiberalism in Constitutional Democracies and Its Unfolding

(Liberal) constitutional democracy and illiberal democracy do not stand as opposites (even if some PLDs end in despotism, which is the opposite of constitutional democracy). In the real world constitutional arrangements, liberal and illiberal (authoritarian) constitutive elements cohabit, and illiberalism and authoritarianism are built into the liberal constitutional order and its institutions.[70] Popular sovereignty (a major building block of populist ideology and power) is the successor of the absolute power of the monarch and state absolutism. Liberal practices are "frail, and vulnerable, and also rife with inequalities and injustices. Indeed, in some ways they have themselves become illiberal or at least incline in this direction."[71] This coexistence is historically determined, and it survives because social authoritarianism provides constant reinforcement. Illiberal democracies only unleash the built-in authoritarianism (see again, the idea of unlimited popular sovereignty).[72] "Illiberal" here means disregarding institutional solutions against the concentration of arbitrary power and disrespecting individual autonomy; "authoritarian" refers to a concentration of power in an oppressive and selfish manner, relying on a forced subordination of subjects to the government.

This survival of illiberalism contradicts the fundamental and foundational liberal hope expressed by John Rawls, that in modern

---

[68] I. Kant, *Anthropology from a Pragmatic Point of View*, ed. H. H. Rudnick, trans. V. L. Dowdell (Southern Illinois University Press, 1996), p. 172.

[69] Passion is an "inclination which can hardly, or not at all, be controlled by reason." Ibid., p. 155.

[70] The charges against liberalism are overblown, even if they allow attractive puns: populism is an "illiberal democratic response to undemocratic liberalism." C. Mudde, "The Problem with Populism," *The Guardian* (February 17, 2015), www.theguardian.com /commentisfree/2015/feb/17/problem-populism-syriza-podemos-dark-side-europe.

[71] Isaac, "Is There Illiberal Democracy?"

[72] Duncan Kennedy reminds us that republican and authoritarian orientations coexist (in conflict) within a constitutional regime. See D. Kennedy, "Authoritarian Constitutionalism in Liberal Democracies," in H. A. García and G. Frankenberg, *Authoritarian Constitutionalism*, p. 161.

constitutional societies an overlapping consensus can be achieved or even exists to an acceptable practical level. This assumes that comprehensive, exclusive doctrines (like religions in the past) "have gradually given way to constitutional government that all citizens ... can endorse."[73] However, populists mobilize citizens with illiberal or authoritarian orientations precisely because consensual doctrines are contrary to their exclusive ones.

Constitutional democracies are imperfect and not only accidentally or occasionally. Given the empirical reality of modern societies, liberal constitutions must provide the opportunity for the cohabitation of liberal and illiberal social structures, and social forces, under *restrained* government power. Liberal polities are "porous."[74] Even a liberal constitutional order must acknowledge that "it is quite misleading to talk of 'liberal' and 'illiberal' cultures, as if the world was divided into completely liberal societies on the one hand, and completely illiberal ones on the other."[75] Of course, in liberal constitutions, liberalism (a commitment to individual rights in a free society) dominates (or at least seems to), and illiberal and authoritarian values are oppressed. However, "[i]f Freud has taught us anything, it is always to be on the lookout for the return of the repressed."[76]

The residual authoritarianism in the institutions of liberal democracies is supposedly constrained and countered by the self-correcting mechanisms of the constitution, but there remains sufficient illiberalism and authoritarianism in liberal constitutionalism (not to speak of other forms of constitutional democracy) that an illiberal constitutional regime can be built upon these elements.[77]

---

[73] Rawls, *Political Liberalism*, p. 10.

[74] C. Taylor, *Multiculturalism: Examining the Politics of Recognition* (Princeton University Press, 1994), p. 63.

[75] W. Kymlicka, *Multicultural Citizenship: A Liberal Theory of Minority Rights* (Oxford University Press, 1995), p. 94. "A constitutional liberal democracy does not require 'liberal' policy choices in the partisan political sense. To the contrary, it is consistent with illiberal policies, such as violations of racial, religious, and sexual-orientation autonomy, grave economic inequality or deprivation, or lack of social services provision." Ginsburg and Huq, *How to Save*, pp. 91–92.

[76] N. Stolzenberg, "The Return of the Repressed: Illiberal Groups in a Liberal State," *Journal of Contemporary Legal Issues*, 12 (2002), p. 899.

[77] Martin Krygier in a personal communication mentioned that there might be a third way of putting it: (1) Liberal and illiberal are not opposites; (2) they *are* opposite, but democracy houses them both; (3) given inherent illiberal tendencies in societies, liberalism is the attempt to tame and contain them. So then it's not so much illiberalism in

Illiberal democracies can simply use the illiberalism already present in constitutionalism (muting the mechanisms and values that limit such potential). The constitutional regime of contemporary plebiscitarianism unfolds the sentiments of religious fundamentalism, conservativism (as traditional conformism and fear of novelty), nationalism, racism, strong leadership, etc., by providing an authoritarian reading of the relevant provisions. The success of populism could build on "the subtle cohabitation of liberal and illiberal norms, with the latter gradually overpowering the former."[78] Such cohabitation is not surprising, given that constitutions are political and ideological (and often unprincipled) compromises, and contain concessions to illiberal forces. They may even be written under the outgoing authoritarian regime[79] (e.g. South Korea, Chile, Myanmar, and South Africa). Perhaps social peace holds more importance for a state than its own foundational principles, and the constitutional order must accommodate various combinations of liberal and illiberal cultures. Constitutions do incorporate and safeguard deeply illiberal social arrangements, often for good constitutional reasons (which have little to do with liberalism – e.g. freezing imposed peace after civil war). They grant indigenous (aboriginal) groups, ethnic and national minorities, etc. cultural exceptions (privileges) that enable illiberal domination, including gender discrimination and racism (see the problem of exclusion from a protected tribe).

The *unfinished* nature of constitutions facilitates the presence and intertwining of these elements. The gaps and shortcomings create opportunities for arch-conservative, populist, and other illiberal forces to bring into the public order illiberal solutions, which for lack of specific rules, will not be unconstitutional.[80] Specific constitutional design errors contribute to the success of populism (see, for example, the electoral premium in Hungary and the ease of amending constitutional provisions by easy to obtain constituent majorities; or the shortcomings of the Polish Constitution, which allow manipulations by simple parliamentary majority, etc.). These

liberal institutions but an attempt (like the ego and the superego) to develop institutions to contain dangerous but perennial tendencies.

[78] J. Dawson and S. Hanley, "What's Wrong with East-Central Europe? The Fading Mirage of the 'Liberal Consensus'," *Journal of Democracy*, 27:1 (2016), p. 23.

[79] M. Albertus and V. Menaldo, *Authoritarianism and the Elite Origins of Democracy* (Cambridge University Press, 2018).

[80] Gaps in the design enable "constitutional retrogression," and facilitate the success of populist power grabs (e.g. making constitutional amendment easy, as in Hungary). A. Huq and T. Ginsburg, "How to Lose a Constitutional Democracy," *University of California Law Review*, 65 (2018), p. 85.

errors were sustained by democratic governments, which could not care less about correcting them at the time.

Many openings within the constitution are technical mistakes, resulting from a lack of foresight or springing from an unwillingness to face unlikely events. It is also possible that safeguarding against a foreseeable unconstitutional development is too costly at the time of drafting. Further, constitutions remain unfinished because historical contingencies force the constituent process to end abruptly. The Declaration of the Rights of Man and of the Citizen does not contain all envisioned rights: after a few weeks of debate, the deputies thought that they had more pressing issues with which to deal. In other instances, insurmountable conflicts among founders are resolved by leaving them undecided or incorporating incompatible positions.[81] The victory of populism, deeply rooted in social discontent and the political mistakes of incumbents, cannot be explained without constitutional contingencies.

In modern societies, illiberal elements are "intertwined in the creation of modern liberal democratic institutions,"[82] and sometimes profoundly illiberal measures are promoted in the name of liberalism. Consider the criminalization of the destruction or disparagement of the national flag and other symbols of authority.[83] The German provisions in force (§ 90a StGB – disparagement, § 104 StGB – destruction) originate from the rather authoritarian Penal Code of Wilhelmine Germany (1876). The current prohibition of disparagement was upheld by the GFCC with the following reasoning:

> As a liberal state, the Federal Republic of Germany ... depends on its citizens' identification with the basic values embodied in the flag. The

---

[81] The 1948 Italian Constitution provided for the "mutual independence" of the Catholic Church and the state, but the same Article 7 recognized the Lateran Pact and apparently exempted its modifications from the constitutional process. This arrangement was the result of a (mistaken) concession by the Communist Party, allowing the Christian Democrats to turn Italy into their regime for forty years, and allowing an illiberal Catholic *reconquista* of the society. Given the constitutional ambiguity of the text, the Catholic Church received special privileges in public education and financing. See A. Pin, "Public Schools, the Italian Crucifix, and the European Court of Human Rights: The Italian Separation of Church and State," *Emory International Law Review*, 25 (2011), pp. 95–149; M. Ventura, "The Rise and Contradictions of Italy as a Secular State," in P. Cumper and T. Lewis (eds.), *Religion, Rights and Secular Society: European Perspectives* (Edward Elgar, 2012).

[82] D. King, *Name of Liberalism: Illiberal Social Policy in the USA and Britain* (Oxford University Press, 1999), p. 3.

[83] The Supreme Court of the United States (SCOTUS) judgment that decriminalized flag burning was decided by one vote. See *Texas v. Johnson* 491 US 397 (1989).

values protected in this sense are reflected in the state colours prescribed
in Article 22 of the Basic Law. They stand for the free democratic basic
order.[84]

This is a hardly liberal justification of an illiberal measure (criminalization of a [harmless] opinion). The justification of criminalization resides
in the need to protect *identification* with values embodied in the flag.
Identity (identification) protection is hardly a classic liberal aspiration
(even if historically nationalism was deeply associated with liberal political movements), but the GFCC took it for granted that the flag is
protected for the sake of the *liberal* constitutional order. This is how
the influence of authoritarian traditions endures within democracy.

Certain authoritarian identity markers are written directly into the
constitution (and allowed to stay there). These markers and institutions
are often premodern and therefore prima facie illiberal. See the privileged
constitutional position of the Orthodox Church in Greece, and in
Russian public law, or certain consequences of the privileged role of the
Catholic Church in Ireland (see first the divorce, and then the abortion,
saga). The emerging illiberal regimes in Europe favor the constitutionalization of traditional identity markers (recently conveniently transformed into "constitutional identity"), as they provide ample
opportunity for nativist mobilization for the constitution.

Successful RoL-based democracies combine liberalism and illiberalism
deliberately and expressly. The US Constitution enabled forms of substantive illiberalism at the state level (slavery, state church) but not
political anti-constitutionalism (i.e. it did not allow non-republican
forms of government). Many consider President F. D. Roosevelt as
a savior of American democracy, but at least in the case of court packing,
he displayed an instrumentalist attitude toward the Constitution that is
common to all populists in power.[85] In 1942 he signed Executive Order
9066, which led to the forced relocation and internment of Japanese
Americans, notwithstanding clear objections, including from his wife.
This is a clear indication of how authoritarian the militarization of the

---

[84] 81 BVerfGE 278. 292. Judgment of March 7, 1990. The actual conviction was held
unconstitutional for lack of proper balancing.

[85] Roosevelt was not indifferent to populism and an important or decisive part of his
electorate consisted of people with existential grievances. He castigated the "new industrial dictatorship" and a large debt write-off was part of his program: the gold clauses in
private contracts were revoked, enabling payment in depreciated dollars. Overall, he
remained a captive of his establishment's constitutional culture and refrained from
attacking institutions in the name of democracy.

executive can be. The US constitutional system remains full of authoritarian hotspots. Admittedly, "current electoral practice is characterized by numerous exclusionary and suppressive practices. Rights-based liberalism is compromised by the systematic underenforcement of many individual rights. Politicians' efforts to entrench themselves are endemic, not occasional. As a result, large gaps remain between the law on the ground and the law on the books."[86] Similar trends are less surprising in nonsecular constitutional systems. The Irish Constitution, as written by de Valera, was certainly not a liberal one (though it respected the individual rights minimum), but it was certainly democratic and satisfied the expectations of constitutionalism. Modern Israel "embodies an equivocal mix of constitutive principles that cannot be resolved in favor of either its liberal or illiberal elements."[87]

Liberal constitutions are constitutions of imperfectly liberal societies. Large segments of the population, even the majority, may feel that the liberal constitution was imposed (and irrelevant for ordinary people); under certain conditions, they acquiesce to it, but this does not result in habit. This seems to be the case in the former European satellites of the Soviet Union, among others.

According to Juan Linz certain constitutional arrangements, namely presidentialism, have by design and nature characteristics that make them receptive to authoritarianism.[88] A president elected by direct popular vote is more likely to govern in a populist, anti-institutionalist fashion. "The feeling of having independent power, a mandate from the people . . . is likely to give a president a sense of power and mission that might be out of proportion to the limited plurality that elected him."[89]

The constitution may preserve the authoritarian tradition of state building and the authoritarian logic of state power (cult of state secrecy, discretionary power, dignity of state institution, military discipline, etc.). For Locke, executive prerogative was a necessity, and he endorsed "the power to act according to discretion, for the public good, without the support of the law and sometimes even against it."[90] Unfortunately, times

[86] Huq and Ginsburg, "How to Lose," pp. 90–91.
[87] Walker, "The Idea," p. 159.
[88] J. Linz, "Presidential or Parliamentary Democracy: Does it Make a Difference?," in J. Linz and A. Valenzuela (eds.), *The Failure of Presidential Democracy* (Johns Hopkins University Press, 1994).
[89] Ibid., p. 19.
[90] J. Locke, *Second Treatise of Government*, ed. C. B. McPherson (Hackett Publishing Company, 1980), chap. IV, XIV.

have not improved. Foreign affairs remain a matter of prerogative, perhaps by another name or nameless. States of emergency still welcome authoritarian rule even if important restrictions on emergency power have been developed in the last seventy years. Institutionalized "hyper-presidentialism" in Latin America is the source of one sort of authoritarianism.[91]

The state relies on a civil service, expecting obedience and loyalty (and these authoritarian elements are enforced even today). The bureaucratic state organization has inherited a clearly authoritarian tradition: the civil service in France and in Prussia were originally conceived as hierarchical, quasi-military, centralized organizations,[92] although efficiency consider-ations (the merit system), the RoL (in the early form of legality review), together with constitutionalization of the administration and modern management resulted in a sea-change. And yet, the state bureaucracy is expected to operate according to the rules of subordination, and in the relationship between authorities and the public, a sort of authoritarian subordination can be detected. The RoL is there to temper but not to undo it.

The logic of *raison d'État* dictates restrictions on access to information: state secrets are expected to be protected as a state interest. The ECtHR has found it necessary in a democratic society to restrict civil servants' freedom of opinion for the sake of loyalty to the state and its constitu-tional order.[93] The toleration of deeply authoritarian submission (pre-sented as duty of loyalty) in the civil service has been decisive in the success of various power grabs. This was the precondition of the concen-tration of power in the hands of the plebiscitarian leader: once he filled

---

[91] C. Nino, "The Debate Over Constitutional Reform in Latin America," *Fordham International Law Journal*, 16:3 (1992), pp. 635–51. Nino used the term "hyperpresiden-tialism" to make a distinction with the term "President," derived from the US Constitution. For Nino, Latin American "Presidents" received many additional powers, which made them – formally – much more powerful, at least in the early days, than US Presidents. These additional powers included the possibility to declare a state of siege, and limit fundamental rights and liberties during those circumstances; the possibility to intervene, even through the use of force, in the internal affairs of the different states that constituted the Union (*intervención federal*); the possibility to appoint and remove its personnel (i.e. Ministers) with absolute discretion, etc.

[92] Prussian civil servants were trained in a feudal and authoritarian tradition developing an attachment to an abstract concept of the state and its authority. M. Broszat, *The Hitler State* (Routledge, 2014), pp. 12–13.

[93] *Glasenapp v. The Federal Republic of Germany*, ECtHR, App. no. 9228/80, Report of 11 May 1984. The Court upheld the German ban although no other country had such stringent restrictions.

the key positions of the public administration with his cadres, the loyal civil service became the tool of domination in his hands.

Beyond the incorporation of illiberal and authoritarian *institutions* into the constitutional order, reflecting illiberal social pressures, a number of *liberal* constitutional *rights* sustain, engender and protect illiberal structures and attitudes. Church autonomy, derived from freedom of religion, represents only the most visible example of nurturing premodern, illiberal structures perpetuating gender bias and authoritarian structures in organization and thought.[94] Freedom of association protects voluntary associations that serve authoritarian forms of cooperation and cultivate authoritarian and other illiberal values; freedom of speech helps propagate authoritarian values. The constitutional protection of parental rights and family autonomy, as well as respect for privacy and the private sphere, accepts patriarchal structures oppressing women. The parental right to educational choice may include despotic decisions to follow the authoritarian convictions of parents.[95]

Many consider private property as central to the liberal order (in the economic sense), and the liberal political order is hardly sustainable without the market economy, but the right to private property enables hierarchical structures and antidemocratic command regimes to be established in the workplace. Further, private property gives the freedom (the material basis) to support authoritarian structures (also as a matter of freedom of expression).[96] On the other hand, the constitutional status of property is determined (limited) by preliberal and antiliberal (e.g. Christian) thought until this day. Article 14 of the German Basic Law, following a preliberal Prussian tradition, provides that property entails

---

[94] See, for example, *Hosanna-Tabor Evangelical Lutheran Church and School* v. *Equal Employment Opportunity Commission*, 565 US 171 (2012). Federal discrimination laws do not apply to religious organizations' selection of their ministers.

[95] The matter remains ambiguous. In *Meyer* v. *Nebraska*, 262 US 390 (1923) and *Pierce* v. *Society of Sisters* 268 US 510 (1925), the state (actually endorsing a campaign of the Ku Klux Klan) intended to apply a restrictive, prejudicial educational policy to all (prohibiting the teaching of German as the language of the enemy). SCOTUS stood up against this totalitarian attitude in the name of private education and the right of "orderly pursuit of happiness by free men."

[96] Privatization of public services removes whole areas of activity from liberal-minded control: "[C]ommingling of government and market forces enables the accretion of State power at the expense of the private sector, *threatening to destabilize the liberal democratic order*. Further, this commingling enables the accretion of political executive power at the expense of Congress and the civil service, *threatening the constitutional and administrative separations of powers*." J. Michaels, *Constitutional Coup: Privatization's Threat to the American Republic* (Harvard University Press, 2017), p. 126.

obligations and that its use shall also serve the public good. Article 43 of the Irish Constitution, famously influenced by Catholic social doctrine, considers property a natural right but requires that its exercise be guided by the principles of social justice. Numerous other jurisdictions echo similar convictions, even without similar constitutional provisions. The only protection that constitutions grant is against confiscation – but the amount of fair compensation often departs from market value.

A level of constitutional openness is inevitable, given that the constitution, as a future-oriented document, tends to create opportunities for adjustment. Constitutions as relational contracts must leave things undecided, including crucial social issues to be determined by the democratic process, allowing the democratic choice to reflect social illiberalism. Criminal libel,[97] blasphemy laws, overcriminalization of harmless behavior, etc., are either such pockets of illiberal choice or simply leftovers.

Beyond incorporating authoritarian rights and institutional structures into the liberal constitutional model, an additional self-defeating element facilitates the success of the illiberal plan. Liberalism remains open and vulnerable to illiberalism because of its own inherent logic. "Liberalism as neutrality ... is consistent with everyone's living very illiberal lives. For everyone could opt into total communities."[98]

The very logic of its tolerance forces liberalism to accommodate illiberal choices as acts of self-determination, allowing forms of life that are incompatible, or at least inconsistent with the liberal requirements of the constitutional order. A society that respects the equality of all, and therefore of all women with all men, cannot tolerate "islands" where equality does not apply. If liberalism "values pluralism, diversity, openness, and tolerance"[99] (what Larry Alexander calls "liberalism as cosmopolitanism"), then illiberals will accuse it of being repressive in its tolerance and imposing diversity. On the other hand, tolerance can also facilitate the destruction of the liberal culture by allowing authoritarian forms of life (groups) to operate.[100] Liberalism enables people to establish

---

[97] Notwithstanding the efforts of the Organization for Security and Cooperation in Europe (OSCE), Western democracies refused to implement the suggested changes.

[98] L. Alexander, "Illiberalism All the Way Down: Illiberal Groups and Two Conceptions of Liberalism," *Journal of Contemporary Legal Issues*, 12 (2002), p. 627.

[99] Ibid., p. 630.

[100] "A central problem for the liberal society's protection of the right to culture – especially if the culture involved is not itself liberal – is that protecting it often requires the state to use illiberal means. For example, granting a particular cultural group the opportunity to preserve its cultural homogeneity in a given region under certain circumstances may

relatively autonomous, self-governing "cultural enclaves within which standard liberal principles can be flouted ... the exercise of individual rights *produces* group rights."[101] The liberal respect of individual choice as a right opens a "space to transmit ... the code of laws and values [of illiberal groups] to new generations."[102]

Constitutional liberalism is ready to protect illiberal exceptionalism. At least for SCOTUS, "intrusion into the internal structure or affairs of an association," like a "regulation that forces the group to accept members it does not desire," is unconstitutional.[103] This means the de facto support of an illiberal life form. To the extent liberalism is tolerant, it will allow illiberal choices to exist at least in a repressed form, in the ghetto of the private realm of associations (including religious associations) and in private relations and family. Of course, this is certainly not the only possibility recognized in liberal constitutionalism. The Swiss and the French (supported by the ECtHR) are less likely to allow illiberal group practices in schools (segregation chosen by the minority – e.g. refusal to participate in common swimming lessons for religious reasons), while courts in Canada and the UK are more permissive to nonmainstream, authoritarian forms of life. The EU seems to grant a narrower exception to churches in the context of antidiscrimination than the United States or Germany, whose constitutional traditions recognize religious authoritarianism.[104]

Constitutionalism tried to contain the illiberal consequences of the freedom to make illiberal personal choices by relegating all potentially authoritarian forms of life to the private sphere, in hope that this would liberate the public sphere, including, at least to some extent, the political as well. Such containment however failed, as the boundaries of a strictly private sphere could not be sustained.

---

exact the price of preventing outsiders from living there." A. Margalit and M. Halbertal, "Liberalism and the Right to Culture," *Social Research*, 61:3 (1994), pp. 491–92.

[101] Stolzenberg, "The Return of the Repressed," p. 899.

[102] Ibid., p. 900.

[103] *Roberts* v. *United States Jaycees*, 468 US 609, 622 (1984). Forcing a group to accept certain members may impair the ability of the group to express those views, and only those views, that it intends to express: admitting a gay member to the Boy Scouts of America stands against the expressed values of the organization. Thirty years later the organization changed its position, allowing gay scouts and gay scoutmasters.

[104] Case C-414/16, *Vera Egenberger* v. *Evangelisches Werk für Diakonie und Entwicklung eV* [2018] EU:C:2018:257. The matter remains pending in the German Federal Constitutional Court.

Unleashed democracy liberates illiberalism (and illiberalism unleashes democracy). Illiberalism here means disrespect for the institutional limits to the concentration of power, intolerance of difference, submissive acceptance of constituted authorities[105] and the imposition of illiberal values (i.e. values that disregard individual freedom). Illiberalism enables a concentration of power that restricts electoral choices and marginalizes increasing numbers of people, limiting the pool of citizens relevant in political decision-making. To the extent that illiberal regimes dismiss obligatory limitations on state power, they fail to satisfy the requirements of normative constitutionalism. Illiberal democracies function within the formal requirements of the democratic process but without the constitutional commitment and democratic culture that would restrict the potential totalitarianism of democracy. More than its manipulated electoral system, creeping illiberalism enables the perpetuation of regimes of democratic shallowness.

This kind of constitutional illiberalism occurs in a cultural environment that favors illiberal social values (and, related to illiberalism, authoritarianism). This illiberal social context raises the prescient question of Graham Walker:

> how to constitute a nontyrannical politics with a decent rule of law, while at the same time affirming in a public, institutionalized way a particular ethos – whether of nationality, moral solidarity, religious tradition, or some more or less alarming combination of all three ... Can the Hungarian state offer its patronage to Magyar identity without fatally undermining its progress toward the rule of law? ... Can Russia constitutionally affirm the historical and cultural centrality of Orthodoxy without inviting a slide to fascism? Can the massively Roman Catholic character of Polish society be enacted in its public institutions in a way that is consistent with constitutionalist aspirations?[106]

The answer seems to be NO. A state that commits first and foremost to the protection of a specific Magyar identity, and accepts personal rule as the allegedly best protector of that identity, inevitably moves away from constitutional neutrality. A democratic theocracy cannot satisfy minimal constitutionalism in the long run.[107] While it cannot be ruled out that

---

[105] On the role of authoritarianism as submission to the leader, see below in Section 1.6.
[106] Walker, "The Idea," p. 156. Walker was right in the sense that the constitutional and political failure of ethnic identity recognition contributed to the success of populists.
[107] See, however, R. Hirschl, *Constitutional Theocracy* (Harvard University Press, 2010). Hirschl thought that theocracy can be incorporated into constitutionalism. Based on the experience of Islamic countries, Saeed warns that "initial containment of 'religious' zeal

a particular ethos may be accommodated in a constitutionalist structure, in the three above-mentioned instances (Hungary, Russia, and Poland), the combination failed. The same applies to Turkey: the illiberalism of (a rather moderate) Islamism may perhaps be compatible with constitutionalism and democracy, but the desire to reimpose it on society has actually destroyed democracy.

The substantive illiberalism (choice of illiberal social values) of the plebiscitarian regime[108] is often described as illiberal mission creep. For example, in Turkey the primary interest of the political power turned out to be its own perpetuation in the service of the greater cause of Islam, which could not be served by any other government. In other words, nonliberal normative constitutionalism is a risky venture at best, and an attempt to delegitimize and destroy constitutionalism at worst.[109] The leader is ready to save, enhance, impose, and perpetuate illiberal means and ways or life. This means a forced return to a patriarchal, nationalist, and religious good life as understood by the leader. The realization of these real or imaginary, inoculated values of the (relative) majority has constitutional implications. "[W]herever people value some aspects of communal identity more than the autonomy of individual choice, such values need to be crafted into a constitutionalist structure, which can simultaneously give them public status and impede their more worrisome expression."[110] The repressed (mildly despised) popular preferences take their revenge in the forms offered by raw democracy. Raw democracy knows no bounds (except to sustain the power of the leader). It will claim that it only answers to the will of the majority, which would allow the expression of all passing desire. This is what plebiscitarianism seems to promise: in reality, the momentary whim is under the strictest control, not of procedures and forms, but of the concerns of the plebiscitarian ruler. He will select the passion that serves the regime, and if no such passion exists – he will generate it.

Contrary to the efforts of many constitutional democracies, which try to keep the public life open to all (with different degrees of diversity),

---

may have the effect of subsequent entrenchment of more moderate, but nevertheless illiberal, rights discourses." S. Saeed, "A Review of Constitutional Theocracy, by Ran Hirschl," *Indiana Journal of Global Legal Studies*, 18:2 (2010), p. 964.

[108] Recall, once again that this illiberalism originates in the democratic nature of the political system. The plebiscitarian leader would like to reflect what is attractive to his people.

[109] For the standard argument (common in feminism, critical theory, Christianity, etc.) that constitutional neutrality privileges a certain individualistic position, oppressing alternative world views, see Chapter 6.

[110] Walker, "The Idea," p. 155.

illiberal democracies encourage illiberal enclaves and encourage their efforts to reconquer the public sphere. This is what animates constitutional policies when public hospitals and schools are transferred to the management of religious organizations. The state remains formally neutral (secular) but becomes increasingly hollow.[111]

1.6 Authoritarian Predispositions

"We know at least since Plato's seminal treatise on the 'Republic' that all political systems rise or fall depending on their goodness of fit to the mental requirements of their citizens."[112] When plebiscitarian regimes enhance illiberal elements of the existing constitutional order, or bring such features into a new constitution, this satisfies popular sentiment among regime supporters. Such responsiveness is a must, given the need for democratic emotional endorsement of the leader.

The personal preferences of the leaders cannot explain the illiberalism of their regimes. Kaczyński may be personally committed to Polish renewal in a Catholic state, but he does not merely impose personal idiosyncrasies on Polish society. Many share his views. Populist voters often cherish authoritarian values, and a good number have nothing against being led by a strongman. These supporters are not simply victims of globalization who are manipulated by populist leaders and dictatorial regimes. Many of them are convinced that by cherishing authoritarian ideas and solutions they affirm a democracy that finally cares for country and nation – and for them.

One should not underestimate the importance, sincerity, and legitimacy of support for the leader and his regime. This is what O'Donnell observed in Latin America over two decades ago:

> The people with whom I spoke were not crooks, or at least did not respond as if they were: they were trying to contribute to some kind of common good even as they trespassed against republican boundaries. They were not alone; their families, fellow party and clique members, and business associates assumed that the officials would behave in this way and would

---

[111] The United States sees increasingly successful attempts to carve out large chunks from general laws as areas of private religious choice. See *Burwell* v. *Hobby Lobby*, 573 US 682 (2014).

[112] J. P. Forgas and D. Lantos, "Collective Narcissism and the Collapse of Democracy in Hungary," in J. P Forgas, W. D Crano and K. Fiedler (eds.), *Applications of social psychology: How social psychology can contribute to the solution of real-world problems* (Routledge, 2020), p. 268.

have strongly condemned them had they not. Everyone matter-of-factly
assumed that informal rules trumped formal ones; I could detect no signs
of bad conscience. Formal rules retained significance, but basically as
hurdles that officials had to learn to circumvent without provoking
damaging consequences for themselves or their affiliates.[113]

In many respects, this kind of understanding characterizes those who say
that the nation's interest remains above the law or constitution. From
Singapore to Venezuela, as well in Hungary and Poland, the majority is
entitled to determine the common good (even if for most people it comes
from believing that "this is the only way"). In this credo, "the good of the
nation is above the law."[114] This often-quoted sentence of MP Kornel
Morawiecki (the father of the Polish Prime Minister) is, however,
a political slogan, not a constitutional theory, and it corresponds to the
old Roman adage *salus populi suprema lex.*

The laws enacted in illiberal democracies in such a spirit rely upon and
reflect the inclinations of an authoritarian social stock. In other words,
there are enough authoritarians among supporters of the charismatic
leader to make authoritarian legal positions welcome. The leader will
select and construe the values and institutions that cater to persons with
authoritarian predispositions, who constitute a sufficient minority to win
elections. The plebiscitarian regime is illiberal precisely because it is
democratic.

The message that mobilized populist voters (in Europe, primarily
right-wing populists) offered an answer to resentment. Already in 1941,
Erich Fromm indicated that where a sense of social insecurity, national
humiliation, etc. prevails, self-esteem can be restored through group
supremacy.[115] By lending his admirers respectability, the leader provides
in-group self-esteem, and by offering a charismatic authoritative figure,
he enables subordination-based conformity. Given the level of this
resentment, ruling in the illiberal state must be an exercise in self-esteem.

Competing but partly overlapping psychological and sociopsychological theories (and empirical findings) explain the success of the political
psychology used by the plebiscitarian leader. This section refers to the

---

[113] G. A. O'Donnell, "Horizontal Accountability in New Democracies," *Journal of Democracy*, 9:3 (1998), p. 118.

[114] "Kornel Morawiecki w Sejmie: Nad prawem jest dobro Narodu! 'Prawo, które nie służy narodowi to bezprawie!' Reakcja? Owacja na stojąco," W polityce (November 26, 2016), www.wpolityce.pl/polityka/273101-kornel-morawiecki-w-sejmie-nad-prawem-jest-dobro-narodu-prawo-ktore-nie-sluzy-narodowi-to-bezprawie-reakcja-owacja-na-sto jaco-wideo.

[115] E. Fromm, *Escape from Freedom* (Holt, Rinehart & Winston, 1941).

relevance of personal authoritarian predispositions in accepting totalitarian democratic political solutions (e.g. treating the opposition and others as treacherous enemies). The collective narcissism of the healing cocktail will be discussed in the context of the leader–people relationship in Chapter 4 and self-esteem in the context of identity building in Chapter 5.

Where the plebiscitarian leader plays the ethnonationalist tune, authoritarian-minded persons will dance in the streets. But others will join them too; not all supporters of populism score high on an authoritarianism scale. There are many reasons to support populist movements other than personality traits, including nationalism as a cultural fact.[116] Many fellow travelers of the regime do not share its illiberal values but accept it because this is the way to make a living, or a very good one. Others are simply too dependent existentially. For different groups, the official recognition of illiberal values merely corresponds to the populist *Zeitgeist* (the culture of narcissism).[117]

Authoritarian predisposition is understood here as a personality trait, measured by child-rearing attitudes.[118] Persons disposed toward authoritarianism favor "suppression of difference and achievement of uniformity necessitate autocratic social arrangements."[119] To quote Adorno's classic formula, the authoritarian personality has a "general disposition to glorify, to be subservient to and remain uncritical toward authoritative

---

[116] K. Dunn, "Preference for Radical Right-Wing Populist Parties among Exclusive-Nationalists and Authoritarians," *Party Politics*, 21:3 (2013), pp. 367–80.

[117] Mudde, "Zeitgeist." On identity see Chapter 4.3.2.

[118] Karen Stenner understands the authoritarian predisposition as one of intolerance against the other, "an individual predisposition concerned with the appropriate balance between group authority and uniformity, on the one hand, and individual autonomy and diversity, on the other." K. Stenner, *The Authoritarian Dynamic* (Cambridge University Press, 2005), p. 14.

Stenner follows here the tradition of T. W. Adorno, E Frenkel-Brunswik, D. J. Levinson and R. N. Sanford, *The Authoritarian Personality* (Harper and Row, 1950), p. 228. On the debates, limits, and contemporary rehabilitation, see among many E. Campo, "Authoritarian Personality," in B. S. Turner (ed.), *The Wiley-Blackwell Encyclopedia of Social Theory* (Wiley Blackwell, 2017).

[119] K. Stenner, "Three Kinds of 'Conservatism,'" *Psychological Inquiry*, 20:2–3 (April–September 2009), p. 142. Scholars who use a different psychological paradigm also find that the populist voter reflects specific personality characteristics, which are against openness and tolerance: "[I]ndividuals low on Agreeableness are more likely to support populist parties." B. N. Bakker, M. Rooduijn, and G. Schumacher, "The Psychological Roots of Populist Voting: Evidence from the United States, the Netherlands and Germany," *European Journal of Political Research*, 55:2 (2016), p. 313. They find that "populist voters do not have an authoritarian personality such as supporters of fascist outfits" (p. 304), but they refer to a different kind of authoritarianism.

figures of the ingroup and to take an attitude of punishing outgroup figures in the name of some moral authority."[120] It is easy to see why a person with such characteristics would be the foundation of "the authentic people" who support the illiberal leader.

Karen Stenner argued that all populations in (Western) societies have a pool of basically authoritarian people, encompassing an estimated one-third of the population.[121] Under most electoral systems, this suffices to win election after election. Empirical data indicate that people with authoritarian predispositions are overrepresented in victorious populist movements. Among the 2016 US Republican candidates, Trump supporters represented a significantly different authoritarianism compared to the constituencies of other candidates.[122] A survey in ten European countries found high rates of authoritarians among populists, many of whom vote for populist parties, although "[t]here are more authoritarian populists than right-wing populist voters."[123] Only in Poland was a single right-wing party able to attract the overwhelming majority of "tribal authoritarians" in the electorate.[124]

What triggers support for a propopulist, and later proplebiscitarian leader, among authoritarian persons? According to Stenner, "[e]nduring authoritarian predisposition interacts with changing environmental conditions – specifically, conditions of 'normative threats' – to produce manifest expressions of intolerance."[125] The conditions most

---

[120] Adorno (et al,), *The Authoritarian Personality*, p. 228. In a modern restatement, Altemeyer claims that the core traits of the authoritarian disposition are aggressiveness, conventionalism, and submissiveness. B. Altemeyer, *Enemies of Freedom: Understanding Right-wing Authoritarianism* (Jossey-Bass, 1988).

[121] K. Stenner and J. Haidt, "Authoritarianism is not a Momentary Madness, but an Eternal Dynamic Within Liberal Democracies," in C. R. Sunstein (ed.), *Can It Happen Here? Authoritarianism in America* (Harper-Collins, 2018), p. 192.

[122] M. C. MacWilliams, *The Rise of Trump. America's Authoritarian Spring* (The Amherst College Press, 2016), pp. 26–27.

[123] J. Bartle, D. Sanders and J. Twyman, "Authoritarian Populist Opinion in Europe," in I. Crewe and D. Sanders (eds.), *Authoritarian Populism and Liberal Democracy* (Palgrave Macmillan, 2019), p. 63.

[124] Ibid., p. 23, Table A4.7: Poland. Hungary was not included.
As to Latin America, see D. Azpuru and M. F. T. Malone, "Parenting Attitudes and Public Support for Political Authoritarianism in Latin America," *International Journal of Public Opinion Research*, 31:3 (2019), pp. 570–87. This work finds that authoritarian parenting attitudes correlate with support of authoritarian measures of governance (e.g. extension of term limits) and perceptions that political minorities threaten the country. Literature debates to what extent authoritarians are present among left-wing populists.

[125] Stenner, *The Authoritarian Dynamic*, p. 8. Some recent empirical studies seem to corroborate the classic position of Adorno, namely that "social and economic dimensions of ideology in general and support for laissez-faire capitalism and racial prejudice, intolerance, and ethnocentrism in particular" are interrelated and originate in

challenging to the oneness and sameness of the social order are "questioned authorities" and a "lack of conformity to or consensus in group values."[126] Under normative threat, authoritarian predispositions increase intolerance toward the different. The populist leader must maintain the sense of threatening out-groups.

What kind of legal arrangements are favored by authoritarians? "Authoritarians consistently favor members of in-groups and discriminate against members of out-groups."[127] Understandably, constitutional positions insist on an exclusive community with strong borders. The law is expected to protect against threatening groups, irrespective of bookish liberal rights.

The authoritarian predisposition has important consequences for the structure of democracy. Submission to the leader (and the act of confirming the leader is an act of submission!), and readiness to reject the outgroup, are dispositions that enable mass support for the illiberal regime. When the regime refuses to recognize the rights of "diverse" people (e.g. migrants or LGBTQ people), it suppresses difference that it finds threatening. This is not simply about massaging identity. It furthers the one-sidedness that undermines democracy as a process of exchange (debate) among reasonable positions. "[A]n authoritarian mind-set . . . is dismissive of counter-opinion and prepared to use all means possible to achieve the populists' (morally suspect) policy goals."[128] Hence the acceptability of plebiscitarian democracy, where democracy is not about common decision-making with results acceptable for all citizens as temporary, reasonable compromises (even when you lose), but an opportunity to express agreement with the leader who has the power to support his people. The leader can count on authoritarian submission. The acceptance of authority is either compelled or embraced for being merely the normal state of affairs: government authority is respected because it has higher standing, as in Singapore, where the authority of the

authoritarian personality traits. F. Azevedo, J. T. Jost, T. Rothmund, and J. Sterling, "Neoliberal Ideology and the Justification of Inequality in Capitalist Societies: Why Social and Economic Dimensions of Ideology Are Intertwined," *Journal of Social Issues*, 75:1 (2019), pp. 49–88. For a contrary finding see Bartle et al., "Authoritarian Populist." (There is left-wing authoritarian populism in Europe.)

126 Stenner, *The Authoritarian Dynamic*, pp. 16–17.

127 J. Mellon and C. Prosser, "Authoritarianism, Social Structure and Economic Policy Preferences," *SSRN* (August 18, 2017), p. 2. See Chapter 4 on the importance of the unity of the people.

128 I. Crewe and D. Sanders, "Introduction," in Crewe and Sanders (eds.), *Authoritarian Populism*, p. 3.

regime stems from the ruling party's consecutive election victories,[129] creating both the impression and the reality of no alternative.

The plebiscitarian form of government (i.e. permanent acclamation that gives continuous legitimacy to the leader and his government) is possible if and when the leader can assume that the citizenry will be deferential to state authority. With a sufficient number of authoritarian-minded people who respect the public authority without further demand for legitimacy, the leader can afford the risks of a contested election: as long as his routinized charisma remains effective (thanks to, among others, the control exercised over mass media and social media), the deferential relative majority will endorse him. People will accept commands from the state simply because such commands originate from the state, and because the leader maintains legitimate authority, and not only in the sense of legality, but also in the plebiscitarian sense of being popularly authorized. For other supporters of illiberal regimes, conformism will suffice, especially where civic resilience does not form part of the local culture.[130]

Authoritarianism is likely more common (or more easily "liberated") where it forms part of the historically determined culture of a country; there will be less resistance to it where the prevalent culture does not support autonomy or republican citizenship, and where, as in Hungary, the prevalent social strategy of survival is traditionally the acceptance of the given.[131] At least in Eastern Europe, the rather mechanically copied constitutional arrangements did not enable the long-term transformative effects that would firmly root basic tenets of constitutional decency into the uncontested shared cultural heritage. The revolutionary institutions could not repress homegrown authoritarianism and tribalism. New freedoms such as freedom of speech and association (and later, the breakdown of the norms of civility) enabled the formation of illiberal-minded groups.[132] Populism

---

[129] J. L. Neo and A. O. H. Xian, "Making the Singapore Constitution: Amendments as Constitution-Making," *Journal of Comparative Law*, 14:1 (2019), p. 76.

[130] This is what makes Poland different: there is a strong tradition of civic resilience, shared among more engaged Law and Justice Party (PiS) and opposition supporters.

[131] It is noteworthy that Hungary is the only EU member state with a Catholic tradition that is close to countries with a Greek Orthodox background. Hungary was low on the values of self-expression (social toleration, life satisfaction, public expression, and aspiration to liberty). Inglehart-Welzel Cultural Map, WVS wave 6 (2010–2014). *World Values Survey*, Figure 6, www.worldvaluessurvey.org/WVSContents.jsp?CMSID=Findings.

[132] In Eastern Europe, illiberal attitudes were inherited from illiberal times through family traditions. A. Pető, "Revisionist Histories, 'Future memories': Far-right Memorialization Practices in Hungary," *European Politics and Society*, 17:1 (2017), pp. 41–51.

only mobilized them and their mentalities, claiming that "people composed of ordinary men and women" were forced to accept liberal impositions.

Where society is short on democratic and liberal experience (not to speak of liberal democracy), and the cultural legacy favors learned acquiescence (a characteristic of the *homo sovieticus*), social resistance to illiberalism and domination is less likely. With such cultural experience, social interactions will likely reinforce acquiescence (conformism) and elevate authoritarian intolerance to the new social normal.

The Emergence of the Illiberal State

In order never to lose power, one must first gain power.

Agnes Heller[1]

2.1 Introduction

Once populist forces win elections, they take similar steps to transform the constitutional structure, following a familiar blueprint. They simply follow the logic of the constitutional state in reverse and obtain control over the institutions that are central to constitutional power. The steps typically include:

> the appointment of party loyalists at all levels of state bureaucracy; empowering the executive at the expense of other branches of state power; the emasculation of state independent authorities and other institutions of horizontal accountability; control over the media, the judiciary, and the education system; crony capitalism; and, ultimately, regime change through the introduction of bold constitutional reform.[2]

In terms of substantive control, this blueprint includes "'grabbing the state' and an expansion of executive power, an onslaught on liberal institutions, and patronage politics."[3]

Scholars have documented the above steps thoroughly.[4] This chapter thus deals with this constitutional demolition purely from a constitutional law perspective, while Chapter 3 will discuss the meaning

---

[1] A. Heller, "Hungary: How Liberty Can Be Lost," *Social Research: An International Quarterly*, 86:1 (2019), p. 6.

[2] T. S. Pappas, *Populism and Liberal Democracy: A Comparative and Theoretical Analysis* (Oxford University Press, 2019), p. 190.

[3] Ibid.

[4] For an excellent comparative summary, see, for example, Ibid.; C. Houle and P. D. Kenny, "The Political and Economic Consequences of Populist Rule in Latin America," *Government and Opposition*, 53:2 (2018), pp. 256–87.

of "grabbing the state" and its relation to domination. This chapter presents the transformation of the pre-existing constitutional system. Populist forces promise authenticity and a government (state) that will cater to the people. These are political projects; the constitutional aspects are secondary. Where constitution-making is possible, it has been used to enable the new state to serve the interests of the new elite formed around the Caesaristic leader. The presentation of this transformation will follow the logic of constitutional law and survey the transformation of key constitutional institutions one by one. There have been important differences in regime building depending on how easy it is to manipulate the constitution, but the logic and mechanisms of institution replacement are similar, irrespective of the ideological orientation (left or right, or religious).[5] Changes in the organization of public life occur rapidly and synchronously in every country concerned. The snowball (avalanche) effect of the transformation makes social resistance nearly impossible. By the time one scandal (a nonsensical proposal or corrupt measure that was thought impossible twenty-four hours earlier) becomes known, the next one has already surpassed it. In Poland, the key legal and resulting personnel changes were in place within three to four months, and the total constitutional transformation of Hungary, Venezuela, and Ecuador took less than eighteen months. The totalitarian nature of the transformation flows from the interaction and celerity of these measures, accompanied by comparably radical changes in business and property relations, as well as public opinion and sentiment, all enabled by the legal transformation.

Inspired by their own populist rhetoric and a strong sense of past betrayal among their supporters, the new rulers claim they have been called to undo the treason and injustices of the (old) elite, who have wronged the ordinary people and the nation. The new rulers promise a clean slate. Both Orbán and Chávez emphasized that they ushered in "a revolution by democratic means against the established liberal institutions" to implement the will of the people/nation.[6] Orbán claimed in 2010 that the people gave him a mandate "to carry out constitutional change and create a new permanent community of national cooperation without ideology."[7] In Poland PiS won the elections of 2015 and 2019

---

[5] See O. Selçuk, "Strong Presidents and Weak Institutions: Populism in Turkey, Venezuela and Ecuador," *Southeast European and Black Sea Studies*, 16:4 (2016), p. 571.

[6] Pappas, *Populism and Liberal Democracy*, p. 152.

[7] V. Orbán, "Orbán Viktor napirend előtti felszólalása" (speech in parliament, July 22, 2010), Prime Minister's Office Website, https://2010-2014.kormany.hu/hu/miniszterelnok

with a comprehensive project of "the good change," offering the repair and reconstruction of the state.

Their popular, nation-building mission required the new rulers immediately to confront the existing constitutional institutions and the people running them, each presented as manifestations of the enemy. These obstacles were to be eliminated by revolutionary rearrangement, without the conditions of a revolution. An anti-institutional sentiment prevailed, but democracy remained an uncontested value. The governments assumed power in a democratic process and functioned in an international environment where the value of democracy could not be challenged.

Today large segments of the population, including many populist voters, support democracy but are ready to accept nondemocratic forms of government.[8] Most supporters of illiberal governments believe that democracy exists in the country and favor it, while the majority of opposition voters believe that there is none.[9]

Under these circumstances, including its original populist commitment to a better democracy, the new power aims to maintain more than

---

seg/miniszterelnok/beszedek-publikaciok-interjuk/orban-viktor-napirend-elotti-felszola lasa-2010-julius-22 (my translation).

By June 2020 the Hungarian government concluded that such a community had been successfully achieved without the opposition. See B. Tamás, "Gulyás: Új fejlemény, hogy az ellenzék nélkül is létrejöhet a nemzeti egység," 444 (June 18, 2020), www.444.hu/2020/06/18/gulyas-uj-fejlemeny-hogy-az-ellenzek-nelkul-is-letrejohet-a-nemzeti-egyseg.

[8] The data are quite contradictory. According to a Pew survey, in 2017, after seven years of Fidesz rule, commitment toward democracy in Hungary was low, comparable, for example, to Senegal or Kenya, and clearly lower than in Western Europe. An overwhelming majority of Hungarians (68 percent) would consider it good to govern the country in a nondemocratic way, especially if governed by experts, with a relatively high acceptance rate of a strong leader (24 percent, a figure that is still considerably less than the popular support for the HPM). R. Wike and K. Simmons (et al.), *Globally, Broad Support for Representative and Direct Democracy* (Pew Research Center, 2017). Another survey noted a similar trend in 2017, though it indicated even higher acceptance of a strong leader among Polish people (35 percent agreeing or tending to agree). P. Krekó and C. Molnár (et al.), *Beyond Populism. Tribalism in Poland and Hungary* (Political Capital Institute, 2018).

The Dalia 2020 survey contradicts this data: 86 percent of Polish people and 78 percent of Hungarian people consider democracy important but absent, resulting in the highest perceived democracy deficit among the 57 countries in the survey. *Democracy Perception Index – 2020*, Dalia Research (2020), https://docs.google.com/spreadsheets/d/17XEqJLw_LDH7Oe48F11u_AsB2gVViki4O7LaXWnB9fs/edit#gid=1912927265.

[9] The survey took place in March 2020. See A. Bíró-Nagy and L. Gergely, *Orbán 10: Az Elmúlt Évtized a Magyar Társadalom Szemével* (Friedrich-Ebert-Stiftung and Policy Solutions, 2020).

a "semblance"[10] of democracy. However, this democracy must serve the interests of the ruler and support his case: to keep the country on the right path forever, whatever the right path might be. It follows that the institutional system must be fixed and quickly, but in a way that maintains popular support and legitimacy. Therefore, democratic and constitutional formalities must be observed, but only in a procedural sense:[11]

> The norm is for them to affirm their commitment to the rule of law, separation of powers, democracy, and constitutional rights of individuals and go from there. Oriented by the genealogies and whatever else, they argue in strictly legal, nonpolitical terms, on the basis of the texts, jurisprudence, and scholarship conventionally available. In so doing, they take advantage of the patchwork or hodgepodge character of actually existing constitutional regimes that were designed by [classic constitutional regimes].[12]

Populist leaders and their voters in what became the illiberal East Central European and Latin American countries had already seen their pre-existing constitutions as illegitimate to a great extent. From day one, right-wing parties in Poland hotly contested the 1997 Constitution, nurturing strong doubts about the validity of the referendum in which it was adopted.[13] Venezuela saw general dissatisfaction with the democratic Constitution in place at the time and all presidential competitors promised a new one in 1998. In Turkey many saw the Constitution as a creation and instrument of the military (as it was written after the 1980 military putsch) and serving the special interests of the secularist-military establishment. There was little political and academic concern about the legitimacy of the Hungarian Constitution, although various regime critiques continuously argued that it was Stalinist, because it was adopted in 1949. The fact that the text was fully rewritten during the 1989–90 transition made no difference.

After their electoral victories, the new populist leaders quickly realized that in order to establish plebiscitarian illiberal rule, they can and must

---

[10] For a contrary view, see S. Levitsky and L. A. Way, "Elections Without Democracy: Rise of Competitive Authoritarianism," *Journal of Democracy*, 13:2 (2002), p. 61.

[11] "Orbán defends his hardline positions as not merely consistent with the EU's fundamental values, but as their true embodiment." M. Mos, "Ambiguity and Interpretive Politics in the Crisis of European Values: Evidence from Hungary," *East European Politics*, 36:2 (2020), p. 276.

[12] D. Kennedy, "Authoritarian Constitutionalism in Liberal Democracies," in H. Alviar García and G. Frankenberg, *Authoritarian Constitutionalism*, p. 173.

[13] See D. H. Cole, "Poland's 1997 Constitution in Its Historical Context," *Articles by Maurer Faculty*, 589 (1998), pp. 3–4.

adopt constitutional forms. The revolutionary creation of the state was not an option, and where there was no constituent majority (as in Poland and for a long time in Turkey), the old straitjacket could not be simply disregarded. However, plebiscitarian leaders also realized that they need not rely on constitutional formalism partly because, once in power, much can be achieved through cheating. Constitutional transformation can use the legal and extralegal opportunities of the "extraordinary situation" (the state of exception required by the transition to a new constitutional order) that has enabled all sorts of extraordinary measures as justified by the (alleged) necessities of social justice.[14] Under this pretext, constitutional transformation could rely on the exceptionalism of the constituent process where power pertains directly to the people (i.e. to the leader who can speak on behalf of them).

Almost a century ago Carl Schmitt was right when he considered a state of emergency (or in our case, a state of exception) the equivalent of a "miracle" in theology.[15] The builder of the illiberal state seeks this miracle, and if it is not forthcoming, he will make it occur. Chávez and Orbán were lucky (the affected population much less so) to have had actual natural disasters at the beginning of their reign. If you pray for a miracle, you will get one: Hitler's jurists called his regime a *gewollte Ausnahmezustand* – a "willed state of exception" – "for the sake of establishing the National Socialist State."[16] The state of exception, like a miracle, gives the leader the opportunity to reveal himself as sovereign: an opportunity in which he can match the challenge of the circumstances with unlimited power. It is also an opportunity to prove that he is the chosen one.

The illiberal state that builds on this "miracle" stands for the disregard of reason (truth, evidence, and proven facts), and this applies to law and legal institutions as well.[17] The emergency, the chaos that illiberal regimes welcome, justifies the transgression of laws and disregards the

---

[14] Emergency situations and emergency powers inherited from colonial rule were considered crucial in postcolonial states for nation-building in ethnically diverse societies. For Singapore see the Internal Security Act. In 1999 the disoriented Venezuelan Congress granted Chávez the power to pursue economic reforms by presidential decree under an "enabling law." The new National Assembly authorized a second enabling law for 18 months, under the pretext of major flooding with 130,000 victims.

[15] C. Schmitt, *Political Theology: Four Chapters on the Concept of Sovereignty* (The University of Chicago Press, 1985), p. 36.

[16] G. Agamben, *The Omnibus Homo Sacer* (Stanford University Press, 2017), p. 169.

[17] Schmitt admitted that the rationality of the Enlightenment and its law refuse miracle for being irrational.

logic of the legal order.[18] Contrary to the totalitarian exceptionalism of Schmitt (and Hitler), such naked disregard is not impossible for contemporary illiberal democracy-making: the power must be grabbed and maintained without expressly renouncing constitutional institutions and legal forms. In order to allow arbitrariness to prevail, the regime must cheat and lie about the laws it uses.

Crucial institutional changes have taken place in the name of perpetually exercised constituent power. In Hungary, constitutional amendments removed constitutional obstacles to regime change, even before the new HFL entered into force. In Venezuela, the Constituent Assembly first stripped the National Assembly of its legislative powers and later its commissions continued to shape the composition of constitutional institutions, even after the Bolivarian Constitution entered into force. All this was justified by the need to undo the fundamental social and political injustices of the previous regime, and all this in the name of the authentic people now exercising majority power. (In Hungary, the Fidesz majority replaced reference to the people with the "system of the national cooperation.")

In some countries the new populist governments had a constituent majority (Hungary and Ecuador), in others there was enough popular support to embark on the path of plebiscitarian constitution-making (Venezuela and Bolivia), while in Turkey there was at least enough of a parliamentary majority to try the plebiscitarian way. However, in Poland the new PiS government did not command a constituent majority in the Sejm and was stuck with the old Constitution. It had to accept the existing constitutional frame, which forced it to make de facto changes constitutional by enacting increasingly suspect legislation, replacing the personnel of state institutions, and creating parallel institutions.[19]

The leaders of these illiberal states have presented the constitutional changes and new constitutions as creating authentic popular and nation-serving democracy. However, the government structures did not significantly change, nor did they necessarily unmask the desire to perpetuate the regime. The dirtier work, the annihilation of the old power, was enacted through transitional legislation. Once the need for regime perpetuation becomes pressing, or the remnants of

---

[18] On chaos, see T. Schabert, "Chaos and Eros. On the Order of Human Existence," *Diogenes*, 42:165 (2014), pp. 111–32.

[19] Chávez loved parallel institutions, though at least in 1999 they enjoyed a dubious constitutional authorization.

constitutionalism present impediments to the higher concentration of power, constitutional prudishness ends abruptly (see Section 8.1.2).

2.2 Constitution-Making and Preconstitutional Changes

These populist parties came to power in legitimate elections in accordance with the existing rules. While in the case of Hungary the election in 2010 resulted in a constituent majority, in Bolivia the Congress was controlled by Movement for Socialism (MAS), the party of the President, making it easy to obtain consent to initiate drafting a new constitution.[20] In some presidential systems the overwhelming victory of a populist president did not translate into a constituent majority in the legislature, consequently leading to conflict between the President and the legislature in Venezuela and Ecuador. However, the legislature authorized the calling of a referendum on the permissibility of a constituent assembly and lost its power during the constitution drafting process. As it will be shown, the new constitutions enjoyed highly strong popular legitimacy.

Poland had no majority for a constitutional amendment, and in its absence, PiS could not wrap its nationalist-sovereigntist ambitions in the cloak of a new constitution. As it could not call a risky referendum, it found no political or legal path for its anti-constitutional aspirations to prevail as general popular will in any formally legal way. It was thus doomed to act against the spirit (and sometimes the letter) of the Constitution in force, relying on revolutionary majoritarianism. PiS stated openly that it had the right to its "own" constitutional tribunal and (later) judiciary, and other public institutions, which until then were controlled by anti-patriotic forces – all in the name of the rights of the people to enact change.

2.2.1 Venezuela

Following his landslide victory in the 1999 presidential elections, Hugo Chávez, in line with his electoral promises, initiated a new constitution to

---

[20] Singapore, the most successful and oldest-living illiberal democracy, is an exception in many respects. The system of governance did not result from a populist victory, and while the government has controlled a constituent majority most of the time, there has been little interest in a specific constitutional design. The Singapore Constitution was an accidental creature in the turmoil of Singapore's secession from Malaysia in 1963. The idea of the originally planned constituent assembly was quickly dropped, and the city-state continued to live with the 1963 State Constitution, with some additions from the Malaysian Federal Constitution.

relegitimize all powers even before taking oath. The idea of a new constitution was popular across society; for Chávez, it needed to come directly from popular power, and he therefore proposed a referendum on convening a Constituent Assembly. He had some less principled reasons as well. The 1961 Constitution granted exclusive amendment powers to Congress, where Chávez had no majority.[21] The Supreme Tribunal of Justice (TSJ) had ruled that the referendum "will not be unconstitutional,"[22] an ambiguous sentence that reflected its ambiguous position; quoting the Abbé Sieyès, it referred to the people's supreme constituent power. The resultant referendum approved the convening of a Constituent Assembly, with 38 percent of the electorate participating (no quorum requirement). Due partly to the opposition being in disarray, and partly to a "smart" electoral system crafted by his experts, the President's movement received 66 percent of the votes, resulting in 94 percent of the Assembly seats. This time, 46 percent of the electorate participated; in other words, the people's will equaled 29 percent of the electorate.

In the name of its original constituent powers, the Constituent Assembly declared that all organs of public power are subordinated to it, and that it can exercise the powers of the National Assembly. The National Assembly tried to resist, but it was physically unable to meet until it agreed that it would not pass legislation hampering the work of the Constituent Assembly. In August 1999 the Constituent Assembly decreed the reorganization of all branches of government; this was upheld by a divided Supreme Court. Chávez decreed a "judicial emergency," and the Constituent Assembly set up a commission to deal with judicial affairs. This emergency decree was supported by eight of the Court's fifteen members but their president, Cecilia Sosa, resigned, declaring that "the Supreme Court was now dead."[23] As Brewer-Carías states, "the court would commit suicide rather than wait to be killed by the Assembly."[24]

---

[21] Article 250 of the 1961 Venezuelan Constitution (in force at the time) rather unequivocally stated that it "shall not lose its effect even … if it is repealed by means other than those provided herein."

[22] A. R. Brewer-Carías, *Dismantling Democracy in Venezuela. The Chávez Authoritarian Experiment* (Cambridge University Press, 2010), p. 52.

[23] R. Gott, *Hugo Chávez and the Bolivarian Revolution* (Verso, 2000), p. 147. The vote of the judges says much about judicial resilience (the lack of it), base opportunism, and the false hope of collaborationists.

[24] Brewer-Carías, *Dismantling Democracy*, p. 55. See further, J. Corrales and M. Penfold, *Dragon in the Tropics: Hugo Chávez and the Political Economy of Revolution in Venezuela* (Brookings Institution Press, 2011).

In less than four months the new Constitution was hurried through the Constituent Assembly without considering the views of the opposition. After the successful referendum, but before the Constitution of the Bolivarian Republic of Venezuela entered into force, the Constituent Assembly enacted a set of transitory rules (the Transitory Constitutional Regime), creating a de facto state of exception. In this transitory regime the outgoing Constituent Assembly, or its Commissions, filled various positions (the new TSJ, Electoral Committee, Prosecutor General, Comptroller). It called new legislative elections, and for half a year, transferred legislative powers to a twenty-one–member commission it elected. Chávez did not ask for a continued mandate, but in line with honest Caesarism, he ran again and received another plebiscitarian endorsement for six (more) years (re-elected with 57 percent of the vote).[25] Three months after his second inauguration, another successful referendum took place, this time to suspend the future election of trade union leaders, whom Chávez accused of corruption. At this moment it seemed that Venezuela would become a Switzerland of the Caribbean, one relying on a permanent constituent power. However, already in 2002, the lack of total popular endorsement became obvious, and when in 2007 Chávez tried to abolish presidential term limits via referendum, together with other regime-invigorating measures, he failed. He thus had to introduce most of these measures by statute, with the complicity of the TSJ. Once again, with their help, he won a new Constitution amending referendum in 2009.

2.2.2   Hungary

In 2010, thanks to the electoral system that was partly proportional, partly first past the post (inspired by the German model), Hungary's former opposition party Fidesz gained a constituent majority in Parliament, with the support of 34 percent of the total electorate. Presenting his government's program in May 2010, the Prime Minister suddenly declared the need for a new constitution, even though this had not been part of his electoral program. The Hungarian Constitution in force was poorly entrenched as it required only a two-third's majority vote in a single chamber for amendments, without any public approval.

---

[25] President Correa of Ecuador followed the lead in 2007. In 2017 President Maduro of Venezuela repeated the Chávez hat trick (via a referendum that approved the call for a Constituent Assembly, which once elected duly declared that it would exercise the powers of (oppositional) legislation).

On April 18, 2011, the Fundamental Law (as the Constitution was to be called) was adopted with little public debate and without the opposition's involvement. It entered into force on January 1, 2012. Fidesz, while repeatedly insisting on its popular mandate, refused to hold a referendum and relied instead on a freshly baked institution, the ex-ante "public consultation" (by which the population receives a set of non-specific questions by mail).[26] Like in Venezuela, the most important institutional and personnel changes took place before the HFL came into force or under the pretext that it necessitated such changes, without changing the structure of government.[27]

2.2.3 Turkey

In Hungary, Venezuela, Ecuador, and Bolivia, the constituent power, as defined by law or at least by a sort of constitutional theory, remained at the service of the freshly elected, popularly endorsed governments. (Likewise, in 1949 Perón could rely on a popular majority when he asked for a constitutional amendment to extend his powers.) In these instances the radical constitutional change, which enabled the concentration of power in the hands of the ruler, occurred suddenly and with popular support. A similar process took many years in Turkey. The first time it came to power in 2003, the AKP obtained a simple majority in the Turkish Grand National Assembly. The Constitution in force was questionable, as it was written two years after the military putsch of 1980 and ultimately served as the backdrop for the de facto military rule. However, constitutional amendment rules required approval by referendum, and the parliamentary opposition and the Turkish Constitutional Court (TCC) resisted several attempts to submit amendments to the people.[28] Finally, in 2007 the mandate of President Sezer came to end (the

---

[26] The government claimed that there was a 15 percent return rate, but there was no way to verify the allegation. An earlier judgment of the Constitutional Court had stated that no referendum is admissible if it intends to change the fundamental structure of the constitution.

[27] Venice Commission Opinion no. 621/2011 on the New Constitution of Hungary, Venice, June 20, 2011, paras. 141–42.

[28] The AKP refused the interparty, consensus-based compromise and in the absence of the supermajority had to turn to the referendum. O. Yegen and Z. Yanaşmayan, "Glass Half Full: Drafting Fundamental Rights in the Turkish Constitution-Making Process (2011–2013)," in F. Petersen and Z, Yanaşmayan (eds.), *The Failure of Popular Constitution Making in Turkey Regressing Towards Constitutional Autocracy* (Cambridge University Press, 2019), pp. 183–217.

President had been an irremovable obstacle to the emerging AKP power, using the highest number of vetoes in Turkish legislative history), and the TCC blocked the AKP candidate to become President of the Republic.[29] While an Amendment by referendum later made the direct election of the President possible, in 2007 the President was still elected by Parliament.

Following the 2016 putsch, a state of emergency consolidated the de facto powers of the President, and Erdoğan could finally push through the changes sought via the 2017 referendum, which succeeded by a narrow and contested majority of 51 percent (44 percent of the total electorate). The 2017 Amendments certainly reinforced the powers of the President, though in the formal sense still respected checks and balances (see Chapter 5).

2.3   Constitutional (Apex) Courts First to Go, the Rest of the Judiciary to Follow

2.3.1   Constitutional Courts

The liberal hope is that constitutional courts function as exemplary deliberative institutions offering (or denying) *legal* justifications to state action, thus elevating legislative measures above the dictate of brute force, power, and the will of a capricious majority.[30] However, according to the agency theory of judicial review, judicial decisions are not only the result of personal judicial preferences (including the preference to serve the regime in power in a legally acceptable form), but also of external political and institutional realities.[31] The social and political design of courts, their institutional and personal vulnerabilities, and the professional expectations interiorized by judges cannot guarantee constitutional resilience. Judges are not designed to be moral crusaders. But the populist zeal, once in power, cannot wait for natural judicial and

---

[29] The TCC concluded that the parliamentary quorum for presidential election was not reached (the secularist opposition boycotted the session). Erdoğan called the judgment "a disgrace to the justice system." Parliament was dissolved and the AKP returned with a sufficient majority that enabled the election of Gül, whom the secularist forces (including the army) considered an Islamist. M. Tran, "Turkey PM accused of insulting court," *The Guardian* (May 30, 2007), www.theguardian.com/world/2007/may/30/turkey.marktran.

[30] J. Rawls, *Political Liberalism* (Columbia University Press, 1993), pp. 231–36.

[31] D. R. Songer, J. A. Segal and C. M. Cameron, "The Hierarchy of Justice: Testing a Principal-Agent Model of Supreme Court–Circuit Court Interactions," *American Journal of Political Science*, 38 (1994), pp. 673–96.

institutional conformity to unfold; if for Lenin the telegraph bureaus were the principal targets in the 1917 Russian Revolution, in the radical restructuring of the constitutional order it is the constitutional (apex) court the first prize.

Although a populist constitutional doctrine may support a radical cutback of judicial power in the name of people's sovereign power – for example, in favor of a commonwealth-type review – because of the new regimes' desire to appear "constitutional," the nuclear option of abolishing constitutional review is not a viable alternative. Still, first and foremost, genuine constitutional control had to be eliminated.

A radical restructuring of the apex court is not a populist invention. In the history of democracy, numerous techniques have aimed to domesticate them.[32] Changing their composition under the pretext of court reform, or via new constitutional design, represent perhaps the most common methods, although changing competence and jurisdiction also feature significantly as possibilities. "Court packing," – creating additional seats filled by government loyalists – serves as a traditional tool for changing the political orientation of apex courts when judges are considered leftovers of the defeated incumbent. The most famous example, which was not implemented but still achieved its goals, can be found in President Franklin D. Roosevelt's plan to add associate justices to the US Supreme Court in order to overcome its resistance to the New Deal reforms.[33] The dismissal of sitting judges is a more drastic version of this, though the latter technique differs in its intensity. Criminal conviction on trumped-up charges is the severest form, followed by disciplinary expulsion, and dismissal for lack of proper qualifications.[34] Perón used

---

[32] A. Castagnola, *Manipulating Courts in New Democracies: Forcing Judges off the Bench in Argentina* (Routledge, 2017); A. Arato, "Populism, Constitutional Courts and Civil Society," in C. Landfried (ed.), *Judicial Power: How Constitutional Courts Affect Political Transformations* (Cambridge University Press, 2019).

[33] Though Roosevelt commanded a majority in the Senate, given the prevailing constitutional culture of the day, the success of the plan cannot taken for granted. W. E. Leuchtenburg, "The Origins of Franklin D. Roosevelt's 'Court-Packing' Plan," *The Supreme Court Review*, 1966 (1966), pp. 347–400.

An early successful example of court packing occurred at the introduction of formal apartheid in South Africa, when the Supreme Court rejected the law depriving the coloreds of their equal voting rights. The Appellate Division Quorum Act, 1955, expanded the size of the Appellate Division to eleven judges.

[34] Dismissal without cause and effective judicial protection are incompatible with judicial independence (irremovability). United Nations Human Rights Committee, General Comment No. 32, Article 14: Right to equality before courts and tribunals and to a fair trial, CCPR/C/GC/32, August 23, 2007, para. 20.

a simple and radical method: he impeached all but one of the Supreme Court judges, whom his parliamentary majority duly found culpable. Mass-scale dismissal may result in collateral damage, but it is faster and more efficient than individual craftsmanship. (Mass-scale solutions are particularly attractive against the ordinary judiciary, with thousands of pieces in the machinery of justice awaiting refurbishment.) In revolutions judges are simply replaced because they are considered politically unreliable servants of past injustice. In "civilized" countries changes are dressed in some kind of reform: for example, a general pension reform might force the judiciary's higher echelon into retirement or judiciary reorganization might improve the efficiency of the administration of justice by eliminating leftovers. The creation of a new body, and the dissolution of the old institution in the name of constitutional reorganization, offers another justification, under the guise of general reform. In non-personnel solutions within the institutional approach, competence can be restricted or transferred, and access and standing rules can be changed.[35] All such measures must be combined with changes in appointment procedures, which will guarantee nomination of the "proper" candidates. All standard methods of selection (except perhaps one which seeks consensus of the political opposition) can yield the desired solution.

"Replace the politically appointed judges!" was the gut reaction of Jefferson's Republican-Democratic Party in March 1801, after the first change of a governing party in the then young history of American democracy. The revolutionary attitude was understandable. After all, during its last days the outgoing Adams administration appointed an entire cohort of "midnight judges" (i.e. political loyalists), hoping to slow the political power grab of its foes. This tradition remains alive and well. Consider Poland in 2015, when the outgoing Sejm filled judicial seats, including some that were not yet vacant. In the same year in Venezuela, after President Maduro's party lost the elections, the outgoing legislature elected thirteen new justices to the TSJ in a lame-duck session, even though there were no actual openings on it. Instead, thirteen of the existing justices, whose terms were to expire in a year, decided to "voluntarily" retire, depriving the new Assembly of the opportunity to elect anti-Maduro judges. "Never mind . . . that the ruling party's bloc in parliament lacked the constitutionally mandated

---

[35] In Hungary *actio popularis* (a bulwark against tyranny introduced after World War II in Bavaria) was replaced with individual constitutional complaint.

two-thirds vote to appoint justices; the supreme court ruled they could do without it."[36]

Perhaps none of these radical measures were necessary. Apex courts are often ready to adapt to new situations; just give them time. After all, the TSJ did not oppose the 1999 constitutional process. However, Chávez did not appreciate the judges' lack of enthusiasm, and the inconsequential reservations dictated by professional considerations actually served the regime's legitimacy. In the transition to the new Constitution, the TSJ got a new name, and the new name duly received new, and more loyal, judges.[37]

In Hungary, immediately after its takeover, Fidesz changed the rules of nomination to the Hungarian Constitutional Court (HCC) purely to fill a pending vacancy. Instead of the previous consensual interparty nomination process, the new system, officially intended "to further independence of the Court," granted the prevailing parliamentary supermajority the full power of nomination.[38] Perhaps not getting the message, soon after, the HCC struck down a special 98 percent retroactive tax on severance payments for dismissed state employees.[39] The next day the government introduced a constitutional amendment restricting the review powers of the HCC. After additional skirmishes, more than a year after its victory, Fidesz introduced comprehensive court reform, in anticipation of the new HFL, not yet in force.[40] The related

---

[36] P. Rosas, "How Venezuela's supreme court triggered one of the biggest political crises in the country's history," *Vox* (May 1, 2017), www.vox.com/world/2017/5/1/15408828/venezuela-protests-maduro-parliament-supreme-court-crisis.

[37] Contrary to the new constitution, the dismissal and appointment of judges was entrusted to a commission (CORJS) set up by the outgoing Constituent Assembly. CORJS was provisionally granted disciplinary jurisdiction, which would have been the competence of disciplinary tribunals. See Article 267 of the new Constitution (which at the time was not in force...).

For the dismissal of the president of the Hungarian Supreme Court see Chapter 7, the *Baka* case. Before then, there were at least five similar instances in postcommunist countries. In most instances the respective courts were able to reinstate the president.

[38] Under ordinary circumstances nomination and election of judges by parliamentary supermajority is a sufficient guarantee of consensus. As Fidesz alone had the supermajority, the scheme did not work after Fidesz abolished the rule that gave equal nomination power to the opposition of the day.

[39] Ending "brazen" severance payments had been a major campaign promise and became a hot issue given the large-scale dismissal.

[40] A. Vincze, "Wrestling with Constitutionalism: The Supermajority and the Hungarian Constitutional Court," *Vienna Journal on International Constitutional Law*, 8:1 (2014), pp. 86–97; M. Bánkuti, G. Halmai and K. L. Scheppele, "Disabling the constitution," *Journal of Democracy*, 23:3 (2012), pp. 138–46; N. Chronowski and F. Gárdos-Orosz,

constitutional amendment (to the Constitution still in force) enabled the overdue court packing (with five new appointments). Between 2010 and 2014 the Fidesz-nominated judges ruled in favor of Fidesz-enacted norms in 80 percent of the cases, while the judges nominated before 2010 by the previous ruling parties found the same rules unconstitutional in roughly 85 percent of the cases.[41] After 2011 the latter group were increasingly in the minority. With a new HCC majority new legal doctrines have prevailed.[42] It has become more respectful of legislative will in view of the separation of powers doctrine, and has cherished deferentialism, relying on theories critical of juristocracy. A concept of national-constitutional identity (further endorsed by a 2018 constitutional amendment) has served to defend sovereignty against the alleged excesses of EU law.

Changing appointment processes may also tame an apex court, with judges anticipating its future in case they do not yield. This anticipation probably determined the path chosen by the Supreme Court of India after Modi and the Bharatiya Janata Party, often described as populist, came to power.[43] Three months after the party's electoral victory in August 2014 the Parliament of India passed the Constitution (Ninety-Ninth Amendment) Act and the 2014 National Judicial Appointments Commission Act, which would have ended the system of quasi-cooptation that existed for Supreme Court appointments. The Constitution of India only states that its judges are appointed by the President of the Union "after consultation with such of the Judges of the Supreme Court and of the High Courts in the States as the President may deem necessary for the purpose." In reality the political branch had limited influence, as the nominations were controlled by a judicial

"The Hungarian Constitutional Court and the financial crisis," *Hungarian Journal of Legal Studies*, 58:2 (2017), pp. 139–54; N. Chronowski and M. Varju, "The Hungarian rule of law Crisis and its European Context," in A. Kellerhals and T. Baumgartner (eds.), *Rule of Law in Europe – Current Challenges* (Schulthess Juristische Medien AG, 2017).

[41] Z. Szente, "Az Alkotmánybírák Politikai Orientációi Magyarországon 2010 és 2014 Között," *Politikatudományi Szemle*, XXIV/1 (2015), pp. 31–57.

[42] G. Halmai, "In Memoriam Magyar Alkotmánybíráskodás. A Pártos Alkotmánybíráskodás Első Éve," *Fundamentum*, 18:1-2 (2014), pp. 36–64.

[43] India under Modi became less liberal. The state and even courts seemingly departed from religious pluralism as secularism, along with increasing state-sponsored or tolerated attacks on academic freedom, independent media, and minority citizens. See S. D. Choudhury, "Can Indian democracy survive Modi's assault on liberalism?," Open Democracy (August 5, 2019). www.opendemocracy.net/en/openindia/can-indian-democracy-survive-modis-assault-on-liberalism/; S. Ganguly, "An Illiberal India?," *Journal of Democracy*, 31:1 (2020), pp. 193–202.

Collegium headed by the Chief Justice. The system may have been corporatist and a creature of the Supreme Court,[44] without grounds in legislation, but at least it was not subject directly to party politics. The ninety-ninth amendment was found unconstitutional,[45] but in the end the Court accepted a memorandum of procedure, signed by the government in September 2019, after Modi's re-election. This memorandum of procedure enables heavy-handed involvement of the executive in the nomination procedure. Moreover, the Court became rather deferential in politically crucial cases (the Kashmir lockdown, the Babri Mosque, and the denaturalization and indefinite detention of alleged immigrants), allowing the government's right-wing populist agenda to prevail.

Populist rulers in Turkey and Poland considered their respective Constitutional Courts a political enemy from the day they came to power. According to Varol, in Turkey "military leaders structured the appointments process to the Court to ensure, to the extent possible, the appointment of justices favorable to their interests."[46] The TCC remained faithful to the antiliberal and repressive Kemalist understanding of the Constitution, which became one of the major obstacles to the political plan of the Islamist AKP. It was the TCC that banned the AKP's predecessor, the Refah Party, in 1998. In its July 2008 judgment, the Court again declared that the governing AKP had exploited religious sentiment for the sake of political interests and "had become the focus of activities" contradicting the principles of a democratic and secular Republic. In contrast to the Refah Party judgment,[47] after five years of consolidation of the Erdoğan regime, the TCC's majority was already short by one vote of the qualified majority needed for party dissolution. The political influence of the army was already melting. Nevertheless,

---

[44] The collegium was a creature of a 1993 judgment (*Supreme Court Advocates-on-Record Association* v. *Union of India* (1993), 4 SCC 441 (Second Judges Case)).

[45] *Supreme Court Advocates-on-Record Association* v. *Union of India* (2015), 11 SCALE 1 (NJAC Judgment).

[46] O. Varol, "The Democratic Coup d'Etat," *Harvard International Law Journal*, 53 (2012), p. 329. The example indicates that abstract models do not provide proper guidance without contextual *consequentialist* analysis (i.e. the probability of how an institutional measure or other judgment contributes to usurpation), which inevitably turns into a political analysis, something that courts are not supposed to do (see, for example, the reluctance to apply such review in the GFCC, where the Court prefers to examine party structure, instead of speculating on the impact an anti-democratic party will have on democracy).

[47] The Turkish judgment was upheld by the ECtHR in 2003, ahead of the AKP victory. *Refah Partisi (The Welfare Party) and Others* v. *Turkey*, ECtHR, App. nos. 41340/98, 41342/98, 41343/98 and 41344/98, Judgment of 13 February 2003.

true to the Kemalist tradition of the Constitution, the Court declared the "Headscarf Amendment" contrary to the unamendable provisions (secularism) of the Constitution. (The formally neutral amendment, dear to the AKP pious, would have enabled students to attend university in religious garb, one of the party's major demands.) The retaliation did not take long. A hotly contested referendum, which included several protective human rights measures,[48] added six new seats to the TCC (on top of the previous eleven). Finally, the 2017 constitutional amendment eliminated the position of military appointees.[49]

In Poland, the conflict between the new government and the Polish Constitutional Tribunal (PCT) started days after the inauguration of the PiS government in November 2015. More precisely, this continued an old conflict: during the first PiS government the PCT opposed some of the party's pet projects. PiS commonly complained that they never had the opportunity to have their own judges in the PCT, whose composition it believed was totally one-sided. Shortly before the 2015 elections, PiS tabled an amendment to the Constitution that would have terminated the mandate of all PCT judges, and proposed replacing majoritarian election with a consensual one.[50] In the absence of a constituent majority, PiS took a less constitutionally aesthetic road.

As in many other contexts, PiS could rely on the constitutional mischief of the outgoing majority,[51] this time in a "midnight judges"

---

[48] The reform was understood to facilitate Turkey's accession to the EU. In one important respect it was clearly a regime-enhancing measure: in reaction to the threatening 2008 AKP judgment, the Amendment increased the party ban quorum.

[49] "Erdoğan appointees virtually always tend to side with the government in cases with heightened political significance to the government and its critics." C. Tecimer, "Why the Turkish Constitutional Court's Wikipedia Decision is No Reason to Celebrate," Verfassungsblog (January 20, 2020), www.verfassungsblog.de/why-the-turkish-constitutional-courts-wikipedia-decision-is-no-reason-to-celebrate.

[50] The draft amendment proposed a supermajority in the election of judges (as in Germany and, on paper, in Hungary). E. Łętowska and A. Wiewiórowska Domagalska, "A 'Good' Change in the Polish Constitutional Tribunal?," *Osteuropa Recht*, 1 (2016), p. 80. In principle, the PiS solution would have ended the majoritarian bias in the appointments, of course in total disregard of the irremovability principle.

The same political-spoils logic appeared in the "compromise" proposal of the then-prime minister in January 2016 (new appointment of all judges, with seats divided between majority and opposition).

[51] This is true in all populist takeovers. When the populists came to power they could also rely on the weaknesses of the constitution in force and/or the reluctance of the constitutional institutions to stand up vigorously for the fundamental liberal structure of the constitution. As mentioned in Chapter 1, constitutions are unfinished ventures. Without democratic willingness to reinforce the constitution we miss one of our last chances to

situation. In the best tradition of President Adams, the outgoing center-right government, sensing a possible loss in the upcoming elections, introduced a special appointment rule in June 2015, and, thirteen days before the elections, filled five vacancies, including two slots that were (in a political interpretation of the law) "reserved" to be filled by the incoming Sejm. A week after the new Sejm members took oath, the new majority repealed the special appointment rule introduced in June, annulled the election of all five judges elected in October by parliamentary resolution, and filled the five vacancies with its "own" judges. A few hours after the new judges were sworn in, in the early hours of December 3, the PCT ruled that the repealed provisions on the election of judges were unconstitutional, and the outgoing Sejm had no power to elect the successors of those two judges whose mandates were to expire during the term of the new Sejm.[52]

As the "old" PCT majority continued to resist the Sejm, the PiS majority enacted laws to paralyze the meritorious work of the PCT. The Repair Act (the second PiS amendment to the Tribunal Act adopted three weeks after the PCT refused to sit three of the November appointees),[53] provided that cases were to be treated in the order of submission, meaning that old cases

---

protect constitutionalism. See A. Sajó, "Militant Constitutionalism," in A. Malkopulou and A. S. Kirshner (eds.), *Militant Democracy and Its Critics: Populism, Parties, Extremism* (Edinburgh University Press, 2019).

[52] In its December 3, 2015 judgment the PCT claimed that there is a "rule that a judge of the Tribunal is chosen by the Sejm during the parliamentary term in the course of which the vacancy occurs" (K 34/15). In its next judgment (K 35/15) the PCT declared the November Amendment which enabled the election of five judges unconstitutional. The PCT did not decide on the actual appointment of these new judges because it had no authority to deal with non-normative acts like individual elections (three judges dissented). The PCT president did not allow three of the new judges to sit on the panels. The three judges who were elected lawfully in October never exercised their function because the President of the Republic refused to swear them in. A year or so later, the term of most judges came to an end. Once the new appointees obtained the majority, the three unseated November judges were admitted to decision-making formations. See L. Garlicki, "Die Ausschaltung des Verfassungsgerichtshofes in Polen? (Disabling the Constitutional Court in Poland?)", in A. Szmyt and B. Banaszak (eds.), *Transformation of Law Systems in Central, Eastern and Southeastern Europe in 1989–2015* (Gdańsk University Press, 2016); M. Bernatt and M. Ziółkowski, "Statutory Anti-constitutionalism," *Washington International Law Journal*, 28 (2019), pp. 485–525; W. Sadurski, *Poland's Constitutional Breakdown* (Oxford University Press, 2019); T. Koncewicz, "The Capture of the Polish Constitutional Tribunal and Beyond: Of Institution(s), Fidelities and the Rule of Law in Flux," *Review of Central and East European Law*, 43:2 (2018), pp. 116–73.

[53] C. Davies, "Hostile Takeover: How Law and Justice Captured Poland's Courts," Freedom House, www.freedomhouse.org/report/special-reports/hostile-takeover-how-law-and-justice-captured-poland-s-courts#_edn17.

were to be treated first, denying the PCT the opportunity to determine the constitutionality of the PiS legislation. Further, tailor-made procedural rules enabled the PiS-elected minority to block or delay decision-making. The Repair Act provided that the full panel of the PCT should have at least thirteen judges for a quorum (previously nine), though only twelve had been recognized.[54] The government refused promulgation of the PCT decisions, including one voiding the Repair Act, claiming that these judgments were rendered by unlawfully constituted formations and therefore nonexistent. This refusal had no basis in law and was taken, formally, by an official at the Prime Minister's office who was responsible for publications in the official gazette. Without promulgation, the decisions were considered to be without legal force and thus inapplicable. Finally, due to the new rules and in disregard of the unamended rules of procedure, a new PCT president was elected. In eighteen months, thanks to the normal process of rotation, the PiS appointees took full control.

Apex courts are supposed to apply the constitution. If the constitution is written by an illiberal regime, the apex court will be bound to protect an illiberal constitution and the illiberal laws that are enacted in conformity with it. Prima facie, they do exactly what most constitutional courts do. Where the constitution is not altered to the wishes of illiberal democracy leaders, and the inherited constitution is relatively neutral, the constitutional court will have a large margin to serve the interests of the illiberal authorities. There is nothing surprising here. As Hirschl has stated, judicial review can provide "an efficient institutional way for hegemonic sociopolitical forces to preserve their hegemony and to secure their policy preferences."[55] Courts will lend legitimacy to legislation (although perhaps at the price of losing their own legitimacy) where legislation and regulations are not faithful even to the constitution of the regime, where even the new constitution is too demanding and too faithful to traditional constitutional values. Where these courts may be found short of their constitutional mandate is in the court of constitutionalism, where they fail to sustain the constitution in the spirit that should animate constitutional design (see Chapters 5, 7 and 8).

---

[54] The Act was declared unconstitutional (K 47/15). See Chapter 8.

[55] R. Hirschl, "The Political Origins of Judicial Empowerment through Constitutionalization: Lessons from four Constitutional Revolutions," *Law & Social Inquiry*, 25:1 (2000), p. 95.

2.3.2   The Ordinary Judiciary

Constitutional courts must be domesticated as the new regime cannot afford the risk that the constitutional court will stand up against the transformative measures needed to consolidate state power, where such a transformation necessitates departure from the constitution in force and constitutionalism. A similar need is less obvious in the context of ordinary courts. The plebiscitarian leader needs the RoL as a pillar of his market economy and not kangaroo courts to eliminate opponents of the regime. The ruler commands legislation, and the simplest way to turn courts subservient to his regime's interests is to change the law that will be observed by the judges. In other instances, the government will bypass courts by enacting legislation that precludes judicial review. The legislator can also create a parallel legal system that would satisfy government interests and protect government clients: for example, a state-of-the-art public procurement system and another system that applies when the government declares that the procurement is a matter of "national economic interest." With these possibilities it seems unnecessary to muzzle the judiciary. However, these less costly solutions are insufficient for the ruler. In all concerned jurisdictions the ruler seems to believe that his rule and client interests are better served with court complicity. The logic of the regime also dictates that powerful organizations must be under central control, and suspect institutions should be colonized.

There is a further rationale behind the attacks on the administration of justice. Standard populist antielitism holds that the judiciary is corrupt, inefficient and indifferent to the plight of ordinary people and, being elitist, continues to play an elitist role even after populism assumes power. At the same time, the new regime opts to play an RoL game rather than act as unmitigated revolutionaries. It will therefore claim that it respects judicial independence, but will take steps to discipline the judiciary so that judges use their independence in favor of the government, even without direct political interference.

As in the case of constitutional court muzzling, standard organizational and procedural techniques can force the administration of justice into submission. Moustafa refers to four major options: "(a) providing institutional incentives that promote judicial self-restraint, (b) engineering fragmented judicial systems, (c) constraining access to justice, and (d) incapacitating judicial support networks."[56] In addition, one can always

---

[56] T. Moustafa, "Law and Courts in Authoritarian Regimes," *Annual Review of Law and Social Science*, 10 (2014), p. 289.

count on judicial socialization and conformism within bureaucratic organizations in a project that intends to bring the judiciary under the leader's spell. Illiberal democracies rely on these possibilities to varying degrees and introduce institutional changes pointing in the above dimensions. In this respect abolishing the institutions of judicial self-government becomes crucial: once the internal dependence of the judge in the judicial organization (court) is increased, and the shield (the self-governance body) that protected the courts from political influence is removed, indirect control over the judiciary is achieved, even if most judges remain free to act independently in their cases (if the right case goes to the right judge).

The first wave of institutional reorganization affects judicial councils and court management (where the power of properly selected presidents will increase). This reorganization aims to carry out changes in personnel. Controlling the judiciary and allowing institutional hierarchies to play their role requires replacing at least part of the judiciary (with chilling effects on the remaining judges). This creates a situation where judges are hierarchically dependent on the people who are loyal to the government.

People are not always reliable, however, and once in a comfortable, officially sheltered position, they may follow their own agenda. Some kind of permanent dependence is needed even at the price of a visible, external dependence. Both Singapore and Poland provide phenomenal examples of this. At the highest levels of the judiciary, dependence is often created by discretionarily extending the terms of judges who should otherwise retire. In the retirement schemes of both countries' supreme courts, upon the judge's request, the President could extend the mandate of judges who had reached retirement age. The extension is granted on a completely discretionary basis.[57] Such dependency fits into the logic of illiberal democracies. (See the notorious reliance on substitute judges [who can be easily dismissed] in Section 2.2.1 below.)

The cleansing and occupation of the ordinary judiciary is executed with the same techniques that are used for apex courts, except that here the occupation of managerial positions (court presidency) is particularly advantageous for the ruler. Judges in civil law systems depend on their court presidents for career advancement, bonuses,

---

[57] See Art. 95(2) of the Singapore Constitution. This power was used regularly. See K. Y. L. Tan, "State and Institution Building through the Singapore Constitution in 1965-2005," in L. Thio and K. Y. L. Tan (eds.), *Evolution of a Revolution: Forty Years of the Singapore Constitution* (Routledge, 2014), pp. 63–64.

discipline,[58] and workload. Further, the court president may determine the outcome of a case by assigning it to the "proper" judge. Even formally neutral performance evaluation can be turned into a tool that limits judicial independence. The appointment and dismissal of court presidents and the appointment of new judges are generally perceived as legitimate (internal) matters of judicial management and thus not considered outright threats to judicial independence. Once court management falls into the hands of government loyalists and conformists, internal dependence within the courts and the administration of justice will do the rest.

Judicial self-government provides the key institutional protection of judicial independence. In Latin America this means that the supreme court exercises control over the whole judiciary. In Venezuela the 1999 Constitution left management of the judicial system in the hands of the TSJ, in line with the prevailing tradition in South America. The 1999 Constitution provided the standard safeguards of judicial independence, with popularly elected judges, and the TSJ was supposed to guarantee independence of the whole system. This standard solution was irrelevant, however, as the outgoing Constituent Assembly elected two transitory commissions to exercise de facto unchecked judicial appointment and removal powers. Originally the interim solution was intended to last for one year, but in the absence of a new law, the commissions remained operational until 2004. In 2004 a Chavezista congressman was elected to run the Judicial Council, a section within the TSJ that oversaw judicial dismissals and appointments. Hundreds of lower-level judges were fired and new people were appointed, under the leadership of the former politician, who in a few years became a fugitive as well. The solely temporary filling of many judicial positions facilitated this round of cleansing; the system had been already weakened.[59] As of 2014 "only some 20% of judges currently in office have security of tenure. The remaining 80% of judges have little or no security of tenure, as they were appointed to provisional

---

[58] In Poland and Venezuela a tailor-made disciplinary system is in place. The actors who can initiate and decide on disciplinary charges are carefully selected. Judges are held criminally responsible for their judgments, and the convictions are used to single out and remove the most vocal opponents of the regime.

[59] *A Decade under Chavez*, Human Rights Watch (2008), section III, www.hrw.org/reports/2008/venezuela0908/3.htm#_ftnref128.

or temporary offices from which they can be removed at will by the Judicial Commission of the [TSJ]."[60]

In continental Europe (excluding Germany), judicial self-government was quite often constitutionalized as a response to the administrative subordination of the judiciary to the executive and/or party in totalitarian states. With the victory of Fidesz in Hungary, the powers of the Judicial Council (where the majority of judicial members were elected by judges) were transferred to a new constitutional institution, the National Office for the Judiciary. This body is responsible for management of the courts, under the leadership of a single person, the President of the Office, elected by a parliamentary supermajority. The President is responsible for appointing court presidents, and can even go against the recommendation of the concerned judges, for example by granting temporary appointments, which increases dependence.[61]

In Poland the Constitution allocated the most important judicial appointment powers to the National Judicial Council (KRS), but the Minister of Justice exercised managerial powers in the administration of justice even before the victory of PiS. At least in that respect there was no need for radical changes to maximize the influence of the executive. As an exception, one new law made the Minister of Justice the head of prosecution, resulting in enormous power over the administration of justice.[62]

In 2017 the Polish government redesigned the KRS within a larger reform. According to the government, popular dissatisfaction with the judiciary, demands for historical justice (removing communist judges) and the inefficiency of the administration of justice necessitated the reform, to "enhance the rule of law and the independence of the judiciary."[63] The government used the standard democratic (populist)

---

[60] *Strengthening the Rule of Law in Venezuela*, International Commission of Jurists (2014), p. 9.

[61] See Act CLXI of 2011 and Act CLXII of 2011.

[62] In Venezuela the Chief Prosecutor's position was vacated under the pretext of having a new constitution. In Hungary a vacant Prosecutor General's post was filled with a Fidesz protégé. The HFL did not change the previous status of the prosecution as an independent body, and the (new) Prosecutor General received de facto unlimited power to determine its structure. Apparently, government influence can be achieved with radically different institutional solutions.

[63] "The Government Presents a White Paper on the Reforms of the Polish Justice System," Prime Minister of Poland Website (March 3, 2018), www.premier.gov.pl/en/news/news/the-government-presents-a-white-paper-on-the-reforms-of-the-polish-justice-system.html.

argument: no public body, not even the judiciary, should be exempt from the democratic requirements of transparency and accountability: it is in the name of these democratic values that the reshuffling occurred.[64]

In this venture, PiS could rely on an imprecision within the Constitution. Article 187 only states that fifteen members of the KRS are to be judges. Since 1989 these judges were elected by their peers; according to the 2017 law, the Sejm should elect them by majority upon the recommendation of at least twenty-five judges (whose identities have never been disclosed).[65] The new KRS speedily filled the vacancies, which were diligently accumulated as the Ministry of Justice failed to allow the vacant seats to be filled until the KRS takeover.[66] The new law further increased ministerial powers, and for a six-month transitory period (transition as a state of exception again!), it granted the Minister of Justice[67] the power to remove common court presidents from their post without cause and irrespective of the terms of their original appointment. The use of this

---

[64] The opposition of democratic and liberal values in the context of judicial independence is not a Polish specialty. See P. H. Russel and D. M. O'Brian (eds.), *Judicial Independence in the Age of Democracy: Critical Perspectives from around the World* (University Press of Virginia, 2001).

[65] Contrary to the March 2019 judgment of the PCT, which found the law constitutional, the Court of Justice of the European Union (CJEU) ruled that the KRS, and consequently a chamber composed of judges selected by the KRS, do not provide guarantees of judicial independence. Joined Cases C-585/18, C-624/18 and C-625/18, *A. K. v. Krajowa Rada Sądownictwa, CP v. Sąd Najwyższy and DO v. Sąd Najwyższy* [2019] EU:C:2019:982.

In a similar manner the Inter-American Court of Human Rights (IACtHR) found that because the Venezuelan body removing the judges was not formed in a way that would guarantee independence, the dismissal is impermissible. *Apitz Barbera et al. ("First Court of Administrative Disputes") v. Venezuela*, IACtHR, Judgment of August 5, 2008.

[66] A. Śledzińska Simon, "The Rise and Fall of Judicial Self Government in Poland: On Judicial Reform Reversing Democratic Transition," *German Law Journal*, 19 (2018), pp. 1839–70. The system follows the Spanish one, where in the process of transition to democracy the law first granted the judicial corps the power to elect the Council members. A few years later this was amended for being a corporatist solution that helps external independence but is contrary to the democratic idea of representative government.

[67] Only the chronicle of scandals provides the proper source for an understanding of the abusive potential of the system in place. In one instance a deputy minister of justice was operating a network from the ministry that was harassing judges and others who opposed the government's judicial reforms. See M. Pankowska, "Why did the Polish deputy minister of justice resign? Everything you need to know about the 'Piebiak scandal,'" Rule of Law (August 27, 2019), www.ruleoflaw.pl/why-did-the-polish-deputy-minister-of -justice-resign-everything-you-need-to-know-about-the-piebiak-scandal;

B. Mikołajewska, "Sędzia Wytrykowski był bohaterem propagandowej akcji Małej Emi. Potem awansował do Sądu Najwyższego," Oko.press (January 31, 2019), www.oko.press /sedzia-wytrykowski-dal-sie-uzyc-w-propagandowej-akcji-malej-emi/.

power had considerable impact on the independence of the judiciary: one-fifth of the positions were filled with new cadres. As in so many instances of the use of power in illiberal democracy, the removal of court presidents as such is not necessarily contrary to the RoL because the guarantees of judicial independence do not necessarily apply to administrative positions. Of course, from the perspective of the separation of powers, interference into the independence of the judiciary is obvious. The dependence was further increased when the Minister of Justice became entitled to remove court presidents for "serious or persistent failure to comply with official duties" and for "other reasons which render remaining in office incompatible with the sound dispensation of justice."[68]

The new system, which transfers control over appointments to a new, politically trustworthy body, makes sense only when there are enough vacancies to be filled. The Hungarians, who were always keen on the RoL (in this case the irremovability principle), designed a neutral system to get rid of the judiciary's higher echelon.[69] Since at least 1869 the retirement age of Hungarian judges was 70; the reform (Act CLXII of 2011) intended to end this "anomaly" by bringing the retirement age in line with the general pensionable age (63, increasing to 65 in 2012), forcing a whole cohort of judges (274 in total, including a disproportionate number in higher managerial positions) into immediate retirement. In July 2012 the HCC declared the measure unconstitutional with retrospective force but without a hint of the applicable remedy.[70] A promptly enacted new law provided that the affected judges could continue to serve for a prolonged period and offered compensation for lost income and moral damage. However, there was no reinstatement to previous managerial posts that were already filled. A few months later the Court of Justice of the European Union (CJEU) found the diminution of the retirement age contrary to EU discrimination law (Directive 2000/78) because it abruptly and significantly lowered the age limit for compulsory retirement, "without introducing transitional measures of such a kind as to protect the legitimate expectations of the persons concerned."[71] The CJEU did not consider the matter from the perspective of judicial

---

[68] Sadurski, *Poland's Constitutional Breakdown*, p. 116.
[69] A formally neutral law was created to remove the President of the Hungarian Supreme Court.
[70] 3/2012 (VII. 17) AB hat.
[71] Case C-286/12, *European Commission v. Hungary* [2012] EU:C:2012:687.

independence; it did find that the law served a legitimate aim (providing opportunities to younger judges).

Poland attempted comparable retirement age reform in 2017. It reduced the statutory retirement age of Supreme Court judges from 70 to 65, immediately affecting twenty-seven of the Court's seventy-two judges. Following intervention by the EU Commission and the CJEU, Poland repealed the law, and the judges continued in their position. This time the CJEU considered that the law violated the requirement of judicial independence as it "reinforced the impression that in fact their aim might be to exclude a pre-determined group of judges."[72]

2.4   Other Institutional Changes

2.4.1   Changes in Personnel

Personnel equals policy. The administration of personnel lies at the heart of all institutional changes. For populists coming to power, reform presents the opportunity to transform public administration personnel (as it did with the judiciary).[73] The creation of a civil service in personal bondage with the ruler is an inherent feature of mass democracy at work, as practiced and heralded by President Jackson.

President Jackson openly admitted that civil service is a matter of spoils and personal loyalty; an opportunity to reward supporters. He thus "removed somewhere between ten to twenty percent [of federal officials] in his first year."[74] This first populist leader of modern democracy believed that his popular election, and alleged mandate for reform, gave him the right to replace those "unfaithful or incompetent hands" who held power, with officers of "diligence and talent" who would be promoted based on their "integrity and zeal."[75] Such a radical mass overhaul characterizes populism, especially where the patronage system is understood as an opportunity to provide public service jobs. Perón consolidated his electoral base with 300,000 new appointments in 10

---

[72] Case C-619/18, *European Commission v. Republic of Poland* [2019] EU:C:2019:615. See further Case C-192/18, *European Commission (II) v. Republic of Poland* [2019] EU: C:2019:924.

[73] Beyond swift changes in leadership positions the nationalization of centrally managed public services offers further opportunity for change of personnel. See Chapter 3.

[74] D. B. Cole, *The Presidency of Andrew Jackson* (University Press of Kansas, 1993), p. 41.

[75] A. Jackson, "First Inaugural Address (March 4, 1829)," in J. Richardson (ed.), *A Compilation of the Messages and Papers of the Presidents*, Project Gutenberg, vol. 3, part 3: Andrew Jackson, March 4, 1829, to March 4, 1833.

years, as did the Panhellenic Socialist Movement (PASOK), once it
became Greece's governing party in 1981, setting the country on
a populist course that all its parties sought to imitate.[76]

In today's democracies, it is 'normal' that certain higher political
positions can be filled with new cadres once a new government comes
to power. What happens after the populists grab control over the state
is a quantitatively and qualitatively "higher" level of spoliation, a
Gleichschaltung of bad reputation. Is this compatible with constitutional
standards? Constitutional history has taught us that mass changes in the
civil service facilitate and normalize the politicization of the bureaucracy.
Where civil servants serve the leader, and not the state, they can be used
for totalitarian purposes. The professional civil service is statutorily,
financially (via severance), or even constitutionally protected against
this possibility, and the constitutional culture sets standards for which
level of the bureaucracy will be affected by governmental change.

The logic of populists is different: the takeover of the state means
control over all state resources beginning with state personnel.
Obtaining control over the institutions of the state first and foremost
means control by government loyalists. This translates into dismissals
and new hires. Unfortunately for the new leader, the inherited law often
protects civil servants against dismissal without cause, at least to some
extent, while the reliable cadres do not necessarily have the formal
qualifications required by law and professionalism. Here creative interpretation will help, and if not – the law can always be changed.[77] Those
dismissed may have some legal recourse, but it is time consuming and the
remedy is generally limited: reinstatement is unlikely.

Most regime-building changes (mass dismissals) can be executed
within the existing possibilities of civil service or labor law. In
Venezuela, beginning in 1999, ten years later in Hungary and again in
Poland in 2015, public administration personnel were replaced with
unprecedented speed and breadth without judicial review of its merit.
Dismissing heads of offices is most difficult where the mandate is

---

[76] Pappas, *Populism and Liberal Democracy*, pp. 191-92.

[77] In Hungary law professors are qualified to be nominated to the HCC. In 2010 Fidesz
elected to the Court a member of the previous Fidesz government who taught political
science at the faculty of law. In the Fidesz interpretation of the law, an appointment to the
law faculty means professor of law. Other examples include appointing someone with no
experience in banking as president of the Hungarian National Bank (claiming that this
general requirement for the banking sector does not apply to the National Bank, which is
regulated in a special law).

statutorily protected, as is the case with constitutional institutions. To overcome this problem legalistically, Venezuela invented an array of new public institutions, while in Hungary the old institutions received a new name. Even a nominal change was enough to conclude that with the cessation of the old institution, the mandate of its head also came to an end. Institutional changes compelling those to vacate office before serving their full term are hardly compatible with the independence of supervisory authorities.[78] Most changes of the guard occurred before the new Constitution entered into force, using the transitory mechanisms presented above in the context of judicial reforms.[79]

Cleansing personnel can be an instrument of revenge too. This was the case in Venezuela, after the 2002–03 strike at the state-owned oil company, PDVSA, where roughly 18,000 workers (and the top management) were fired.[80] In Hungary, the cleansing of the civil service started practically overnight after the Fidesz victory; dismissals were most often without cause, thanks to Act LVIII of 2010 (June 21), which amended the law on the status of higher civil servants. Though found unconstitutional eight months later, the law itself was held applicable until a new law could be enacted within three months.[81] In other words, the HCC left the cleansing untouched for all practical purposes and later ruled that the unconstitutional law must be applied in labor law proceedings initiated by dismissed civil servants, depriving them of all protection.[82] Moreover, to play the social justice card, another law deprived the fired civil servants of their severance pay, as the 2010 Fidesz electoral campaign promised to end the so-called "brazen severity" clauses, in the best populist tradition.[83] Putting

---

[78] Case C 288/12, *Commission* v. *Hungary* [2014] EU:C:2014:237 (regarding the dismissal of the Hungarian data-protection supervisor, whose mandate had been terminated because the HFL reorganized the data protection office).

[79] L. Castaldi, "Judicial Independence Threatened in Venezuela: The Removal of Venezuelan Judges and the Complications of Rule of Law Reform," *Georgetown Journal of International Law*, 37 (2005), p. 477; M. J. Garcia-Serra, "The 'Enabling Law': The Demise of the Separation of Powers in Hugo Chavez's Venezuela," *The University of Miami Inter-American Law Review*, 32 (2001), pp. 275–76. The most radical transitory solution was developed in Ecuador, where an all-powerful special appointments body was created in the constitution (the Council of Citizens' Participation and Social Control).

[80] K. A. Hawkins, *Venezuela's Chavismo and Populism in Comparative Perspective* (Cambridge University Press, 2010), p. 22.

[81] 8/2011 (II. 8) AB hat.

[82] 34/2012 (VII. 17) AB hat. This is how the HCC tried not to cause serious political harm to the government even where it had to declare a law unconstitutional.

[83] A high-visibility scandal regarding excessive severance in the public sector was used as evidence of the corrupt nature of the socialist-liberal government.

up a RoL façade, severance was nominally paid to avoid accusations of retrospective legislation, but Act x c of 2010 imposed a special 98 percent tax on public sector severance payments in excess of €13,000 (at the exchange rate at the time). This was considerable in a country where the average annual income was around €10,000. The tax targeted the higher- and mid-level cadres of the previous socialist regime (including former members of Parliament but also teachers with sufficiently long service). This satisfied the populist logic of envy and "common sense" reductionism: why should anyone receive more than a year's salary for not working?[84] The solution was found repeatedly unconstitutional, until Fidesz intro- duced an amendment that rescinded the HCC's competence in the matter (affecting the budget).

Polish legislation relied on a different trick to maintain the semblance of the RoL. Instead of an individualistic approach, the PiS government applied a general measure (acting even faster than the Hungarians). By the end of 2015 the Civil Service Act of 2008 was amended to abolish public competition for civil service positions in favor of appointments. The law terminated around 1,600 higher civil service positions with one month's notice and abolished qualification requirements for new appointments.[85]

2.4.2   Broadcasting and the Press

Hegemony is based on the manufacture of consent. Even before the mass purges in the public administration, the Caesaristic leader must take control over broadcasting, and public broadcasting in particular, so that the purges will be properly presented as acts of social justice. Public broadcasting had been the most influential player in the broad- casting market in all Eastern European countries at the time the populists came to power.[86] In Hungary, in less than two months after Orbán became Prime Minister, a temporary law enabled the parliamentary majority to exercise decisive influence in the Media Council, without even terminating the mandate of the sitting members. This was followed by a complete overhaul of the broadcasting and telecommunications

---

[84] On the resulting litigations as an example of constitutional chicanery see Chapter 8.
[85] Łętowska and Wiewiórowska Domagalska, "A 'Good' Change," p. 80.
[86] The phenomenon is not limited to illiberal democracies. For control of the media by a tycoon close to the government, dismissals in the public broadcaster, etc., see Bulgaria in 2019. Safety of Journalists Platform, *Annual Report: Hands off Press Freedom: Attacks on Media in Europe Must Not Become a New Normal* (Council of Europe, 2020), p. 36.

sector at the end of Year One of the "New Era."[87] While until 2010 the parliamentary opposition had veto powers on the Board of Public Broadcasting, the new system guaranteed government control over public service broadcasting through its decisive influence on the Board. Within a few weeks after the interim law came into force, the public broadcasters were purged, and their programs turned toward directly serving the political interests of Fidesz. In addition, the law endowed the Media Council with new, enhanced powers (severe sanctions and discretionary power), to protect children, the public interest, and national community values, among others. While innocuous, even laudable goals, the resulting discretionary sanctioning power granted the Media Council the means necessary to "domesticate" private media, which were rightly afraid of the selective ire of the Council.[88]

Article 213 of the Polish Constitution requires an independent broadcasting authority in charge of "safeguard[ing] the freedom of speech, the right to information as well as safeguard[ing] the public interest." The specific powers and competences of this authority, the National Council of Radio Broadcasting and Television (known as KRRiT), were left to legislation. It was therefore possible to transfer most of the important competences to a new, loyalist body, without formally curtailing the constitutional mandate of the KRRiT. (Contrary to Hungary, the PiS has a certain preference to create dead souls and empty shells: it must keep institutions and their leaders in place but deprive them of power.

---

[87] Act LXXXII of 2010 (amending the Broadcasting Act); Act CLXXXV of 2010 (new law on media services and mass communication). According to the pre-2010 law a board elected by Parliament, with seats divided equally among government and opposition candidates, was in charge of public broadcasting regulation. The new system did not touch on the paritarian appointments, but the president and a second member were elected by the Media Council, another revamped body composed of members elected by the majority in Parliament. The freshly appointed President of the National Media and Infocommunications Authority, an organ of the public administration, became a voting member of the Media Council with a decisive vote. In this Russian doll system, the partisanship of the ex officio members in the one body guarantees a government majority in all other entities. The complicated system aimed to preserve the impression that institutional independence, pluralism, and neutrality remain respected, as required by EU law.

While the Hungarian model observed all the guarantees of irremovability, impartiality, etc. (a politically convenient system as the outcomes of the impartial body's decisions can be taken for granted), in Venezuela a nominally independent body, whose board served at the pleasure of the President, was in charge of media regulation.

[88] For the situation ten years later see, for example, *Conclusions on the Joint International Press Freedom Mission to Hungary*, International Press Institute, Article 19 et al. (December 3, 2019).

This is what happened with the ombudsperson and the PCT.)[89] The Act on Public Service Media Governance, of December 30, 2015, transferred the KRRiT's appointment powers for public media boards to the Treasury, of all places. The theory was that public media are state assets, and managing public assets pertains to the Treasury.[90] The transition law terminated the mandate of board members and abolished certain membership qualification requirements. The competent minister duly replaced all members of the supervisory and management boards of Polish Television and Polish Radio, and the new board implemented the expected changes at the operative level (many managers and journalists simply resigned).

Like their counterparts in liberal democracies, the government-friendly media regulatory authorities of the illiberal state enjoy a whole arsenal of means to influence private media. This includes the selective and discretionary use of the law, including disproportionate penalties for minor violations of programming rules, threats of license revocation, license non-renewal (as in Hungary), or actual license revocation,[91] threats of criminal processes, and even actual seizure of assets under the pretext that owners have breached the law (in non-media related activities), to convince license holders of the advantages of license transfer (Russia and Turkey). Beyond media outlet owners, threats of coercion as well as harassment, and civil and criminal libel cases target journalists in their personal capacity.[92] Muzzling (self-censorship) is often achieved

---

[89] See also the 2015 PiS constitutional amendment proposal regarding the Constitutional Tribunal in Section 2.3.1 above.

[90] The idea of financial accountability is extensively used to curtail institutional autonomy in organizations using public funds. It was in the name of accountability that the Hungarian government obtained direct control over academic institutions.

[91] In the case of Venezuela, where the press and broadcasters had a large audience and financially strong (partly foreign) ownership, nonrenewal of the most popular private station, producing the most popular telenovela series, resulted in popular resistance. In the longer run, harassment ultimately impacted the rather independent private media, which was more interested in viewers than audience-losing progovernment propaganda, see "Concentración y Abuso de Poder en la Venezuela de Chávez," Human Rights Watch (July 17, 2012), www.hrw.org/es/report/2012/07/17/concentracion-y-abuso-de-poder-en -la-venezuela-de-chavez.

[92] See the prohibition of "false, deceitful, or tendentious news," "inciting rebellion or lack of respect" and subversive propaganda clauses of the Venezuelan Constitution and the extension of the scope of insult and incitement laws to sanction private media. "Venezuela" in *World Report 2003*, Human Rights Watch (2003), www.hrw.org /reports/2003/venezuela/venez0503-03.htm; *A Decade under Chavez*, Human Rights Watch (September 2008), www.hrw.org/sites/default/files/reports/venezuela0908web .pdf.

by "creative" legal interpretation. For example, in 2001 Venezuela's TSJ found that:

> [A]rticle 58 of the Constitution guaranteeing the right to "timely, truthful, and impartial information" imposed enforceable obligations on the media. The court held that media outlets must avoid "publishing false news or news that is manipulated with half truths; disinformation that denies the opportunity to know the reality of the news; and speculation or biased information to obtain a goal with regard to someone or something." The court also concluded that article 58 required publications to be ideologically pluralistic unless their editorial line was made explicit.[93]

Government-friendly ownership represents the safest way to control media outlets. Singapore long ago found the simplest commercial solution. The law institutionalized so-called "management shares," which are held by government-approved directors (among them former high-ranking government officials.)[94] Other illiberal democracies prefer more complicated, informal solutions without direct legislative intervention, closer to the Russian model. In order to have political influence, some of the most influential Russian oligarchs took control of media outlets during the 1990s, used their press and broadcasting outlets for blackmail and manipulated the public via scandalmongering. When Putin came to power he merely followed the existing logic of oligarchic rule, speedily forcing the oligarchs to sell their media assets to other, more reliable oligarchs or to companies (Gazprom) close to the Kremlin. This was facilitated by the overwhelming, legally nearly unconstrained power of the state administration, including law enforcement.[95] Illiberal

---

[93] "The Supreme Court ruling raised fears that article 58 would be used to gag press critics of the government. Indeed, in October, the National Commission of Telecommunications began an investigation into the conduct of the Venezuelan television network Globovisión, for allegedly broadcasting 'false, misleading or tendentious information', an offense under Venezuela's Radiocommunications Regulations. In September, the network aired the statement of a taxi driver who claimed that nine colleagues had been killed by criminals, when in fact only one had died. President Chávez urged the station to 'reflect before it is too late', and threatened to 'apply mechanisms for the defense of the national interest, the truth, and public order.' For its error, which it promptly corrected, the station was potentially liable for a fine or the suspension of its broadcasting license." "Venezuela" in *World Report 2002*, Human Rights Watch (2002). www.hrw.org/legacy/wr2k2/americas10.html.

[94] Mark Tushnet, "Authoritarian Constitutionalism," *Cornell Law Review*, 100 (2015), p. 407.

[95] "Yet the Kremlin has stopped short of owning outright every important media outlet in the country. Rather, plausible deniability about the extent of state control is maintained by encouraging Kremlin-friendly business-men to invest in the media." S. Gehlbach, "Reflections on Putin and the Media," *Post-Soviet Affairs*, 26:1 (2010), p. 81.

democracies, with more constrained, inhibition-ridden states, and sizable foreign ownership, have used a combination of economic pressure (including blackmail) and actual market acquisition.[96] The end result is the same: once a media outlet lands in proper hands, and after the obligatory press release that editorial freedom will be fully respected, the power inherent in ownership is turned into censorial editorial power. Most editors don't wait to be fired.

In Hungary, after the government cronies diligently acquired the targeted media outlets, they suddenly – during the same week – decided to donate these assets (altogether roughly 800 outlets) to KESMA, a public fund dedicated to supporting media that reinforce national identity. Such a concentration of entities would have required review by the competition office. The government declared this fusion to be a matter of special national economic interest and therefore exempt from competition law review. The fund runs a coordinated national propaganda factory using the media it owns (see Chapter 8).

Like so many building blocks of the illiberal regime, achieving political control over media outlets through legal harassment is not specific to illiberal democracies. It also pertains to the illiberal (authoritarian) potential of constitutional democracies. As a Spanish example:[97] when the People's Party came to power in 1996, it used nearly all of what would later become the main ingredients of the illiberal democracy recipe. The Spanish government targeted PRISA, a liberal-left private media group, which intended at that time to launch a digital TV platform that could control the broadcasting of Real Madrid and Barcelona games (fans know that this is no small treat):

---

[96] In 2008 "Turkish state-owned banks had stepped in to provide $750 million in loans to Calik Holding, which is owned by a close friend of Prime Minister Recep Tayyip Erdoğan, in order to enable it to purchase the second largest media group in Turkey." G. Jenkins, "Turkish Banks make huge Loans to Friend of Erdoğan," *Eurasia Daily Monitor* 5:78 (2008).

[97] Italy too was found to disregard the requirement of media pluralism for decades. Case C-380/05, *Centro Europa 7 Srl* v. *Ministero dello Comunicazioni* [2008] EU:C:2008:59; *Centro Europa 7 S.r.l. and Di Stefano* v. *Italy*, ECtHR (GCh), App. no. 38433/09, Judgment of 7 June 2012.

As for India, under Modi "senior government officials have pressed news outlets – berating editors, cutting off advertising, ordering tax investigations – to ignore the uglier side of his party's campaign to transform India from a tolerant, religiously diverse country into an assertively Hindu one." V. Goel and J. Gettleman, "Media Dissent Fades as Modi Tightens Grip," *The New York Times* (April 3, 2020), Section A, p. 1. In this case too, governmental pressure on the media was a long-established tradition of Indian democracy.

The government declared illegal, as a starter, the decodifier for the new TV, passing a decree-law on the grounds of "exceptional urgency"; it then increased by ten percentage points the value added tax that this new TV was required to pay; and, finally, a law was passed that snatched soccer matches from this TV on the grounds of the "public interest."[98]

This effort was complemented by a criminal investigation against PRISA. The magistrate carrying out the political order was later convicted for abuse of judicial power but pardoned by the Prime Minister.

While in illiberal democracies, all public and government controlled media is expected to enthusiastically support the government directly, for the purposes of domination, it suffices if the press not controlled by the government remains silent about embarrassing facts. Commercial enterprises are often ready to cut deals with the government but profit-driven programming cannot afford too many concessions: if an outlet becomes a tool of government propaganda its ratings will suffer. Foreign control of the media can also be an obstacle to state control as large media conglomerates have the resources to resist government pressure and are less dependent on government support. Such regimes present foreign ownership as destroying national culture and serving foreign political interests.[99]

In many places, including those Latin American countries were populism prevailed, the media remain vulnerable, as private outlets depend on "political favors to ensure governmental advertising and other funds." Sometimes, the populist (but not only the populist) government subsidizes both media and journalists. Most populist leaders in Latin America "brought into office with them aggressive media reforms that either attempted to tackle media concentration and restrict the power of media elites, and/or proposed a model of public (state) communication, albeit with varying degrees of success and political support."[100]

Surprising as it is, independent voices are still heard. This is the hallmark of power in illiberal democracy: it aims for hegemony but insists that freedom is sustained and the authorities carefully remind the remaining independent press about the limits of their freedom.

---

[98] J. M. Maravall, "The Rule of Law as a Political Weapon," in J. M. Maravall and A. Przeworski (eds.), *Democracy and the Rule of Law* (Cambridge University Press, 2003), p. 294.

[99] For the Philippines see C. Fonbuena, "Duterte Steps up Attack on Philippines' Largest Broadcaster," *The Guardian* (February 11, 2020), p. 25.

[100] M. Guerrero and M. Márquez-Ramírez, "Media Systems and Communication Policies in Latin America," *The International Journal of Hispanic Media*, 7:1 (2014), p. 2; S. Waisbord, *Watchdog Journalism in South America: News, Accountability, and Democracy* (Columbia University Press, 2000).

Independent journalists are disciplined with libel suits.[101] Increasingly strict rules protect the public against "terrorist propaganda," whatever it may be. They aim to protect "truth" as well, with legislation against spreading fake news; illiberal governments tend to consider fake news their monopoly.[102] Singapore was one of the pioneers of such legislation, but France and Germany were also willing to join the club, once again showing the blurred demarcation between "good" and "bad" democracies. However, even writing the truth can be made irrelevant when the government has successfully promoted a sense of relativism. "The provision of multiple, contradictory alternatives to the truth serves the purpose of undermining trust in objective reporting."[103]

2.4.3   Independent Agencies

According to Cas Mudde, illiberal democracy is (among other things) a response to the undemocratic components of constitutional democracy: "Crucial economic and financial powers were externalized to independent institutions, like central banks, governed by technocrats and without significant democratic oversight. Similarly, many controversial issues were legalized out of politics, such as abortion or the death penalty, never to be campaigned on again."[104] This understanding of the political is detrimental to democratic accountability. "[T]here must exist state agencies that are authorized and willing to oversee, control, redress, and if need be sanction unlawful actions by other state

---

[101] In illiberal democracies, in contrast to despotism, libel law cuts both ways, and opposition figures and independent media win dozens of libel cases against government propaganda machines (which seem to have infinite resources to pay damages).

[102] For a recent example of muzzling in the name of fighting misinformation in Singapore, see the Protection from Online Falsehoods and Manipulation Act 2019.

[103] K. Giles, *"New" Tools for Confronting the West: Continuity and Innovation in Moscow's Exercise of Power* (Chatham House, 2016), p. 37. The Russian government was famous for inventing a new form of mind control: instill in public opinion the conviction that facts are always fabricated, and every piece of information is a suspicious narrative! However, outright patriotic propaganda has increasingly taken over.

[104] C. Mudde, "When illiberal forces win, the answer is more – not less – democracy," *The Guardian* (June 6, 2018), www.theguardian.com/commentisfree/2018/jun/06/when-illiberal-forces-win-the-answer-is-more-not-less-democracy.

See also M. F. Plattner, "Illiberal Democracy and the Struggle on the Right," *Journal of Democracy*, 30:1 (2019), pp. 5–19.

In this train of thought "undemocratic liberalism" left national and international autonomous agencies without democratic control and is blamed for the success of populism and illiberal democracy. In fact, these agencies were overwhelmingly created to correct democratically elected profligate bodies.

agencies."[105] Populists have always attacked these institutions for the usual reasons (elitist, non-accountable, unelected, and "imposed upon the society"). Populism as illiberalism contests these constitutionally imposed liberal taboos; populist governments bring these matters directly back to politics and use legislation to destroy the liberal taboo.

Notwithstanding populist aversion, these governments do not abolish independent agencies and other institutions of internal state accountability, as happens with most constitutional institutions. Instead, they put these institutions to the use of the government. Hungary even increased their powers. Although, of course, the agencies were purged first. Once the political loyalty of the heads of nondemocratic, unelected accountability and policy agencies is guaranteed, the agencies become a source of legitimation as well as a source of harassment for the opposition.[106] "Independent" electoral commissions work hard to disqualify opposition candidates[107] and reject popular initiatives; the Hungarian State Audit Office, an independent parliamentary body, reviews the financing of opposition parties and imposes choking fines, while the ruling party just happens to be left off the list of this year's audit plan. (An independent agency follows its own, certainly neutral planning.) The new ombudsperson certifies government policies (or better, concludes that it has no competence). So it goes.

---

[105] G. A. O"Donnell, "Horizontal Accountability in New Democracies," *Journal of Democracy*, 9:3 (1998), p. 119. O'Donnell calls this horizontal accountability.

[106] In important exceptions the constitution is more in line with populist ideas. Bolivia introduced the popular election of judges, only to allow the President to fill the slots with what he thought would be "his" people. A. Driscoll and M. J. Nelson, "Judicial Selection and the Democratization of Justice: Lessons from the Bolivian Judicial Elections," *Journal of Law and Courts*, 3:1 (2015), pp. 115–48.

[107] This is true of Hungary and Venezuela. In Poland the Electoral Committee still refused PiS recount requests in 2018.

3

Creating Dependence

The example of the prince "is followed by the masses, who keep their eyes always turned upon their chief."

Machiavelli, quoting Lorenzo de Medici.[1]

3.1 Introduction

Machiavelli believed fear should be the primary tool of the Prince. Fear requires reliance on armed forces and secret services, but the authoritarian dictator may not have sufficiently gathered these resources, which remain potentially threatening to him.[2] Illiberal democracies do not have such properties and are unlikely to use them.[3] Because illiberal democracies are personalistic leader democracies, the leader must sustain his routinized charisma. "The legislator therefore, being unable to appeal to either force or reason, must have recourse to an authority of a different order, capable of constraining without violence and persuading without convincing."[4] He must offer "constant proof of merit through struggle, articulation of new norms and values, and responsibilities."[5] In order to

---

[1] N. Machiavelli, *Discourse on the First Ten Books of Titus Livius in The Historical, Political, and Diplomatic Writings of Niccolo Machiavelli*, trans. C. E. Detmold, vol. 2 (J. R. Osgood and Company, 1882), p. 396.

[2] M. W. Svolik, *The Politics of Authoritarian Rule* (Cambridge University Press, 2012).

[3] The Turkish army, an authoritarian institution, served as checks and balances against AKP rule.

The Turkish illiberal democracy experience remains relevant for the present discussion, even if Turkey, at least since 2017, arguably does not qualify as a democracy.

[4] J.-J. Rousseau, *The Social Contract and Discourses*, trans. G. D. H. Cole (Dent and Sons, 1923), p. 37.

[5] J. E. Green, *The Eyes of the People: Democracy in an Age of Spectatorship* (Oxford University Press, 2010), p. 154. On personalistic leadership and charisma see also K. Weyland, "Latin America's Authoritarian Drift. The Threat from Populist Left," *Journal of Democracy*, 24:3 (2013), p. 20.

prove his merit, the leader creates chaos. He then becomes the savior from it; the protector and restorer of virtue.

The prevailing force that generates and sustains illiberal power is not tied to specific social and economic conditions.[6] In illiberal democracies, the political shapes society by creating and reinforcing specific mindsets and dependencies.[7] "Populism first and foremost shapes patterns of political rule, not the allocation of socioeconomic benefits or losses."[8] The political and resulting social power of the plebiscitarian leader originates from a system of personal dependencies and from the belief that the leader is indispensable in the permanent chaos. The leader's political power enables him to set the rules of the game, defining who is both friend and enemy. "Populism first and foremost shapes patterns of political rule, not the allocation of socioeconomic benefits or losses."[9]

This chapter discusses the system of personal dependencies and role of law in creating and sustaining them. Chapter 4 will show how popular support emerges from the chaos (and resulting fear).

3.2 Neopatrimonial Patronage

Ideally, in a constitutional democracy power is exercised within formal, legally prescribed forms. In contrast most authoritarian rulers "behaved in ways that, following Max Weber and Juan Linz, can be called neopatrimonialist, if not sultanistic. They claimed to rule *for* the common good, but held themselves above the law, and often ignored for their personal advantage the ethical injunctions of republicanism."[10] In the context of illiberal democracies Scheppele confirms that for the populists [the victorious leader] "the drive for power, plain and simple" is the principal motive. "Populists may appear to valorize elections, but underneath they have no intention of leaving office."[11] Illiberal democracies are

---

[6] C. de la Torre, "Populism in Latin American Politics," *The Many Faces of Populism: Current Perspectives. Research in Political Sociology*, 22 (2014), pp. 79–100.

[7] The illiberal regimes of Eastern Europe are not sustainable without the support and complicity of the EU. However, this book deals only with the endogenous roots of government power in illiberal democracies.

[8] K. Weyland, "Clarifying a Contested Concept," *Comparative Politics*, 34:1 (2001), p. 11.

[9] Ibid.

[10] G. A. O"Donnell, "Horizontal Accountability in New Democracies," *Journal of Democracy*, 9:3 (1998), p. 117.

[11] K. L. Scheppele, "The Opportunism of Populists and the Defense of Constitutional Liberalism," *German Law Journal*. 20:3 (2019), p. 330.

neopatrimonial regimes,[12] but here personal rule exists hand in hand with a bureaucratic, formal, rationalistic system. The ruler pretends not to be above the law, and his state and its officials act as authorized by law.

Using public resources the plebiscitarian leader operates a *patronage* system in accordance with the rules he has created.[13] The leader determines who gets what from the state, but the beneficiary may hold state resources as a "prebenda" only.[14] Control over the state enables an effective patronage system that will serve the leader and his party, and first and foremost enables him to hold on to power. The privileged access to state resources, the possibility to shape decisions of the state in favor of oligarchs, etc., depends on the holders of political power.[15] Private interests are subordinated to the public interest of maintaining power. Or to use the elegant formula of Professor György Schöpflin, MEP for Fidesz for fifteen years, these intermediaries appear to Brussels as private actors, while in reality they "carry out (manage) the economic policy of the state."[16]

Max Weber distinguished between patrimonial rule and the feudal estate system: "The ruler recruits his officials in the beginning and foremost from those who are his subjects by virtue of personal dependence (slaves and serfs), for of their obedience he can be absolutely sure."[17] These elements appeared atypically in Western feudalism but resemble certain elements of Ottoman rule, where military and administrative officers were granted possession until the end of their service, as a matter of discretion. "In contrast to bureaucracy, therefore, the position

---

[12] According to Erdmann and Engel, neopatrimonialism is a hybrid of Weber's patrimonial and legal–rational forms of domination. Legal–rational institutions are intertwined with the informality of clientelism, patronage, and rent-seeking. G. Erdmann and U. Engel, "Neo-patrimonialism Revisited – Beyond a Catch-All Concept," German Institute of Global and Area Studies Working Papers No.16 (2006).

[13] Of course, patronage is not specific to illiberal populist regimes.

[14] A. Innes, "The Political Economy of State Capture in Central Europe," *Journal of Common Market Studies*, 52:1 (2014), pp. 88–104, quoted in R. Sata and I. P. Karolewski, "Caesarean Politics in Hungary and Poland," *East European Politics*, 36:2 (2019), p. 208.

In medieval ecclesiastical law, prebenda is an endowment of land or other wealth set aside as the provender (prebenda) of an ecclesiastical official (prebendary).

[15] This applies to domestic players. Some large foreign investors (especially in automobile manufacturing) in Hungary do not depend on the state but receive considerable benefits. On the other hand, no such exceptions were made to foreign investors in Venezuela, where Chávez continued with nationalization to create clientelistic opportunities.

[16] "Vendégünk Schöpflin György," HetiVálasz podcast (May 7, 2020), https://open.spotify.com/episode/04x4eSxHpcfl3ujb4VKjGu.

[17] M. Weber, *Economy and Society* (University of California Press, 1968), p. 1026.

of the patrimonial official derives from his purely personal submission to the ruler."[18]

Patronage forms the social basis of the leader's domination; any analysis of the constitutional order of the regime, or of illiberal democracy, is doomed to fail if it does not consider the interrelation between the patronage-enabling legal structure, and the informal structures, norms, and exchanges of patronage that support, alter, and replace formal legal structures.[19] The legal sphere is guided by the formal, general rules of the law, but it will be overwhelmingly influenced by private considerations, in particular the preservation of power and the spoils, preferably via democratic means. Yet private interest can be legalized under the pretext of the common good, and this indeed happens in many illiberal democracies.

Patronage systems predate illiberal democracies, which have merely revitalized the model.[20] Patronage systems are structured around the "personalized exchange of concrete rewards and punishments, and not primarily around abstract, impersonal principles such as ideological belief or categorizations that include many people one has not actually met in person. ... The centrality of personalized, as opposed to impersonal, exchange explains why ... weak rule of law, nepotism, and corruption all tend to be common in highly patronalistic societies."[21]

The power of the political leader over his clients, who are entrusted with governing and managing the country as well as parts of the economy, and increasingly culture, is the real power behind the constitutionally granted authority of the prime minister or president who acts as the plebiscitarian leader. The patron-in-chief is the one who is elected and who possesses the popular support that legitimizes the regime and

---

[18] Ibid., p. 1030.

[19] For a similar position regarding presidential systems in Latin America see G. A. O'Donnell, "Illusions about Consolidation," *Journal of Democracy*, 7:2 (1996), pp. 39–40.

[20] In Singapore, traditionally, "the party was the vehicle of patronage. Today, it is the control of the state, its resources and institutions that give the dominant parties their power . . . . Arguably their allies in the economy are dependent on distribution of state-connected favours." B. Welsh and G. Lopez, "Conclusions. Challenges and Resilience in Malaysia and Singapore," in G. Lopez and B. Welsh (eds.), *Regime Resilience in Malaysia and Singapore* (Rowman & Littlefield, 2018), p. 286.

[21] H. E. Hale, "Russian Patronal Politics Beyond Putin," *Daedalus* 146:2 (2017), p. 31. In Hale's typology the patronage system can be hierarchical or competitive, p. 32.

On the relation between patronage and distorted democracy see T. Carothers, "The End of the Transition Paradigm," *Journal of Democracy*, 13:1 (2002), pp. 2–21; for Latin America see O'Donnell, "Illusions About Consolidation."

enables his cronies to benefit from it.[22] The leader's lieutenants (who are selected by the leader from his loyal cronies or simply appointed to formal governmental leadership positions) depend completely on him. When in 1994 Berlusconi succeeded in having fifty of his media managers elected to the Italian Parliament, he boasted that "I'm like Prince Charming. They were pumpkins and I turned them into parliamentarians."[23] The HPM was able to conjure a whole supermajority out of his pumpkins.

The core supporters of the regime receive entitlements, including long-term transfers and promises of future benefit. The most vulnerable and most dependent citizens are offered one-off handouts.[24] The patronage system is not limited to an inner circle of vice-regents who control and deliver certain spheres in exchange for services rendered. Patronage in a plebiscitarian democracy must benefit a sufficient part of the constituency to produce extended popular acclamation. Venezuela was famous for socialist-style social services for those among the poor who could be deemed Chávez supporters (others were denied them). The PiS government did not hesitate to engage in large-scale redistribution in favor of families with children, an example followed by the Hungarians. The Turkish housing agency has built approximately 500,000 homes, "literally constructing its own constituency."[25] The AKP is well-known for providing gifts to its supporters, especially during election campaigns (this follows from the general political culture). AKP patronage turns Turkey into a "charity economy,"[26] but patronage meant that the state had to deliver services: the health care system was unified and extended, ending the privilege of government-sector employees. When it came to vote maximization, the AKP was ready to sacrifice the rationality of its own project, and before the 2007 election, it abolished the referral

---

[22] In Poland the leader's legitimacy does not derive from being directly elected. Kaczyński was only the President of the governing party, and the "center for political command," the de facto ruling entity is formed around him. See W. Sadurski, *Poland's Constitutional Breakdown* (Oxford University Press, 2019).

[23] Quoted after T. S. Pappas, *Populism and Liberal Democracy. A Comparative and Theoretical Analysis* (Oxford University Press, 2019), p. 148.

[24] I. Mares and L. E. Young, "The Core Voter's Curse: Clientelistic Threats and Promises in Hungarian Elections," *Comparative Political Studies*, 51:11 (2018), pp. 1441–471.

[25] A. Finkel, *Turkey: What Everyone Needs to Know* (Oxford University Press, 2012), p. 71.

[26] M. Çınar, "Explaining the Popular Appeal and Durability of the Justice and Development Party in Turkey," in E. Massicard and N. Watts (eds.), *Negotiating Political Power in Turkey. Breaking up the Party* (Routledge, 2013), p. 50.

requirement for tertiary health care, under pressure from its constituency.[27]

The patronage system reinforces mental and existential dependency necessary for political domination. The political power of the center is converted into economic power in the private economy, which is then used to consolidate political power through elections as well as mind control. It is within the constitutional structure that *refeudalization* occurs through public law.[28] The neofeudal relations emerge in a capitalist system where "domination is independent of market mechanisms."[29] Here the political powerholder maintains domination over a network of loyalists who receive administrative or economic positions and wealth (prebenda). The leader exercises control over others in exchange for loyalty to both the supreme powerholder and the local patron. According to Max Weber, "under prebendal authority, property (benefice) [is] given to the followers for their services, but rulers can revoke this property at any time." In many illiberal centralizing regimes, property (as "benefice") was "redistributed to owners who were believed to loyally serve the political powers. In regard of the Hungarian system neo-prebendalism ... operates with a much-reduced system of legal-rational authority."[30]

[27] "[A]bolishing the referral system has increased the AKP's electoral votes by about 5 percent." H. H. Yildirim and T. Yildirim, "Healthcare Financing Reform in Turkey: Context and Salient Features," *Journal of European Social Policy*, 21:2 (2011), p. 190.

[28] The term refeudalization was used in J. Habermas, *The Structural Transformation of the Public Sphere: An Inquiry into a Category of Bourgeois Society*, trans. T. Burger (Polity Press, 1989). It has resurfaced among critics of globalized capitalism. The present use of the term, as applied to Hungary, obviously differs from those uses. Feudalism is characterized by a very formal set of traditions and rules defining the duties of the subordinates, and positions, privileges and duties are inherited. See A. Ágh, "The Bumpy Road of Civil Society in the New Member states: From State Capture to the Renewal of Civil Society," *Politics in Central Europe*, 11:2 (2015), pp. 7–21. Ágh argues that these networks can be liked to "a modernised system of 'feudal' dependence or 'vassalage,' or to some kind of subordination pyramid providing mutual support and protection in exchange for certain privileges. In this kleptocratic system, the 'vassals,' clients or subordinates are organised into a large, nationwide political family. In this perverse world, everything is 'legal,' including corruption through public tenders." Ibid., p. 12. See further Z. Ádám, "Re-feudalizing Democracy: An Approach to Authoritarian Populism Taken from Institutional Economics," *Journal of Institutional Economics*, 16:1 (2020), pp. 105–18. Authoritarian populists bring back private political contracting as a dominant political coordination mechanism, effectively refeudalizing democracy.

[29] T. W. Adorno, "Late Capitalism or Industrial Society?," in F. van Gelder (trans.), V. Meja, D. Misgeld, and N. Stehr (eds.), *Modern German Sociology* (Columbia University Press, 1987), p. 244.

[30] T. Csillag and I. Szelényi, "Drifting from Illiberal Democracy: Traditionalist/Neo-conservative Ideology of Managed Illiberal Democratic Capitalism in Post-communist Europe," *Intersections*, 1:1 (2015), p. 27.

With the help of the law, state assets are mobilized to maximize power and perpetuate service to the leader and his clique.[31] The legal structures are shaped in order to enable and sustain a patronage system.[32] Once the leader controls state power, he will be able to keep his supporters and others dependent of him. The clients placed in key positions, both in the state administration and outside it, must remain obedient. Contrary to classical feudalism, this is democratic or majoritarian clientelism, as a sizable number of beneficiaries express loyalty at election time.[33] Breaching loyalty would mean loss of the rent opportunity. However, loyalty is more than a simple economic calculation. In many respects, breaching it is simply unthinkable in the leader's inner circle (as well as for supporters who are loyal to the leader as a tribal leader). "If there is only one common good and only one way to represent it faithfully ... then disagreement within the party that claims to be the sole legitimate representative of the common good obviously cannot be permissible."[34]

Control over the state is centralized and personal: at the top of the hierarchy of command stands the head of the executive, the Caesaristic leader surrounded by his entourage. Control over the state means control over the state bureaucracy. More control does not require more bureaucracy,[35] only that most of the public bureaucracy be under central control. The Caesar is the master of the civil service. He knows no impediment, as legal constraints are summarily eliminated by legislation.[36] The leader works with an

---

[31] Carothers assumes that "[t]he state tends to be ... weak and poorly performing." Carothers, "The End," pp. 11–12. In Hungary and Poland, it is precisely the relatively good performance of the state that enables the leader's effective long-term rule.

[32] On the importance of state capture and patronage in Hungary and Poland as part of "Caesarean politics," see Sata and Karolewski, "Caesarean"; Z. Enyedi, "Populist Polarization and Party System Institutionalization: The Role of Party Politics in De-Democratization," *Problems of Post-Communism*, 63:4 (2016), pp. 210–20.

[33] On clientelism in Poland and the higher acceptance of this form of social organization among PiS voters, see R. Markowski, "Creating Authoritarian Clientelism: Poland After 2015," *Hague Journal on the Rule Law*, 11 (2019), pp. 111–32. "[A] thorough test of the support for the clientelistic authoritarian project in Poland stems not so much from the heritage of communism as from either the deep historical traditions or from recent reactions to the socialist blueprint in the form of distrust towards institutions, ... and their axiological foundations in the form of low tolerance, dogmatism and paternalism in social relations." Ibid. p. 125.

[34] See J.-W. Müller "'The People Must be Extracted from Within the People': Reflections on Populism," *Constellations*, 21:4 (2014), p. 487.

[35] The growth in the number of civil servants occurs where jobs serve to reward supporters.

[36] "Such 'rule of the personal genius,' however, stands in conflict with the formally 'democratic' principle of a generally elected officialdom." Weber, *Economy and Society*, pp. 961–62.

apparatus of officials who were appointed by him and who depend on him. Parallel to the process of administrative centralization, the ruler relies on non-majoritarian, expert public bodies.[37] The specialty of illiberal democracy is that the neutral role of "experts" is only a façade: who counts as an expert will be determined on the grounds of partisan loyalty.

It is through the state that the leader controls the public service, economy, and culture (mind control). This occurs in the best Caesaristic tradition: as Machiavelli, otherwise not immune to the attractions of Caesaristic leadership, observed, Caesar "complete[d Rome's] spoliation."[38] To create loyalty and dependence, a selective system of access to state services and resources is established. Only the chosen few have access to privileged benefits.[39] The state resources that are used discriminatorily are *material, regulatory* and *coercive*. At the heart of illiberal democracy lies the leader's control over them.[40] These include:

- the state bureaucracy;
- the regulatory power (including control over parliament as a legislative factory), thereby determining the conditions of access to, and the use of, assets under state influence as well as tax advantages;
- control over material assets, including transferring state property, the favors and privileges resulting from economic policies, and confiscating assets via nationalization or license revocation;[41]
- control over administrative resources (who receives quality medical care or building permits);
- *coercive* means (using the power of constraint, police action, criminal proceedings, and prison);

---

[37] P. Mair, *Ruling the Void. The Hollowing of our Western Democracy* (Verso, 2013), p. 51, called it "politics of depoliticization."

[38] N. Machiavelli, *The Discourses* (Penguin, 1970), p. 138.

[39] K. A. Hawkins, *Venezuela's Chavismo and Populism in Comparative Perspective* (Cambridge University Press, 2010), p. 27. This was one of the sources of Chávez's power.

[40] Müller identifies three populist techniques of governing: the colonization of the state, discriminatory legalism, and the repression of civil society. J.-W. Müller, *What is Populism?* (University of Pennsylvania Press, 2016), p. 44.

[41] There is no single populist economic policy; however, because of strong nationalism, sovereignty-enhancing economic policies like protectionism, reindustrialization and fiscal permissiveness are often advocated. For the plebiscitarian leader, the decisive economic consideration is winning the next election. There seems to be a tendency to favor debtors in the name of justice to the detriment of creditors, who are often presented as agents of multinational conspiracies. Nativist population policies (serving the middle class) are also common.

- control over the production of ideas and beliefs (directly, by national-izing institutions of ideological production like schools and public media, and indirectly, by controlling private outlets); and
- control over the means of constraint as well as monopolized violence.

Statism is the name of the game. "Authoritarian statism" increases the importance of the state to the detriment of the market and civil society, as well as individual autonomy. Such a regime is characterized by "intensi-fied state control over every sphere of socio-economic life combined with a radical decline of the institutions of political democracy."[42] A statist system is oriented toward maximizing the power of the state, where "the control of surplus is external to the economic sphere."[43]

In order to extend the leader's administrative power, illiberal democ-racy tends to extend the state. Therefore, it nationalizes foreign-owned public services, utilities, and media (especially where the multinational tries to resist regulatory intervention).[44] This is done with some self-restraint in Europe (but not in Latin America).[45] To control the state and to direct public administration, proper legal rules are produced. The domination over the public administration is rational-legalistic (in the Weberian sense). Feudalistic domination, relying on the redistributive, regulatory, and coercive power of a beefed-up state, needs the instrumen-tal and biased use of the law to guarantee that the formally law-bound state serves the patronage system, which is the socioeconomic foundation of the Caesaristic political regime.[46] However, behind the semblance of legal rationality, legally authorized discretionary use and non-use of legal resources prevails.

The leader rules with the unscrupulous use of constitutional executive powers: some newly minted, others inherited and "normal" in a democracy. Even if these powers are normal, the constitutional (and

---

[42] N. Poulantzas, *State, Power, Socialism* (Verso, 2014), p. 229.

[43] M. Castells, *The Rise of the Network Society* (Wiley-Blackwell, 2009), p. 16.

[44] In Venezuela, ExxonMobil and ConocoPhillips were expropriated in 2007, when they refused a restructuring that would have offered their shares to PDVSA (the national oil company). Other companies accepted the minority shareholder's position.

[45] In Hungary, the share of the state-controlled economy is high but not excessive in comparison with Western economies. According to OECD data, the percentage of employees in state-owned companies in Hungary was slightly higher than in the Czech Republic, or in the historically etatist France, and considerably higher than in Poland. See, *Hungary: Public Administration and Public Service Development Strategy, 2014–2020*, OECD Public Governance Reviews (2017).

[46] How modern law (a principally equality and predictability-based, neutral instrument) is used in illiberal regimes is discussed in Chapters 5, 7, and 8.

social) balances are eliminated. Be it a parliamentary or presidential regime, the Caesaristic leader "sees himself (and is seen by his many supporters) as a strong leader who, at least metaphorically, holds a whip in his hand and is in no sense controlled by a formal party apparatus. He seemingly regards himself as the primary, if not the unique, fount of legitimate policy initiatives."[47]

How does legal control over the state contribute to the hegemonic position of the ruler in politics and (increasingly) in social life? The rules, and their interpretation by loyal servants under the threatening eyes of their frightened superiors, will allocate the material resources to the first tier of trusted clients. Their duty is to extend the leader's control. For this reason, existing institutions are captured by the governing party cadres: "a phenomenon coupled with selective, yet widespread nepotism and corruption."[48] The new system in the making is thus much more clientelism than populism proper. Consider, for example, the situation of a manager of a cultural complex. The auditorium in this public building will be made available during the electoral campaign only to the ruling party, and not for the opposition, because on the day of the opposition's rally mandatory cleaning has been scheduled (and something else legally necessitated will occur each and every time the opposition party tries to exercise its right to access the facility).

The competences of the state are extended so that the leader can reach all of society through his obedient servants, who carry out his will, which then transforms into formally (more or less) correct law. In this respect, the leader is reminiscent of the Schmittian dictator of the total state:[49] everything that is "state" is politically determined by the leader, therefore the bigger the state's influence is, the better it is for the leader's personal power.

The state's ever-increasing power can guarantee hegemonistic domination over people, the economy, the manufacturing of ideas, and ultimately society. The more control over society, the more likely that the regime can sustain itself through elections: this is how the totalitarianism of democracy unfolds. If most resources are controlled by the state, there will be little autonomy and no effective political competitor left. No

---

[47] J. Ober, "Joseph Schumpeter's Caesarist Democracy," *Critical Review*, 29:4 (2017), p. 490. (referring to President Trump).

[48] Markowski, "Creating," p. 120.

[49] See D. Schneiderman, "Parliamentarism and Its Adversaries: Legislatures in an Era of Illiberal Executives," in A. Sajó, S. Holmes, and R. Uitz, *Routledge Handbook of Illiberalism* (Routledge, in press).

reasonable businessman will sponsor an opposition party if his future contracts and tax audits depend on the incumbent government.

In order to provide access to state resources, in the form of non-refundable (government/state) subsidies, one would expect increased redistribution. The Hungarian government has often used the general budget reserve (intended to cover expenditures for extraordinary events) to non-transparently fund the HPM's pet projects (see also sports-related expenditures supported by tax transfers). However, in terms of government spending, centralization is not excessive, and the level of fiscal redistribution through Hungary's budget has not exceeded the OECD average. Hungary's spending ratio hovers around the EU average, while Poland's is below.[50] Noticeable in Hungary, however, is that redistribution favors the upper-middle classes, thanks to the flat tax rate, among other things, while social welfare is reduced for the poorest, who have become even more dependent on the government's public-works program.[51] Poland introduced an important redistributive measure favoring families with children and reduced the retirement age.

Two of the most characteristic techniques of the Hungarian patronage system are public procurement and the distribution of subventions (including EU structural funds).[52] Because of the tailor-made bid criteria in public procurement calls, the preselected bidder inevitably wins the tender. Between 2010 and 2016, 5 percent of public procurement went to a group of five friends and family members of the HPM, at contract prices exceeding roughly 20 percent of the average competitive bids.[53] Among the many legal tricks used to achieve this result, lower bids are declared

---

[50] "Country List Government Spending to GDP | Europe," Trading Economics, www.tradingeconomics.com/country-list/government-spending-to-gdp?continent=europe.
     Poland's public deficit has been set at 60 percent. At least in the past, it had a policy of limiting discretionary spending.

[51] In 2019 the Hungarian government started a program to boost childbirth with loans that would not be paid back after a fourth child is born. Mothers with four children will enjoy lifelong personal income tax exemption. According to a 2020 survey, this was the most important achievement of the Fidesz government, a distant second being that the country was protected against migrants (45 percent). See *Orbán 10: Az Elmúlt Évtized a Magyar Társadalom Szemével*, Friedrich-Ebert-Stiftung and Policy Solutions (2020).

[52] EU funds play the same role that oil did in Venezuela (with similar consequences for market distortion and economic development).

[53] I. J. Tóth and M. Hajdu, *How does the Kleptocratic State Work in Hungary?*, Corruption Research Center (January 26, 2018). For a similar use of public procurement in Turkey see E. Ç. Gürakar and T. Bircan, "Redistribution or Crony Capitalism? Favoritism in Public Procurement Contract Award Processes," in E.Ç. Gürakar (ed.), *Politics of Favoritism in Public Procurement in Turkey. Reconfigurations of Dependency Networks in the AKP Era* (Palgrave Macmillan, 2016). See further Chapter 7.

formally faulty or the bid is considered unreasonably low. Commonly, the winning government-friendly bidder presents additional claims after the contract is signed, citing "unforeseen" expenses, or the public entity will ask for extra services without a bid. The extent of discretionary powers granted to the authorities is considerable, and the formal criteria are determined in a discriminatory manner.

While the Hungarian public sector is not large enough to control the entire economy, with 50 percent of the GDP centrally redistributed, the government is in the position to grant important economic opportunities, which serve as the basis of patronage and resulting domination.[54] The nationalization without compensation of tobacco sale licenses, and their redistribution through public bids, represents a textbook example of the use of state power to reward a clientele that remains dependent on the benefactor.[55] Tobacco retail redistribution was overnight made subject to a licensing system with a limited number of licenses. Tens of thousands of distributors in grocery stores owned by small entrepreneurs were deprived of their right to sell tobacco. The number of sales points was radically reduced in the name of protecting health. At the end of a nontransparent and arbitrary public competition, many of the new licenses went to "friends" of the regime.[56]

In exchange for procurement contracts or other perks, clients of the regime provide the resources necessary to win elections, particularly through controlling the media but also by using the employment opportunities that government cronies (including political appointees in the public sector) can offer to extract political loyalty from dependent employees. The concentration of power comes at considerable cost. Political powerholders and their clients invade the market to convert political power into rent-seeking opportunities. The market is

[54] M. Fazekas and I. J. Tóth, "From Corruption to State Capture: A New Analytical Framework with Empirical Applications from Hungary," *Political Research Quarterly*, 69:2 (2016), pp. 320–34.

[55] *Vékony v. Hungary*, ECtHR, App. no. 65681/13, Judgment of 13 January 2015. For details see Chapter 8.

[56] The literature on Poland does not emphasize the importance of patronage to the same degree. See, however, in the area of subsidies, G. Makowski. "Poland's hidden corruption," Notes from Poland (February 28, 2020), www.notesfrompoland.com/2020/02/28/polands-hidden-corruption/. Compared to Hungary, PiS cadres are more frequently held legally responsible for abusing their position, partly because Kaczyński cares about the party's purity. P. M. Kaczyński, "Four Corruption Waves Hit PiS," Political Europe (January 29, 2019), www.political-europe.com/2019/01/29/how-corruption-eats-pis/; Markowski, "Creating," p. 125.

characterized by under-the-counter business transactions just like democratic exchange is replaced by under-the-counter political deals.

Some economies may not be able to sustain the inefficiency resulting
from parasitic clientelistic structures and direct transfers to privileged
loyalists. A distorted market means insufficient information, arbitrary
decisions, and a politically high price: depending on the conditions, and
wrong choices, in arbitrary public transfers (e.g. not providing enough to
pensioners), public dissatisfaction may grow, increasing the risk of unrest.
However, some regimes are lucky to receive subsidies (from the EU) or
have natural resources that make the costs of the regime (more) affordable.

What, then, is the advantage of controlling society through the state,
notwithstanding the high social costs of such a centralized venture? In
this model of social control, the state's regulative, redistributive, and
disciplinary powers can be easily mobilized relatively freely in support
of domination. "Access to and control of public office and state authority
continue to greatly influence how private wealth and social power are
accumulated and distributed."[57] This quote ends with the words "in
Indonesia," but it applies to illiberal state-centered regimes in too many
countries under the spell of populism-based leader democracy.

The patronage system does not result in state capture but capture by
the state (*reverse state capture*),[58] except when it comes to large foreign
investments.[59] It is the Caesaristic ruler (through the state) who captures

---

[57] V. R. Hadiz, "Indonesia's Year of Democratic Setbacks: Towards a New Phase of
Deepening Illiberalism?," *Bulletin of Indonesian Economic Studies*, 53:3 (2017), p. 262.

[58] "Instead of classic state capture where economic interests take over a weak executive, in
Hungary a powerful executive cooperates in a nontransparent manner with business
circles that it has itself created." Bertelsmann Stiftung, *BTI 2020 Country Report –
Hungary*, Bertelsmann Stiftung (2020), p. 4.

In *state capture* situations, oligarchic business groups exercise control over the state and
its resources through control over political parties. However, Berlusconi in Italy and Babiš
in the Czech Republic became prime ministers using their own economic intelligence and
media resources (with Berlusconi also using state power to shield his investments), though
these events appear to be one-man attempts. S. Hanley and M. A. Vachudova,
"Understanding the Illiberal Turn: Democratic Backsliding in the Czech Republic," *East
European Politics*, 34:3 (2018), pp. 276–96.

Putin's power is based on his successful reversal of state capture in 2000, although the
oligarchs never did "substantively dominate policy making for any extended period."
R. Sakwa, "Putin and the Oligarchs," *New Political Economy*, 13:2 (2008), p. 186.

[59] Following the example of their predecessors, the nationalist Hungarian and Polish
governments have been ready to create a "friendly" business environment for large
investors, but contrary to the state capture model, the investors do not have to take
control of the party. Latin American populist regimes took the opposite position and
squeezed out foreign influence in the natural resources sector.

his oligarchs, and other privileged users of the state, and designates the beneficiaries of state rents for his own purposes. The state-appointed or approved oligarchs must show their loyalty by all sorts of contributions and presence. The expectation of such acclamative support applies to major multinational corporations too (in exchange for special tax and other benefits). One does business in full respect of local traditions.

In Italy, Berlusconi bought AC Milan, a world-class football team, way before he entered politics with his own money (whatever the origin of that money was). In Hungary, the HPM "bought" the whole of Hungarian football with public money, although only one Hungarian football team reached even a qualifying round in European cups during his reign – a real indicator of the regime's inefficiency.[60] Never mind; as the Trainer in Chief told us: "Football was always consolation [among others for the territorial loss caused by the 1920 Treaty of Trianon] and redress for the Hungarian."[61]

3.3 Reducing Autonomy

For purposes of domination, control over assets is not only about providing access to (loyal) beneficiaries who will, in exchange, support the regime. It is equally about dependence by *deprivation*.

---

[60] Act LXXXI of 1996, as amended from 2011 onwards, provides that companies can transfer to certain sporting activities up to 80 percent of their taxes and receive a 7.5 percent tax credit. (For the sake of comparison, two percent of personal income tax can be dedicated to religious and charitable purposes, without credit.) Companies (among them state-owned companies) are "expected" to take advantage of this opportunity. In less than ten years, more than two billion (!) euros were transferred. The football club that was founded by the HPM received 55–100 million euros (not including the stadium built across the HPM's family home). The bulk of the contribution came from the HPM's number one trustee and childhood friend, but Coca-Cola also considered it important to support the team of this village of 500 souls. Beginning in 2019, the previous possibility to transfer a part of corporate tax for cultural purposes (like theaters) was abolished, and only sport activities can be supported by donors using the partial tax credit. The HPM considers football an art, so from his perspective there is no loss to cultural activities. K. Erdélyi, "Fidesz-közeli, állami, és multinacionális cégek öntik a TAO-pénzt a kormány kedvenc futballklubjaiba – itt vannak a nevek és a számok." *Átlátszó* (July 17, 2018), www.atlatszo .hu/2018/07/18/Fidesz-kozeli-allami-es-multinacionalis-cegek-ontik-a-tao-penzt-a-kor many-kedvenc-futballklubjaiba-itt-vannak-a-nevek-es-a-szamok/
The EU is of the opinion that this is not state aid.

[61] V. Orbán, "Orbán Viktor nyilatkozata a „Labdarúgás és tudomány" című sportszakmai tankönyv bemutatásakor" (Speech, May 30, 2020), Prime Minister's Office Website, http://www.miniszterelnok.hu/orban-viktor-nyilatkozata-a-labdarugas-es-tudomany-cimu-sportszakmai-tankonyv-bemutatasakor/ (my translation). For the relevance of the constant victimhood identity in the leader-people relation see Chapter 4.

Centralization means that resources of institutional and personal autonomy are eliminated. Local self-government powers are transferred to an unelected, nonresponsive central administration; and social services (e.g. education) provided by local self-governments are taken over by the central government.[62] Public schools, originally managed by municipalities, were first deprived of proper finances; when some municipalities faced difficulties in covering expenses, all the municipal schools were transformed into state-owned schools under a single national management, with total control over appointments and curriculum, officially to reduce inequality in education. Local self-governments were made financially dependent on the state (if necessary, changing their constitutionally protected status), being deprived of local revenues.

Allegedly relying on a UK model of financial responsibility (service for money), commissars (so-called chancellors) are appointed to each university with exclusive power over financial decisions. As a result, academic freedom is curtailed. The chancellor has full financial control over university decisions with financial implications.

The power of the state is used to take control over knowledge-based resources of independent thought. Legal regulation in the hands of biased executors of the law is intended to create a government-friendly monopoly over media outlets. The material (ownership-based) and regulatory control over media outlets enables the unhindered manufacture of messages about constant threats (terrorism, migrants, or foreign conspiracies).[63] In Hungary, the public service broadcaster unabashedly continued, throughout the year, to cover the story of a crime committed in January by a "migrant" in Germany, as if it were a fresh news item. Existing fears are sustained and increased. This public sentiment of fear is turned into the demand for protection, and the authorities, under the guidance of the leader, are presented as protectors of the national ethnic community against the threats posed by "aliens."

Where the state controls investment, employment, educational, and health care opportunities, the material resources, knowledge, and security,

---

[62] See also the dissolution of the Laender at the beginning of Hitler's rule and the submission of the regional governors to presidential power in Russia at the beginning of the consolidation of Putin's power.

[63] D. Canetti-Nisim, E. Halperin, S. E. Hobfoll, and O. Shapira, "A New Stress-Based Model of Political Extremism: Personal Exposure to Terrorism, Psychological Distress, and Exclusionist Political Attitude," *Journal of Conflict Resolution*, 53:3 (2009), pp. 363–89. This is true even if Hungarians highly distrust the media (85 percent). See *Beyond Populism? Two Years After*, IPSOS Public Affairs, 2018.

social capital that can sustain action against oppression becomes scarce. In order to understand the effects of the totalizing political domination over most spheres of life, picture the fate of a small-town public-school teacher who serves as a local election observer on behalf of one of the opposition parties. She will be dismissed from the school on trumped-up charges. Some of her colleagues will expressly condemn her for making fuss and jeopardizing the fate of her children. Most will remain silent, trying to avoid eye contact; a few will whisper words of compassion (but not solidarity). There is no other school in the village, and the few private employers (all or most with contracts with the municipality) refuse to hire her. Her children are ostracized at their school for having an unemployed mother and for not having enough money to join the school excursion.

This is the real effect of domination.

In this world of submission and personal dependence even the poorest members of the active electorate vote for the leader, even if their conditions do not much improve and certainly far less than the economic possibilities would permit. In Hungary, 80 percent of the voters living in the poorest villages voted for the government in 2018; support for PiS is strongest in the poorest southeastern and eastern parts of Poland.

"Vibrant organs of civil society" and "meaningful political intermediaries" are indispensable for liberal democracy.[64] In illiberal democracies civil society has a very different "vibration." Civil society and NGOs depend to a great extent on government largesse, even in advanced welfare states. This inherent vulnerability creates the opportunity for state domination in countries where there is insufficient private wealth to enable the autonomous existence of civil society organizations and interactions. Without tax benefits, state subsidies and state service contracts, civil society organizations are particularly vulnerable. At the same time, the illiberal state uses its financial and administrative resources to discipline civil society, often in the guise of support: Caesaristic regimes from Venezuela to Hungary extend their financial largesse to their loyalist NGOs. Not even religious organizations are exempt. The Catholic Church in Poland is different; the state served it even before PiS came to power, and the Church remains a (perhaps senior) partner of the state, which willingly supports the Church's conservative agenda and benefits from its political support. In exchange for financial support,

---

[64] S. Issacharoff, *Fragile Democracies: Contested Power in the Era of Constitutional Courts* (Cambridge University Press, 2015), p. 270.

religious organizations will provide their moral support to the government (e.g. progovernment sermons) or engage in mass mobilization.
Where civil initiatives insist on their independence and appear critical
of the regime, they might be persecuted with the tools of the law (from
fiscal audits to criminalization),[65] as happened with the decisively anti-
Chávez Catholic Church in Venezuela,[66] or they may be forced to serve
the regime, as happened with the trade unions, again in Venezuela.

Beyond the destruction of the material grounds of personal autonomy
emerges a state-induced loss of personal orientation. In a bourgeois
society of independent individuals, the "market is a point of reference
for all aspects of life,"[67] but the markets available for orienting the citizen
in an illiberal democracy are mostly distorted and manipulated. The
consequence is the loss of a sense of agency. Swiftly, a sense of no
alternative becomes "common knowledge."[68] That common knowledge
is based on the everyday experience that the powers that be can be
arbitrary, and that the promise of the law is unreliable, inefficient, or
false.

In an (ideal) democracy, to believe what the competitive leaders assert
is (in principle) a matter of rational, evidence-based personal choice. In
a consolidated illiberal democracy, the capacity to choose among beliefs
disappears in a growing number of minds, or at least ceases to function in
the public, political sphere. Instead of a rational choice, belief in the
legitimacy of the leader stems from enhanced authoritarianism, from the

---

[65] On the Hungarian "foreign NGO" law, see Case C-78/18, *Commission v. Hungary* [2020]
EU:C:2020:476, para. 1. ("By imposing obligations of registration, declaration and publication on certain categories of civil society organisations directly or indirectly receiving
support from abroad exceeding a certain threshold and providing for the possibility of
applying penalties to organisations that do not comply with those obligations, Hungary
had introduced discriminatory and unjustified restrictions.")
    In August 2018, Polish authorities also created a blacklist against government-critical
NGOs. K. Zbytniewska. "Poland's deportation of human rights activist: The back story."
Euractiv (August 21, 2018), www.euractiv.com/section/justice-home-affairs/news/
polands-deportation-of-human-rights-activist-the-back-story/.

[66] The Chávez government tried to support evangelical Protestant churches to counter the
Catholic Church (traditionally, financially dependent on the state). D. Smilde and
C. Pagan, "Christianity and Politics in Venezuela's Bolivarian Democracy," in
D. Smilde and D. Hellinger (eds.), *Venezuela's Bolivarian Democracy. Participation,
Politics, and Culture under Chávez* (Duke University Press, 2011), pp. 317–341, p. 337
in particular.

[67] O. Nachtwey, "Decivilization: On Regressive Tendencies in Western Societies," in
H. Geiselberger (ed.), *The Great Regression* (Polity, 2017), p. 85.

[68] P. Petit, *Republicanism: A Theory of Freedom and Government* (Oxford University Press,
1997), pp. 58–59. See further Chapter 6.

wish to accept authority without question, solely for being *the* authority. Unconditional acceptance is not without proper rewards. The advantages are partly material, partly emotional, and identity based: acceptance proves to populist-traditionalist-nationalists that they have the right identity: that they are part of the chosen, authentic people.

Constitutionally embedded plebiscitarian state power is used to create and sustain dependency, not only among beneficiaries of the regime, but also among those who lost their autonomy due to (more or less) lawful measures of deprivation. For effective domination, the ruler must control the ruled and reward and keep at bay his own accomplices. How is this achieved?

In his discussion of the routinization of charisma Weber states that "It is not possible for the costs of permanent, routine administration to be met by 'booty,' contributions, gifts, and hospitality."[69] Certainly, the routine administration of state affairs requires a rational, law-based system. But "booty" remains crucial for the patronage-based regime. The legally sanctioned position of power grants the leader and his entourage access to spoils and "hospitality" in a system of reciprocal favors: you get a bank, but in exchange you provide loans for my friends and our political (e.g. electoral) purposes. At the same time, the selective use of governmental advantages and coercion, the power to grant and revoke rights, provides opportunities for extortion: irresistible offers can entice private owners to transfer their property; the buyer makes a below-the-market offer more "attractive" by referring to the possibility of tax inspection. Even independent business must join the club and serve the economic (and political, including party political) goals of the state.[70] The monopoly of constraint (extortion) in the hands of the leader and his cronies[71] means more than a simple opportunity to threaten and pressure; it provides immunity. But even immunity creates further dependence because nonpunishment of the wrongdoing is not final. At any moment, the prosecution or police may discover the lost file, new evidence may be found relevant, and so on.

---

[69] Weber, *Economy and Society*, p. 252.

[70] In the case of EU member states, dependence on EU transfers and direct investment (primarily from Germany) limits the capacity to extort.

[71] A. Sajó, "From corruption to extortion: Conceptualization of post-communist corruption," *Crime, Law and Social Change*, 40 (2003), pp. 171–94. In the disorder of the early postcommunist transition, every street police officer had extorsion opportunities; he could threaten all drivers with a speeding ticket or other fine for a real or imaginary violation. The centralized state power would not tolerate such challenges to its own monopoly of extortion.

Depending on the extent of the progress toward despotism, constraint, and violence (including the use of progovernment thugs) will become increasingly prominent. Law is used beyond disciplining, as a tool of revenge. In the mildest forms of the punitive state, those believed to be related to the opposition and other enemies of the people, people with known critical attitudes, are dismissed and blacklisted. All citizens who had signed the 2004 recall petition against Chávez were "catalogued" (*lista Tascón*), becoming ineligible for participating in the government's missions and, thus, receiving state aid.[72]

Dependence among the beneficiaries of the patronage system generates electoral loyalty. Those who are deprived of an autonomous existence or are simply vulnerable due to their social conditions will also be loyal, as they are susceptible to regime pressure. The quasi-feudal system of dependencies results in a functioning and relatively stable regime.[73] Political and administrative coordination (together with patronage networks) are a substitute for other forms of social coordination, like the free market, when the spontaneous order of civil society does not function or is made dysfunctional.

The domination over society by a central, personal, political power is not just about opportunities for redistribution and corruption. It serves a special need of the plebiscitarian regime, namely, to generate popular support to renew and perpetuate itself. Elections remain crucial for the illiberal regime, perhaps too much so. The leader must win all coming elections, and all resources held in trust by his clients are mobilized for victory. Elections are the payback day for patronage. Of course, full support is not just a matter of loyalty. The clients depend totally on the political regime: victory of the leader is a matter of life and death (or years in prison) for the client.[74] The most prominent example of the duty to promote governmental interests is the private control of the media. In feudalism, the lord was obligated to mobilize a number of soldiers in exchange for land ownership. In Hungary the recipient of a lucrative

---

[72] J. Corrales and M. Penfold, "Venezuela: Crowding Out the Opposition," *Journal of Democracy*, 18:2 (2007), pp. 99–113.

[73] These regimes remain stable as long as external factors (e.g. oil revenue) counter the costs of corruption. Once such support disappears (as in Venezuela, due to a radical drop in oil prices), discontent starts to eat into the system.

[74] The key problem of dictatorship is that "promises made at one point by the dictator, his allies, or the regime's repressive agents may be broken later, when they become inconvenient." A similar problem may emerge in illiberal regimes. Svolik, *The Politics*, p. 14.

license is expected to run a progovernment broadcast station or other loss-producing media outlet.

For the purposes of plebiscitarian acclamation (including elections), the state uses its resources to mobilize those citizens who depend on the state.[75] Civil servants provide administrative resources. The poor, who have become dependent on government services, either under the control of the public administration or as temporary workers subject to the will of an employer (e.g. landowner), will be mobilized via benefits and threats. Out of their pockets, clients distribute food and small sums of money to the most needy; people will be fired if they do not vote properly, irrespective of the secrecy of the vote.[76] It remains "an optimization problem of the government in any autocracy, including populism, how much fiscal redistribution is needed to the benefit of the poor so that they stay content while the elite maximize their utility."[77] This is a matter for anticipatory transfers (certainly much more important than small-scale vote buying). Modern democracies in welfare societies are also driven by anticipatory transfers whereby the governing party not only follows its pre-election commitments of transfer and redistribution but modifies its commitments in view of the forthcoming election. Such anticipatory, election-oriented transfers become predominant in illiberal democracies, with the regime fixated on winning elections.

Of course, contrary to an authoritarian regime, many citizens remain independent of the government and its cronies. However, the system of domination will affect their decisions. The collapse of the liberal expectations and individual free choice sustaining public institutions (e.g. autonomous education, accessible free press, etc.) facilitates the perpetuation of power through elections. In Hungary (but not in Poland or even Venezuela), there is a sense that there is no alternative. And at that point, electoral democracy becomes meaningless.

---

[75] S. Handlin, "Mass organization and the durability of competitive authoritarian regimes: Evidence from Venezuela," *Comparative Political Studies*, 49:9 (2016), pp. 1238–269.

[76] For empirical evidence on Hungary see Mares and Young, "The Core Voter's Curse."

[77] Z. Ádám, *Gerrymandering the Nation. A Political Transaction Cost Theory of Populism Mimeo* (Corvinus University of Budapest, 2017), p.16.

4

They, the People

> I declare the people to be the only and the true owners of their sovereignty.
> I declare the Venezuelan people the true owners of their own history.
>
> Hugo Chávez[1]
>
> There can be nothing better for a Perónist than another Perónist.
>
> Juan Perón[2]

4.1 Introduction

Illiberal democracies offer a public order that originates in populism. The ruler ascends to power as the leader of a populist movement, and his legitimacy relies on the tenets of populism: the people versus an elite opposition, and the promise that this time the government will follow the will of the authentic people. The primacy of popular will turns the regime against the self-constraining institutions of democracy. While it would be unfair to claim that a radical reliance on the people runs contrary to democracy, populism as a movement and ideology is based on exclusion. Its anti-institutionalism and rejection of political mediation[3] are contrary to democracy as rational decision-making. This rough democracy is deprived of its constitutional protection against the arbitrariness of the genuine will of genuine people. With

---

[1] Chávez quoted after F. Panizza, "Introduction," in F. Panizza (ed.), *Populism and the Mirror of Democracy* (Verso, 2005), p. 4.

[2] J.D. Perón, "The Twenty Truths of the Perónist Justicialism" (speech at Plaza de Mayo, Buenos Aires (October 17, 1950), in *Perónist Doctrine* (Partido Perónista, 1952), p. 87.

[3] "These are non-partisan leaders with a non-partisan program running a non-partisan government in the interests of the people as a whole. This is, in short, partyless democracy." Tony Blair, quoted in P. Mair, "Populist Democracy vs. Party Democracy," in Y. Mény and Y. Surel (eds.), *Democracy and the Populist Challenge* (Palgrave Macmillan, 2002), p. 96.

this point of departure, the natural choice is to turn the regime plebiscitarian.

The people and popular sovereignty are crucial concepts and points of reference for populism and determine the constitution of PLD. The leader claims that there is a direct relation between government and people.[4] In a way, PLD realizes a Rousseauist vision of democracy, with much pragmatism and little messianism. However, when it comes to actual power, in the emerging illiberal democracy the sovereign people has as little involvement in governing as possible, in accordance with Rousseau's totalitarian vision.[5]

"The people," as a concept used by populists, is highly problematic for constitutional culture, even if the collective action of citizens (under specific circumstances) forms a bulwark of the constitutional system and the citizens' properly institutionalized action plays an indispensable role in the system of modern checks and balances. Those who make a living from glorifying the people and democracy are outraged by similar constitutional reservations about the people. However, a certain disrespect of "the people" does not conflict with the fundamental emancipatory assumption of liberalism:[6] it does not affect the principled respect for our fellow citizens as human beings with the equal capacity to choose freely. But a normatively embedded duty to respect free choice does not entail the duty to respect the very choices actually made.

Idolatry of the sovereign people is a remnant of "nineteenth century romanticism" and communist and democratic propaganda. The related assumption that the people will act as a noble and just savior once "liberated" and true to itself, is both naive and manipulative, if not an outright lie, evoking the irrational elements of popular (vulgar) culture and individual prejudice. By delegitimizing the "elite" (a catch-all false notion), populism removes important cultural and legal constraints and endorses the forces that disrupt civilization. By allegedly enabling a people (in reality, the leader of people) to rule unencumbered, populism allows democracy to become what Tocqueville feared it would be:

---

[4] E. Shils, *The Torment of Secrecy. The Background and Consequences of American Security Policies* (I. R. Dee, 1956), pp. 98–103.

[5] R. Tuck, *The Sleeping Sovereign* (Cambridge University Press, 2015).

[6] On the positive role of the people in constitutional checks and balances, see A. Sajó and R. Uitz, *The Constitution of Freedom: An Introduction to Legal Constitutionalism* (Oxford University Press, 2017).

a formless equality catering to a tasteless (and impervious) relative majority of the leader's liking.[7]

This chapter reflects upon the contribution of people and "the people" (as both an abstraction and the interaction of actual citizens) to the contemporary difficulties of democracy. Section 4.2 will discuss the ambiguities of the concept of the people (4.2.1) and that of popular sovereignty in democratic theory and political ideology (4.2.2). Section 4.3 will indicate how these concepts are used and finally transformed (abused) in populist illiberal regimes (4.3.1) and in the name of homogeneity (4.3.2.) as part of identity politics animated by *ressentiment*. It will show how majoritarianism (a primitive concept of democracy) plays into the hands of populism (4.3.3), and how the emerging Caesarist rule perpetuates the passivity of Caesar's people (4.3.4). Section 4.4 concludes that these conceptual changes (and related practices) undermine democracy.

4.2 The People and Its Sovereignty

4.2.1 Meanings of People

The meaning of "people" has often changed throughout history[8] (this is nothing special). Because of its ambiguity, political philosophers find that it is a notion without foundation,[9] corresponds to no reality, is a fiction, remains too flexible,[10] or is used for propaganda purposes. The word "people," the Marquis de Mirabeau noticed long ago (during debates on naming the body that became the French National Assembly of 1789) "necessarily means too much or too little . . . . It is a word open to any use."[11] Today, "the people" refers to an abstract notion of constitutional and political theory, often with normative characteristics. "A people" refers to an active political actor, capable of tangible action, or at least

---

[7] See S. Bilakovics, *Democracy without Politics* (Harvard University Press, 2012).

[8] M. Canovan, *The People* (Polity Press, 2005), p. 16.

[9] According to Habermas: "The people from whom all governmental authority is supposed to derive does not comprise a subject with will and consciousness. It only appears in the plural, and as a people it is capable of neither decision nor action as a whole." J. Habermas, *Between Facts and Norms: Contributions to a Discourse Theory of Law and Democracy* (The MIT Press, 1996), p. 469.

[10] L.-A. Blanqui, quoted in P. Rosanvallon, "Histoire moderne et contemporaine du politique," in *Cours: La démocratie: esquisse d'une théorie générale* (College de France, 2012), p. 681.

[11] P. Rosanvallon, "Revolutionary Democracy," in P. Rosanvallon, *Democracy Past and Future* (Columbia University Press, 2006), p. 83.

an actual collective assumption that generates social action (a coordinated action with meaning).

Irrespective of the difficulties arising from its fictive nature and putative empirical presence, the people is both an assumption and an actor. It is indispensable for democracy in both meanings. It is needed to fill the space when "the locus of power becomes an empty place" by the absence of a divine monarch.[12] "The people" excludes all other pretenders to power. This secular turn is emancipatory: there is no one above the people, which can therefore exercise self-rule and self-government. For a moment, it could seem that by filling the void, the individual would be set free: the monarch is gone, and with no one else filling the command post, there is no one above the individual. This is a short-lived hope, a chimera: the people, the collectivity, the people's representative will remain above the individual, while the citizens are told that they are the master of their fate as part of this supreme will.

The reference to an obscure entity or abstraction (often replaced with the nation[13]) implies a body that seems to exist only in presentation;[14] as if it would exist as a mirror image of the represented. Indeed, the celebrated "people" of populism is but a shadow of the leader. Or perhaps the people is a logical necessity: where there is a representative like the plebiscitarian leader (and his physical existence is beyond doubt), there must be something represented too. After all, a representative must represent someone, by definition. In the real world, impostors represent an invented thing.

Constitutional theory refers to the sovereign people as an artificial entity and an abstraction, "ungrounded in the structure of society," and "based exclusively on the ability of a leader (and his intellectuals) to exploit the dissatisfaction of a variety of groups."[15] From a more empirical perspective, "people" refers to a reality characterized by many names depending on its structure, behavior, and social status (mob, crowd, multitude, etc.). In its actual appearance as multitude or crowd, it hardly ever endorses constitutional or even democratic values. It is important

---

[12] C. Lefort, *Democracy and Political Theory* (University of Minneapolis, 1988), p. 225.

[13] Reference to the "nation" is even more nebulous than "the people" and facilitates further ethnonationalism. It is easier to monopolize power if the leader speaks on behalf of the nation than of the people.

[14] U. Sarcinelli, "Von der Räpresentativen zur Präsentativen Demokratie. Politische Stilbildung im Medienzeitalter," in H. Vorländer (ed.), *Zur Ästhetik der Demokratie. Formen der politischen Selbstdarstellung* (Deutsche Verlags-Anstalt, 2003), pp. 187–99.

[15] N. Urbinati, "Political Theory of Populism," *Annual Review of Political Science*, 22 (2019), p. 118.

for a community how it conceives of itself: the very conceptualization forms the community. Imagination[16] is crucial for the social construction and existence of the people as the possibility of a political community: the nature (quality) and sustainability of democracy (as a popular political community) depend on the nature of this imagination. The concept of the people enables the community (the coordinated actors) to imagine itself as autonomous and united and therefore even sovereign.[17] The people's self-imagination involves a competition of ideas and life forms: in the right-wing populist imagination, the people (a select group of the citizenry) restores itself to the true national identity.

The above empirical people is not unrelated to the abstract (legal) concept of people in the world of law and politics. The abstract concept offers a normative frame: the empirical people should structure itself accordingly in order to give its own acts legal legitimacy. The normative frame intends to determine how the acts of a multitude are socially ascribed to a people as a social actor.

Preconstitutional assumptions about the nature of real people influence the abstract concept (and vice versa): consider the regulation of citizenship (who pertains to the legal people?). The choice of *ius soli* versus *ius sanguinis* as acts of imagination reflects deeply held assumptions about "who belongs" to the political community. In between the abstract concept of the people, and the multitude of individuals in search of their collective formation, stands the legal structures that enable the empirical multitude to structure itself (e.g. electoral procedures and methods, voting rights; different forms of representation).

With the advent of modernity, representation of an abstract people as the source of power, without some kind of popular influence or involvement, became politically unsustainable, as it contradicted the commitment to equality. The denial of voting rights offended the self-respect of all nonvoters, who (beginning with the Chartists) increasingly insisted on political recognition after realizing the political and personal advantages of having a decisive say in who represents them (and their interests).

The problem with the empirical people is that they are not as neutral as abstract legal theories imply, nor as magnanimous and decent as favor-seeking politicians, some republican virtue theorists and political

---

[16] P. Rosanvallon, *Le Peuple Introuvable: Histoire de la Représentation Démocratique en France* (Gallimard, 1998), p. 16.

[17] See R. Geenens, "Sovereignty as Autonomy," *Law and Philosophy*, 36 (2017), p. 495 (especially p. 503). A common assumption is needed for collective action, but this does not require a common identity, as claimed by populists.

correctness might suggest. People (individuals) and "the people" can be manifold and mutable; populism's problem (among others) is that it tends to rouse destructive characteristics in individuals (particularly intolerance, in the name of restored self-esteem and pride) and their interactions. These emotional and somewhat irrational (biased and mistaken) and intolerant features become constitutive parts of illiberal democracy. Emotionalism forms an inevitable part of human life and politics, but populists select the socially destructive emotions that undermine deliberation-based democracy.

The acts of an actor, if called (represented or imagined as) the "people," carry a specific power of legitimation. What remains ambiguous or contested is whose acts, or what kind, count as the people's acts. Not all acts in the name of the people are socially or legally recognized as acts of the sovereign people, not even where actors claim that they are the people or that they act on its behalf. Large but short-lived demonstrations may not be recognized as expressing a people's binding will. The people is a self-constituting entity and only *ex post*, after a politically successful act, does it count as established or constituted. The constituted people (on whose behalf the very act of constitution was taken) will also include those who did not participate in the constituent act, or even stood against it. As the story goes, during the American War of Independence, one-third of the colonists were patriots, another third loyalists and the remaining third indifferent.[18] In such circumstances, who counts as the American people who have created the Union? The minority who constituted the new Union with acts of rebellion and ratification? To pose this in a fundamentally troubling context: did those who were present at the annual Nuremberg rallies, or the million at Vienna's *Heldenplatz* who enthusiastically greeted Hitler, constitute a new German people?

4.2.2   People's Authority and Legitimacy

The term "the people" carries a positive connotation in the popular mass culture of democracies and beyond. Historically the term ennobled the multitude of the wretched of the earth. Its legitimacy originates in historical mythologies and romanticism.

---

[18] This distribution is attributed to John Adams. On the uncertainty see P. H. Smith, "The American Loyalists: Notes on Their Organization and Numerical Strength," *The William and Mary Quarterly*, 25:2 (1968), p. 259. Roughly one inhabitant (family) out of forty had emigrated. See M. Jasanoff, *Liberty's Exiles: American Loyalists in the Revolutionary World* (Alfred A. Knopf, 2011).

Mandatory respect for the good people results in the legitimacy of whatever is deemed to be done by the people. In a democracy, "the people" has the Midas touch. Classical republican theory is more nuanced: "[T]he general will is always rightful and always tends to the public good; but it does not follow that the deliberations of the people are always equally right. We always want what is advantageous to us but we do not always discern it. The people is never corrupted, but it is often misled, and only then does it seem to will what is bad."[19] Unconditional respect for the people, especially as *the sovereign* (source of) power, is theoretically unsound, as it does not recognize the complexity of "people" and the resulting uncertainties.[20]

"The people" as an abstraction has no qualities. Contrary to Urbinati, it was not populism that "succeeded by making the citizenry an unqualified and undefined public of individual voters, with no party affiliation and loyalty."[21] This is what follows from the abstract concept of the people as accepted in legal theory. Constitutional democracies are socially diverse and democracy is plural. Populism, bringing to fruition democracy's totalitarian potential, stands firmly for unity, claiming that the fragmentation enabled by pluralism destroys nation and virtue. The French revolutionaries famously tried to prohibit intermediary formations, and clubs were suspect: as to populism in power, here no autonomous body is welcome, because it visibly endangers the people's unity.

It is never fully clear who the autonomous people is. Different (especially violent) groups may claim that they act on behalf of the people, or that they *are* the people given the nature of their action. Outside legal abstraction, presence matters (large-scale demonstrations, successful resistance to state constraint – e.g. Indians are those who refuse the salt tax; Americans are those who refuse the Stamp Act). Sometimes the people is thought to be what is seen of it: the multitude on the square, especially if broadcast, or acts against the center of state power (the storming of the Bastille, Paris women marching on Versailles, etc.). The people is a visual theatrical reality.[22] It is not a silent movie. Voiceover

---

[19] J.-J. Rousseau, *The Social Contract* (Penguin, 1972), p. 72.

[20] Unconditional reliance enables the antiegalitarian, and totalitarian, potential. Rousseau devised precautions: in order to avoid the people being misled, he welcomed the dictatorship of the providential man.

[21] N. Urbinati, "Unpolitical Democracy," *Political Theory*, 38:1 (2010), p. 71. Urbinati reached this conclusion on the basis of the Berlusconi experience.

[22] F. Millar, *The Crowd in Rome in Late Republic* (Ann Arbor, 1998). Millar indicated the theatrical element in people's political participation. He famously emphasized the role of *contiones*, where people could listen to orators and often reacted violently. Votes,

matters: when large crowds with common goals appear on television, and when they chant that "we are the people" (rather than just trade unionists or pride parade participants, etc.), they may credibly claim that they are the people. This is all the more so if a sympathetic commentator refers to the crowd as the people (this clearly indicates the *externally* construed, biased nature of the empirical people). However, the multitude may elevate and turn itself a genuine political actor. On April 9, 2002, a mass demonstration (along with the dubious position of the military) forced Chávez to resign. Two days later a larger, spontaneous demonstration (with the support of some elites) reversed his fortune.[23] The latter, successful crowd counted as the people.

Constitutionalism provides legal forms, procedures, and institutions that structure and fragment the people as powerholder. Contrary to early liberals, modern liberal constitutions willingly accept (in more or less restrictive formulations) that the people is (at least the ultimate) source of power. Constitutionalism and its structures accept the foundational legitimating power of the people; constitutional democracy respects human self-government in its collective forms, based on the assumption of equal worth of all human beings (or at least citizens). Constitutional procedures determine how popular will can be constituted, albeit that the multitude occasionally disregards such prescriptions and forces the acceptance of its actions as the people's will through unstructured, even violent, mass pressure.

4.2.3 Popular Sovereignty

Like all concepts in the present equation, meanings of sovereignty vary with the chancellor's foot. Yet for republicans and populists alike, sovereignty refers to the unlimited use of state power. In democracies this unlimited, absolute power pertains to and is (allegedly) used by the people.[24] For constitutional theory, the people may well be a fiction, but it is inevitable for logical consistency, just as Kelsen's assumption

---

however, were cast at a separate meeting (*comitia*). The parallelism between Millar's Roman plebs and the people of populism is striking.

[23] R. Brading, *Populism in Venezuela* (Routledge, 2013), pp. 72–74.

[24] E. Lauterpacht, "Sovereignty-Myth or Reality?," *International Affairs*, 73:1 (1997), p. 40. Lauterpacht calls sovereignty "a largely meaningless concept." This Chapter does not discuss the absurdity of absolute power: not even the most powerful state, not even the most absolute ruler, has such power in an interdependent world.

regarding the *Grundnorm* is a prerequisite for the legal order, fallacious as it may be.

Recognition of the people as the source of state or sovereign power is not just a logical necessity for theory building. It is an act of emancipation, especially if it relates to the concept of self-government. Sovereignty is the utmost form of autonomy: subjects shall be in the position to determine what is best for themselves. There is no place, in principle, for any master above the autonomous people. But this makes little sense for imaginary collective entities and legal fictions like the people: a fiction does not possess the capacity for autonomous choice (among other reasons, because people are not, or are not only, unified).

Margaret Canovan has noted that popular sovereignty lies at the heart of democracy. However, this heart (the claim that sovereignty relates to an uncertain concept and empirical mass of real people) is perhaps what makes democracy problematic as a practice in the first place. For its own sake, democracy must be liberated from its idolatry of the people. All idolatries are intellectually wrong, and adoration of an idol with the attributes of an absolute sovereign is particularly problematic.

Popular sovereignty has met increasing professional skepticism in the recent past.[25] A decade ago it seemed to be "no longer a viable concept" and incompatible with the RoL.[26] Fear of globalization has changed the equation. Once again, it appears it may serve as "the starting point for justifications for more democratic forms of government," though, as Yack has argued, it would be a "mistake to identify the modern doctrine of popular sovereignty with commitment to democratic forms of government."[27] Noting that universalism has become a source of concern for large masses, populism has deliberately sided with popular sovereignty, which seems to provide protection against "alien" forces.[28] Popular sovereignty was to be reclaimed by populists in the name of democracy. Not surprisingly, it is attractive to a democracy that tends toward totalitarianism: for the fullest satisfaction of genuine human interests, "the extreme forms of popular sovereignty became the essential

[25] See M. Loughlin, "Ten Tenets of Sovereignty," in N. Walker (ed.), *Sovereignty in Transition* (Oxford Hart, 2003), p. 55.

[26] F. G. Jacobs, *The Sovereignty of Law: The European Way* (Cambridge University Press, 2007), p. 5.

[27] B. Yack, "Popular Sovereignty and Nationalism," *Political Theory*, 29:4 (2001), p. 518.

[28] N. Walker, "Illiberalism and National Sovereignty," A. Sajó, S. Holmes, and R. Uitz, *Routledge Handbook of Illiberalism* (Routledge, in press). Walker refers to A. Vincent, "Chapter 2: Liberalism," in A. Vincent, *Modern Political Ideologies* (John Wiley and Sons Ltd., 2002).

concomitant of this absolute purpose."[29] Populism promises that sovereignty will be regained for country and for people, but sovereign debt does not disappear except by defaulting on the debt – and that sovereign act has the most unpleasant consequences for many people, including the have-nots.

However, the empirical people (both at the ballot box and on the street) are an unreliable "master, commanding and insatiable at the same time."[30] The legal concept of the people enables a multitude to take decisions in matters where the participants are incompetent (the same applies to their allegedly wise representatives). "Thus the typical citizen drops down to a lower level of mental performance as soon as he enters the political field. ... His thinking becomes associative and affective. ... The weakness of the rational processes he applies to politics and the absence of effective logical control over the results he arrives at would in themselves suffice to account for that."[31]

Nevertheless, it is assumed that this sovereign entity has a will of its own (good and trustworthy), and law (and other decisions) shall respect and reflect the will of the people. This is a fundamental tenet in many democratic theories, although in many respects the people's will is a myth,[32] a matter invented by elites or used for elite purposes, like the concept of *populus* was invented in Rome so that the patriciate could control the plebs.

By endowing the people with unlimited power, democracy takes a serious risk: without constitutional and cultural restraints, popular sovereignty liberates a power that will threaten ... people. Moreover, the idea that the people is sovereign produces arrogance (of those who claim to speak for them): sovereignty is understood as the authorization to defy and flout everything outside of the people, *including* people (individuals, groups). Once again, populism benefits enormously from this feature of people's power. It insists on continued popular constituent power, which enables the constant rewriting of society, the political community, and even history.[33] Here, the constitution, or even the entire

---

[29] J. L. Talmon, *The Origins of Totalitarian Democracy* (W. W. Norton & Company, 1970), p. 2.

[30] Rosanvallon, *Le peuple introuvable*, p. 12.

[31] J. Schumpeter, *Capitalism, Socialism and Democracy* (Harper's Torch Book, 1950), p. 262.

[32] A. Weale, *The Will of the People: A Modern Myth* (Polity, 2018).

[33] C. Schmitt, *Constitutional Theory* (Duke University Press, 2008), p. 75.
   Pappas reminds us that all contemporary political systems are people-centered; however, it is in the populist imagination that the people has permanent constituent power. The people (an abstraction) has an unmediated relationship with the ruler. T. S. Pappas,

legal system, becomes the actual existential expression of the will of the people, a matter of *permanent* political unity[34] (and how could a legal notion or fiction be split or reflect diversity and conflict?).

To attribute such an active and decisive role to the people is popular because the traditional system of popular representation (representative government) has discredited itself, and politics is represented as a source of discord that undermines people's unity. Populism is embedded in deep feelings of discontent, not only with politics but also with daily life in general.[35] The people is an emotional unity based on *ressentiment*, fear, and longing for recognition through collective membership: plebiscitarian rule is predominantly emotional politics to the detriment of the rational elements of democratic decision-making.

Once in power, the plebiscitarian leader will try to manage the permanent constituent power. The constitutional theory of populism in power may differ considerably from movement populism, and Caesarism (as we will see) has little use for its people. While the idea of regained national sovereignty, which pertains to the nation of good patriots, remains an important point of reference, actual reliance on the people and its constituent power fades away. (On the ambiguous relationship to referendums, see Chapter 5.)

While populist movements endorsed popular sovereignty where the people is permanently in action, once in power populists seemingly follow Rousseau, who (like other, but nondemocratic classics) distinguished between sovereignty and government. Rousseau thought that the individual citizen, a bourgeois, does not have the time to participate in government; moreover, to govern is technically impossible for the people. In a republic (as opposed to ancient democracy), the people's role is limited to determining the outlines of political government (i.e. the

---

Populism and Liberal Democracy: A Comparative and Theoretical Analysis (Oxford University Press, 2019), p. 23.

[34] See for all, President Moreno: "We will go to all courts of international law, but above all to the unity of the people to reject this insulting meddling in our democratic system and sovereign right to decide." "Ecuador: Moreno Government to Defend Referendum at OAS After Protest," Telesur (February 8, 2018), www.telesurenglish.net/news/Ecuador-To-Send-Delegation-to-OAS-to-Defend-Referendum-20180208-0002.html

The permanent presence of the people contradicts Rousseau, who explains that once the proper laws are in place, there is no need for the people. Rousseau, *The Social Contract*, book 2, chap. 7.

[35] B. Spruyt, G. Keppens, and F. Van Droogenbroeck, "Who Supports Populism and What Attracts People to It?," *Political Research Quarterly*, 69:2 (2016), p. 335.

constitution).[36] In PLDs, government becomes the exclusive function of the ruler.

Sovereignty claims absolute power. But power over what? Popular sovereignty is a claim over state power. The state is considered sovereign in its own right, both internationally and domestically. Here lies the difficulty of popular sovereignty. Let's assume that the people is the only source of power in, or over, the state. It does not follow that the instrument over which the people claims sovereign power should have absolute sovereign power. The people has no power over the individual (which constitutes it), except to the extent that the state has such power. Some absolutist theories of the state (advocated in the early days of sovereignty theory, regarding royal power) claimed such absolute state power. These theories are without democratic or other justification and contradict the very idea of the constitutional state, where the state with its administrative machinery exists legally within the constraints of the constitution. Popular sovereignty is limited by the very object of this unbound power.

Popular sovereignty can be national only (i.e. limited to a state territory). The sovereignty receives a specific meaning, standing for a specific form of life and interest. For an illiberal democracy that is rooted in populism, the constitutional restrictions on the state also restrict the nation's (the ethnonationalist people's) sovereign power. In the populist discourse, constitutional institutions are inevitably an elite imposition, a way in which the elite attempts to control people.

4.3   The Use of the People in Victorious Populism

Today, reference to the people is attractive, even irresistible, in most countries of the world. This sentiment predates the rise of populism but (re)gained influence when traditional party politics and representative government (particularly the work of parliaments) became a matter of disrespect. Populism as an antiestablishment movement has granted a central role to betrayed and humiliated people seeking revenge.

What matters for populists movements is that the people be in power, not how the people is governed (and even less that it would rule). However, what the populist movements mean by "the people" is not fixed. Perón referred to a despised group among Argentinians as the object of his personal concern, while Orbán gradually replaced the people first with

---

[36] This follows Tuck, *The Sleeping Sovereign.*

the Hungarian nation and then increasingly (even in the new HFL) with the "Hungarian person" ("*magyar ember*"). Chávez, on the other hand, seems to have included anyone who was not with the elite.

Populist movements contrast the unspoiled, authentic, betrayed people (the only authentic element in an institutionally inept democracy) with the traitors of democracy, namely the ruling elite. The rejuvenation of the system requires the re-creation of the people. This reconstruction requires purification even at the individual level. Exclusion and inclusion are traditional processes in the making of peoples and the operation of democracies (see the legal definition of citizenship as inclusion and exclusion in nation building). Populism is radical in this respect, ready to exclude from its people any force that is dangerous to victory and alien to the values that mark people's identity.

In most illiberal democracies, the cleansing of the people is not based on deprivation of citizenship: it is a cultural exclusion with practical consequences. Independent cultural entities that do not serve the "authentic" people (e.g. unreformed universities, media outlets, theaters, etc.) are gradually excluded from state-supported entities for being alien to the national values that animate the authentic people. The state as service provider serves the authentic people only, albeit according to "objective" (i.e. authentic people–prone) criteria. To the extent necessary to perpetuate power through elections, the voice of the authentic people receives the (extra) weight it merits. Access to mass media, and gerrymandering, is the name of the game. Voices alien to the people are expelled from the public space, which is cleansed just like the people. Only the voice of the authentic people, only authentic people, are to be heard.

4.3.1   People's Unity: Homogeneity

Claims of sovereignty insist on unity. Only a single entity can be sovereign. This serves a very specific political agenda. In a revolutionary moment, the Abbé Sieyès stated: "France is and must be a single whole."[37] Through representation the nation becomes a political union.[38] The people is an

---

[37] Quoted in M. G. Forsyth, *Reason and Revolution: The Political Thought of the Abbé Sieyès* (Leicester University Press, 1987), p. 87.

[38] E.-J. Sieyès, "Qu'est-ce que le Tiers-État?," in *Écrits politiques* (Éditions des archives contemporaines, 1985), p. 121. See L. Scuccimarra, "Généalogie de la nation. Sieyès comme fondateur de la communauté politique," *Revue Française d'Histoire des Idées Politiques*, 33:1 (2011), pp. 27–45.

empty construct of constitutional law.[39] It can be filled legally and politically with different subjects and values (where the subjects are determined
by the value). Right-wing populism fills the vacuum with a somewhat
fictitious selection, increasingly on grounds related to ethnicity (national
provenance) or religion. Here, the people's populist liberation means that
the people will reclaim national sovereignty. At this juncture, populism will
be reinforced by the nationalism inherent in national-popular sovereignty:
"the spread of popular sovereignty doctrines seems to promote the discov-
ery or rediscovery of national loyalties,"[40] even outside of the specific
context of illiberal democracies.

Populist leaders often claim that the unity of the people originates
from the people's homogeneity.[41] Unity is fictitious and nonspecific.
The populist claim "is of a moral and symbolic – not an empirical –
nature, it cannot be disproven."[42] This mythical homogeneity disregards actual social stratification and it is eminently emotional.[43] Social
class has been "eliminated" and replaced with identity-related
concerns.[44] In Poland Dr. Zybertowicz, a leading PiS ideologue and
presidential adviser, claimed that those who refuse a patriotic minimum
renege on Polishness. The criteria of Polishness, includes the need for
an effective state, recognition of the importance of the Catholic Church
and acknowledgment of a certain Polish history.[45] In the sociology of

[39] In modernity, from the early days of the French revolution, "people" served as a referent
of unity without a specific subject. People was "faceless." Rosanvallon, "Revolutionary
Democracy," p. 79.

[40] Yack, "Popular Sovereignty," p. 518.

[41] See Perón's view: "In Argentina there should not be more than one single class of men:
men who work together for the welfare of the nation, without any discrimination
whatever." In reality, he was ready to expel his opposition from Congress and (like
Chávez and populist leaders in Europe) polarize the citizenry. J. D. Perón "What is
Perónism?," Perónist Doctrine (Partido Perónista, 1952), p. 55.
   In Turkey, a similar tradition was present for many decades: "Erdoğan's emphasis on
a homogenous and infallible national will is the continuation of Turkey's center-right
tradition from the 1950s to the 1970s." O. Selçuk, "Strong Presidents and Weak
Institutions: Populism in Turkey, Venezuela and Ecuador," Southeast European and
Black Sea Studies, 16:4 (2016), p. 577.

[42] J.-W. Müller, What is Populism? (University of Pennsylvania Press, 2016), p. 39.

[43] Umberto Eco refers to the "fear of difference marker" as a constituent element of fascism.
U. Eco, "Ur-Fascism," New York Review of Books (June 22, 1955).

[44] In the post-structuralist perspective, social stratification is a matter of social construction:
it is the discourse that is "the primary terrain within which the social is constituted."
E. Laclau, "Populism? What's in a name?," in F. Panizza (ed.) in Populism and the Mirror
of Democracy (Verso, 2005), p. 49.

[45] Quoted in W. Sadurski, Poland's Constitutional Breakdown (Oxford University Press,
2019), p. 264.

populism there is no place for social difference: populism proposes an essentialist sociology.[46] The vision of homogeneity caters to expectations of equality (motivated by a mixture of envy and a wish for self-respect). But first and foremost, it resonates in the sentiments of a growing number of citizens who are concerned about the loss of national culture (identity) due to real or imaginary immigration and minority privileges.[47] Against the threat arising from minority protection ("favoritism"), and the tyranny of the minority the victimized majority reacts by presenting a single identity. Against the threat of diversity, it finds refuge in majoritarian democracy, where only the majority counts. Populist demagoguery creates the impression that constitutional democracies favor the tyranny of minorities, which undermines a promise of homogeneity that is attractive enough to insist on this self-deception. Those who "feel at home" with this imagery have good reason: not for the first time in history, too many people have lost a consistent, safe, common-sense world where they could feel confident.[48] Moreover, the demand for oneness and sameness corresponds to the "intolerance of difference" – the normal authoritarian response to a "normative threat." The normative threat challenges the sameness of the social order, in particular, "disrespect for leaders or leaders unworthy of respect, and lack of conformity to ... group values."[49] Such threats were certainly present in societies where

---

[46] P. Rosanvallon, *Counter-Democracy: Politics in an Age of Distrust* (Cambridge University Press, 2008), p. 256.

[47] For a review of the surveys, see R. Eatwell and M. Goodwin, *National Populism: The Revolt Against Liberal Democracy* (Pelican Books, 2018), pp. 151–56. In 2017, 55 percent of Europeans agreed that further immigration from Muslim countries should be stopped, with Hungary, Poland, and Austria rating the highest. It was in 2017 that the right-wing populist Freedom Party received 26 percent of the vote in Austria, entering into a government coalition with the conservative People's Party (also categorically anti-immigration).

[48] H. Arendt, *The Origins of Totalitarianism* (Houghton Mifflin Harcourt, 1994), pp. 352–53.

[49] K. Stenner, *The Authoritarian Dynamic* (Cambridge University Press, 2005), p. 17.
   Some recent empirical studies seem to corroborate the classic position of Adorno, namely that "social and economic dimensions of ideology in general and support for laissez-faire capitalism and racial prejudice, intolerance, and ethnocentrism in particular" are interrelated and originate in authoritarian personality traits. F. Azevedo, J. T. Jost, T. Rothmund, and J. Sterling, "Neoliberal Ideology and the Justification of Inequality in Capitalist Societies: Why Social and Economic Dimensions of Ideology Are Intertwined," *Journal of Social Issues*, 75:4 (2019), pp. 49–88. For a contrary finding, see J. Bartle, D. Sanders, and J. Twyman, "Authoritarian Populist Opinion in Europe," in I. Crewe and D. Sanders (eds.), *Authoritarian Populism and Liberal Democracy* (Springer, 2019).

populism became powerful, particularly in the periods leading to populist movement victories.

The promise and delivery of homogeneity satisfies the demand for "common authority (oneness) and shared values (sameness),"[50] which provides the togetherness ("us") that was disappearing or threatened in a diverse and changing society. Of course, the "common authority" facilitates acceptance of the plebiscitarian Caesar.

The people becomes homogeneous via identification of the enemy. Anyone who is not elite, and does not serve as lackeys of the elite, can be the people. This is vital for exercising populist power:

> In populist systems, therefore, polarization is deliberately constructed for political purposes. Especially once they have colonized the state and are in control of the state resources, strategic polarization becomes for the populists their best viable strategy for holding on to power.
>
> Secondly, strategic polarization creates a new cleavage in society that subsumes all previous cleavages, including ideological ones.[51]

Growing polarization makes plebiscitarian support a matter of course; you vote for the leader as a matter of your identity. It is at this point that tribalism enters, where "sectarian loyalty or nativist hatred override civic bonds."[52] In fact, the mindset of a currently decisive minority of Polish and Hungarian peoples goes hand in glove with the aims and means of a tribal form of populism and a plebiscitarian illiberal constitutional arrangement.[53] Tribalism is systematically sustained in the politics (propaganda and agenda setting) of the plebiscitarian leader. "Tribalism is about rallying around the leader of the tribe and rejecting the other tribe."[54]

This is vital for the victory of populism: given that "a crucial skill for politicians is learning to speak the language of personality – namely, to

---

[50] K. Stenner and J. Haidt, "Authoritarianism is Not a Momentary Madness, but an Eternal Dynamic within Liberal Democracy," in C. Sunstein (ed.), *Can it Happen Here?: Authoritarianism in America* (Harper Collins, 2018), p. 185.

[51] Pappas, *Populism and Liberal Democracy*, p. 213.

[52] P. Mishra, "The Globalization of Rage," *Foreign Affairs* (November/December 2016), p. 49.

[53] R. Wike and K. Simmons et al., *Globally, Broad Support for Representative and Direct Democracy* (Pew Research Center, 2017).

[54] P. Krekó and C. Molnár et al., *Beyond Populism Tribalism in Poland and Hungary* (Political Capital Institute, 2018), p. 12. Tribalism is defined here as a combination of Manichean populism and belief in a strong leader. The proportion of tribalists is 10 percent in Hungary and 15 percent in Poland. Tribalists are overrepresented toward the governmental, especially in Hungary: 59 percent of tribalists would vote for Fidesz.

navigate properly in the domain of personality attributes by identifying and conveying those individual characteristics that are most appealing at a certain time to a particular constituency"[55] – all that the populist leader had to do was play the tribal and authoritarian[56] card, which was close to his beliefs in any case. The message of the populist party (the leader) matched the authoritarian predispositions that were already mobilized by the insecure social environment.[57] This is exactly what happened in Hungary, where authoritarianism as a trait of both personality and culture was widespread; authoritarians primarily but not exclusively identified themselves with right-wing political authoritarianism[58] (a matter that was also part of the historical legacy). The authoritarian predisposition in waiting was mobilized with the ethnopopulist discourse of Fidesz, leading to its victory in 2010.[59] The *demos* ended up as *ethnos*.

---

[55] G.V. Caprara and P.G. Zimbardo, "Personalizing Politics: A Congruency Model of Political Preference," *American Psychologist*, 59:7 (2004), p. 584. See further on the leader-voter personality congruence G. V. Caprara, "The Personalization of Modern Politics," *European Review*, 15:2 (2007), pp. 151–64.

[56] Consider the relatively high occurrence of authoritarian attitudes among Hungarians (see footnote 54).

[57] M. Salmela and C. von Scheve, "Emotional Roots of Right-Wing Political Populism," *Social Science Information*, 56:4 (2017), pp. 567–95.

[58] B. Todosijević and Z. Enyedi, "Authoritarianism Without Dominant Ideology: Political Manifestations of Authoritarian Attitudes in Hungary," *Political Psychology*, 29:5 (2008), pp. 767–87. More recently J.T. Jost and A. Kende, "Setting the Record Straight: System Justification and Rigidity of the Right in Contemporary Hungarian Politics," *International Journal of Psychology*, 55:S1 (2020), pp. 96–115. (Self-identified rightists [Fidesz supporters] scored higher than leftists on the needs for order, structure and system justification.)

In Poland, the "most strongly-held value is that everyone in Poland should live by Polish national values and norms – 80 percent of respondents believe this." F. Pazderski, *In the Grip of Authoritarian Populism. Polish Attitudes to an Open Society*, Voices on Values Report (2019). Note the importance of Catholicism in the success of PiS. A. Modrzejewski, "Catholic and Nationalist Populism in the Current Poland," *Perspectives in Politics*, 10:1 (2017), pp. 21–31.

[59] This is not to say that Fidesz is the party of authoritarians, and even among Fidesz-supporting authoritarians, there is commitment to democracy (which they most likely identify with the current plebiscitarian rule).

For the relevance of authoritarian predisposition in the United States, see M. MacWilliams, "The One Weird Trait That Predicts Whether You're a Trump Supporter," *Politico Magazine* (January 17, 2016), www.politico.com/magazine/story/2016/01/donald-trump-2016-authoritarian-213533 (In 2016, 49 percent of likely Republican primary voters scored in the top quarter of the authoritarian scale – more than twice as many as Democratic voters.) Authoritarian predisposition was determined using the most traditional child-rearing attitude, and not group prejudice.

The grounds for homogeneity, other than not being elite (or some other enemy serving the elite), remain somewhat obscure in the populist dream. Who constitutes the real, authentic people depends on the circumstances, but the people is composed always of ordinary men and women.[60] In Latin America, and in Trump's rhetoric, the people are some kind of neglected outcasts, while in Europe they are often more mainstream socially but feel culturally oppressed. They believe they are not allowed to express genuine national and Christian feelings and habits, or at least, are looked down upon for being what ordinary people are.[61]

The prevailing legal concept of the people facilitates acceptance of the homogeneity myth. Here the people as a fiction, an abstract entity without properties, inevitably points toward a conceptual unity. Of course, the allegation that the people is indivisible becomes inevitably the source of social division and intolerance, especially in diverse societies (and one way or another, most societies are plural). Diversity signifies betrayal. The formerly "neglected" may feel included or at home in the authentic people offered by the populist leader, but the inclusion of the previous left-outs and left-behinds goes hand in hand with the squeezing out of others. Homogeneity results in polarization and fragmentation.

Those who do not share the proper features of authentic people are to be disregarded or even discarded. "Such a locus of power attributes 'national homogeneity' to a mere portion of the electorate."[62] In the Rousseauist tradition, every individual "would have to be transformed into part of a greater whole from which he receives his life and being."[63] Homogeneity becomes a normative expectation, that is to say, there is no place for divergence, nor for partial interests. In some versions of the populist rhetoric, homogeneity as a "single will" means some kind of common identity as the source or dictate of the general will, i.e. the "will" emanates from the identity, in the worst Rousseauist unanimity.[64]

---

[60] C. de la Torre, "Populism and Nationalism in Latin America," *Javnost/The Public*, 24:4 (2017), pp. 375–84.

[61] Christian is not necessarily used in a fundamentalist religious sense.

[62] O. Kirchheimer, "Remarks on Carl Schmitt's Legality and Legitimacy," in W. E. Scheuerman (ed.), *The Rule of Law Under Siege: Selected Essays of Franz L. Neumann and Otto Kirchheimer* (University of California Press, 1996), p. 68.

[63] Quoted after Talmon, *The Origins*, p. 2.

[64] This is not to say that in the case of Rousseau unity originates in some kind of national identity, as Talmon seems to imply. See S. T. Engel, "Rousseau and Imagined Communities," *The Review of Politics*, 67:3 (2005), pp. 515–37.

While the people's homogeneity is taken for granted, its origins may differ. The authentic people live in a mythical place, the heartland.[65] Homogeneity can be based on ethnicity or nationality or originate from some other victimhood.

Myth or not, the populist dream of unity has practical consequences for constitutional matters. Contrary to Rousseau's expressed preference,[66] there is no place here for the separation of powers and social autonomy (autonomous organizations), because these are the seeds of division and discord. In order to have unity, the leader needs to produce the appropriate uniform voter. This is achieved through brainwashing, made possible by control over mass media and the strategic positions of cultural production (e.g. education). Emigration of independent-minded (and therefore not trustworthy) citizens is welcome.

In the populist mythology discontent, partisanship and competition are fatally divisive and divergences result in paralysis in parliamentary affairs. There is nothing new here: the evolution of modern democracy is a history of the "moral disdain for partisans" and "partisanship."[67] Populism promises the end of the parliamentary paralysis that originated in discord. In the leader–people symbiosis, the people stands for national unity and concord: an early declaration of the Fidesz government, the Program of National Cooperation (later integrated into the HFL) expressly established "concord" as a state goal.[68] As Orbán, still in the opposition then but clearly the future winner of forthcoming elections, stated in 2009:

> Today it is realistically conceivable that in the coming fifteen-twenty years the Hungarian politics should be determined not by the dualistic field of force bringing with it never-conclusive and divisive value debates, which quite unnecessarily generate social problems. Instead, a great governing party comes in place, a central field of force, which will be able to articulate the national issues and to stand for these policies as a natural course of

---

[65] M. Canovan "'People,' Politicians and Populism," *Government and Opposition*, 19:3 (1984), p. 312.

[66] "Rome, when it was most prosperous, suffered a revival of all the crimes of tyranny, and was brought to the verge of destruction, because it put the legislative authority and the sovereign power into the same hands." Rousseau, *The Social Contract*, p. 36.

[67] N. Rosenblum, *On the Side of the Angels: An Appreciation of Parties and Partisanship* (Princeton University Press, 2008), pp. 25–26.

[68] The Constitution of Singapore (a classic of illiberal democracy) insists on harmony, which became an important source of illiberalism.

things to be taken for granted without the constantly ongoing wrangling.[69]

For the flesh-and-blood people of the populist state, the separation of powers and the institutional limits of popular power are "alien," running contrary to the assumption of unitary power[70] and the direct, authentic expressions of the will of authentic people.

The structuring of the people (i.e. predetermined forms and procedures for the expression of people's preferences) conflicts with homogeneity. The myth of unity diverges from democracy as it denies polyarchy.[71] In poly-archy, different groups permanently compete and reach compromise instead of there being a final victory of the strongest over the enemy. Carl Schmitt provided an ideal theory of people's unity under the leader.[72] The president (or any other leader with Caesaristic power and charisma) is affirmed by the entire people in a plebiscitarian form. (Parliamentary elections, a remnant of past formalities, are rearranged into acclamation.) There is no need, there-fore, for checks over the state and its power. The leader embodies the unitary people's sovereign will and is therefore legitimate. In the context of the Weimar Constitution, Schmitt argued that it "presupposes the entire German people as a unity which is immediately ready for action and not first mediated through social-group organization."[73]

4.3.2 Unity Is Identitarian

Unity is based on the homogeneous identity of the people, again as emphasized by Carl Schmitt:

> Political democracy cannot rest on the lack of difference between people, but only on the belonging to a certain people, where this belonging to a people can be determined by very different moments (ideas of common race, belief, common fate or tradition).[74]

---

[69] Viktor Orbán's speech at a Fidesz picnic in Kötcse, September 2009 quoted after Z. Bretter, "The Name of the Game: The Regime of National Collaboration," in B. Pająk-Patkowska and M. Rachwał (eds.), Hungary and Poland in Times of Political Transition (Faculty of Political Science and Journalism Adam Mickiewicz University Poznań, 2016), p. 48.

[70] F. E. Schnapp, "Staatsgrundlagen; Wiederstandrecht," in I. Von Münch and P. Kunig (eds.), Grundgesetz-Kommentar. Bd.1.6. Aufl (C. H. Beck, 2012), p. 1411.

[71] R. A Dahl, Polyarchy (Yale University Press, 1971).

[72] The constitution is "the substantial homogeneity of the identity and the will of the people." Schmitt, Constitutional Theory, pp. 125-26.

[73] C. Schmitt, Der Hüter der Verfassung (Duncker & Humblot, 1996), p. 159.

[74] C. Schmitt, Verfassungslehre (Duncker & Humblot, 1928), p. 228.

Given the emotionality and polarization in the social and political life of illiberal democracies, citizens and the very concept of the authentic people are malleable in the hands of the leader and the state apparatus under his control.

"Only some of the people are really the people."[75] What this authentic people is, and who belongs to it, is shaped by the populist leader. In his choice, the leader must find attractive popular characteristics for a sufficient number of voters.[76] He must respond to large-scale frustration, particularly to a sense of loss of self-respect and "unmet demands, where 'people do not know how to name what they are lacking.'"[77]

While shaped and framed by the leader, the people as an empirical reality is an act of collective imagination. When the leader's people finds its identity decisively in ethnicity, this is not simply the consequence of populist manipulation.[78] It results from the imagination of flesh-and-blood, interacting individuals. In their imagination, their (imaginary) community is not just a multitude living in a territory demarcated by accidental boundaries. There is an element of choice by a political community, the construction of values and even a belief in a common identity. Even if mistaken, the sociological fact of integration remains based on how members of society, in their interaction, imagine their community. Unsurprisingly, European plebiscitarians tend to fill the empty ideological vessel of populism with nationalism (or some other single identity), hoping that "in 'open confrontation' the national myth of

---

[75] Ibid., p. 21.

[76] The leader reflects the identity of his subjects; to show nativist identity elements is an act of loyalty. The President of the Chamber of Pharmacists, humbly complaining to Orbán because pharmacists did not receive a COVID-19 bonus, starts as follows: "Before anyone misinterprets, I want to make it clear: my writing is not an attack coming from opposition. I am a Hungarian (more precisely Szekler-Hungarian), a person with national commitment, a believer, a person with a conservative value system, and the head of a professional advocacy organization, which has been a strategic partner of the Hungarian Government since 2010. Don't get me wrong, as President of the Chamber of Pharmacists, I remain committed to continuing our strategic collaboration with the Government. After all, based on the experience of the last thirty years, there is no other alternative for us." Nationalist and religious characteristics make the humble petitioner worthy of membership in the people, a loyalist beneficiary of the regime, whose loyalty is guaranteed by the fact that there is no alternative. Confessions of the people, first hand.

[77] Panizza, "Introduction," p. 10.

[78] Since 2015, Poland's PiS "has consistently applauded 'unity' and 'community' as paramount social values, and at the same time depicted the opposition as enemy, evil, illegitimate." W. Sadurski, "How Democracy Dies (in Poland): A Case Study of Anti-Constitutional Populist Backsliding," *Sydney Law School Research Paper No. 18/01* (2018), p. 15.

race and nation always wins out over class."[79] Understandably, this undermines the liberal qualities of the political community. When you "bring the people into political life . . . they arrive marching in tribal ranks and orders."[80] "Populists strive in polarization and artificially increase and perpetuate it. In polarized societies, ordinary people become pro- or anti-Chávez, Orbán, or Erdoğan first, and democrats only second."[81]

That someone pertains to the people of the leader (i.e. to the authentic people) defines identity, and identity defines truth in the postmodern world. There is no place for persuasion, no place for the very idea of a deliberative democracy. Discourse is futile where "each of us has our own truth."[82] Which narrative is accepted is unrelated to evidence: evidence is selected as a matter of identity and loyalty. For a member of the authentic people, truth is what other members of the people consider to be true, especially if the truth is formulated by the leader. The mentality that enables such attitudes resembles the one described by Hannah Arendt:

> They do not believe in anything visible, in the reality of their own experience; they do not trust their eyes and ears but only their imaginations, which may be caught by anything that is at once universal and consistent in itself. What convinces masses are not facts, and not even invented facts, but only the consistency of the system of which they are presumably part.[83]

The revolt that forged the new people reflected a moral outrage, as the incumbent political forces were seen, correctly to a great extent, as corrupt.[84] "End corruption!" was crucial in the electoral victory of populism. But the moral outrage was channeled by the populist into identity politics.[85] Identity politics flourishes in societies where the primary

---

[79] C. Schmitt, *The Crisis of Parliamentary Democracy* (The MIT Press, 1985), p. 75.
[80] M. Walzer, "The New Tribalism: Notes on a Difficult Problem," in R. Beiner (ed.), *Theorizing Nationalism* (State University of New York Press, 1998), p. 206.
[81] M. W Svolik, "Polarization versus Democracy," *Journal of Democracy*, 30:3 (2019), p. 21.
[82] A. Przeworski, *Crises of Democracy* (Cambridge University Press, 2019), pp. 118–19. Przeworski provides a summary of the post-truth world. The impossibility of truth was an important element of Russian government propaganda even before Putin came to power.
[83] Arendt, *The Origins*, p. 352. The masses that endorsed totalitarianism resemble contemporary populists in their bitterness and lack of discernment.
[84] See Hungary, Poland, Russia, and even Venezuela.
[85] In the words of Kaczyński: "If you don't have a strong identity, you can really do anything with society. And we must defend our sovereignty . . . not to fall into this vortex." See "Kaczyński: mamy do czynienia z buntem, mamy rebelię," TVN24 (video, June 4, 2016), www.tvn24.pl/polska/zjazd-okregowy-pis-w-warszawie-przemowienie-jaroslawa-kaczynskiego-ra649572-3186955.

concern of individuals is increasingly to find their "true" identity and live accordingly.

This identity-centered life form has been facilitated by a cultural shift that occurred in many Western societies, namely by the arrival and acceptance of a narcissistic culture that legitimizes a self-directed interest and approves self-admiration. This has led to the growth of a number of clinically narcissistic personalities (who are perfectly functional in society). According to a body of research, illiberal right-wing populism, and even more so right-wing plebiscitarian leaders, are successful because they offer a coherent vision of national identity that provides a convincing response to the challenged expectations of self-importance. The ruling Eastern European plebiscitarian leaders cater to "national collective narcissism" based on victimhood and related resentment. This is why Orbán and Kaczyński, both in and out of power, emphasize that the chosen people, or "in-group," is "exceptional and entitled to privileged treatment, but it is not sufficiently recognized by others."[86] The plebiscitarian leader must sustain this feeling even after his people emerges victorious and becomes in charge of the nation's fate. Hence, the constant reference to the lack of well-merited recognition by more successful Western or Northern countries (not only in Eastern Europe but in Greece and Italy, too). To understand the leader–people relationship, it is important that the leader selects and indulges collective narcissism, with the promise of overcoming the undeserved neglect by outsiders in order to restore wounded collective self-esteem (complete with a strong sense of self-righteousness based on moral indignation). In Poland and Hungary, and in Trump's America, the populist leader becomes successful because he appeals to an offended self-esteem. The leader will make the *plebs* feel right and proud of themselves.

The populist identity cult in Central Europe is "identity retrenchment,"[87] meaning a search for a backward-oriented identity

---

[86] A. Golec de Zavala and O. Keenan, "Collective Narcissism as a Framework for Understanding Populism," *Journal of Theoretical Social Psychology* (2020), p. 1. On Hungary see J. P. Forgas and D Lantos, "Collective Narcissism and the Collapse of Democracy in Hungary," in J. P. Forgas, W. D. Crano, and K. Fiedler (eds.), *Applications of Social Psychology: How Social Psychology can Contribute to the Solution of Real-world Problems* (Routledge, 2020). Collective narcissism is more common amongst Fidesz supporters.

[87] D. Caramani and C. Wagemann, "A Transnational Political Culture? The Alpine Region and its Relationship to European Integration," *German Politics*, 14:1 (2005), p. 74. The characteristics of Alpine populism are more or less identical with the populist national identity of East Central Europe: (a) the idea of "the people" as a natural entity that needs

that offers security in an uncertain age. The populist identity is "anti-pluralist," and anti-Enlightenment, and consequently unfit for the complexities of reason-based democracy in a multicultural society.[88] Adherents to populist movements search for confirmation of their challenged and shaken or disrespected identity. This reaffirmation occurs through the election of the leader and via hatred of the "other": in rejecting the abnormal possibility that a life that differs from that of "normal" people can be legitimate. The identity will be reinforced through the elected leader, who affirms and designates the values of the people. As Andrew Arato observes, "The role of elections here is to confirm identity and identification."[89] The leader and his people operate in a mutually reinforcing bind. Recall that under plebiscitarian conditions, "it is not the politically passive 'mass' which gives birth to the leader; rather the political leader recruits his following and wins over the mass by 'demagogy.'"[90]

The charismatic leader readily accommodates popular illiberalism, producing and endorsing sentiments that respond to popular demand. But again, this is also (more or less) within the constitutional limits of the liberal state: notwithstanding popular demand, the death penalty, to the regret of the HPM, cannot be reintroduced due to international pressure (foreign elites, again!).[91]

The Caesarist leader selects his people and finds legitimacy in their wishes, or in the Hungarian case, "Hungarian men and women." The use of the gender-neutral term "*magyar ember*" ("Hungarian person") carries a traditional connotation (non-Jewish, non-Roma and bound to an ethnic tradition). It includes strong traditional behavior stereotypes, like "a Hungarian man does

to be protected from outside threats; (b) the idea that the ethnic and religious roots of the people – and the feelings of "community" that follow from them – are threatened by an over-generous, universalistic, and multicultural idea of citizenship; and (c) the idea that this longing for a feeling of "home" justifies the rejection of others who . . . are perceived as otherwise invading a culturally closed "homeland."

[88] Persons of authoritarian predisposition glorify uniformity and disparage difference. Stenner and Haidt, "Authoritarianism is Not a Momentary Madness," p. 184.

[89] A. Arato, "Populism, Constitutional Courts and Civil Society," in C. Landfried (ed.), *Judicial Power: How Constitutional Courts Affect Political Transformations* (Cambridge University Press, 2019), p. 329.

[90] M. Weber, "Parliament and Government in Germany," in M. Weber, *Weber: Political Writings*, eds. P. Lassman and R. Speirs (Cambridge University Press, 1994), p. 228.

[91] I. Traynor, "EU chief warns Hungary over return of death penalty comments," *The Guardian* (April 30, 2015), www.theguardian.com/world/2015/apr/30/eu-jean-claude-juncker-viktor-orban-hungary-death-penalty-return.

not speak while eating."[92] The use of cultural stereotypes embedded in familiar sentences ("speaking the language of ordinary people") provides a head-start advantage in the fight for hearts and minds, and references to nonspecific traditions, historical independence and anticommunism in the HFL reflect and facilitate such social representations.

However, it is not only up to the leader to select his people rooted in the life form reflecting an imagined past. When the authentic people votes for the leader, it selects itself (and its identity); at the same time, by affirming the leader, it accepts with complicity whatever the leader will affirm to be the authentic people. The specific mixture of identitarian elements varies according to local conditions and it changes through time.

It is all circular. What is known, and affirmed, is who *does not* count as the people.

Populism relies upon, endorses and perpetuates tribalism. In consequence, the people's plebiscitarian homogenization begets social and political polarization; interest-based rational politics goes to the dogs. Identity politics is certainly not a unique feature of less-than-established democracies. It is inherently intolerant and notoriously divisive everywhere. The identitarian's primary concern is who he is, instead of what one does. He seeks the answer in terms of group membership – and the result is tribalism. Nationalists are concerned about their origins ("where do you come from?"), strongly emphasizing past and present historical victimhood.[93]

As Hofstadter observed in the American context, the "victimized populace" is central to populism.[94] According to the respective leaders of Hungary and Poland, Hungarian and Polish people are eternal, innocent victims of foreign aggression and domestic treason (bonus: the Polish people are martyrs). In the leftist populist agenda, people are the victims of inequality and exclusion. A strong sense of victimhood breeds resentment. The populist political agenda relies on a people with *ressentiment*. The resentment is directed against the treacherous elite, or at least the populist leader turns it against the elite, who can be blamed for all the neglect and humiliation. The leader promises respect for the threatened identity. This representation is attractive to those who have felt despised

---

[92] The reference to "Hungarian person" appears already in the HFL. There is no gender difference in the Hungarian language.
[93] See A.G. Slama, "Au nom du peuple : de 'populaire' à 'populiste'," *Le Débat*, 166:4 (2011), p. 64; Müller, *What is Populism?*, p. 31.
[94] R. Hofstadter, *The Age of Reform: From Bryan to F.D.R.* (Vintage Books, 1955), p. 35.

for what they are.[95] The populist leader exempts the individual of responsibility and promises respect to people irrespective of merit, simply for belonging to the group.

In order to maintain homogeneity (a feeling of unity and interdependence), it is imperative to protect identity and an inherited way of life against existential threats, like foreigners with a different skin color or religion (or merely allegedly in competition with locals for jobs and social security).[96] Elsewhere, the invisible forces of global elites present the unifying threat. Of course, a people that needs enemies in order to remain a people will become hostile, antagonistic, and intolerant; surely not the best features for a democratic citizen and their political community. The populist solution of social and political conflicts knows no compromise, only total victory. This certainly does not mean the total annihilation of the enemy but their interests, being "alien," are illegitimate, necessitating their exclusion of any meaningful role in politics.

4.3.3 The (Relative) Majority as People: The Rule of the Part as a Whole

In the exercise of power, populism relies extensively on the majoritarian principle, claiming that the application of this decision-making tool actually means the expression of popular will. What actually counts as the people is the will of the relative majority supporting the populists. As mentioned above, this is a logical strategy of the relative majority against the opportunities of a liberal constitutionalism that enables diversity. It is also against the fundamental tolerance of pluralism that is inherent in all constitutional democracies. Of course, the dictate of a (relative) majority of the population can be fair in the sense of respecting the equality of citizens in decision-making; further, it is based on an ex ante agreement (or at least, acceptance of a habit of decision-making by acquiescence).[97] Nevertheless, majoritarianism results in impositions on the individual

---

[95] Commentators, mostly of left-leaning tendencies, claim that support for populism comes from those who were omitted from the social fabric, due to neoliberal globalization. The model is contested in view of empirical findings, see Y. Margalit, "Economic Insecurity and the Causes of Populism, Reconsidered," *Journal of Economic Perspectives*, 33:4 (2019), pp. 152–70; see further S. van der Walt, "Populism and the Yearning for Closure: From Economic to Cultural Fragility," *European Journal of Social Theory*, 23:4 (2019), pp. 1–16; for Poland see M. Gdula, *Nowy Autorytaryzm* (Wydawnictwo Krytyki Politycznej, 2018).

[96] Eatwell and Goodwin, *National Populism*, p. ix.

[97] On nondomination in majority decisions in democracy see, for example, T. Christiano, *The Constitution of Equality* (Oxford University Press, 2008).

and therefore shall be subject to limitations according to individual-respecting constitutionalism in a democracy. Illiberal democracies readily disregard these constitutional concerns. Moreover, majoritarianism is replaced by the decision-making principle of majority rule, with the justification that such decisions express the will of the authentic people. (Those who voted against are not members of the people or are mistaken about the will of the people.)

Not all populist leaders are supported by an absolute majority of the people, or such support may quickly diminish, as happened to Chávez. However, thanks to the peculiarities of the electoral system and other forms of acclamation, even a relative majority of the citizenry is enough to claim popular authorization for law-making and even constituent power. Democracies rely on relative majorities. Except in countries where proportional representation applies, representatives of a relative popular majority run parliament or the presidential office.[98] In "mature" democracies it is common, even standard, that as little as one-third of the population can serve as the majority.[99]

Majoritarianism (without constitutional counter-strategies) disregards foundational social agreements on values and – as a result – endangers minorities. Further, majoritarianism results in suboptimal decisions, though these are not a major concern in illiberal democracies. It is charismatic legitimacy that matters, and the leader, being identical to the people, is always right. Of course, contrary to dictatorship, the leader's decisions are carefully crafted to avoid antagonizing supporters. If there is a mistaken decision (mistaken because of destructive consequences or popular dislike, or because the temperature in the room was wrongly taken), the leader is not accountable. First, the mischief is always caused by the never-fully eliminated antagonistic elite. Second, accountability mechanisms were long eradicated.

Once again, majoritarianism under the decisive influence of a Caesaristic leader does not contradict regular democratic practices.

[98] Hitler never received more than one-third of the votes of the total electorate in free elections; in 2015, PiS in Poland could form a government with 16 percent of the votes of the electorate. Only about a third of the French population endorsed the 1946 Constitution and no party in the U.K. (or position in a referendum, like Brexit) has secured a majority of the popular vote, except perhaps in 1931, etc.

[99] Distinctions between electoral systems do not make a fundamental difference. True, mandatory participation in proportional representation-based elections may provide a government by representatives of an actual majority of the population. The price of PR is fragmentation that endangers governability. At the end of the day, in a coalition government the representatives of the strongest minority may run the show.

Professional politicians were always "able to fashion and, within very wide limits, even to create the will of the people ... a manufactured will."[100] Nevertheless the minority dictatorship, disguised as the people's majoritarian will, is fundamentally problematic for constitutionalism: it claims to be above the constitutional values that are affirmed by the constituent power and the established traditions of living together.

The people is a minority (relative majority) that stands for the whole. It is a self-selected group; the members of the people elevate themselves to the people by casting the vote for the leader or the cause he designed. Urbinati described this reduction of the people masterfully:

> The logic of populism is the glorification of one part. The legal fiction of *pars pro toto* was intended to characterize representative institutions in their generality and does not apply to populism, which rejects the notion of generality. Populist government is *pars pro parte*. It is essentially factional government: government by a part (defined as the best) that rules openly for its own good, satisfying its own needs and interests.[101]

Such elevation of the partial to the total may have emancipatory effects, especially compared to the de facto exclusion that exists in some representative systems. Perón's chosen people, the "true Argentinian people," were the *descamisados* (literally, "the shirtless"), the Perónist segment of the working class whom he granted fair(er) labor conditions and self-respect. At the end of the day, emancipation only served the needs of Perón's personal rule, moving toward corporatism and dictatorship in the footsteps of European fascist leaders. (Compare with *"le petit peuple toujours malheureux,"*[102] a creation of Robespierre: they were perhaps liberated, but to serve totalitarian purposes.)

What about those who are left out of the authentic people? Rousseau had the answer: those who took the wrong position and did not vote with the majority were mistaken. They may think and feel that they too are part of the people and the nation, but they are mistaken: they have excluded themselves from the people by not belonging to the putative majority. They had the chance to join the leader's people on the leader's terms. They failed to do so, therefore the leader will not stand up for them. Putin does not intend to represent gays and lesbians; he intends to

---

[100] Schumpeter, *Capitalism, Socialism and Democracy*, p. 263.
[101] Urbinati, "Political Theory," p. 123.
[102] R. Scruton, *The Palgrave Macmillan Dictionary of Political Thought* (Palgrave Macmillan, 2007), p. 517.

be President for authentic Russians, even if gays and lesbians will have their (modest) place in the country.

The relative majority, as the people, needs the reaffirmation that only they are the people. The authentic people is purified but not based on formal exclusion (though exclusion was the favorite form of democratic rule in Athens, in the shape of ostracism). Instead of formal exclusion, an array of techniques for disadvantaging voting (gerrymandering and mass media manipulation, etc.) and forming cultural identity is used to grant extra weight to the authentic people. It is the historical right of the authentic people to silence the nonpeople in the public space. It is fake, anyway. Only the voice of the authentic people must be heard!

4.3.4   The Democratic Legitimacy of Populist Popular Sovereignty

In the last decades, elections have been decreasingly less about interparty competition, where parties represent different interests, and increasingly more about personalities who rely on identity programs (to be good Hungarians, Poles, etc.). Democratic politics is replaced by the personalization of politics. Hence, politics moves toward personalism and personal competition, which increases the importance of emotional elements. Populists, with their inevitable leader cult, present only the logical conclusion of the transformation of program-oriented, interest-based electoral democracy.[103] The cult of personality in populism (where the movement needs a leader who gives it character, legitimacy, and a point for emotional identification) is inevitable, and once victorious, it is transferred into PLD.

Personalism results in the Caesaristic centralization of power (both as state control as well as broader control over the economy and culture through patronage). Is the exercise of state power by victorious populist movements compatible with democratic government?

Scholars in the tradition of Laclau claim that populism, and the government created by its victory, makes democracy more robust, for example, by including oppressed views and people in politics. Laclau argued that all politics is to a degree always populist, and Margaret Canovan has indicated that "populism has a characteristic of core concepts that it asserts . . . – democracy, popular sovereignty, the people . . .

---

[103] In 2018 Fidesz substituted the party program, which is produced habitually before elections, with a simple, ambiguous but evocative slogan: "we will continue!"

these cannot be dismissed as empty rhetorical flourishes."[104] The elected leader of the emerging illiberal regime claims that the people continuously, and democratically, supports his policies. The plebiscitarian leader stands for the people's rule (with the unpleasant consequence that the regime takes drastic measures to generate a majority). In addition, he provides the authentic representation of the authentic people. He can reflect the people's deeper values, which cannot be formed in rational deliberation, but rather exist organically, or in the national and/or religious tradition, as understood and shaped by the leader. The leader continuously refers to his popular election. This proves that he acts for the people, and it is the people that acts through him. But popular self-rule is a fiction here: "'Plebiscitary democracy' ... conceals itself under the form of legitimacy which is derived from the will of the ruled and only sustained by them."[105] The legitimacy of the regime is emotional: it relies on identifying between a quasi-charismatic leader and his chosen people, often mixed with nationalism. At this point, the superabundance of authoritarian personalities will explain the success of plebiscitarian illiberalism. Populism mobilizes the pool of persons with authoritarian predispositions, and populism in power will rely on the submission to a higher authority (the acceptance of the regime merely for being in command) that comes "naturally" for the authoritarian personality. "The leader's autocratic image validates the followers' twofold wish to submit to authority and to be authority [themselves]."[106]

Plebiscitarian leader democracy is all for democracy. What it finds irrelevant and frustrating is deliberation. Following Rousseau, populism in power is suspicious of popular deliberation and deliberation among citizens (including deliberation between the government and the opposition or within public opinion). Deliberation is between us and our

---

[104] M. Canovan, "Taking Politics to the People: Populism as the Ideology of Democracy," in Y. Meny and Y. Surel (eds.), *Democracies and the Populist Challenge* (Palgrave Macmillan, 2002), p. 33.

[105] M. Weber, *Economy and Society*, eds. G. Roth and C. Wittich (University of California Press, 1978), p. 268.

[106] G. Frankenberg, "Authoritarian Constitutionalism: Coming to Terms with Modernity's Nightmares," in H. A. García and G. Frankenberg (eds.), *Authoritarian Constitutionalism*, p. 25, quoting from T. W. Adorno, "Freudian Theory and the Pattern of Fascist Propaganda," in A. Arato and E. Gebhardt, *The Essential Frankfurt School Reader* (Urizen Books, 1978), p. 127. Robert O. Paxton, in his classic *The Anatomy of Fascism*, defines a cult of leadership as one in which the followers believe the leader's instincts are better than the logic used by elites. The followers are willing to give up their individuality and freedom in exchange for the leader's "protection." See R. O. Paxton, *The Anatomy of Fascism* (Penguin Books, 2005).

opponents; but for populism, there is no room for opponents and hence none for pluralism. This is once again totalitarian democratic theory as advocated by Rousseau; democracy at its worse.

There is no pre-set right choice in deliberative democracy, and whatever emerges in a proper process of deliberation must be considered the genuine choice of the people, though this is a choice without finality, and it does not totally disregard the losers' perspective and interests. Only the preconditions of deliberation are normatively pre-established, and not the outcome. This lack of preordained substantive values in deliberative democracy is unacceptable for populists.

What is the problem with deliberation from a populist perspective? Rousseau admits that popular deliberation may have been practical in ancient democracy, but people in a modern republic should be kept isolated. Political interaction is detrimental to political decision-making: "it was the activity of communicating with one another that gave rise eventually to what [Rousseau] called 'partial associations' and *the eventual corruption of the state*."[107]

The fear of corrupting deliberation in autonomous organizations (i.e. organizations not controlled by the ruler) animates illiberal democracies. Such uncontrolled deliberation could indeed "corrupt" the regime by developing dissent and an alternative people; it is for this reason that illiberal regimes prefer and foster atomization while they praise communitarian virtue and a homogenous people. The people is unified and the leader is capable of sensing and shaping this unity. Deliberation is superfluous even among his own people. Instead of deliberation there is support by acclamation.

There is a clear deliberative democracy deficit here, but according to constitutional and international law standards, popular will can be legitimately formed by elections and plebiscite. An additional, overlapping source of democratic legitimacy is the people's power. This is what boosts the democratic credentials of populism and illiberal democracies. What matters is not how decisions are taken (a matter of restrictive formalism) but who takes the decision.

In the past 200 years, political rule was made legitimate (and popular in many senses of the word) by the popular nature of political regimes, the assumption that the people has supreme, sovereign power. The popular (even *völkisch*) nature of the political system became the norm. Instead of the burdensome civic virtues and alien abstract values of constitutionalism, the

---

[107] Tuck, *The Sleeping Sovereign*, p. 6.

cultural habits of the "deplorables" and "disposables," Perón's *descamisados*, become respectable. The popular (vulgar) is the norm. Berlusconi or Trump are beloved for their politically incorrect views and manners, which were earlier quarantined but are now shared by their constituencies, who feel liberated once their previous "shortcomings" become appropriate. Hence the resurgence of machoism, the respect for "old-time order" (authoritarianism or patriarchy). Values and patterns of behavior, originating in premodern or religious tradition, which seemed anachronistic and a matter of shame in the elitist dictatorship of modernity and postmodernity, are now celebrated: the dirty language and knowing smiles in the gym and behind them, xenophobia, misogyny, and homophobia, are normalized. This return to the "roots" boosts the self-confidence of the authentic people.

4.3.5   The People of the Leader and Total (Unbound) Popular Sovereignty

Popular sovereignty promises absolute power to whomever can act on behalf of the people – as long as he can maintain the belief that he acts on their behalf. The homogeneity of the people (an act of imagination followed by exclusion and *Gleichschaltung*) cannot exist without personification in the leader. Representing *his* people, the people will be homogenous through him. The elected leader has the advantage to the state (another unitary entity) too, which triggers respect, authority, and obedience (especially among authoritarian-minded citizens).[108]

The ruler acts as if he were the people: that is the source of his power. He achieves this role as unifier of the people. In this capacity the ruler serves the "crystallization of common affects," a process in which "affective bounds with a leader can play an important role."[109] Power, here, "is not 'a thing' empirically determined, but is inseparable from its representation," and this representation "is constitutive of social identity."[110] As a leading apologist of Fidesz stated in 2015:

---

[108] PiS was able to attract the overwhelming majority of Polish "tribal authoritarians." Bartle, Sanders, and Tywman, "Authoritarian Populist Opinion in Europe," p. 23, Table A4.7: Poland.

For Latin America see D. Azpuru and M. F. T. Malone, "Parenting Attitudes and Public Support for Political Authoritarianism in Latin America," *International Journal of Public Opinion Research*, 31:3 (2019), pp. 570–87.

[109] M. Calderbank, "For A Left Populism: An interview with Chantal Mouffe," *Red Pepper* (September 22, 2018), http://www.redpepper.org.uk/for-a-left-populism-an-interview-with-chantal-mouffe.

[110] C. Lefort, *The Political Forms of Modern Society* (The MIT Press, 1986), p. 188.

> For some, politics is the realm of institutions, regulated mechanisms and impersonal machineries. Everything ought to be official and statutory. In my opinion, the politics doesn't work like this. Politics is the lore of man. It tells us how to guide people. If I am the ruler, I have to achieve that people want the same what I want.[111]

The citizen of illiberal democracy, the authentic people, has no will without the leader: "There is no democratic popular will independent of political manipulation . . . . In a contingent political situation, political leaders determine the political space(s) and dimension(s) in which voter preferences are formed."[112]

The leader, too, has specific features. As Weber explains, "pure charisma does not know any 'legitimacy' other than that flowing from personal *strength*, that is, one which is constantly being *proved*."[113] In order to prove himself, he needs crisis. Where there is none, he will create one. Hence the constant threat of migrants at the border. Crisis comes from the enemy; hence the need for creating an enemy outside the people. Political power stems from the ability to construe the enemy (see the role of the leader in Section 4.3.5). The vagueness of the elite-as-enemy allows groups with different grievances to believe that they are united against a common enemy.

The leader of illiberal democracy is elevated to his position by empty heroism in a self-generated struggle and a simple, obstinate wish and hunger for power. His justification for leadership, his qualification, is that he dared to lead, and that he dared successfully.[114] This is the charisma of daring in an emaciated political world. The leader of the plebiscitarian illiberal democracy will be a "princely figure"; the prince of democracy governs in crisis by organizing the *conditions of power* by *divide et impera.*[115]

---

[111] G. G. Fodor, quoted after the excellent essay of Bretter, "The Name of the Game," p. 45. Fodor relied on T. Schabert, *Boston Politics: The Creativity of Power* (De Gruyter, 1989). See further, G. G. Fodor, "The Two 'Faces' of Political Creativity. Two Paradigms of Political Leadership," in J. Femia, A. Korosenyi, and G. Stomp (eds.), *Political Leadership in Liberal and Democratic Theory* (Imprint Academic, 2009).

[112] A. Körösényi, "Stuck in Escher's Staircase. Leadership, Manipulation and Democracy," *Österreichische Zeitschrift für Politikwissenschaft*, 39:3 (2010), p. 298.

[113] M. Weber, *From Max Weber: Essays in Sociology*, eds. H. H. Gerth and C. Wright Mills (Oxford University Press, 1946), p. 248 (emphasis added).

[114] Professor Körösényi, a prophet of Orbán's second coming in 2009, singled out determination, risk taking, willpower and some vision of the national interest as leader-making characteristics. See A. Körösényi, "Political Leadership. Classical v Leadership Democracy," in Femia, et al (eds.), *Political Leadership*, p. 92.

[115] G. G. Fodor, "The Two Faces," pp. 179–80.

The people of populism exist in symbiosis with the leader. "People always ask for their own Caesar."[116] Because the people exists only through the leader, the leader, in order to perpetuate the people in its homogenous unity, must perpetuate his own power. Hence the problem of term limits in illiberal presidential regimes: there is a constant fight to abolish or bypass them, from Julius Caesar to Vladimir Putin.

Perón's interaction with his supporters at the previously quoted 1945 pre-election rally is the quintessential example of the leader/(select) people symbiosis:

> AUDIENCE: *outburst of cries and cheers.* This is the people! This is the people!
> PERÓN: This is the people. This is the suffering people that represent the pain of our motherland, which we have to defend. And we...
> AUDIENCE: *outburst of cries and cheers.* Perón! Perón! This is the people of... This is the people of Perón! This people of Perón! *(In unison with increasing strength).*
> PERÓN: This... This is the people of the fatherland.[117]

Note that the crowd spontaneously identified itself as the people *of* the leader.

In the Weberian sense, an act is social in the sense that a shared social meaning can be attributed to it. In order to attribute the meaning of "the people's act" to a political decision, the agent and/or observers must see that the actor is the people. The act of ruling, in order to be attributed to the people, must be structured according to pre-existing expectations (e.g. the decision results from a plebiscite that is carried out according to rules and therefore is understood as the people's will). In populist regimes, the necessary structuring will be determined by the leader (and the regime ends if there is a successful action attributable to a people that is construed/ perceived under different presuppositions).[118]

---

[116] This is what Francisco Campos, the Brazilian Carl Schmitt (Minister of Justice under Getulio Vargas, the populist dictator of Brazil) stated in 1937. Quoted in R. Gargarella, "Latin America Breathing: Liberalism and Illiberalism, Once and Again" in A. Sajó, S. Holmes, and R. Uitz, *Routledge Handbook of Illiberalism* (Routledge, in press).

[117] J. D. Perón (speech of October 17, 1945), in M.A. Vitale, "This Is the Suffering People that Represent the Pain of the Motherland: Argentina-Argentine Voices," *African Yearbook of Rhetoric*, 6:2 (2015), p. 57.

[118] The people's will "is articulated by the plebiscitary leader himself, who, relying on his power as party leader and the disciplined Fidesz parliamentary group, conveys it to the legislature, as well as to domestic and foreign policies." A. Körösényi, "The Theory and

Elections are a feast of self-affirmation for the self-chosen people. The leader insists on elections not only to reaffirm his leadership but also to show to the whole electorate (opposition included) that his majority is the only relevant people. As Hugo Chávez stated in his 2006 closing campaign speech: "You are going to reelect yourselves, the people will reelect the people. Chávez is nothing but an instrument of the people."[119] Here again the totalitarian (Rousseauist) potential of democracy manifests itself; "the idea of a people becomes naturally restricted to those who identify themselves with the general will . . . . Those outside are not really of the nation."[120]

Caesarism relies on elections because it operates within the framework of the people's supremacy, but the leader is the natural representative of the people, and therefore democratic forms of popular will formation hold little practical relevance. Moving in the direction of despotism, the leader will "figure out" popular will and will find it in his own desire. "The real people, or *rather their leadership*, once triumphant in their insurrection, become Rousseau's Legislator, who surveys clearly the whole panorama, without being swayed by partial interests and passions, and shapes the 'young nation' with the help of laws derived from his superior wisdom. He prepares it to will the general will."[121]

Beyond participation in elections and occasionally in progovernment rallies, the people's role is limited to that of the spectator in the tradition of the Roman *populus*. This people is not expected to be a decision-maker and is involved in decision-making only for propaganda purposes.[122] The people exists "in the act of cheering or booing those who competed for a political post or tried to conquer people's support for their cause."[123] Acclamation becomes complicity.

The ruler communicates with his people directly, without institutional mediation. This looks democratic in the sense of direct and participatory democracy, but it is essentially contrary to constitutionalism. While the

Practice of Plebiscitary Leadership: Weber and the Orbán Regime," *East European Politics and Societies and Cultures*, 33:2 (2019), p. 290.

[119] K. A. Hawkins, "Is Chávez Populist? Measuring Populist Discourse in Comparative Perspective," *Comparative Political Studies*, 42:8 (2009), p. 1040.

[120] Talmon, *The Origins*, p. 48.

[121] Ibid., p. 49.

[122] After the 2000 elections, in the transformative period of the Bolivarian Revolution, Chávez ruled by decree for a year, excluding deliberation even within his own movement. R. Brading, "From Passive to Radical Revolution in Venezuela's Populist Project," *Latin American Perspectives*, 41:6 (2014), p. 56.

[123] N. Urbinati, "The Populist Phenomenon," *Raisons politiques*, 51:3 (2013), p. 151.

guardians of a constitutional order are there "to withstand the temporary delusion" of people "to give them time and opportunity for more cool and sedate reflection," the populist leader who must cater to public emotions may show "unqualified complaisance to every sudden breeze of passion."[124] Especially so, when the leader was the one to generate that passion. Moreover, the leader needs happy spectator-voters. "There is nothing so joyful as despotism. The sight of human miseries, the unhappy are its natural enemies. It loves on the contrary to find the image of joy everywhere in its path, and it is pleased with games and spectacles. ... No one desires more than it does that peoples enjoy themselves, provided that they think only about enjoying themselves."[125]

The leader needs happy spectator-voters.

Political regimes emerging from the victory of populism are PLDs by nature: this is what they inherit from the populist movement phase. The people that emerges from the struggles of populism can exist only through the leader, and in symbiosis with the leader, and would not have identity without him.[126] The role of the authentic people is to be united around the leader, therefore its role is apolitical or antipolitical.[127] The leader is "the trustee of the masses, self-elected by the masses themselves to whom they will subordinate themselves as long as he enjoys their trust."[128] The masses elect the leader to elect themselves. Notwithstanding the democratic rhetoric, elections in illiberal democracies provide a representation of the people in a nondemocratic sense, as understood in conservative theories of people's rule. Burke held that nonparticipatory forms are the most adequate forms for expressing people's sovereignty: for Burke, the limited English electorate, and the select few leaders, guarantee the best representation of the English people; the English people at its best.[129]

Caesarism (leader's democracy) offers an essentially nonparticipatory form of people's sovereignty. The leader's competence (his intuitive "knowledge" of what people desire) makes popular participation in

---

[124] A. Hamilton, J. Madison, and J. Jay, *The Federalist Papers. No. 71* (Mentor Book, 1961), p. 432.

[125] A. de Tocqueville, *Democracy in America*, vol. 4 (Liberty Fund, 2010), p. 1249.

[126] For a leader-centered power system emerging from populism in Latin America, see C. de la Torre, *Populist Seduction in Latin America* (Ohio University Press, 2010), p. 200.

[127] I. Berlin, "To Define Populism," *Government and Opposition*, 3:2 (1968), p. 137, emphasized the apolitical nature of the concept of the people.

[128] M. Weber, "The President of the Reich," in Weber, *Political Writings*, p. 305. The translation has been changed to follow Weber's original term "selbstgewählten Vertrauensmann der Massen."

[129] Urbinati, "Unpolitical Democracy," p. 66.

government superfluous. The leader's competence means that he can hear and echo the grief of the people and speak the language of the voiceless. The leader promises that the voice of the authentic and offended people will be heard and that "he will care about the ordinary people" at a time of economic or other anxiety.[130] "[T]he leader who will succeed is the one who best senses and delivers what an audience already desires."[131] This is exactly what a populist people desires: "While the populists of the 'silent revolution' wanted more participation and less leadership, the populists of the 'silent counter-revolution' want more leadership and less participation."[132]

The leader may have predetermined conceptions of the will of the people, and he will try to rally people around that imaginary will, which is his own desire dictated by the primary need of the regime: self-perpetuation. But the leader is a realist. As Perón noticed: "In government to do fifty percent of what you want, you have to let the rest of the people do the fifty percent in the way they want."[133] The advocates of leader democracy (the intellectual-courtiers in Orbán's court) consider leader democracy a system where the leader "through the manipulation of voters' preferences" is "able to shape the collective choices," and here, "instead of people's will, it is the volition of political leaders that prevails in the political process."[134] This may be true, but most Caesarist leaders are pragmatic (contrary to full-blown totalitarian dictators). They will impose their preconception of the people's will with caution: that will is construed and changed if necessary, after proper sniffing of public sentiment (the Orbán government spends a remarkable amount of public money on public opinion research and brainwashing campaigns). The leader selects successfully from the obscure desires of his electorate and liberates oppressed identity components that were suppressed as inappropriate by the cultural censorship of liberal democracy.[135] He

---

[130] President Obama claimed that he is not a populist merely because he cared: populists are those who add nativism and xenophobia.

[131] Panizza, "Introduction," p. 10.

[132] C. Mudde, "The Populist *Zeitgeist*," *Government and Opposition*, 39:4 (2004), pp. 557–58.

[133] J. D. Perón, *Conducción Politica* (Editorial Freeland, 1971), p. 36; quoted after F.J. Mc Lynn, "The Political Thought of Juan Domingo Perón," *Boletín De Estudios Latinoamericanos y Del Caribe*, 32 (1982), p. 18.

[134] Körösényi, "Political Leadership," pp. 92–93.

[135] I. Krastev and S. Holmes, "Explaining Eastern Europe: Imitation and Its Discontents," *Journal of Democracy*, 29:3 (2018), pp. 117–28 ("a deep-seated disgust at the post-1989 'imitation imperative,' with all its demeaning and humiliating implications," p. 118).

will reinforce what he personally finds attractive. Here is Orbán's ideal, which resonates with what many people find virtuous and appropriate, even if it is far from their own, much more modern, life world:

> The archetype of the Hungarian male (*férfiember*) is the yeoman farmer (*gazda*).[136] The man [person] from the countryside has this way of thinking that there is a territory with a boundary, a clear extension, and he is responsible for the quality of life there, for order, for making a living from the territory and for how things go. This sense of responsibility explains why the Hungarian province gave so many good leaders to Hungarian politics, because that needs the same kind of way of thinking.[137]

The ruler in plebiscitarian democracy "will attempt to consolidate the loyalty of those he governs either by winning glory and honor in war or by promoting their material welfare, or under certain circumstances, by attempting to combine both. Success in these will be regarded as proof of the charisma."[138] Putin and Erdoğan are courting glory by engaging in limited wars, while populist leaders like Perón, Kaczyński, or Chávez are outstanding (at least in the short run) in providing material benefits to their chosen people and protecting them against enemies.[139] Illiberal regimes promise governing for the people and protection not only against the elite, like the Caesars of Rome,[140] but also against enemies

---

[136] "*Gazda*" resembles the populist yeoman ideal "who owned a small farm and worked it with the aid of his family, was the incarnation of the simple, honest, independent, healthy, happy human being," except that the Hungarian yeoman had some servants and day laborers, of course treated severely but fairly. Hofstadter, *The Age of Reform*, pp. 24-25.

[137] See V. Orbán, "Orbán Viktor beszéde a „Mindent a magyar vidék jövőjéért" című könyv bemutató sajtótájékoztatóján," Miniszterelnok.hu (July 9, 2020), www.miniszterelnok.hu/orban-viktor-beszede-a-mindent-a-magyar-videk-jovojeert-cimu-konyv-bemutato-sajtotajekoztatojan/. The HPM added: "I am pleased to see here these Hungarian faces and these heads facing me reminding us of a noble Szekler." The Caesar establishes complicity with allusions to premodern identity markers.

[138] Weber, *Economy and Society*, p. 269.
Once again, the populist leader in power is providing services (even if at high costs due to clientelistic corruption). The illiberal regimes are neopatrimonial, which means that goodies are distributed to the constituency. See Chapter 3.

[139] It is argued that the second victory of Modi in India is intimately related to the distributions of benefits to the electorate. Y. Aiyar, "Modi Consolidates Power: Leveraging Welfare Politics," *Journal of Democracy*, 30 (2019), pp. 78–88. As long as the economy allows it, democracy tends to reward the incumbent, who materially supports its welfare-dependent constituency.

[140] See Y. Roman, *Empereurs et Sénateurs. Une Histoire Politique de l'empire Romain* (Fayard, 2001), pp. 221–22. The Roman plebs supported Caesar because he protected them against the aristocracy.

that exist in the Caesar's imagination (e.g. "migrants"). This is "an illiberal move whereby the rulers care about popular support."[141] "A perpetually frustrated and perpetually fearful populace is one that will continue to lend support to demagoguery. The policies adopted by an Erdoğan or a Duterte are not meant to solve problems, but to keep the fear of them alive."[142] Once imaginary threats threaten the group and the authority that keeps it together, the supporters "will actually augment their commitment to and defense of this normative order."[143] But relying on fear only, *pace* Machiavelli, is not enough. The frustrated will constantly search for the source of the frustration, and one day they may conclude that it is Caesar himself.

The electoral success of populist movements is based to a great extent on the promise of recognition. True to the legacy of populism, all leaders provide a cause for self-respect,[144] "a restoration of control ... on social and cultural matters,"[145] and continuously promise the restoration of the greatness of the people (nation). Finally, the popular demand for recognition is satisfied, to a great extent, in the endorsement of the authentic people's way of life.

4.4   Populism as Democracy?

Popular sovereignty creates the opportunity for the absolutization of power, the enforcement of the will or consent of an electoral minority (a relative majority of the voters) with little consideration for other members of the political community (electorate). Populism unashamedly makes use of this possibility. But populist majoritarianism remains a democratic exercise of power,[146] based on popular sovereignty, even

---

[141] Sadurski, "How Democracy Dies," p. 14.

[142] J. T. Levy, "The Sovereign Myth," Niskanen Center (June 15, 2017), www .niskanencenter.org/sovereign-myth.

[143] Stenner, *The Authoritarian Dynamic*, p. 19.

[144] D. James, *Resistance and Integration: Perónism and the Argentine Working Class, 1946–1976* (Cambridge University Press, 1988), pp. 24, 30–33.

Populism in ancient Rome meant the enlargement of the political constituency by including the *populus*. Chávez did redistribute oil revenues, Morales did help the indigenous to live in accordance with their traditional forms of life (beyond constitutionalizing coca), PiS did pay family subsidies, and the HPM did reduce the tax burden of his middle-class supporters.

[145] J. T. Levy, "The Sovereign Myth," Niskanen Center (June 15, 2017), www.niskanencenter.org /sovereign-myth.

[146] This can be embellished, and one can say, following Urbinati that it is "a perverse inversion of the ideals and procedures of democracy." See Urbinati, "Political Theory,"

if a dubious or suspect theory and practice of democracy. It celebrates the people, but in a way that forces them to collide with constitutional democracy.

Populism in power reinterprets the idea of government in the service of the people. Government is not a function of the people. The people is sovereign, but exactly for this reason, the people do not govern. The state squeezes out autonomous institutions that produce collective goods, or makes them dependent. This is logical from the perspective of domination, as polyarchy may undermine the construction of a single center of power. The power is not interested in finding partners in the determination and service of a common good; it is not interested in dialogue in order to reach consensus. Consensus is taken for granted: it is achieved charismatically but also with manipulation. At a certain point, of course, those who refuse the consensus (on the leader's terms) will not become part of the authentic, relevant people. This has practical consequences: no jobs, and no entrepreneurial opportunities. The strong state itself (i.e. the leader) will determine what the problems of the people are and how to solve them.

This mode of government, with its plebiscitarian acclamation, precludes governmental accountability, the Schumpeterian minimum of democracy. Governing (ruling) is not the business of the people, so it cannot hold anyone accountable. Not only are the techniques of ruling mobilized to prevent the leader's dismissal in elections, but the whole idea of political accountability becomes nonsensical, because "there is no objective standard to evaluate governmental policy. In the absence of such standards it makes no sense to come forward with claims of governmental accountability."[147]

Populism in power exposes the inherent contradictions and weaknesses of democracy. Even where it was unable to take control of the state administration so far, it has undermined otherwise solid democracies, simply by its increasingly hegemonic influence on politics and public thought. It is for this reason (and not just for constitutional shortcomings) that illiberal regimes are increasingly normalized, even

p. 113. Even if "populism in power is a transmutation of democratic principles, though not (yet) an exit from democracy." See Urbinati, "Political Theory," p. 118. See further Rosanvallon, *Counter-Democracy*, p. 265.

[147] F. G. Gábor, "Jó és rossz kormányzás Magyarországon," *Politikatudományi Szemle*, 17:1 (2007), p. 132. This is contrary to what Weber assumed about the Caesaristic ruler, who in his assumption was ready to be held popularly responsible for his choices if unsuccessful.

in the European Union. They are normalized also professionally as the following quote illustrates: "The populist parties do not entail the destruction of democracy. They often propose a different version of democracy, but they are also characterised by respect for some of the basic principles of democratic majority rule. . . . One can even claim that they to at least a limited extent vitalize democracy."[148] Certainly, the plebiscitarian regime has been normalized as democracy in Hungary, at least among the supporters of Fidesz. They are committed to democracy and believe that there is democracy in Hungary.

Populism stands against the institutional limits on state power. This counter-constitutionalism is based on the assumption that the people's power in the state is sovereign. This is the despotic program that is realized in illiberal democracies: they do not intend to structure the people and its power, in contrast to constitutionalism, which recognizes the people by structuring and thereby taming it. Populism in power relies on the inherent inconsistencies of democracy, but at a certain point, it parts way with it. The popular success of populism indicates with utmost clarity the constitutionally destructive potential of the people as a concept. And not only that – it reminds us of the destructive potential of people (i.e. human beings in community).

---

[148] *Timbro Authoritarian Populism Index* (Timbro, 2019).

5

Constitutional Structure

The accretion of dangerous power does not come in a day. It does come, however slowly, from the generative force of unchecked disregard of the restrictions that fence in even the most disinterested assertion of authority.

Youngstown Sheet & Tube Co. v. *Sawyer*[1]

5.1 Introduction

Illiberal democracies do not depart from the known *formal* structures of constitutional government. As Pinelli notes, "neither the representative system nor the referendum have been questioned as such."[2] In terms of ordinary comparative constitutional law, they may be presidential systems, semipresidential or textbook Westminster parliamentary regimes. However, their presentation and analysis cannot be confined to a description of their institutional structures, processes, and legal assumptions.

Bugarič claims that "[p]aradoxically, constitutional democracy can play its 'counter-majoritarian' role only when a majority of the people believe that it is the only game in town."[3] In countries where populism has gained control over the state, this is precisely the shared belief. Democracy *is* the only game in town – but it does not play a counter-majoritarian goal. Beyond its different constitutional forms, its law serves plebiscitarian democracy. The Caesar leads, rules and governs by the people's will (which is his own), but democracy is not a straitjacket for the populist leader. On the contrary, it is a Savile Row, tailor-made shirt (worn unbuttoned and with no tie, naturally); it enhances the illiberal

---

[1] *Youngstown Sheet & Tube Co.* v. *Sawyer*, 343 US 579, 594 (1952) (concurring opinion).
[2] C. Pinelli, "The Populist Challenge to Constitutional Democracy," *European Constitutional Law Review*, 7:1 (2011), p. 11.
[3] B. Bugarič, "Central Europe's Descent into Autocracy: A Constitutional Analysis of Authoritarian Populism," *International Journal of Constitutional Law*, 17:2 (2019), p. 600.

power of the charismatic ruler, who finds in his people the source of his increasingly unlimited power.

The Caesaristic leader rules by cheating. Constitutional and other public law arrangements profess that the regime fits into classic parliamentarism, presidentialism, or semipresidentialism. These arrangements make little difference in an illiberal democracy, as institutional solutions are intentionally introduced to facilitate regime perpetuation and personal rule. Once illiberal democracy is consolidated and realizes that its existence is sustainable, mimicry becomes a dwindling necessity. The regime can afford to unmask itself as opportunistic and, if required, despotic. However, at least initially, the regime continues to operate behind and *with* a façade of constitutionalism and democracy. In many cases, it may reach a certain stable equilibrium, like in Singapore: this constitutional form (or stage, if one accepts that this leads to despotism) is the subject of the present chapter.

Some argue (in a dynamic context, i.e. how democracies retrogress) that democratic decay results from piecemeal deviations from key elements of constitutional democracy, where the shifts "complied with the existing, liberal constitution."[4] "[I]t necessarily involves many incremental changes to legal regimes and institutions. Each of these changes may be innocuous or even defensible in isolation. It is only by their cumulative, interactive effect that retrogression occurs."[5] This effectively captures the difference between a populist illiberal democracy and pre-power grab democracy, but examining solely the constitutional text reveals little that is troubling. Arguably, the constitutional system of illiberal democracies collects antiquated, antiliberal institutions, "constitutional worst practices,"[6] and solutions of democracies that do not even function as written. However, many of these solutions are venerated in the country of origin (e.g. Poland adopted the Spanish model of judicial council elections). What matters is that the changes (increase of presidential powers, limits to judicial review, exceedingly long mandates, etc.) were intended for potential abuse even if

---

[4] M. Tushnet, "Authoritarian Constitutionalism," *Cornell Law Review*, 100 (2015), p. 437. Tushnet seems to believe that the content of the rules is "authoritarian."

[5] A. Huq and T. Ginsburg, "How to Lose a Constitutional Democracy," *University of California Law Review*, 65:78 (2018), p. 97; For a similar argument, see K. L. Scheppele, "The Rule of Law and the Frankenstate: Why Governance Checklists Do Not Work," *Governance*, 26:4 (2013), pp. 560–62.

[6] K. L. Scheppele, "Worst Practices and the Transnational Legal Order (Or How to Build A Constitutional 'Democratorship' in Plain Sight)," in T. Ginsburg, T. C. Halliday, and G. Shaffer (eds.), *Constitution-Making and Transnational Legal Order* (Cambridge University Press, 2019), p. 5.

these solutions conform to the constitutional canon, while others reinforce democracy. Based on comparative law, one could not object to the Hungarian government's plan for a separate administrative court system except that under local circumstances, selection of the new judges would very likely be highly political, undermining the RoL. Moreover, many of the reforms enhance democracy, at least in principle. In several Latin American countries (beginning with Perón in Argentina), the regimes extended the franchise, which became the very source of entrenched one-party rule.[7] Seemingly, the new institutions and their relations do not cause a "system effect":[8] the fundamental changes occur at the level of *personnel*. However, in certain areas that are decisive for perpetuating plebiscitarian political power (elections, where the rules of competition, administration, parties, and media are all changed in the same restrictive direction) and domination (procurement and subsidies), the system effects are undeniable.

5.2 The Spirit of Constitutionalism and Its Absence

5.2.1 Constitutional Background Assumptions

Illiberal democracy is a special constitutional arrangement: it is a plebiscitarian democracy unfolding the totalitarian potential within a democratic system. As a centralized power, it intends to perpetuate the rulers' monopoly over the state, relying on the falsification of classical (liberal) constitutionalism. These features offer sufficient family resemblance to treat them together for the purposes of constitutional theory. Within this resemblance are historically defined differences regarding the norms of socially acceptable constitutional behavior: e.g. the degree of reliance on violence and its acceptance, the demand for transparency, social solidarity in resistance, patterns of acquiescence, etc. For example, Singapore's constitutional reality is determined by the laws of

---

[7] The HFL represents one of the most multiculturalist, national minority-endorsing constitutional documents in Europe, stating twice that "the national minorities living with us form part of the Hungarian political community" and "are constituent parts of the State," with language rights, reserved parliamentary seats and a preferential vote (resulting in additional parliamentary support to the government). The Fidesz government extended citizenship and voting rights to ethnic Hungarians living abroad, another generous gesture of recognition – with the power-perpetuation effects seen in Latin America. Fidesz takes for granted that diaspora Hungarians will vote for them.

[8] A. Vermeule, P. S. Karlan, L. Lessig, and P. J. White, "The Supreme Court, 2008 Term," *Harvard Law Review*, 123 (2009), pp. 1–151. "A system effect arises when the properties of an aggregate differ from the properties of its members, taken one by one." Ibid., p. 6.

emergency,[9] rather than populism; in other countries, a state of emergency does not play a central role (although it can be useful), or it is used only in the transition period.

The specificity that fosters the family resemblance among illiberal democracies becomes clearer when comparing them with established constitutional democracies: it   is   the   absence/presence   of a *constitutional spirit* (replaced by the primary concern for maintaining political power and social domination) that sets the two families apart. All constitutional regimes depend on shared constituent beliefs, even if many are uncertain and some conflict with each other. "Spirit is actual only as that which it knows itself to be, and the state, as the spirit of a people, is both the law *permeating all relationships within the state* and also at the same time the customs and consciousness of its citizens. ... A people's constitution must embody its feeling for its rights and its condition."[10]

The populist, nationalist beliefs that animate illiberal regimes do not necessitate the decency that is essential for constitutionalism. On the contrary, the regime is animated by a spirit of constitutional instrumentalism that justifies the use of the constitution to deceive the world, including its own subjects and supporters. The claim that the specificity of illiberal democracies can be found in the spirit of "unconstitutionalism" (illiberalism) makes constitutional scholars feel ill at ease. When analysts discuss spirits, they often tend to describe ghosts. "The problem with spirits is that they tend to reflect less the views of the world whence they come than the views of those who seek their advice."[11] Montesquieu famously referred to the spirit of the laws, only to devise a series of misunderstandings regarding institutional structures; for Montesquieu, "spirit" was a shorthand for (partly sociopsychological) assumptions to explain the successes and failures of different governments, primarily in terms of their stability. Yet one can make sense out of spirit: informal institutions such as routines, roles, and norms characterize the functioning of all institutions.[12] Tribe describes an invisible aspect of the

---

[9] See, for example, Article 9(6) of the Singapore Constitution: "Nothing in this article shall invalidate any law ... in force before 16 Sep 1963 which authorizes the arrest and detention of any person in the interests of public safety, peace and good order."

[10] G. W. F. Hegel, *Outlines of the Philosophy of Right* (Oxford University Press, 2008), p. 263.

[11] *Public Citizen* v. *United States Department of Justice Washington Legal Foundation* 491 US 440, 473 (1989).

[12] J. March and J. Olsen, *Rediscovering Institutions: The Organisational Basis of Politics* (Free Press, 1989), p. 52.

constitution, as "a complex superstructure of rules, doctrines, standards, legal tests, judicial precedents, legislative and executive practices, and cultural and social traditions."[13] In this respect, Ernst Fraenkel referred to an unwritten command of *fairness*, and beyond it, a code of values containing a moral minimum of social living-together. This minimum means a minimum of accepted social decency.[14] Unwritten norms (and maxims of law) are to be observed even if inconvenient.[15]

The difficulties of the catching the spirit of the constitution is aggravated by a specific problem of legal/constitutional interpretation. In the practical search for the constitution's "spirit," reference to underlying values will enforce the bias of the legislator or, even worse, that of the interpreter, as in the case of Justice Scalia's favorite exhibition item, *Church of the Holy Trinity v. United States*. The 1885 Alien Contract Labor Law prohibited "the importation and migration of foreigners and aliens under contract or agreement to perform labor or service of any kind in the United States." SCOTUS examined the underlying assumptions, the spirit behind the text of the act, and concluded that "this is a Christian nation. In the face of all these, shall it be believed that a Congress of the United States intended to make it a misdemeanor for a church of this country to contract for the services of a Christian

---

[13] L. H. Tribe, *The Invisible Constitution* (Oxford University Press, 2008), p. 10. See further R. Dixon and A. Stone (eds.), *The Invisible Constitution in Comparative Perspective* (Cambridge University Press, 2018). Unwritten norms were famously important in English constitutionalism, but respect for these uncertain practices has dissipated in the last few decades (see L. Siedentop, *Democracy in Europe* [Columbia University Press, 2001], pp. 71–72). Populism had its field day with Brexit, but it is still unthinkable, even at this moment of regained English parochialism, that any political leader of an established democracy would dare to use the holes of the constitution to perpetuate his power or consider the opposition as the enemy of the people. Of course, the day the unthinkable becomes a legitimate possibility, constitutional democracy can no longer be taken for granted.

[14] E. Fraenkel, "Strukturdefekte der Demokratie und deren Überwindung," in E. Fraenkel and K. Sontheimer, *Zur Theorie der Pluralistischen* (Bundeszentrale für Politische Bildung, Demokratie, 1964), p. 117; E. Fraenkel, "Möglichkeiten und Grenzen Politischer Mitarbeit des Bürgers in einer Modernen Parlamentarischen Demokratie. Besinnung auf das Wesen Politischer Erziehung und Bildung," *Aus Politik und Zeitgeschichte: Bundeszentrale für Politische Bildung*, 16:14 (1966), pp. 1–13. Quoted after F. Schorkopf, *Staat und Diversität* (Brill, 2017), p. 81.

[15] American constitutional theory often refers to *faithfulness* to the Constitution, especially when it comes to its interpretation/application. A. Amar, *America's Unwritten Constitution* (Basic Books, 2012), p. 5. During the drafting of the US Constitution, and debates on the *ex post facto* clause, the argument against inclusion was that it was "unnecessary and would reflect poorly on the legal sophistication of the draftsmen." Certain principles of natural justice are obvious without being stated. Ibid., p. 7.

minister residing in another nation?"[16] The answer was a resounding NO, contrary to the plain meaning of the law. For Scalia, this kind of reasoning makes law unpredictable, increases judicial discretion and compromises democratic values as through it the interpreter becomes the legislator.[17]

Spirit is not the only constitutional background consideration. Admittedly, "the interpretation of a constitution cannot be separated from the interrelationship of political forces to which it is applied. If the interrelationship varies, the structure and the functioning of the government established by the constitution vary at the same time."[18] The more hegemonic one of the political forces is, the less it will feel bound by conventions and spirit. This is exactly the problem in some illiberal democracies, where the government as a political force towers over society. But the problem goes beyond constitutional interpretation; it is about decency in the use of public power. "These populist governments also have made a point of undermining informal democratic norms, which include conflict of interest laws, financial transparency, respect for opposition, access and accountability to media, and the meritocratic awarding of jobs, tenders, and contracts. Levitsky and Ziblatt have identified the mutual toleration of the opposition and the government, and forbearance from using the law as a weapon, as critical informal norms of liberal democracy."[19]

The assumptions animating the contemporary liberal constitutional order (as an ideal but also as a practice) correspond *grosso modo* to basic

---

[16] *Church of the Holy Trinity* v. *United States*, 143 US 457 at 471 (1892). The Church contracted an alien, intending to bring him to the United States to serve as its pastor. SCOTUS applied the "soft plain meaning rule": "a thing may be within the letter of the statute and yet not within the statute, because not within its *spirit*, nor within the intention of its makers."

[17] A. Scalia, "Common-Law Courts in a Civil-Law System: The Role of United States Federal Courts in Interpreting the Constitution and Laws," in A. Scalia, *A Matter of Interpretation: Federal Courts and the Law*, ed. A. Gutmann (Princeton University Press, 1997), pp. 9–12.

In the UK, unless expressly stated, the legislator cannot intend unreasonable consequences, and the interpretation will avoid such meanings. D. Lowe and C. Potter, *Understanding Legislation: A Practical Guide to Statutory Interpretation* (Bloomsbury, 2018), pp. 60–61.

[18] Duverger made this remark with regard to semipresidentialism. M. Duverger, "A New Political System: Semi-Presidential Government," *European Journal of Political Research*, 8:2 (1980), p. 165, p. 167.

[19] A. Grzymala-Busse, "How Populists Rule: The Consequences for Democratic Governance," *Polity*, 51:4 (2019), p. 712., referring to S. Levitsky and D. Ziblatt, *How Democracies Die* (Crown, 2018).

tenets of liberal theory. In this "background culture" (as Rawls calls it), "acceptance of the burdens of judgment, tolerance and the virtue of civility must be assumed."[20] A liberal constitutional system presupposes that certain underlying assumptions and principles (like decency and the command of self-limitation, including reluctance to interfere into private affairs and adherence to evidence-based reason and justification) form part of the constitution. Among these beliefs is also the assumption that these principles will be observed by the powers that be.

The constitutional "theory"[21] of the illiberal state reflects a substantive (primarily collectivist) understanding of state functions. Limiting state power is not a concern: wherever substantive goals require, state powers shall increase. The most commonly referenced substantive value is the "common good." This reference is most obvious in Poland as PiS is strongly influenced by Catholic social doctrine, which intends to restore a Christian (Catholic) order in the state.[22] Likewise Hungary (at least in the professional literature) takes interest in the common good, within the context of the good governance versus good government debate. In public statements, the "national interest," in a nationalist sense, is closest to a common good; the interests of Hungarians certainly stand ahead of and above constitutional niceties. Chávez also referred to the need to serve the common good, though in a far more class-oriented, socialistic understanding.[23]

---

[20] A. Ferrara, "Can Political Liberalism Help Us Rescue 'the People' from Populism?," *Philosophy & Social Criticism*, 44:4 (2018), p. 471.

[21] The existence of a specific theory is doubtful. For the regime, the principal assumption is that the constitutional order is within the tradition of constitutionalism and a conservative or popular participatory version of "ordinary" constitutional theory applies. The present reconstruction of the constitutional theory of the illiberal state is a non-theory: it argues that it describes a practice of cheats. It is a parasite of constitutional theory.

[22] On the Catholic concepts of the common good, see e.g. W. A. Barbieri, "Beyond the Nations: The Expansion of the Common Good in Catholic Social Thought," *The Review of Politics*, 63:4 (2001), pp. 723–54; J. Sniegocki, "The Social Ethics of Pope John Paul II: A Critique of Neoconservative Interpretations," *Horizons*, 33:1 (2006), pp. 7–32.

[23] Recently Professor Vermeule advocated a "common-good constitutionalism" as a theory of interpretation for SCOTUS. This "should be based on the principles that government helps direct persons, associations, and society generally toward the common good, and that strong rule in the interest of attaining the common good is entirely legitimate." A. Vermeule, "Beyond Originalism," *The Atlantic* (March 31, 2020), http://www.theatlantic.com/ideas/archive/2020/03/common-good-constitutionalism /609037. Vermeule, a defender of Hungary's "mild autocracy" advocates "illiberal legalism" and expects from the interpreter of the Constitution a moral reading that respects

In an ideal constitutional democracy, all actors respect constitutional aims to a decisive extent, and in case of a serious break, most actors refuse cooperation and defy deviation from constitutional principles. A constitutionalist constitution is a commitment that power will be accountable and not perpetual, and a constitutional commitment means that the constitutional foundations cannot be disregarded with the majority's mood swings, even if it were a constituent or overwhelming majority.[24] With the ascending power of plebiscitarian democracy, institutional commitments and the background culture of constitutionalism are windswept by populism; the norms of reality TV prevail. As Ruth Wodak has stated (primarily on the basis of Austrian developments), "shamelessness, humiliation of other participants, defamation, lies and ad hominem attacks dominate."[25] Constitutional shamelessness is becoming widespread; it suffices to consider the neglect of constitutional decency in the separation of powers in North Carolina, a de facto one-party state in the better part of the twentieth century. In both cases, the constitutional chicanery and the use of sheer partisan power intend to perpetuate partisan rule.[26]

5.2.2   Illiberalism as a Consequence of Identity Politics

In a postmaterial culture, social and personal issues are increasingly expressed as issues of identity. Plebiscitarian illiberal regimes rise to power in a world where identitarian antagonism sets the framework for public discourse and private self-esteem. This identity-centered culture changes politics: "not only does your identity give you reasons to do things [a matter that can be destructive of collective action serving a common good, if one believes in it, but at least undermines effective social coordination], it can give others reasons to do things to you. . . . [A]mong the most significant things people do with identities is use

---

"the hierarchies needed for society to function." For Max Weber this would be the end of the RoL. See further Chapter 1 on authoritarianism.

[24] For the various theories of unamendability see Y. Roznai, *Unconstitutional Constitutional Amendments, The Limits of Amendment Powers* (Oxford University Press, 2017).

[25] R. Wodak, "Entering the 'Post-shame era': The Rise of Illiberal Democracy, Populism and Neo-authoritarianism in Europe," *Global Discourse*, 9:1 (2019), p. 197.

[26] North Carolina has been a one-party state for most of the 20th century, so partisan constitutional chicanery cannot be surprising. C. Jarvis, "North Carolina Governor Signs Bill Limiting His Successor's Power," Governing (December 19, 2016), www .governing.com/topics/politics/tns-mccrory-cooper-bill.html.
  See further *Rucho* v. *Common Cause*, No. 18-422, 588 US ___ (2019), and Chapter 7

them as the basis of hierarchies of states and respect and of structures of power."[27] Claims based on identity are increasingly considered the only legitimate and authentic claim.

Identity politics relies on the mobilization of concerns with the self, celebrating the satisfaction that comes from recognition for who one is and not for what one does. Self-evaluation depends on the social evaluation of the group to which a person belongs. Some previously self-confident groups feel that their privileged, or at least protected, status is under threat and that they are being abandoned by the political elite. These cultural developments frustrate majorities (or relative majorities or important voting blocs), especially where material conditions become less comforting. The beneficiaries of the "old" status quo, and particularly those whose main source of social advantage was that they belonged to the majority, feel increasingly insecure and frustrated. For many people in certain contemporary cultures, some sources of self-esteem and pride that were previously taken for granted no longer exist, including heroic national history and Christian (traditional) values.

Those who voted for Fidesz or PiS (and continue to vote for them) and the voters of other populists are not necessarily "left behind" in the economic sense but are "left out" and "left behind" culturally, feeling that their traditional (strongly nationalist) values and related ways of life are threatened, while "alien life forms," they feel, have been promoted or tolerated by prepopulist governments.[28] The complaint is that "unusual" others threaten the majority's way of life (or that of the group that claims privilege), and the identity that had been uncontested and taken for granted loses recognition (among other reasons, because other identities are treated as equal). Insufficient respect for the old dominant identity was (and remains) a major factor leading to populist victories in Europe

---

[27] K. A. Appiah, *The Lies that Bind: Rethinking Identity* (Liveright Publishing Corporation, 2018), pp. 10–11. See further M. Lilla, *The Once and Future Liberal: After Identity Politics* (Harper, 2017).

Note that defense of Poland's unbound sovereignty against a multicultural Europe is justified by the need to protect Polish identity. "If you don't have a strong identity, you can really do anything with society. And we must defend our sovereignty ... not to fall into this vortex." "Kaczyński: mamy do czynienia z buntem, mamy rebelię," Tvn24 (June 4, 2016), www.tvn24.pl/polska/zjazd-okregowy-pis-w-warszawie-przemowienie-jaroslawa-Kaczyńskiego-ra649572-3186955.

[28] Sociodemographic indicators in Hungary "predict receptivity to populism poorly," while "identity-based fears and nationalist sentiments" have a stronger explanatory power for the success of populism (in the post-2010 period). P. Krekó and C. Molnár et al., *Beyond Populism. Tribalism in Poland and Hungary* (Political Capital Institute, 2018).

and elsewhere (the United States), and it remains formative for the political and constitutional arrangements of illiberal democracy. (Arguably, resentment of the socially and culturally excluded in Latin America has had similar consequences.)

The *ressentiment* of those who feel left behind serves as the breeding ground of populism, channeling their emerging frustration and rage.[29] Populist movements have mobilized such groups, capitalizing on their fears and their perceived loss of identity and social status. Those who feel left behind believe that other, relatively successful, identity groups have improved standing at the former's expense. They feel that the hegemony of their world, for many their only source of pride and social advantage, is increasingly endangered. The welfare services needed for new identity groups (like migrants and refugees) threaten the less well-to-do who had been the previous beneficiaries. They fear that their benefits will diminish as a result (e.g. when the children of minorities attend the schools of "ordinary" citizens). To what extent these concerns are based on facts is irrelevant: the populists (as well as extreme and mainstream political parties and cultural entrepreneurs) successfully instill and reinforce such sentiments.

The competitors of the putative losers have been minorities or otherwise disempowered groups of individuals. As minorities, they have had few chances to receive political recognition (and a resulting protection of their interests) in a traditional majoritarian representative democracy. Their (often successful) strategy has been to incorporate direct identity recognition into special protective laws that prove they deserve to be victims of social (majoritarian) injustice. Recall that "being a victim" has become a winning claim in the culture of competing vulnerabilities.[30] This success threatened the putative losers who quickly adopted the strategy of their competitors and turned their resentment into another demand of victim-identity recognition. This was a claim of re-recognition, a return to the "normal" order of things. The populist (and extreme left and right) strategy mobilized the resentment that results

---

[29] Resentment lies at the heart of populism. Its cultivation helps the leader to maintain his legitimacy and popularity. Often, resentment originates in genuine injustice or social exclusion. Since 1945, in many instances in Latin America "widespread injustice and the absence of the rule of law ... were the necessary conditions for successful populist movements to emerge." K. A. Hawkins, *Venezuela's Chavismo and Populism in Comparative Perspective* (Cambridge University Press, 2010), p. 233.

[30] Even majorities present themselves as victims. See the use of the victim narrative by the Christian Right.

from victim status. Underlying the complaint of all victims has been a strong antiliberal bias: according their complaint the pseudoneutrality and individualism of the liberal constitutional order dismissed their specific identities.

Identity-based resentment politics has important consequences for democratic legitimacy. Politics within the traditional constitutional frame does not offer sufficient answers to resentment claims. Many[31] among the politically dissatisfied feel that they are left behind by the political system, which promises equal representation for all citizens. They consider politicians to be nonresponsive, corrupt, and sympathetic to minorities and foreign international forces. The litany of dissatisfaction reads like a script from Carl Schmitt.[32] Sensing this alienation, populist movements have attacked the idea of representative government as nonfunctional and elitist, doing so in the name of real democracy of the people. This decisive element in populism will determine future constitutional structures. (Forms of representative democracy survived, but under the tutelage of the plebiscitarian leader.) Concentrated power

---

[31] However, the "left behind" explanation of the success of populism is one sided. Maciej Gdula has concluded that PiS supporters are neither left behind nor frustrated; they simply find pride in the nationalist program offered. M. Gdula, K. Dębska and K. Trepka, *Dobra Zmiana w Miastku. Neoautorytaryzm w Polskiej Polityce z Perspektywy Małego Miasta* (Instytut Studiów Zaawansowanych, Warszawa, 2017); M. Gdula, *Nowy autorytaryzm* (Krytyki Politycznej, 2018).

A survey of party preferences in Hungary in the 2002–12 period indicated that political polarization was primarily ideological. Z. Enyedi, Z. Fábián and R. Tardos, *Pártok és Szavazók 2002–2014*, Társadalmi Riport (2014). After seven years of Fidesz rule, identity concerns continued to hold greater importance than the presumed economic situation. While Fidesz is most popular among low-income groups (who are more likely to be "left behinds"), it remains the party of the satisfied. Sixty-eight percent of Fidesz voters are described as "satisfied rightists" – they trust their future and are satisfied with the current democratic system. M. Gerő and A. Szabó, "A Társadalom Politikai Integrációja. A Politikai Értékcsoportok," in I. Kovách (ed.), *Társadalmi Integráció. Az Egyenlőtlenségek, az Együttműködés, az Újraelosztás és a Hatalom Szerkezete a Magyar Társadalomban* (Belvedere Meridionale Kiadó, 2017).

In Italy, when Cinque Stelle was at the zenith of its popularity (2017), there was low support among the more vulnerable (those over 65 years old). "Sondaggio, M5s 'partito pigliatutti': piace agli elettori di sinistra come ai leghisti, a operai e imprenditori," Il Fatto Quotidiano (April 10, 2017), www.ilfattoquotidiano.it/2017/04/10/sondaggio-m5s-partito-pigliatutti-piace-agli-elettori-di-sinistra-come-ai-leghisti-a-operai-e-imprenditori/3512273. When Lega Nord was at the zenith of its popularity and still in government in the spring of 2019, it gained support from state employees (the least vulnerable group in Italy), even in the South. G. Macchi, "Più della metà degli elettori della Lega non va oltre la licenza media: i dati," TPI.it (May 23, 2019), www.tpi.it/politica/chi-vota-lega-e-salvini-dati-20190523322545.

[32] C. Schmitt, *The Crisis of Parliamentary Democracy* (MIT Press, 1985).

through the state, which is the dream of all populist leaders (with or without a sense of a higher mission) cannot be but plebiscitarian, given the premise, or, in other words, democracy. The commitment to democracy makes the difference between populism in power and fascism, whichever way democracy is used. The difference is between respectful abuse and hateful denial. Even if the populist leaders were neo-Bolsheviks,[33] they become leaders of authoritarian regimes *only* when forced to be authoritarian, when democracy betrays them.

Citizens in democracies are told that they are equal politically and in dignity. Populist citizens derive both their self-confidence and their frustration from this encouraging news. Their frustration will increase when they are faced with the reality that they are not equal in terms of political influence. This equality of influence is attractive to voters, especially where the demagogue fills this void with conviction, building nationalist pride and fear of difference. Armed with the moral indignation that results from the humiliation of inequality in influence in a world that promised "one person, one vote," populism as a democracy booster promises to undo this disparity. This is what keeps populism morally alive. In this perspective, the people emerges not simply as the opposite of a corrupt elite but as the only theoretical possibility of equal influence: the people is the theoretical assumption that all have equal political influence. "Everybody's views shall count equally!" Thus, the voice of the people's representatives and experts shall not be privileged: legitimate authorization (mandate) or knowledge does not justify privilege in decision-making.

If all views are equal, there can be no better argument and no compromise to reach an optimal solution, which is the negation of democracy as a form of superior decision-making. Information-based deliberation becomes suspect or irrelevant at best. Instead, there is a willingness to impose a value-laden social vision that is at least supported or willed by the authentic people. "The more exalted or limitless the constitutive aspirations, the more vulnerable are institutionalized, structural limits on power."[34] Constitutional aspirationalism, the imposition of a specific social or economic arrangement,[35] or way of life, as the mandatory result

---

[33] A. Applebaum, "100 years later, Bolshevism is back. And we should be worried," *The Washington Post* (November 6, 2017), www.washingtonpost.com/opinions/global-opin ions/bolshevism-then-and-now/2017/11/06/830aecaa-bf41-11e7-959c-fe2b598d8c00_s tory.html.

[34] G. Walker, "The Idea of Nonliberal Constitutionalism," *Nomos*, 39 (1997), p. 168.

[35] Not all social arrangements are aspirational. A set of constitutional rules abolishing the caste system are simply guarantees to maintain the neutral status of equality.

(an enemy per se of liberal neutral constitutionalism) characterizes most illiberal democracies of populist origin, except perhaps in Hungary, where even nationalism is pragmatic. Aspirationalism, unleashed as majority will (or better, the will of the true people), unleashes the totalitarian in democracy. This result is demonstrated in the creation of "LGBT-[ideology]-free zones" declared by majority vote in Polish municipalities.[36]

Identity politics results in appeals to tribal togetherness. Where politics is understood as a tribal conflict, social issues cannot be construed in a way where commonalities can be found or developed.[37] This is not a populist invention, but populists have been successful in imposing their own patterns of identity discourse on others. Here the sovereign and authentic people stands against the elite (a bunch of traitors). There is nothing to discuss: for in a policy that flows from identity, there is nothing to concede (fortunately, the identity hides some flexibility). An identity group will first police the identity of their peers within their identity community; subsequently, especially once in power, it will render this "service" for (or against) outsiders.

This kind of discourse without dialogue conquers the public space. In Poland and Hungary, both the government and opposition parties use the same antagonistic cognitive frames, and in the Netherlands, Prime Minister Rutte won re-election after he absorbed part of the populist's antimigrant rhetoric.[38] Once both the relative majorities and minorities conclude that they are the victims in a political system that does not recognize them properly or provide representation, the pressure grows to replace liberal (individualist) majoritarian representative democracy

---

[36] Such municipal resolutions were found discriminatory by a first instance court in 2020.

[37] In Poland and Hungary, the host ideology of the populist forces was ethnonationalist. Democratic backsliding may, however, rely on other host ideologies: in the Czech Republic, Babiš used a technocratic discourse. However, it did not prevent him from attacking "the corrupt elites" and constantly promising protection against migrants. S. Hanley and M. A. Vachudova, "Understanding the Illiberal turn: Democratic Backsliding in the Czech Republic," *East European Politics*, 34:3 (2018), pp. 276–96.

[38] "[O]n election night [of the 2017 elections] Rutte declared in his victory speech that the Netherlands had put a halt to 'the wrong kind of populism', implying that there is a good kind of populism." C. Mudde, "'Good' populism beat 'bad' in Dutch election,": *The Guardian* (March 19, 2017), www.theguardian.com/world/2017/mar/19/dutch-election-rutte-wilders-good-populism-bad. Rutte ran on a program that promised the defense of Christian traditions; compare with the HPM's defense of "our Christian roots."

On the serious impact of populism on Western European "mainstream" parties see M. Rooduijn, S. L. De Lange and W. Van der Brug, "A populist Zeitgeist? Programmatic Contagion by Populist Parties in Western Europe," *Party politics*, 20:4 (2014), pp. 563–75.

with identity group representation, a position that is[39] increasingly endorsed by traditional (establishment) parties and governments. Certain identity-based ideas of democracy clearly conflict with the assumptions prevailing in liberal constitutionalism. Group identity demands require a kind of identity-estate representation, an understanding of the democratic political organization that runs contrary to the individualism, equality, and universalism of liberal constitutional democracy. Singapore's electoral system demonstrates how the constitutionally guaranteed representation of ethnic minorities contributes to the discipline of parliamentary opposition and the ruling party's perpetuation of power.[40] This seems irrelevant for the European countries[41] under populist rule. The identitarian (relative) majority claims exclusive identity representation, asserting that before the right-wing populist came to power, the nation, the majority, and the authentic people were not represented.

The plebiscitarian constitutional "theory," with its abstraction of an authentic people, reproduces the position of its identitarian competitors: democracy must represent group identity. In the populist vision, adopted in plebiscitarian regimes, only one group will be represented, namely the authentic people. And only one politically relevant identity (that of the true people, whatever that may mean at any given moment) is automatically represented by the charismatic leader. It is the culmination and logical conclusion of identity politics that hollers for total recognition without compromise. The dictates of the only correct, genuine identity should be imposed on all of society; but given the pragmatic, even opportunistic, nature of illiberal democracies and the external constraints, the leader is satisfied with the hegemony of the preferred identity.[42] The identity of the authentic people is

---

[39] Various forms of corporativism were part of the constitutional reality in a number of democracies (see in particular Austria and the Netherlands), although these were always strange bedfellows.

[40] There should be a minority candidate in all competing teams in the "group representation constituencies," with the candidates properly pre-selected. L.-A. Thio, "The Passage of a Generation: Revisiting the Report of the 1966 Constitutional Commission," in L.-A. Thio and K. Y. L. Tan (eds.), *Evolution of a Revolution: Forty Years of the Singapore Constitution* (Routledge, 2009), pp. 36–37.

[41] It did result in the constitutionalization of identity group representation in Bolivia.

[42] Obviously, such absolutism is not part of all identity-based political programs. A level of diversity can be built into individualistic liberal constitutionalism. It is also possible that a society will choose a constitutional system that stands for diversity; it can be argued that such a system will be both constitutional and at least minimally liberal, with guarantees for individual autonomy (within the person's group).

protected in a way that excludes the relevance of its competitors (e.g. migrants and cosmopolitan elites). Successful European populists could rely here on a right-wing tradition that has claimed a monopoly over the imagined community of the entire nation.

It is unlikely that a liberal democracy of autonomous individuals will remain attractive where the name of the game is competitive victimhood.[43] In victimhood competitions, all groups and individuals claim they are more disadvantaged than others due to some past injustice, with the prize-winning victim group deserving special treatment.

A quarter of century ago, Hobsbawm identified the features that hamper the combination of identitarianism (and hence its monopolist version, populism) and constitutional democracy:

> [C]ollective identities are defined negatively; that is to say against others. "We" recognize ourselves as "us" because we are different from "Them." If there were no "They" from whom we are different, we wouldn't have to ask ourselves who "We" were. Without Outsiders there are no Insiders. In other words, collective identities are based not on what their members have in common – they may have very little in common except not being the "Others." . . . In short, exclusive identity politics do not come naturally to people. It is more likely to be forced upon them from outside.[44]

Identity politics denies (or renders irrelevant) common universal values; it creates and sustains an antagonistic divide by the "us versus them" frame of the political world and forces individuals to make exclusive identity choices. In the illiberal democracy, one is either part of the authentic people or is nobody. This is exactly what one gets back after the populist takeover: a shallow communitarianism and mockery of universalism (which was first attacked as an imposition on other cultures [neocolonialism] – see the assault on human rights, Chapter 6) and an oppressive dismissal of identitarian diversity.

The logic of the culture of identitarianism runs fundamentally against the assumptions of *liberal* constitutionalism: identitarians are *essentialists*. They can stand for freedom but not for freedom for all. They champion the freedom of *their group*, and yet often attack liberal constitutionalism for being *individuum*-centered (see the HPM on human rights in Chapter 6). This is how the inheritance of identitarianism

---

[43] "[R]oughly two-thirds (66 percent) of white working-class Americans agree that discrimination against whites is as big a problem today as discrimination against blacks and other minorities." R. P. Jones, B. Cooper, D. Cox et al., *How Immigration and Concerns about Cultural Change Are Shaping the 2016 Election*, PRRI/Brookings Survey (PRRI, 2016).

[44] E. Hobsbawm, "Identity Politics and the Left," *New Left Review*, I:217 (1996), p. 41.

influences the spirit of the constitution, which can develop into illiberal democracy.

Beyond the incompatibility of an equality-based democracy with the illiberal state's identity monopoly, populist identitarianism further runs contrary to another element of constitutional democracy, namely the rationality assumption of democratic political decision-making. Once populism has gained control over state power, it continues to attack the already undermined rationality that is the precondition of democratic politics and liberal constitutionalism.

Populism is a revolt of the masses against what Burke calls "all the solemn plausibilities of the world,"[45] like "rank, office and title." Identity concerns define the new common sense, with important cognitive consequences. Identity determines how information is evaluated. Fake news does not alone distort contemporary understanding of the world and public discourse. Even true or likely correct information will become "fake" if it does not conform to the dictates of identity or reinforce the self, increasing self-esteem. Information that hurts cannot be true, and if true, it cannot be relevant. The oversensitive (and increasingly narcissistic)[46] identity will reject evidence-based information as fake, merely because it is unpleasant or challenges the tenets of identity. Any information on the past historical misdeeds of a nation (e.g. an official genocidal policy) will be rejected as fake and considered an intentional attack on the group and its personal identity (as elevated to law in Poland[47] and in the Preamble of the HFL). Facts that do not fit into this self-representation will be rebuffed even at the peril of personal

---

[45] H. Arendt, *The Origins of Totalitarianism* (Houghton Mifflin, 1994), pp. 352–53.

[46] J. M. Twenge, *Generation me: Why Today's Young Americans are more Confident, Assertive, Entitled – and more Miserable than ever Before* (Free Press, 2006). On the increase on narcissism in America see J. M. Twenge and J. D. Foster, "Birth Cohort Increases in Narcissistic Personality Traits Among American College Students, 1982–2009," *Social Psychological and Personality Science*, 1:1 (2010), pp. 99–106.

[47] The Polish government and many Polish people are rightly outraged at talk of "Polish death camps." Polish people had little to do with them, except that they were the first martyrs in Auschwitz. Only turning this concern into a matter of criminal law is where authoritarianism appears. (See the Amendment to the Act on the Institute of National Remembrance, 2018.) An earlier PiS law protecting the honor of the Nation was declared unconstitutional in 2008 (TK judgment of 8 September 2008, Case no. K 5/07) but only on strictly procedural grounds. A. Gliszczynska-Grabias and A. Sledzinska-Simon, "Victimhood of the Nation as a Legally Protected Value in Transitional States – Poland as a Case Study," *SSRN* (2018); J. Hackmann, "Defending the 'Good Name' of the Polish Nation: Politics of History as a Battlefield in Poland, 2015–18," *Journal of Genocide Research*, 20:4 (2018), pp. 587–606. After a few months of turmoil, the "crime of Polish co-responsibility for the Nazi crimes" was replaced with a civil cause of action.

interest. "Where you stand on COVID-19 depends not on facts but on whether you see yourself as red or blue, and the desire to be part of that identity overrides even personal self-interest in health or safety."[48] Democracy as a decision-making and leader-selection mechanism assumes that collective choices are the outcome of a relatively reasonable discourse where facts matter. A democratic society can exist only where, as a minimum, all individuals are intellectually capable and free to participate in forming the public opinion that influences public policy. The assumption is that public debate will contribute (or even lead) to rational discourse and rational outcomes. This assumption may not be sustainable due to the fragmentation of opinion formation in the modern world of social media, with its echo chambers, polarization, and attractive irrationality.

This assault on rational discourse is aggravated when a non-neutral government, interested in power perpetuation, obtains monopolistic control over the media and uses it to promote its (often irrational) propaganda, economical with the truth. Identity cults and culture, and related identity politics, render the rationality assumption even less sustainable. It is hard to have genuine democracy (with or without free and fair elections) when the core issue is who is a good Hungarian or a good Pole.

Tolerance, a crucial assumption of constitutionalism, falls as another victim of identity politics. The authoritarianism mobilized by government-induced fear pushes the constitutional structure toward xenophobia. Right-wing populists construe migration and migrants as a threat to the identity (way of life) of an imagined majority. This becomes the center of their campaigns and policies (once in power),[49] and other parties follow suit. This can have constitutional consequences: the HFL, for example, was amended to enhance the protection of constitutional identity by prohibiting the "settlement of aliens."[50]

---

[48] F. Fukuyama, "The Wages of American Political Decay," The American Interest (May 4, 2020), www.the-american-interest.com/2020/05/04/the-wages-of-american-political-decay.

[49] C. de Vries and I. Hoffman, Fear not Values. Public Opinion and the Populist vote in Europe (Eupinions, 2016).

[50] This was possible and welcomed due to existing authoritarianism within the population. The rate of xenophobes (i.e. those who would not allow any refugees to enter Hungary) was 60 percent in November 2017, compared to 39 percent in 2014, before the 2015 refugee crisis and the related governmental hate propaganda. According to results from the European Social Survey Round 8, 48 percent of Hungarian people would not allow anyone of a different race/ethnic group to live in Hungary, and 62 percent would not allow anyone from poorer countries outside of Europe to settle there. See B. Hunyadi,

Identity politics generates claims about forms of life that are hard to reconcile. Identity claims are often based on the assumption that common values are only impositions of the values of the majority and not minimal conditions of living together.[51] This kind of suspicion increasingly denies the possibility of universal norms: each identity becomes a law unto itself. The credo of identity politicians and their followers asserts: "We want a political life ... that fully answers our deepest longings."[52] This is certainly single-minded in a complex world – but this is what "common sense" has come to mean.[53]

5.3 Majoritarianism, Anti-institutionalism, and Instrumentalism

5.3.1 How Populism in Power Tries to Solve the Problem of Democracy

The emerging plebiscitarian regime's primary constitutional goal is self-preservation: the preservation of the state for the ruler.[54] However, the original populist attitudes shape plebiscitarian democracy: power serves first and foremost to preserve itself, but to the extent possible, in the form of a plebiscitarian constitutional system.

For this kind of plebiscitarian arrangement, democracy carries certain specificities:

- Those who are not with us are against us: therefore, democracy is not about rational compromise but the uninhibited will of the majority.
- The constitutional subject (the source of power) is the homogeneous people (often understood in ethnic terms with special cultural markers).

C. Molnár, and V. Wessenauer, *Committed to Rights, but Longing for Stability. Hungarians' Attitudes to an Open Society*, Voices on Values Report (Open Society European Policy Institute, 2019).

[51] "Living together" is used in a neutral sense, not in the French sense, which refers to a value-laden way of life, as in the case of the burqa prohibition.

[52] P. Simpson, *Political Illiberalism: A Defense of Freedom* (Transaction Books, 2015), pp. 67–68. From this position Simpson concludes that illiberalism (in his case, religious) is appropriate, requiring the state to suppress rival religions. Ibid., p. 103.

[53] Note that authoritarians are "simple-minded avoiders of complexity." K. Stenner and J. Haidt, "Authoritarianism is not a Momentary Madness, but an Eternal Dynamic within Liberal Democracies," in C. R. Sunstein (ed.), *Can It Happen Here?: Authoritarianism in America* (Harper-Collins, 2018), p. 183.

[54] K. L. Scheppele, "The Opportunism of Populists and the Defense of Constitutional Liberalism," *German Law Journal*, 20:3 (2019), pp. 314–31. "In Orbán's world, power is all that matters." Ibid., p. 329.

- The constitutional order is understood within a relation of "the authentic people against an elite enemy," where the political opposition is the enemy of the people.[55]

These constitutional assumptions have practical consequences: in Hungary, the regime-serving constitutional institutions receive particular protection: laws can be amended only with a supermajority and leaders of independent agencies enjoy extended mandates. Limiting the possibility of an ordinary majority offers safeguards against the enemy (i.e. the opposition) regaining power. (However, the single-chamber Hungarian Parliament has constitutionally required a qualified majority in a number of legislative subject matters, even beyond fundamental rights.)

In a democracy people either decide (govern) themselves or authorize a government to rule. Populism advocates for the former, but once the populist leader controls his government, the logic of centralized personal power no longer allows government by the people. Technically, the much-maligned representative democracy remains in place, serving as the façade of plebiscitarian acclamation. (Parliamentary election is a matter of acclamation: elections provide an opportunity to express trust and devotion to the leader.)

For democratic constitutions, the people is sovereign and the ultimate source of power. The guiding principle is popular supremacy – and the populists cannot agree more. Or perhaps they will agree even more than fully: the "people's will" is supreme *at every moment*, not just at constitution making. The "people's will" is always available as majority will. This corresponds to popular expectations: according to two-thirds of Hungarian and Polish people, the will of the people should be the highest principle in their country.[56] This is reflected in the thinking of the PLD leaders. As Lech Kaczyński has stated: "In a democracy, the sovereign is the people, their representative parliament and, in the Polish case, the elected president. If we are to have a democratic state of law, no state authority, including the PCT, can disregard legislation."[57] In the populist

---

[55] Singapore, where the regime is not a populist creature, prefers to co-opt the opposition.
[56] Krekó and Molnár et al., *Beyond Populism*, p. 22.
[57] "Kaczyński: mamy do czynienia z buntem, mamy rebelię," Tvn24 (June 4, 2016), www .tvn24.pl/wiadomosci-z-kraju,3/zjazd-okregowy-pis-w-warszawie-przemowienie-jaro slawa-Kaczyńskiego,649572.html. Quoted after C. Davies, "Hostile Takeover: How Law and Justice Captured Poland's Courts," Freedom House, www.freedomhouse.org/report/ special-reports/hostile-takeover-how-law-and-justice-captured-poland-s-court s#_edn17. The ambiguity remains: Kaczyński did not say that people's sovereign will is above the constitution.

ideal, the constitution is supreme only in a formal sense: the people can
change at any moment at will, or strategically bypass if formal amendment is not possible. The unlimited power of the people as majority is
evident from the history of power aggrandizement. The first populist
leader in power, US President Jackson, declared in his 1829 State of the
Union Address that "[t]he first principle of our system" is "that the
majority is to govern."[58] Majoritarianism provides a theory of the constitution that grants unfettered powers to the people.

The overwhelming majority of illiberal democracies originate in some
kind of populism. The arising political structure responds to the forces that
animate populists. These forces and their expectations will shape the constitution in an illiberal and popular way; this is what the emerging plebiscitarian constitutional practice will undoubtably reflect. Illiberal regimes, while
following the populist path of plebiscitarianism, serve patronage-based
domination. This will determine their instrumental relationship to their
own law. The anticonstitutional instrumentalism (opportunism), and the
constant need to cheat, originates from the needs of this domination.

State power means the capacity to compel government bureaucrats and
citizens to act according to the wishes of those who control (dominate) the
state, even against their interests. The law of illiberal democracy creates and
endorses such state power. The influence of the belief in the legitimacy of
power (legality) is considerable in legalistic cultures (such as Central
Europe) but cannot explain on its own the popular acceptance that is needed
for effective state power. The role of law and constitutional institutions in
the emerging domination calls for reviewing the social factors that enable
the success of these kinds of legal arrangements. For example, if authoritarianism as a psychological trait and a cultural pattern is widespread in society,
it will facilitate the acceptance and endorsement of authoritarian legal
solutions. This seems to be the case in most illiberal democracies (and it is
unknown to what extent a similar disposition awaits in other countries).

5.3.2   Instrumentalism

Illiberal democracy takes an instrumental attitude to constitutional
institutions.[59] Amendments to the constitution take place according to
the momentary interests of the political power, like in any democracy

---

[58] A. Jackson, "First Annual Message to Congress (Dec. 8, 1829)," in J. Richardson (ed.),
Messages and Papers of the Presidents, 1789–1897 (Authority of Congress, 1896) p. 448.
[59] C. Mudde, *Are Populists Friends or Foes of Constitutionalism?* (The Foundation for Law,
Justice and Society, 2013).

where the constitution has no cumbersome amendment rules. The ultimate attachment to the spirit of the constitution, the idea of respecting an unamendable core, is missing. Some amendments are technical, others simply defiant acts by the majority to show the unruly judiciary that popular will stands above judicial pettiness: the will of the people ranks higher than constitutional obscurities. In this spirit the Singapore Constitution was amended in response to a High Court order indicating that the courts should apply the RoL even when detention occurs under the Security Act. Likewise, the HFL was amended without hesitation every time a stubbornly resilient political institution or social group seriously defied the regime of the HFL – by applying its provisions which have not foreseen a future complication, embarassing the governing power. In Venezuela, Chávez, and later Maduro, used constitution-making to employ extraordinary powers in order to paralyze the National Assembly.

There is no commitment to underlying principles; appearances matter, not authenticity. Hence the inevitable duplicity and deceit in the constitutional and legal system of illiberal democracy. Legal forms are sustained but only with the intent to cheat. Like in a marriage where the stronger partner continually cheats on the other or marital rape is common; nevertheless, the couple claims that this is a respectable, sacred union. The honestly held, underlying and observed constitutional (i.e. constituent) principle is that institutions and individuals shall accept the ruler's leadership, including the extension of his power, because that is what the majority requires for the greater good of the nation. Any such principles are certainly not liberal.

Given the populist commitment to simple, pragmatic answers, the "instrumental attitude towards the constitution"[60] is not surprising. The constitution is not an entrenched, higher order law but a practical tool to solve emerging conflicts in an illiberal and nondemocratic way (imposing arbitrary will as supreme command). Consider for example Singapore, where in 1965 (two years after secession), the entrenchment of the amendment rule was repealed.[61] The formal centrality of the

---

[60] Venice Commission Opinion no. 720/2013 on the Fourth Amendment to the Fundamental Law of Hungary (Venice, 17 June 2013), pp. 18 and 30.

[61] Since 1979, a two-third's majority is again needed to amend the Singapore Constitution. Perhaps a permanent constituent majority (popular or parliamentary) is the quintessential precondition of a consolidated illiberal democracy (see Chávez [most of the time], Orbán, Lee Kuan Yew, Putin; contrast with PiS). But note that "If the PAP's seats in Parliament [in Singapore] more closely tracked their share of the popular vote, then they would not have been able to pass constitutional amendments on a straight party vote in five of the eleven Parliaments that have formed since the first General Election."

Parliament and the resulting lack of checks and balances, with de facto supremacy of the executive, prompted Harding to conclude that "The [Singapore] Constitution is not the grundnorm. The grundnorm is the supremacy of the legislature."[62] (At least in the formal sense.)

In countries where illiberal democracy has sprung from the victory of populist movements, the new leader faces a fundamental constitutional dilemma. He led an antiestablishment movement that relied on the people. This was a visible people who emerged both loudly and physically in mass demonstrations as well as virtually as popular opposition on the internet. The people was a nonnegligible reality. "In Hungary, the blocked political system . . ., in which the holders of power disregard or disdain popular aspirations, has turned the street into a political institution."[63] The plebiscitarian leader carries in his baggage a deep-seated popular ambivalence vis-a-vis constitutional arrangements, particularly those noninstitutional elements that are beyond his majoritarian-legislative control, like the culture of the RoL.

Populism stands for simplicity and directness. According to its own mantra, the "common man" abhors complexity and abstraction. "Right thinking people demand straight answers." This is echoed in the populist predilection for majoritarianism, which abhors entrenched and unamendable constitutional provisions. Majoritarianism breeds anticonstitutional instrumentalism: the constitution does not exist to limit legislation but acts merely as a source of authorization for it. Instrumentalism excludes respect for the underlying values of constitutionalism. "[A] legal order with a living constitution that promptly adapts to the changing orientation of the majority of citizens is no different from a polity with no constitution at all. Populism leads to an implicit *deconstitutionalization* of our democratic polities."[64]

The constitution serves local needs (later embellished by the Asian values doctrine), not abstract foreign doctrines. At least, this is what Lee Kuan Yew loved to emphasize whenever he felt the need to justify departure from what seemed to be acceptable constitutional wisdom on

G. Silverstein, "Singapore's Constitutionalism: A Model, But of What Sort?," *Cornell Law Review*, 100 (2015), p. 21.

[62] A. Harding, "Parliament and the Grundnorm in Singapore," *Malayan Law Review*, XXV (1983), p. 366. Today it seems that the prevailing doctrine in Singapore claims the supremacy of the Constitution.

[63] G. Schöpflin, "Democracy, populism, and the political crisis in Hungary. A response to Thomas von Ahn," *Eurozine* (May, 2007), http://www.eurozine.com/democracy-populism-and-the-political-crisis-in-hungary.

[64] Ferrara, "Can Political Liberalism Help Us?" p. 469.

checks and balances and fundamental rights. If the constitution is local and corresponds to local preferences, international standards – with their universalist flair – are allegedly not applicable, at least not without considerable flexibility.

The populist suspicion against checks and balances, relying on the actual shortcomings of and frustration with parliamentary ("failed representative") government, has led to the acceptance of plebiscitarianism, a permanent popular supremacy acting through the leader as the embodiment of his people (see Chapter 4). In the plebiscitarian democracy (in contrast to RoL-governed representative government), the legitimacy and charisma of the ruler depends on continuous, demonstrable popular support expressed in various forms (not necessarily via referenda, recall, and direct democracy). The need to prove perpetual popular support necessitates systematic constitutional chicanery.

5.4 From Separation of Powers to Executive Domination

The populist promise was that the people's victory would end the delegation of power to international and domestic nonmajoritarian, expert, and neutral institutions and would restore national sovereignty.[65] Chávez and his followers in Latin America were clearly against liberal constitutionalism (a tool of the oligarchy) and intended to create a "postliberal" constitution.[66] Where legally possible, and with sufficient political support, the new populist governments ventured into constitution-making immediately following their electoral victory. A new constitution signals a break with the previous corrupt regime. It offers a strategic advantage as well: the transition facilitates the preconditioned institutional restructuring that allows the new leader to gain total control over the state.

Certainly, the new constitutions differ from their predecessors, especially linguistically. The preambles are full of references to glorious history, community, and national honor, all this with new ideological priorities.[67] Further, some Latin American populist constitutions reinforced

---

[65] See W. Streeck, *How Will Capitalism End? Essays on a Failing System* (Verso, 2016), chap. 2.

[66] C. de la Torre, *Populist Seduction in Latin America* (Ohio University Press, 2010).

[67] See also the Irish Constitution of 1937, "a combination of nationalist aspirations and a religious ... ethos." A. Kavanagh, "The Irish Constitution at 75 years: Natural law, Christian Values and the Ideal of Justice," *Irish Jurist*, 48 (2012), p. 71.

superpresidentialism.[68] Novel popular institutions ("branches of power") are invented, capable of blocking the autonomy of other, more traditional constitutional branches (legislation, judiciary).

The Venice Commission has argued that "a new, self-serving constitution was passed in 2011 by the Fidesz-dominated parliament, which included extensive supermajority requirements and created a power for establishing autonomous bodies that could 'curtail the parliament's powers.'"[69] True, these features did contribute to power maximization in the specific context, but they are innocuous, even laudable, constitutional instruments in a single chamber system. Supermajority requirements had been part of the existing Constitution and for good reason in the single-chamber Parliament, as it pushed for consensus in a political system where a minority of the popular vote could be transformed into a comfortable parliamentary majority. The mere fact that neutral institutions can curtail the Parliament's profligate powers is not in itself detrimental to checks and balances.[70] There is relatively little at the level of separation of powers that would depart from the constitutional traditions of the country concerned.[71] Neither the rewritten nor the newborn constitutions are antidemocratic, nor spectacularly illiberal. What makes them noteworthy is how they demonstrate palpable interest in a plebiscitarian leader at the head of the executive.[72]

Both presidentialism and parliamentarism are capable of accommodating the personalization of power, a crucial matter for plebiscitarian systems where the regime's legitimacy depends on the charisma of the

[68] The 1949 amendment of the Argentinean Constitution extended Perón's presidential powers, including the power to veto laws and declare a state of siege. In turn, parliamentary control over the Executive was reduced.

[69] Grzymala-Busse, "How Populists Rule," p. 712. The above conclusions are based on the presentation made by K. Scheppele.

[70] As it happens, populists are outraged by the power of such unelected institutions restricting popular power. It is one of the most disliked elements of the constitutional structure.

[71] Existing democratic forms of government structures can serve illiberalism very well. Under the uncontested rule of Chief Minister Lee Kuan Yew, Singapore remained a parliamentary system with a standard list of fundamental rights where law and order relied on emergency powers. Singapore offers a semblance of constitutionality resulting in proud illiberalism with its constitutional reference to social harmony, a major ground for rights restriction. See *Shared Values*, adopted by the Singapore Parliament on 15 January 1991: "1) Nation before community and society above self, 2) Family as the basic unit of society, 3) Regard and community support for the individual, 4) Consensus instead of contention, and 5) Racial and religious harmony."

[72] For a contrary view, see T. Drinóczi and A. Bień-Kacała, "Illiberal Constitutionalism: The Case of Hungary and Poland," *German Law Journal*, 20:8 (2019), pp. 1140–166.

leader.[73] In Hungary, the HFL follows the previous parliamentary model influenced by German parliamentary democracy, although the HPM found it important to formalize the Prime Minister's commanding position in the cabinet,[74] allowing the government to become "the general organ of the executive branch" with a general authorization to act. The previous Constitution applied an enumerated powers solution.[75] However, in reality, the leader's power is "presidentialized" everywhere, even if he is not popularly elected.[76] In Italy, where populism was widespread even before populist parties came to power, this was elucidated by the 2005, and especially the 2016, failed constitutional reforms. In particular, Prime Minister Renzi revealed an initiative to enhance executive power with a popularly elected prime minister, an idea that was tested and failed in Israel. The entire constitutional referendum was presented as a vote of confidence in Renzi, leader-in-making. This first step toward a fully plebiscitarian regime failed when Renzi's charisma evaporated.[77] The much criticized 2017 amendments in Turkey offer another version of power grab through presidentialization. Technically, the amended Turkish system resembles semipresidentialism combined

---

[73] "Leader-centered state executives emerging in the Westminster systems" seem "analogous to monarch-courtier relations" where decision-making involves only a handful of key actors. J. Pakulski and A. Körösényi, *Toward Leader Democracy* (Anthem Press, 2012), p. 76, quoting D. J. Savoie, *Court Government and the Collapse of Accountability in Canada and the United Kingdom* (University of Toronto Press, 2008) p. 16.

[74] Article 18(1) HFL: "The Prime Minister shall define the general policy of the Government. (2) Ministers ... shall perform the tasks determined by the Government or the Prime Minister. (4) ... Ministers shall be accountable to the Prime Minister."

[75] Article 15(1) HFL.

[76] Centralization in Poland is realized at the level of the ruling party, which has a rather centralized structure. Recentralization had already begun in Poland in the 1990s. J. Regulska, "Decentralization or (Re)Centralization: Struggle for Political Power in Poland. Environment and Planning," *Government and Policy*, 15:2 (1997), pp. 187–207.

[77] The arguments for and against the reform were rather populist, such as the concern that the Senate was losing power and therefore checks and balances would not guarantee executive accountability, or that it was undemocratic not to have Senators elected. In a less critical reading, the efforts of Berlusconi and Renzi promised a reasonable solution to the weakness of the government, originating in the electorally inevitable coalition and the impossibility to control intraparty divisions (in the case of Renzi). See further P. Blokker, "Populism and Constitutional Reform. The Case of Italy," in G. Delledonne (et al.), *Italian Populism and Constitutional Law. Strategies, Conflicts and Dilemma* (Palgrave Macmillan, 2020).

Some elements of the Renzi project were resurrected thanks to the 2020 September referendum, seeking to reduce the size of Parliament and make it more efficient (i.e. more majoritarian).

with a mutual parliament/president veto. In the present situation it only enhances the autocratic use of presidential powers.[78]

Not unsurprisingly, populists clearly respect the pre-existing, standard constitutional forms. The "standardized design and vocabulary is perfectly capable to hide the political subtext, where this is advantageous and has the merit of traditional legitimacy that is due to the constitutional form."[79] That was exactly the case with the HFL, which satisfied the standards of the high-prestige expert group, the Venice Commission.[80] What the Venice Commission was not ready to discern at the time was that the forms hide "usurpation" (to use Benjamin Constant's classic expression): "Despotism banishes all forms of liberty; usurpation needs these forms in order to justify the overturning of what it replaces; but in appropriating them it profanes them."[81]

The illiberal constitutions are written in an "anti-Rawlsian" situation, behind a veil of omniscience. The seemingly neutral texts are calibrated first and foremost to protect the newly gained power. For example, the HFL's perfectly standard solutions guarantee the best possible self-protection for the regime to come.[82] The hand that was drawing the hand was the hand that was drawn. The Constitution provides the guidelines for the majority to determine the substance of the very institutions it has created.[83] Most importantly, what the hand drew intended

[78] The fact that Parliament can bring down the President at the cost of its own dissolution can be seen as a genuine element of checks and balances (or a destabilizing design in case of cohabitation). The President has original decree-making powers and is not limited to the faithful execution of the law. However, in principle, the Turkish Parliament can always overrule presidential decrees.

The constitutional solution is silent on the subconstitutional reality of the security state: the police have been equipped with heavy arms, and religious practices are now expected in the armed forces. H. Eissenstat, *Snapshot – Uneasy Rests the Crown: Erdoğan and "Revolutionary Security" in Turkey*, Project on Middle East Democracy (December 2017).

[79] G. Frankenberg, "Authoritarian Constitutionalism: Coming to Terms with Modernity's Nightmares," in H. A. García and G. Frankenberg, *Authoritarian Constitutionalism*, p. 26.

[80] Venice Commission Opinion no. 621/2011 on the New Constitution of Hungary, Venice, June 20, 2011, paras. 141–142.

[81] B. Constant, *Political Writings* (Cambridge University Press, 1993), p. 95.

[82] The HFL provides an extraordinarily long mandate to constitutional veto players (heads of prosecution, judicial administration, national audit, HCC) with a nine to twelve year mandate to guarantee the survival of the regime.

[83] For this reason the Constitutional Court of Columbia found unconstitutional an amendment that would have allowed the incumbent President to run for a third term: all differently staggered appointments would have been made by the President. The longer the mandate, the better the chances of power accumulation.

to facilitate permanent rule. Of course, constitutions are designed to be lasting and binding for future generations. But here, the constituent ruler with his entourage aspires to cross the gates of eternity using specifically designed constitutional institutions. In an alternative reading, this serves totalitarian democracy,[84] as proudly admitted by revolutionary populists: "Of course, we want to install . . . the true dictatorship of true democracy and the democracy is the dictatorship of everyone . . . to be installed forever."[85] Or, to quote the HPM in 2011: "I make no secret of the fact that [by using the two-thirds law] I would like to tie the hands of the next government. And not only the next one, but the next ten governments!"[86] The leader and his cronies will have too much to lose if the opposition comes to power; therefore, perpetuation of the leader's power is necessary and welcomed. Consequently, "the losers of today [do not] have a credible chance to reorganize and perhaps emerge as the winners of tomorrow."[87]

The maxim of liberal constitutional design is contained in the famous admonition: "All would be lost if the same man or the same body of principal men . . . exercised these three powers: that of the making the laws, that of executing public resolutions, and that of judging."[88] One cannot definitively say that separation of powers or checks and balances are not recognized in populist constitutions. For example, the 2017 Turkish amendments were developed partly in line with the US model, while the Venezuelan Constitution is explicit on the matter (Articles 136–139).[89] Likewise, according to its text, the HFL has enhanced the powers of Parliament and the autonomy of independent agencies.

---

[84] J. L. Talmon, *The Origins of Totalitarian Democracy* (W. W. Norton & Co, 1970). Rousseau would force all citizens to be part of the people to will the general will, while the leader of the illiberal democracy simply omits the hopeless, so that the remaining authentic people will be sufficient for the general will (which is formulated by the leader).

[85] Jorge Rodriguez, Vice President of Venezuela, January 2007, quoted in A. R. Brewer-Carías, *Dismantling Democracy in Venezuela. The Chávez Authoritarian Experiment* (Cambridge University Press, 2010), p. 25.

[86] Quoted in P. Lendvai, *Orbán: Hungary's Strongman* (Oxford University Press, 2018), p. 98.

[87] S. Issacharoff, *Fragile Democracies: Contested Power in the Era of Constitutional Courts* (Cambridge University Press, 2015), p. 270.

[88] Montesquieu, *The Spirit of Laws* (Cambridge University Press, 1989), p. 157.

[89] One could even argue that in Venezuela, checks and balances were maintained by strengthening the power of the National Assembly and enabling the possibility of a popular recall; however, in other respects, presidential powers were extended (longer term, delegated law-making power without limits, and exceptional dissolution power). On the reality see M. J. Garcia-Sierra, "The 'Enabling Law': The Demise of the Separation

The perpetuation of power presents special problems in presidential systems. In the original versions of the illiberal Latin American constitutions, strict term limits had conformed with both populist and constitutionalist logic.[90] After a few years in power, with new presidential elections approaching, leaders realize the necessity of "fine-tuning." The revolution must continue; government achievements must be preserved for the sake of the nation. Otherwise, the despised elites, the enemies of the people, will return to power to the detriment of the nation-people. Perpetuation of power is the militant democracy of the illiberal leader.[91] Setting the example for future generations of populists, Perón's Argentine constitutional amendment of 1949 permitted the immediate re-election of the President (justified with references to Hamilton's view in the *Federalist Papers!*).[92] Chávez, Moreno, and Erdoğan followed the example.

The texts of the new constitutions may have been comforting to a point but were certainly not keen on stopping the tacit collusion between branches (already a major concern for Madison). The formal powers of the emerging leader are not constitutionally enhanced. The

---

of Powers in Hugo Chávez's Venezuela," *University of Miami Inter-American Law Review*, 32:2 (2001), pp. 265–93; Brewer-Carías, *Dismantling Democracy in Venezuela*, p. 123; M. López and M.-L. E. Lander, "Participatory Democracy in Venezuela: Origins, Ideas, and Implementation," in D. Smilde and D. Hellinger (eds.), *Venezuela's Bolivarian Democracy: Participation, Politics and Culture under Chávez* (Duke University Press, 2011), p. 61.

[90] One of the most eloquent justifications of the *antiperpetuation principle* originates from a great constitutionalist who did everything to perpetuate his presidential powers. This is what Bolívar had to say in his Address at the Congress of Angostura (1819): "The continuance of authority in the same individual has frequently meant the end of democratic governments. Repeated elections are essential in popular systems of government, for nothing is more perilous than to permit one citizen to retain power for an extended period. The people become accustomed to obeying him, and he forms the habit of commanding them; herein lie the origins of usurpation and tyranny. A just zeal is the guarantee of republican liberty. Our citizens must with good reason learn to fear lest the magistrate who has governed them long will govern them forever." Quoted after G. A. Sherwell, *Simon Bolivar* (1st World Publishing, 2005), p. 110.

[91] The easing of term limit rules is also common in other forms of government. It was proposed in the Philippines long before Duterte (and rejected on technical grounds by the *Supreme Court, Santiago v. Commission on Elections* 270 SCRA 106 [1997]). In Columbia, the Constitutional Court found the second term acceptable, but not a third one.

[92] L. L. Ilsley, "The Argentine Constitutional Revision of 1949," *The Journal of Politics*, 14:2 (1952), pp. 224–40. In Brazil Getulio Vargas, who ruled under a constitution that was created under his putschist regime, moved to an *autogolpe* in 1937 when his presidential term was nearing its end. Under the very constitution enacted under his control, he was no longer eligible for re-election.

constitutional reality for the plebiscitarian leader in a democracy is that checks and balances must be paralyzed. No system of separation of powers can counter the executive, unless the contingencies of political forces provide help.[93] The lack of a single-party majority creates veto powers in coalition governments; internal divisions in the governing party limit the power of the prime minister; while a dual executive is an obvious constraint in semipresidential systems.[94]

The standard solutions of constitutional design enable the rule of the charismatic plebiscitarian leader. In most cases, the leader is the head of the executive branch, though this is not necessary: Kaczyński, for example, could rule Poland de facto as President of the governing party, staying away from higher constitutional offices. The formal independence and powers of the legislative branch matter little for checks and balances once the majority is personally dependent on the plebiscitarian leader. This is the case where the leader's authority results from popular acclamation – no branch of power or anyone within the governing party can challenge it. The HPM has regarded elections as tools that grant him authorization, a so-called *personal mandate* to govern according to "the people's will."[95] No political force is capable of countering the leader: neither the army, civil society, oligarchy nor fourth estate has the power to play a balancing role.

Personal power does not derive only from the formal and informal concentration of decision-making powers. It is based on the shared belief among members of parliament and members of the executive, who have independent decision-making power and yet the duty that no important decision can be taken without the leader's consent, a decision that they should be able to accurately anticipate. This reflects a corresponding popular conviction: "the electors proclaim their faith in a leader's ability to act for the national interest, rather than mandating him to carry out a concrete program."[96]

---

[93] R. Uitz, "Can You Tell When an Illiberal Democracy Is in the Making? An Appeal to Comparative Constitutional Law Scholarship from Hungary," *International Journal of Constitutional Law*, 13:1 (2015), p. 292. For an attempt to concentrate power in Parliament against the President see Romania in 2012 (Chapter 8).

[94] The demand for power concentration convinced the French to synchronize presidential and parliamentary elections in the name of efficient governance. This kind of concern for efficiency helps the Caesar in plebiscitarian democracies.

[95] A. Körösényi, G. Illés, and A. Gyulai, *The Orbán Regime: Plebiscitary Leader Democracy in the Making* (Routledge, 2020).

[96] Ibid., p. 36.

The concentration of power means that other branches and institutions of power depend completely on the leader. He will decide on the distribution of perks and determine who can run for which public office and when. With the muzzling of the opposition, parliament cannot operate as a counterbalance. In the absence of a culture that respects checks and balances by *self-restraint* among the power holders, no ambition remains to counter that of the leader. Once the legislative branch is dominated by the leader's party, and once the party or its delegates in parliament depend completely upon the leader, the fundamental constitutional solution offered by the separation of powers cannot work. The political branches (and consequently, autonomous bodies and gradually the judiciary) can remain separate from each other but will continue to defer to all decisions from the leader. The plebiscitarian ruler without checks and balances will be tempted to forgo all compromise. Even if he were inclined to seek one, no one remains to cut deals or engage in dialogue, as the opposition has been labeled the enemy.

The concentration of power in the hands of the ruler tends toward an "unbound executive," which facilitates and prepares self-aggrandizement.[97] This is not an illiberal peculiarity. It fits into a common trend that prevails in democracies: "elected executives weaken checks on executive power one by one, undertaking a series of institutional changes that hamper the power of opposition forces to challenge executive preferences."[98] In the United States, the use of regulatory agencies for presidential policy was the only logical conclusion from a fifty-year-old trend toward an imperial presidency. When panicked observers conclude today that the US presidency is moving toward despotism, they forget that the executive departments merely use powers they obtained under previous administrations.[99]

The expansion of executive power is justified in democracies by the superior capacity of the executive to handle complex problems with knowledge, determination, and speed. In illiberal democracies, charisma and a "natural" understanding of the wishes of the people are the sources

---

[97] This trend started with the emergence of mass democracy. President Jackson "re-energized the Presidency by marrying its constitutional powers to a theory of the Executive as the focal point for national majority rule, a role that was not obvious, to say the least, from the constitutional text." J. Yoo, "Andrew Jackson and Presidential Power," *Charleston Law Review*, 2 (2008), p. 106.

[98] N. Bermeo, "On Democratic Backsliding," *Journal of Democracy*, 27:5 (2016), p. 10.

[99] Huq and Ginsburg argue that the current retrogression is analytically distinct from executive aggrandizement. Huq and Ginsburg, "How to Lose a Constitutional Democracy," p. 84.

of the leader's superior capacities. This kind of personalization provides a "super-legitimacy ... that cannot help but encourage a certain illiberalism."[100] A populist understanding of the people begs for a strong, powerful leader who guarantees its unity and identity. The power of the state will be vested in the person of the leader, eliminating the possibility for any competitor or institution to challenge him.[101] Aggrandized power will be used to perpetuate itself.[102]

The constitutional-governmental construct of personal rule results in princely government, perhaps an inherent feature of centralized and concentrated power. With his personalized power, the head of the executive is supreme to the parliament, as he represents the whole nation, while the parliament is only an ad hoc elected body, a tool of the majority.[103] The HPM's number one admirer has seen the consequences of this princely rule once institutional and cultural restrictions disappeared: "Thus the leader becomes the master of the paradox of power by creating within the framework of constitutional government, a para-institutional configuration of personal power. Against the shattered pieces of constitutional government, he sets off monocratic powers – an autocracy with the help of the power of friends."[104] Thus, personalism leads to despotism (autocracy).

5.4.1 Constitutional Courts

As demonstrated in Chapter 2, notwithstanding the populist tenet that elected bodies shall be supreme, the constitutional courts have maintained their formal legal power. This power is now used to protect the constitutional order of illiberalism and the actual political interests of the regime, even if some judgments void norms enacted by the regime. Such rulings are limited to politically irrelevant cases (which may still be important for individual rights protection or legal

---

[100] P. Rosanvallon, *Good Government: Democracy Beyond Elections* (Harvard University Press, 2018), p. 55.

[101] In the 1990s, populist presidents Abdala Bucaram of Ecuador and Fernando Collor of Brazil were removed from power due to the resistance from the legislative branch.

[102] See in this sense D. Schneiderman, "Parliamentarism and its Adversaries: Legislatures in an Era of Illiberal Executives," A. Sajó, S. Holmes, and R. Uitz (eds.) in *Routledge Handbook of Illiberalism* (Routledge, in press).

[103] Ibid.

[104] G. G. Fodor, "The Two 'Faces' of Political Creativity. Two Paradigms of Political Leadership," in J. Femia, A. Körösényi, and G. Stomp (eds.), *Political Leadership in Liberal and Democratic Theory* (Imprint Academic, 2009), p. 183.

consistency).[105] However, finding for or against legislation is not a reliable indicator. The "new" PCT found an earlier act of the Sejm unconstitutional, only to legitimize the planned action of the government to dismiss the politically "untrustworthy" Judicial Council with its inherited composition.[106]

Government-friendly adjudication comes easy when loyalist judges can apply a constitution that was tailor-made for illiberalism. The task is not significantly more difficult where the constitution is neutral, as it should be. Political loyalty will be coated in the logic of formalistic, legitimate judicial reasoning. Legal and constitutional positivism, reinforced by traditional techniques of legal interpretation, turn judges into instruments of oppressive and/or arbitrary law. Still claiming the role of "Defender of the Constitution," the HCC became proudly deferential (as expressed in concurring opinions). The leading principle is this: dare to be insignificant, especially when the parliamentary majority has spoken; respect parliament and the national interest and reduce the role of the court. Separation of powers is often considered together with the argument that parliament is the popularly endorsed organ of lawmaking.[107]

Formalism helps, too: sensitive applications are declared inadmissible, or at least the decision is delayed in order to avoid embarrassing situations. (Lawyers know that you don't have to win on the merits, if you can win on procedure.) To keep a semblance of principled adjudication associated with precedent, the judgments are increasingly self-referential and do not aim to provide arguments accessible to public reason. However, if needed, even positivist judges will refer to material justice and collectivist constitutional values, as in the Hungarian "No resettlement of migrants" case, where the HCC suddenly found that a new concept of constitutional identity is applicable.[108]

The aesthetic imperfections and authoritarian categoricity of the judgment's language and the reference to patriotic values and constitutional

---

[105] Regime-supportive interpretation or reinterpretation of the constitution is not unique to illiberal democracy. It uses status quo–friendly doctrines, like constitution-conform interpretation to save otherwise problematic legislation, and judicial self-restraint.

[106] See Chapter 2.

[107] According to important academic positions ("political constitutionalism"), the new deference to the legislative branch simply restores a different constitutional balance, where courts play a much more restrained role. In this view, the antidemocratic colonization of the political by the judiciary must end. If checks and balances are not working, only the democratic process can restore the balance.

[108] Decision 22/2016 (XII. 5) AB hat. (HCC).

identity are quite telling: the judgments' rumbling voice indicates the difficulty of convincingly justifying the government's arbitrary and greedy measures. However, even obviously fraudulent explanations may well serve the new function of the constitutional courts, which instead of defending the constitution defend the cause of the nation and its protector, the government.[109] Summarizing his earlier writing, Brewer-Carías concluded in 2014 that the Venezuelan TSJ distorted the Constitution rather than protected it. With regard to Poland, Martin Krygier has identified the new role of the PCT as one of regime legitimation against the Constitution: "The government sends petitions to the Tribunal so that it can lend legal legitimacy to purely political inroads on the system of justice and the Polish Constitution."[110] The constitutional courts "cooperate" with the political branches. This is nothing special: "[J]udges could be transformed into instruments to destroy competitors, rather than to protect democracy."[111]

5.4.2 Parliament without Deliberation

Before their power grab, populists constantly and consistently attack parliament in the name of a crude and rude theory of democracy, claiming that parliaments are both impotent and serve the elite, in breach of their popular mandate.[112]

Populists rise to power dreaming of parliaments that express the people's will (i.e. the dictate of the righteous majority). The parliament that serves the unitary will of the rejuvenated nation now has the right or even duty to fulfill the will of the majority, exposing the totalitarian within democracy, transitioning into despotism. There is only one correct will of the unitary people, and it cannot and shall not respect the

---

[109] However, for a number of reasons (e.g. professional self-esteem, international credibility), where judges do not sense that government authority is at stake, they will continue to act as if they are enforcing the constitution.

[110] M. Krygier, "The Challenge of Institutionalisation: Post-Communist 'Transitions', Populism, and the Rule of Law," *European Constitutional Law Review*, 15:3 (2019), p. 547. The PCT's finding of unconstitutionality eminently serves to justify legislative reforms that enable control over one or another institution.

[111] J. M. Maravall, "The Rule of Law as a Political Weapon," *Estudio/Working Paper 2001/ 160* (2001), p. 9.

[112] In 2017, future Czech Prime Minister Babiš ran a campaign that promised limited powers to a streamlined Czech Parliament. T. Boros, D. Bartha, R. Cuperus, et al. (eds.), *The State of Populism in Europe* (FEPS, Policy Solutions and FES Budapest, December 2017), p. 77.

opposition, which serves as an obstacle in achieving the common good. Yet the opposition continues to exist, because the regime remains true to its formal commitments to democracy, including the RoL, even if in a form that curtails the opposition. For example, opposition parties receive public funding, which is subject to neutral norms, though selectively applied by the authorities. Opposition parties are thus often found to be violating these formalities, resulting in sanctions and providing a convenient opportunity for the media to depict them as corrupt.

Constitutional theorists reject the assumption that a parliamentary majority can be identified with the popular will.[113] Parliament should be understood as a mediating institution where politicians seek dialogue and optimize interests. It is no accident that laws are enacted in the name of all members of the assembly "who claim in their diversity to represent all the major disagreements about justice in their society."[114] However, such considerations bear no weight in the totalitarian tradition of democracy, where there is no place for disagreement and even less for considering such potential.

Nevertheless, only de Gaulle as a plebiscitarian leader dared to openly diminish the legislative and supervisory powers of the French National Assembly in the 1958 Constitution. He sought to limit the powers of an institution that had been the rallying point of his opponents.[115] In Venezuela, Chávez, though distrustful of a future National Assembly, granted it considerable balancing power in the 1999 Constitution; he simultaneously weakened the legislative branch using a backdoor strategy, by submitting all parties (including MAS, the President's movement) to various forms of control in the name of internal party democracy. This controlling supervision was exercised by the Electoral Committee, perhaps the most loyal Chavezista body. (The weaker the party and parliamentary faction, the stronger the leader of the party.)

All in all, the texts of populism-inspired constitutions have not radically changed the role of the legislative branch and attributed to it, at least formally, primacy in legislative matters with a strong emphasis on matters being regulated at the level of statutory law. For example, Hungary continued with "overparliamentarization."[116]

---

[113] A. Voßkuhle, "Demokratie und Populismus," *Der Staat*, 57:1 (2018), pp. 119–34.

[114] J. Waldron, *Law and Disagreement* (Oxford University Press, 1999), p. 10.

[115] The despotic potential manifested in post-Soviet constitutions, which have adopted the model.

[116] The term was invented by Professor Kukorelli, judge of the HCC. In the communist practice the Presidium of the Parliament legislated on the basis of a general

However, though the powers of the legislative branch have been nearly unchanged on paper, they have been clearly eroded in reality. The situation results in "complete executive supremacy in the legislative process, severely limited opportunities for general debates criticizing government, virtually no opportunities for scrutinizing executive acts and making the executive give an account of them [. . .] executive power is a little too immune from proper scrutiny."[117] While this remark refers to France, it applies to Hungary and Poland as well. As to the legislative branch in populist Latin presidentialism, its weakness originates from the fragmented party system; there was thus no need for a formal process to weaken the branch within the constitution. The frailty of the legislative branch characterizes Latin American *presidencialismo* and the already weak party system, combined with the electoral system. Partly in response to inefficient legislation, populist Latin American presidents wield overwhelming legislative privileges (exclusive introduction of bills in specific areas, government by decree powers, and legislative veto).[118]

The decisive role of parliaments in matters of legislation is constitutionally recognized, but the legislation occurs in highly rationalized parliaments,[119] resulting in the de facto supremacy of the executive. The rationalized parliament fails to exercise its supervisory role, and as such, embodies the proverbial three monkeys in one: see no evil, hear no evil, speak no evil. "[A]s Max Weber warned, institutions deprived of real power and responsibility tend to act in ways that seem to confirm the reasons adduced for this deprivation."[120] Rationalization of the parliament is a 100-year-old phenomenon, which the populist leader continues to excessively use. Parliament is primed to constrain

constitutional delegation of power. For this reason the demand for parliamentary legislation became a formative element in the constitutional changes in the transition to democracy in 1989, something that Fidesz had to respect even two decades later.

[117] J. Frears, "The French Parliament: Loyal Workhorse, Poor Watchdog," *West European Politics*, 13:3 (1990), p. 33.

[118] M. Shugart and J. Carey, *Presidents and Assemblies: Constitutional Design and Electoral Dynamics* (Cambridge University Press, 1992).

[119] B. Mirkine-Guetzevitch, *Les Constitutions de l'Europe Nouvelle* (Delagrave, 1928), p. 19. The term originally refers to the reorganization of parliamentary work in the logic of party domination. In de Gaulle's system, it was a set of parliamentary (procedural) rules enabling the executive to govern even without a majority. J. D. Levy and C. Skatch, "The Return to a Strong Presidency," in A. Cole, P. le Galès, and J. Levy, *Developments in French Politics*, 4 (Palgrave Macmillan, 2008), p. 113.

[120] G. A. O'Donnell, "Illusions About Consolidation," *Journal of Democracy*, 7:2 (1996), p. 45.

itself.[121] In the legislation of the illiberal democracy, the will of the executive leader is de facto supreme. In Hungary, the government's final bills are always accepted, while in the history of the UK House of Commons government bills have been defeated more than a hundred times since 1945 and the bills submitted by government are regularly modified in the legislative process.[122]

The rationalization of parliament satisfies the populist dream of the primacy of the common sense of the ordinary people: the complexity of regulatory matters that would require extended discussion disappears and formal processes are simplified (even if the laws are complex or presented as hundreds of pages of amendments, precluding transparency). Efficiency is confused with celerity, and the dictates of the moment receive the stamp of legislated eternity. It is in this spirit of popular aversion for the legislative branch that Fidesz radically streamlined Parliament, partly because this enabled tight control over the opposition.[123] Equally important, it served to discipline the majority (Fidesz) rank and file and create further dependencies on the leader.

In quantitative terms, legislation can be quite active in illiberal democracy. In the first cycle of Fidesz rule (2010–2014), the Hungarian Parliament adopted 859 acts, an increase of 46 percent compared to the preceding cycle. Twelve percent of these acts were adopted in fewer than 10 days.[124] Yet the total time spent on parliamentary debate did not decrease in Fidesz's first two cycles (2010–2018). In this transition period to illiberal democracy, Parliament was in plenary session 50 percent more than the average of the 1990–2018 period.[125] However, after 2018, the time dedicated to plenary debates has been less than half of the comparable previous periods. Parliament is losing its importance even in statistical terms.

---

[121] Should parliament not accept that role, the executive will try to annihilate it (see President Maduro's action in 2015).

[122] P. Norton, "Government Defeats in the House of Commons: The British Experience," *Canadian Parliamentary Review*, 8:4 (1985), pp. 6–9.

[123] 2012. Act xxxvi of 2012 on the Parliament. The Preamble declares that Parliament is the highest organ of popular representation, "the most important constitutional institution of our democracy" and the depository of people's sovereignty.

 Streamlining the legislative body is a populist classic (see Venezuela, Italy, and Bulgaria).

[124] A. B. Orbán, "Pillanatkép az Országgyűlés Törvényalkotási Tevékenységéről - 2014," *Pro Publico Bono. Magyar Közigazgatás*, 4 (2014), p. 93; Scheppele, "The Rule of Law," pp. 559–62.

[125] "A plenáris ülések tárgyalási idejének megoszlása típusonként 1990-2018," Országgyűlés, www.parlament.hu/a-plenaris-ulesek-targyalasi-ideje.

Constitutionalists agree that the quality of parliamentarism depends on deliberation, giving justifications and exchanging reasons for choosing public policies. This is quintessential for political accountability.[126] Deliberation requires the *meaningful* participation of the opposition, even if "research ... has suggested that legislative speech is used by political parties to communicate with their voters."[127]

Without deliberation parliament becomes a legislative factory. This has been achieved with the same trick in Hungary and Poland: while rules provide for proper transparency, government-submitted bills require debate and cost-benefit analysis, etc., parliamentarians can submit government-prepared bills in their personal capacity circumventing the rules of parliamentary procedure in order to avoid such "complications."[128] As one example: some of the 2018 amendments to the HFL were submitted as a private bill to the competent committee after 5 p.m. on a Friday, to be debated for an hour the following Monday morning. The process of adopting the whole amendment (which now requires the state to protect Christian values and constitutional identity) entailed only two and a half working days.

Celerity serves more than the efficient production of the legislative chain gang. It silences or eradicates the opposition;[129] while formally their rights are protected, in reality the extensive use of legalistic gimmicks turn these rights into mere formalities.[130] For the government

---

[126] J. Dryzek, *Deliberative Democracy and Beyond: Liberals, Critics and Contestations* (Oxford University Press, 2000).

At least, this is the theory. In reality, even in the Westminster tradition, "[a]s the late Sir Patrick Nairne, a widely respected mandarin, was honest enough to admit: 'economy with the truth is the essence of a professional reply to a parliamentary question.'" R. Norton-Taylor, "A Dominic Cummings coup will not oust the Whitehall mandarins," *The Guardian* (February 9, 2020), www.theguardian.com/politics/2020/feb/09/how-whitehall-will-fend-off-dominic-cummings-culture-of-secrecy.

[127] H. Bäck, M. Baumann, M. Debus, and J. Müller, "The Unequal Distribution of Speaking Time in Parliamentary-Party Groups," *Legislative Studies Quarterly*, 44:1 (2019), p. 165.

[128] For a similar practice in Poland, see "Poland's Ruling Law and Justice Party is doing Lasting Damage," *The Economist* (April 21, 2018), www.economist.com/europe/2018/04/21/polands-ruling-law-and-justice-party-is-doing-lasting-damage.

[129] A 2014 amendment of the House Rules limited the number of two-minute interventions, essential for direct debate; reduced the total amount of debate time; and "disciplined" the debate at second reading. Moreover, most propositions are debated in one committee only and the number of committees had also been reduced.

[130] In Hungary, the HCC intervened in 1998 when an extreme right-wing party could not form a faction (on the basis of a pre-existing rule that the party list did not reach the mandatory five percent threshold); however, in 2012, when the new (clearly *ad personam*) amendment to the House Rules precluded the formation of a new faction, the HCC

majority this is appropriate: the opposition is widely considered to be a bunch of traitors and evil incarnate. In some instances, limits on the opposition are expressed: according to 24. § (2) of the Parliament Act (Act xxxvi of 2012), it is no longer mandatory to establish an inquiry committee upon the initiative of one-fifth of the members. The discreet obscurity of the formulation characterizes the prudish deceit preferred in Hungary: the provision states that "1/5 of the MPs may initiate the setting up of a committee of inquiry." Hear no evil. The opposition has the right to initiate, but the majority decides. There are no effective sanctions for failing to appear at the inquiry committee, except that the committee president will report on the matter during the next plenary. Similar tricks typify the work of the Polish Sejm. "The abusive use of *vacatio legis* or intertemporal provisions, the midnight voting, the voting's repetition until expected results, the reopening of closed voting as well as harsh MPs disciplinary penalties may serve as perfect examples."[131]

Yet again, the rules seem to fit into traditional parliamentarism. One could even think that compared to the German Bundestag, the Hungarian rules are generous. For example, while in Germany the threshold for faction formation is 5 percent, it is only 2.5 percent of the total number of delegates in Hungary. In important supervisory committees, like national security, the chairperson must come from the opposition. It is at the level of practice, determined by parliamentary culture, where illiberalism prevails. Members of the majority have no scruples in boycotting committee meetings called by the opposition, because in their absence, short of a quorum, the meetings cannot be held. Question hours (when the executive must answer questions from members of parliament) are regularly held and even broadcast online (albeit not in public-service media, as had previously been the case), but ministers refuse to answer the opposition's questions, claiming their party is unworthy of an answer; the friend/enemy division thus makes political community and compromise impossible. When an offended minister leaves the chamber without answering an inconvenient question, the public does not perceive this as a sign of weakness or breach of duty, but rather as the normal treatment the opposition deserves.

---

found it constitutional, claiming (rather surprisingly) that the parliamentarians who were unable to join a faction continue to enjoy equal rights with other MPs. 10/2013 (iv. 25) AB hat.

[131] M. Ziółkowski, "Undemocratic but Formally Lawful: The Suspension of the Polish Parliament," Verfassungsblog (September 25, 2019), http://www.verfassungsblog.de /undemocratic-but-formally-lawful-the-suspension-of-the-polish-parliament.

The fewer opportunities the opposition has to influence public opinion, the better the chances to strip assets and build unfettered permanent power. In rationalized legislation, there is no place for public debate, especially not rational discourse or deliberation. The government-controlled media provides only distorted snippets of discussion, and the opposition has no opportunity to hold the government accountable. With diminishing visibility, the opposition desperately tries to be seen. Relying on theatrical protests inside and outside the premises of parliament, they also depart from the logic of rational discourse, which the majority has already abandoned. The increasingly radical, desperate actions of the opposition result in increasingly harsher sanctions for "trouble-making" members who "offend the dignity of the institution," a concept inviting politically biased application. According to the HFL, the Speaker enforces the dignity of the Parliament. This rule corresponds to the authoritarian tradition of many parliaments but was only introduced in Hungary in 2012 to discipline the opposition. Government propaganda and examples of unruliness enable denouncement of the irresponsible, clownish opposition; even if the chaos undermines public trust in Parliament, it helps to consolidate trust in the Caesar as the only responsible and dignified political actor.

Through the fraudulent restrictions on debate (and, more importantly, rendering debate and decision-making "invisible"), the classic assumption of parliamentarism, that parliament serves as a permanent link between representative government and public opinion, is destroyed. Populist leaders do not need such mediation: they prefer a more direct connection with the people.

5.4.3 Electoral Law

The Caesar's power stems from the people, and the regime's legitimacy is based on plebiscitarian support for the leader. Hence the importance of formal institutions of popular self-expression combined with "institutions of domination."[132] For this to succeed, plebiscitarian democracies must hold "regular elections, which are 'broadly inclusive' (respecting universal suffrage), minimally competitive (whereby different parties are allowed to compete for votes), and minimally open (there is no massive repression)."[133] It is not voter intimidation or electoral fraud that keeps

---

[132] A. Schedler, *The Politics of Uncertainty* (Oxford University Press, 2013), p. 55 on electoral authoritarian regimes.
[133] Ibid., p. 2.

the governing party in power but identification with the leader and fragmentation of the opposition, facilitated by tricky legal design.[134] It is better to disqualify a party for financial inappropriateness, creating petty criminals, than to jail its leaders, turning them into martyrs. If there is intimidation, it must be legal. "Suing an opponent for libel or pursuing him for tax evasion, gets far less ink than throwing him in prison, and it is every bit as effective. In Singapore, only those who are willing to risk financial ruin dare to challenge the government openly."[135] This trend is not limited to Singapore.[136]

Within this framework, it becomes a crucial constitutive issue for the illiberal constitutional system to neutralize democratic popular control while maintaining popular endorsement. More prosaically, the legal system must guarantee that its rule be based on elections without running too much risk that the Caesar will be voted out. "Institutional uncertainty" (i.e. the possibility that any governing party can realistically be defeated) is the inherent characteristic of any democracy.[137] Through legal means, such uncertainty must be reduced to the greatest possible extent. One day perhaps, even this manipulation will not be necessary, when the incumbent becomes the dominant power (the party of power, as seen in Russia, where most people are hesitant to vote against it). This situation may occur when the fragmented opposition becomes permanently under-resourced and has lost credibility as a possible alternative (all this thanks also to various tricks of the hegemonic party).

Elections must remain free (as this gives credibility to the affirmation of the leader in the eyes of his supporters, and to some extent, those who oppose him), as well as enjoy a certain level of fairness. In order to remain within the democratic game, the powerholder must assume certain risks inherent to democratic representation. The opposition must feel that they have at least a minimal chance to win future elections, and the cost of accepting loss in the present does not appear excessive given the prospect of an eventual victory at a later point in time. "The calculus may go either way so long as the policies imposed by the winners are not too

---

[134] Hungary was eager to reform its electoral system; Poland was less so until the presidential elections of 2020, when COVID-19 caused unexpected difficulties for the incumbent.

[135] Silverstein, "Singapore's Constitutionalism," p. 21, quoting M. Gee, "International Affairs: The Singapore Suits," *Globe and Mail* (March 12, 1997), p. A-15.

[136] However, in Latin American illiberal democracies, with their backs to the wall, the middle class and business sector have had no choice but confrontation.

[137] A. Przewroski, *Democracy and the Market: Political and Economic Reforms in Eastern Europe and Latin America* (Oxford University Press, 1991).

extreme or so long as their chance to win at the next opportunity is sufficiently high."[138] This is how illiberal democracy differs from despotism and what keeps it in the democratic family. It is not out of the question that the incumbent will lose. In Hungary, a genuine joining of opposition forces could have resulted in an actual chance of victory. In Poland, the 2020 presidential elections were undeniably competitive, despite administrative resources favoring the incumbent. The opposition won numerous municipal elections in all the countries concerned. In Venezuela, the 2015 National Assembly elections resulted in a landslide opposition victory (forcing, however, the regime into naked authoritarian dictatorship). Correa and Morales were also forced to quit, a consequence of losing popular support.

Several techniques in electoral design can award additional seats to the incumbent party or president, including gerrymandering, granting premium seats to the relative majority, restricting media access, financial constraints, limited review of the election's legality, etc.[139] The results are often spectacular. In 2010 in Venezuela, a difference of 80,000 votes gave MAS 98 National Assembly seats out of a total of 165.[140] In Singapore, even though the governing party (the PAP) received on some occasions only 60 percent of the vote, they always controlled more than 90 percent of the seats. Laws written by the majority of the day always try to provide advantage to the incumbent, and there is not much originalism in this illiberal electoral tinkering: "Repression, intimidation, manipulation of rules, abuse of state apparatus, and fraud are standard instruments of electoral technology."[141] International observers consider the Hungarian

---

[138] A. Przeworski, *Crises of Democracy* (Cambridge University Press, 2019), p. 161. For example, on the use of state resources in the 2017 Turkish constitutional referendum, see *Republic of Turkey Early Presidential and Parliamentary Elections 24 June 2018: ODIHR Election Observation Mission Final Report*, Organization for Security and Co-operation in Europe (September 2018).

[139] See, for example, *Hungary, Parliamentary Elections, 6 April 2014: Final Report*, Organization for Security and Co-operation in Europe (July 2014); M. Bánkuti, G. Halmai, and K. L. Scheppele, "Disabling the Constitution," *Journal of Democracy*, 23:3 (2012), pp. 138–46.

In politics, as in other types of competitive activities, bending and circumventing the rules may sometimes be considered "part of the game." A. Schedler, "Elections Without Democracy: The Menu of Manipulation," *Journal of Democracy*, 13:2 (2002), pp. 36–50.

[140] A. Tarre, "Venezuela's Legislative Elections: Arm wrestling with Hugo Chávez," *Fletcher Forum of World Affairs*, 35:1 (2011), p. 139. In some countries, the president can be elected by a relative majority in a single round. In Nicaragua, in the process of perpetuating Ortega's presidency, even the minimum vote requirement was abolished in 2014.

[141] A. Przeworski, *Why Bother with Elections?* (Cambridge University Press, 2018), p. 50.

electoral system and its elections free but not fair,[142] though in terms of the Gallagher index, the Hungarian system is far less distortive than in the UK (in at least at some elections).[143]

What matters is not who votes how, but who counts the ballots (per Joseph Stalin). It is perhaps here that the most important support is built in the illiberal regime's electoral system. National electoral boards are granted enormous powers (see Venezuela) and are stacked with well-paid government loyalists who use an entire arsenal of twisted legal interpretations and other forms of legalized cheating (see Chapter 8). The fundamental problem with electoral changes lies in their goal: the intentional design and redesign of an electoral system that perpetuates the regime and its leader runs counter to the constitutional truism that "no government should set the rules by which it retains power."[144]

5.4.4   Referendum

Populism advocates for popular participation and enhanced control of unresponsive and alienated representative bodies. Legislation by direct democracy enjoys more popularity among supporters of populist parties in Western Europe than among nonpopulists.[145] Populists in opposition use popular initiatives to delegitimize the government via referendum (as in Hungary 2004–2010; see also Brexit). They rely on the ritualistic physical presence of the people: the people exist *en masse* at antigovernment demonstrations. However, the plebiscitarian nature of illiberal democracies does not result in the endorsement of direct democracy. After the populist takeover, the reliance on the electorate varies according to local circumstances. While the populist logic would suggest heavy

---

[142] *Hungary Parliamentary Elections 8 April 2018. Limited Election Observation Mission Final Report*, Organization for Security and Co-operation in Europe (June 2018).

[143] See. M. Gallagher and P. Mitchell (eds.), *The Politics of Electoral Systems* (Oxford University Press, 2008).

[144] E. A. Reese, "Or the People: Popular Sovereignty and the Power to Choose a Government," *Cardozo Law Review*, 39 (2018), p. 2059.

[145] Of course, this is before the state is "carried away" by a populist monopoly. As of December 2019, 58 percent of the supporters of the Lega (outside of government) and 50 percent of M5S supporters (in government, and originally an absolute supporter of direct democracy) claim that all important issues should be decided by referendum. "Rapporto gli Italiani e lo Stato – Rapporto 2019," Demos & Pi (December 23, 2019), www.demos.it/rapporto.php

Max Weber opposed direct democracy because it "does not know compromise." M. Weber, *Weber Political Writings*, eds. P. Lassman and R. Speirs (Cambridge University Press, 1994), p. 225.

reliance on referendum, it is instead used strategically when the ruler, short of total constituent power, has no proper means to overcome constitutional and political obstacles, as seen in the case of the term limits amendment.

Illiberal democracies are not enthusiastic about direct democracy, and public support for direct democracy in Hungary, Poland, and Venezuela corresponds to the regional median.[146] The plebiscitarian leader must demonstrate that he is in a permanent relationship with his supportive people,[147] but populist leaders are reluctant to allow popular initiatives. After all, the popular initiative may be used by the opposition, or it may express popular discontent. Moreover, there is no real need for referendum as the charismatic leader feels and knows naturally what his people desire is: the people *should* just feel and know what the leader knows already. (Of course, propaganda works hard to validate this *petitio principi*.)

The 1999 Venezuelan Constitution formally favored direct democracy, providing for consultative, approbatory and abrogative referendum as well as recall.[148] In contrast, the Hungarian populists, who were quite radical in opposition, were more careful. Contrary to the populist theory

---

[146] R. Wike and K. Simmons (et al.), *Globally, Broad Support for Representative and Direct Democracy* (Pew Research Center, 2017).

[147] In the unlikely case that a leader-initiated plebiscite does not produce the expected confirmation of the ruler's position, constitutional tribunals can still interpret the result. See, among others, the judicial "correction" of the rejection of party financing reform in Venezuela, the judicial override of the refusal to abolish term limits in Venezuela and Bolivia, and the dismissal of the outcome of the Greek government's austerity referendum. When the "no alien resettlement" referendum did not produce the required quorum in Hungary, the Constitution was amended to reflect the choice of the Hungarian people (i.e. the majority of the minority who participated in the referendum). Ironically, traditional constitutional institutions come to the rescue of the populist plebiscitarian project.

[148] According to Brewer-Carías, when a sufficient number of people recalled the President in 2004, the Electoral Committee requalified the referendum as a "ratification referendum," which "does not exist in the Constitution," and claimed that the votes must be counted differently. In this innovative interpretation, which contradicted the Constitution, they could simply consider which way the majority of the vote went. Much of the vote was cast in favor of Chávez. Brewer-Carías, *Dismantling Democracy*, pp. 113–14.

The French Constitutional Council was equally unwilling in 1961 to nullify the constitutional amendment that de Gaulle had called in clear violation of the Constitution, because at the time of the decision, the popular vote had been cast in favor of the initiative. See also the constitutional amendment referendum in France. J. E. Beardsley, "The Constitutional Council and Constitutional Liberties in France," *The American Journal of Comparative Law*, 20:3 (1972), pp. 431–52.

of popular sovereignty, the HFL endorsed the long-established position of the HCC, namely that parliamentary representation is the *primary* form of the expression of popular sovereignty.[149] The referendum has an auxiliary character, and according to the text of the HCC, is an exceptional instrument. The quorum rule (50 percent) is demanding and limits the possibilities for popular decision-making. The rule was conveniently inherited from the socialist government and can be justified in constitutional theory. Where the constitution opts for the primacy of representative government, considerable weight is needed to overcome the position of parliament, which represents a sizable portion of the population. There has only been one referendum in Hungary since 2010, called by the government to prohibit the settling of migrants; however, the initiative failed because only 44 percent of the electorate participated.[150] Citizen legislative initiatives (which obligate Parliament to discuss) have now been abolished (since 2014).

At the same time, the HFL did not make popular initiatives more cumbersome. Compared to Venezuela, the solution can be called magnanimous.[151] A valid initiative only requires the signature of approximately 2.5 percent of registered voters, which is comparable to Switzerland, the model country for the popular initiative. However, in a system of illusionary democracy (where even populism becomes delusionary), the hard reality is construed at the level of subconstitutional norms, which enable creative application by trusted law enforcers. The most important defense against popular initiative is found in the formal requirements for admissibility of the referendum, as interpreted (restrictively) by national electoral committees, which are staffed with a carefully selected progovernment majority. Of course, as one would expect in illiberal regimes bound by legality, there is judicial recourse, but the competent chambers regularly endorse the position of this committee,

---

[149] 2/1993 (1.22) AB hat. The HCC (in the same composition) modified its view in 1997: "the direct exercise of power is an exceptional form of exercising popular sovereignty, but in exceptional cases when it is actually realized it stands above the exercise of power through representatives." Decision 52/1997 (x. 14) AB hat.

[150] MEP József Szájer, a principal draftsman of the HFL, claimed that after the consolidation of democracy there is a need for greater representative government, and the restriction serves to mitigate the danger of populism (!). "Szájer József: Erre az alkotmányra fel lehet nézni," Infostart/InfoRádió (April 18, 2011), www.infostart.hu/belfold/2011/04/18/szajer-jozsef-erre-az-alkotmanyra-fel-lehet-nezni-427922.

[151] In Venezuela, the petition must be signed by no less than 10 to 15 percent of the registered voters (20 percent for recall).

relying on hairsplitting legalistic and judicial fictions. For example, the Hungarian National Electoral Committee refused popular initiatives against a Fidesz-introduced Sunday observance law, claiming that none were sufficiently clear, which was further endorsed by the Kúria (the Hungarian Supreme Court) for fourteen months.[152]

The HPM prefers a substitute plebiscite, invented by the government: the so-called national consultation process. In ten years, there have been seven national consultations. These are not regulated by law and no fairness or transparency rule applies. Following a government propaganda campaign, the population receives a set of questions by mail, and the answers are returned in a prepaid envelope and evaluated in a nontransparent, unvalidated process that is then used to justify existing government programs and policies.[153]

At the end of the day, plebiscitarian regimes do not favor plebiscite. When one is in the business of expressing the will of the people – it is best not to ask what the people think.

---

[152] Following a major scandal, when the submission of the initiative request was physically obstructed by progovernment thugs, the Supreme Court found one of the initiatives admissible. In order not to lose popularity, the government reversed course on Sunday closing within six days. According to this new Gospel the people (and especially good Hungarian families) deserve the right to shop on Sundays.

See Kúria, "A Választási és Népszavazási Eljárásokkal Kapcsolatos Jogorvoslat Tárgyában Létrejött Joggyakorlat-elemző Csoport," *Összefoglaló vélemény* (2018).

[153] For example, the national consultation "On the Soros plan" (Fall 2017) asked respondents for their views on a supposed effort to convince "Brussels" to settle in Europe one million African and Middle Eastern migrants per year. According to the never-validated results, the HPM could declare that the overwhelming majority of Hungarian men and women did not agree with this. Consequently, the HFL was duly amended in 2018, after elections returned Fidesz to power with a constituent majority.

6

The Fate of Human Rights

Human rights have nothing but friends.

Michel Villey[1]

6.1 Introduction

This chapter claims that diminishing government and public respect for civil liberties and human rights in illiberal democracies is embedded in a broader, even global, backlash against human rights protection.

Increasingly, one hears about the disregard of, or even crisis in, international human rights law. Some contend that "[w]ith populism sweeping the world and new superpowers in the ascendant, post-Westphalian visions of a shared global order are giving way to an era of resurgent sovereignty. Unchecked globalization and liberal internationalism are giving way to a post-human rights world."[2] This chapter does not argue that human rights are more often violated now than they were ten years ago. A lack of adequate methodology and data makes proving such allegations quite difficult. However, the *authority* of human rights *has* diminished, even in liberal constitutional systems, international relations, and international human rights law. At times these developments are described as a "change" or "shift" in language or emphasis. For example, under Chinese pressure in the UN Human Rights Council, accountability for human rights violations is replaced with "dialogue."[3]

---

[1] M. Villey, *Le Droit et les Droits de L'homme* (Presses Universitaires de France, 1983), p. 17 (my translation).

[2] S. Strangio, "Welcome to the Post-Human Rights World," Foreign Policy (March 7, 2017), www.foreignpolicy.com/2017/03/07/welcome-to-the-post-human-rights-world.

[3] "As China's Grip Tightens, Global Institutions Gasp Limiting Beijing's Influence Over Accountability and Justice," Human Rights Watch (2019), www.hrw.org/world-report /2019/country-chapters/global-3. This is not an isolated event. On March 19, 2018, the

The term "change" disguises a process of reducing the significance and value of classic civil and political rights.[4]

The loss of such status carries obvious practical consequences, both in international relations and human rights adjudication and – more broadly – in their protection and respect. Human rights become irrelevant as standards capable of guiding interstate relations, including diplomatic recognition, cooperation, state aid, or sanctions. As to adjudication, once human rights (understood as a shortlist of fundamental concerns) are removed from their pedestal, other values and considerations can easily prevail, to their detriment. One can see this in the case law of the ECtHR, which extends the grounds for human rights limitations beyond those enumerated in the European Convention on Human Rights (ECHR) and formally kept as a finite list.

For example, the ECtHR, following its consistent case law, held in *S.A. S. v. France* (the burqa ban case) that the "enumeration of the exceptions to the individual's freedom to manifest his or her religion or beliefs, as listed in Article 9(2), is exhaustive and that their definition is restrictive."[5] Nevertheless, the same case elevated "living together in society" to a right of others, rendering it compatible with the enumerated grounds for rights limitation. The Court interpreted the assumption that the rights of others could provide grounds for limitation by satisfying an abstract concern rather than an individual human rights claim. A few years later, the Court went even further, by stating that "for it to be compatible with the ECHR, a limitation on this freedom must therefore pursue an aim that *can be linked* to one of those listed in this provision."[6] Allowing any aim linked to a permitted ground to suffice in limiting a human right in effect elevated a myriad of interests above human rights.

This chapter does not claim that the world once saw a golden age of human rights protection; the analysis here concentrates on the international, national, and social *authority* of the concept (which of course has considerable influence on actual rights protection). The authority of human rights has increased since World War ii, and globally the

Russian Federation representative opposed the inclusion of a Human Rights High Commissioner report on Syria into the agenda of the UN Security Council.

[4] Classic (or "first generation") human rights are those listed in the US Bill of Rights, the French Declaration of the Rights of Man and Citizen, or the European Convention on Human Rights.

[5] See *S.A.S. v. France*, ECtHR, App. no. 43835/11, Judgment of 1 July 2014, para. 113.

[6] *Hamidović v. Bosnia and Herzegovina*, ECtHR, App. no. 57792/15, Judgment of 5 March 2018, para. 34 (emphasis added).

underlying idea became practically uncontested after 1989. Instead of challenging it, governments have limited their resistance to reinterpretation (see the Cairo Declaration on Human Rights in Islam, 1990). The human rights situation did not improve, notwithstanding the higher number of democracies worldwide.[7] With the current growth of illiberal democracies and other hybrid regimes, the erosion of the authority of human rights seems to accelerate. Localism becomes stronger and revision of the meaning and priorities of human rights continues.

6.2   Diminishing International Respect (Authority) of Human Rights

In 2000, Michael Ignatieff could still correctly state that human rights had become nothing short of "the dominant language of the public good around the globe."[8] A generation earlier, Michel Villey observed that "human rights have nothing but friends."[9] Today, this is considered a thing of the past, a not-so-noble lie. It is held against human rights that it dared to be the dominant language. To be dominant is a sin, because dominance is imperialistic. Human rights were and are the tool of ruling elites, and classic civil rights are the worthy tool of elite privilege.[10]

The old demagoguery roars again: it is increasingly common to label human rights defenders as criminals.[11] Public opinion does not appear to be worried about it. Human rights discourse is redesigned and marginalized in Western societies; in the rest of the world, where human rights served as the mobilizing idea in revolts against tyranny, little enthusiasm likely remains after the failure of the Arab Spring.

A generation ago, a state that would have openly challenged universal human rights ran the risk of becoming a pariah. Today, disregarding

---

[7] R. Clark, "A Tale of Two Trends: Democracy and Human Rights 1981–2010," *Journal of Human Rights*, 13:4 (2014), pp. 395–413. Clark found that "democracy ratings have both increased and converged considerably, while human rights ratings have worsened and diverged slightly."

[8] M. Ignatieff, *The Rights Revolution* (House of Anansi Press, 2007), p. 176.

[9] M. Villey, *Le Droit et les Droits*, p. 17 (my translation). Villey was very critical of the use of human rights in law.

[10] This fits into the populist delegitimation of human rights (an imposition from a global conspiracy).

[11] In 2018, Italian Vice-Prime Minister Salvini called the high sea rescuers of asylum seekers "criminals." See A. Giuffrida, "Italian Government Approves Salvini Bill Targeting Migrants," *The Guardian* (September 24, 2018), www.theguardian.com/world/2018/sep/24/italian-government-approves-bill-anti-migrant-measures-matteo-salvini.

human rights in international relations has become common, even normal.[12] Doing business with dictators goes without saying: human rights are not a precondition for economic ties with China. To the extent that domestic protection of human rights is a matter of international relations (which has formed part of the equation even in stable democracies – see the foreign policy sides of desegregation in the United States), the changes are discouraging. Post-1989, it seemed that democracies committed to human rights would push other countries toward greater respect for them, and the latter would have little choice but to accept the corresponding hegemonic language. (Of course, this was not a strong push, and even development aid was not tied to the human rights record of a recipient country.) Today, with new political and economic dependencies, this pressure is diminishing.

The international human rights protection system runs the risk of disintegration, even if some events point in the opposite direction.[13] The UK openly refused to implement the ECtHR judgment on prisoner voting rights and threatened withdrawal from the European system.[14] The Russian Constitutional Court followed suit, declaring that it has the constitutional duty to determine which judgments of the ECtHR are compatible with the Russian constitutional order.[15] This position was endorsed by Russian legislation requiring the Constitutional Court to exercise the ultimate review of constitutionality. Country after country deserts the jurisdiction of the International Criminal Court, and the ECtHR is under increasing stress. Earlier in Latin America, after the IACtHR found that a dismissal of judges in Venezuela violated the Inter-American Convention,[16] the Venezuelan TSJ held that the Convention and the rights protected by it, "under the pretext of universal legalities,"

---

[12] The UK, which only twenty years ago copied the ECHR into its constitutional system to fill a major gap, now conducts a relentless war against this very Convention, which was the brainchild of Winston Churchill.

[13] On the disregard for international judgments in illiberal democracies, see Chapter 8.

[14] State Obligations Concerning Change of Name, Gender Identity, and Rights Derived from a Relationship Between Same-Sex Couples (Interpretation and Scope of Articles 1(1), 3, 7, 11(2), 13, 17, 18 and 24, in relation to Article 1, of the American Convention on Human Rights (1978), Advisory Opinion OC-24/17, IACtHR (ser. A) No. 24 (November 24, 2017).

[15] See L. Mälksoo, "Russia's Constitutional Court Defies the European Court of Human Rights: Constitutional Court of the Russian Federation Judgment of 14 July 2015, No 21-П/2015," *European Constitutional Law Review*, 12:2 (2016), pp. 377–95.

[16] *Apitz Barbera et al ("First Court of Administrative Disputes") v. Venezuela*, IACtHR, Judgment of 5 August 2008. See Chapter 7.

cannot be supreme compared to the Constitution, and thus refused to execute the judgment.[17]

While most of the backlash against human rights resembles erosion and decline, there has been progress for certain human rights and related claims, at least in many countries. Instead of a general backlash, we may be facing an important readjustment, a shift *within* human rights, a restructuring and re-evaluation of their priorities and content. Human rights are universal but not immutable, and certainly not exempt from social adjustment. Or perhaps they must be local. Perhaps classic civil and political rights are less important today compared to the age of bourgeois elite rule, and only traditionalists interpret such loss of importance as decay. After all, fundamental human rights have always been subject to change. Cultural shifts matter both for the meaning (interpretation) of human rights and their social acceptability. While liberal constitutionalism and early rights declarations centered on freedom, today this no longer holds the same importance for a majority that takes liberty for granted: it is not concerned with liberation from specific forms of despotic oppression. Liberty appears too burdensome for ordinary use. As Tocqueville had already noticed: "To live in freedom one must grow used to a life full of agitation, change and danger; . . . that is the price of freedom."[18] Today, freedom means: "no more politics. I'm in the land of the free!"[19] However, if confronted with authoritarian ideas and practices, this might change.

The emerging indifference to civil and political rights reflects a shift toward identity concerns in the contemporary narcissistic Western culture. Narcissism and related consumerism have already altered the focus on freedom-oriented human rights.[20] As Nina Power, author of *One Dimensional Woman*, has stated following Laing's theory of (personal) liberation: to live freely means "to live as freely and honestly as possible,

---

[17] In a similar situation, Peru took the same position earlier with respect to *Castillo Petruzzi et al. v. Peru*, IACtHR, Judgment of 10 May 1999. In the end, Trinidad and Tobago and Venezuela (in 2012) denounced the Convention.

[18] A. de Tocqueville, *Journeys to England and Ireland*, ed. J.P. Mayer (Yale University Press, 1958), p. 116.

[19] The quote comes from Mrs. Schoolland, who survived China's many vicissitudes. See J. Stossel, "China's Tech Totalitarianism," Rasmussen Reports Political (April 15, 2020), www.rasmussenreports.com/public_content/political_commentary/commentary_by_john_stossel/china_s_tech_totalitarianism.

[20] On the negative social consequences of the cult of identity see M. Lilla, *The Once and Future Liberal: After Identity Politics* (Harper Collins, 2017); F. Fukuyama, *Identity: The Demand for Dignity and the Politics of Resentment* (Macmillan, 2018).

to coincide with oneself as much as possible, to not feel anxious or guilty, or ashamed, to not dwell in negative feelings."[21] Freedom has become a problem of identity and feeling good: it means the right to an authentic (narcissistic) identity. Hence a specific understanding of privacy that insists on combining exhibitionism with governmental protection from its negative consequences (e.g. the right to be forgotten). Privacy and the right to private life have become the shelter of personal weakness and vulnerability (see Section 6.4.1), often impairing political rights and transparency, which are necessary for a robust democracy. Other fundamental rights – like the right to freely practice religion – become expressions of identity: a manifestation that is not protected as part of a collective belief but because a person claims that an idiosyncratic behavior that is important to their identity just happens to be religious.

The citizens are satisfied with their "cage-free" status. By industry standard, to be "cage free" means able to nest, perch, and dust-bathe, with a minimum average space (as in the case of prisoners, who should enjoy on average three to six square meters per person in a prison cell). This is freedom *in* the cage; the cage is mistaken for an essential protective device or even a necessity to maintain the community within it, which would otherwise disappear in competition with other hen cultures.

This new understanding harms not only classic civil, political, and even socioeconomic rights but the very idea underlying human rights as such: the possibility that there are inherent limits to state power.

How did we get here? The shift is partly generational. It is difficult to understand and feel the importance of fundamental freedom-enhancing rights without the experience of totalitarianism. Other, actual injustices – frustrations due to inequality – capture the imagination. The fate of endangered species in faraway lands may stir the democratic public more than a lack of freedom for apostates in Bangladesh. Dolphins look more fun than prisoners.

Survey results indicate that both in stable democracies and transitional countries increasing numbers of people identify themselves with values that are incompatible with human rights. Nationalism and fear of the "other" turn against human rights. People show little interest in rights that pertain to all and demonstrate increasing hostility to rights that seem to benefit specific groups for which they find little sympathy. Majorities are solely interested in rights from which they individually benefit, like

---

[21] N. Power, "Untitled," *Nina Power* (blog, March 14, 2019), www.ninapower.net/2019/03/14/248.

freedom of conscience (but not freedom of religion for unusual and foreign groups), the right to certain elements of private life and privacy (related to freedom of consumption), and the collective rights of the majority. The resurgent idolatry of the sovereign nation state prevails (especially after the takeover of right-wing populism). The idolatry of sovereignty and the nationalist cult of provincial localism is antithetical to the international protection of human rights; it denies transnational human solidarity and refuses international human rights protection.

How was it possible that demagogy could once again undermine the results and foundations of three centuries of civilization? The complacency of self-evident truths (proudly professed long ago in the US Constitution and the French Declaration of 1789) has backfired. The last great reaffirmation of the obvious necessity of human rights came from the experience of totalitarianism. The lesson that civilization may easily collapse seems to be on the road to oblivion.

6.3   The Many Sources of Delegitimation

This chapter hypothesizes that the fate of human rights and fundamental constitutional rights in illiberal democracies is determined by the needs of plebiscitarian rule, while the instrumentalism and reinterpretation of human rights reflects broader, worldwide changes that facilitate the demise noticeable in illiberal democracies. It is not Eastern European authoritarianism but various Western ideologies, and geopolitical Western cultural changes, that undermine respect for human rights. Many scholars, activists, and ordinary citizens in stable democracies do not mind this loss. For them, human rights is not part of the solution but part of the (social) problem. For many critics, human rights are supposedly apolitical and thus unable to solve social conflicts. (Never mind that this has never been the ambition or purpose of human rights.)

Over the last seventy years (and for far longer, as natural rights), human rights were unquestionable or even sacred. Human rights "stand as the last remnant of the Enlightenment to retain its universal character. . . . Human rights thus function as a normative imperative that is beyond politics and law."[22] Today, when populist movements and governments base their power on denying Enlightenment and reason in the name of alternative facts, and where the possibility of community is

---

[22] R. Salecl, *The Spoils of Freedom: Psychoanalysis and Feminism after the Fall of Socialism* (Routledge, 1994), p. 112.

denied through the claim that "everything is political," the relevance of this attack is more obvious than ever and so are the stakes. A new wave of human rights revisionism is readjusting the field of liberty.[23]

Only a few years ago, Professor Moyn gained a certain celebrity status, which says little about his book's scholarly value but much about academia's state of mind in matters of human rights.[24] According to Moyn's thesis, the international recognition of human rights was neither a universalistic claim of the last two or three hundred years, nor a specific reaction to the barbarity of totalitarianism and World War II; it was a Cold War in(ter)vention, an apolitical, "moral" tool developed to respond to communism and enable interference into the domestic affairs of communist and other states.[25]

This kind of human rights revisionism is propelled by American (French, etc.) self-hatred, or more properly, hatred, dislike, or suspicion of the establishment, inspired eminently by President George W. Bush's unsuccessful invasion of Iraq. Moyn's earlier scholarly "conversion" paper is quite telling in this respect:

> The shift in political debate has been impossible to miss. Even those who retain an investment in human rights cannot treat them as an unquestionable good, mainly because the America that once seemed to many enthusiasts to be the prospective servant of universality abroad all too quickly became the America pursuing low-minded imperial ambitions in high-minded humanitarian tones.[26]

---

[23] P. Alston, "Does the Past Matter? On the Origins of Human Rights," *Harvard Law Review*, 126 (2013), pp. 2043–81.

[24] S. Moyn, *The Last Utopia: Human Rights in History* (Harvard University Press, 2012). See further, following a more openly leftist-egalitarian agenda at the expense of "liberal" human rights: S. Moyn, *Not Enough: Human Rights in an Unequal World* (Harvard University Press, 2018). For a general criticism of Moyn's attempt to destroy human rights and liberal democracy, see J. Lacroix and J.-Y. Pranchère, *Human Rights on Trial: A Genealogy of the Critique of Human Rights* (Cambridge University Press, 2018). For a historically and morally more accurate narrative on human rights see L. Hunt, *Inventing Human Rights: A History* (W. W. Norton & Company, 2007).

[25] The thesis reflects the 1960s state-of-the-art Soviet position, and yet Professor Moyn is not alone. Some of these attacks (stirred by leftist dissatisfaction – see Alain Badiou in Section 6.6) confuse the occasional or even systemic disregard of human rights with their legitimacy. E. A. Posner, *The Twilight of Human Rights Law* (Oxford University Press, 2014) and S. Hopgood, *The Endtimes of Human Rights* (Cornell University Press, 2014) are part of what Langford calls an "eschatological trilogy." M. Langford, "Critiques of Human Rights," *Annual Review of Law and Social Science*, 14 (2018), pp. 69–89.

[26] S. Moyn, "On the Genealogy of Morals," *The Nation* (April 16, 2007), www .thenation.com/article/archive/genealogy-morals.

This is a simple replica of the old Carl Schmitt line:

> The concept of humanity is an especially useful ideological instrument of imperialist expansion, and in its ethical-humanitarian form it is a specific vehicle of economic imperialism. Here one is reminded of a somewhat modified expression of Proudhon's: whoever invokes humanity wants to cheat.[27]

In Moyn's imagination, human rights, which are allegedly apolitical or suprapolitical, serve unacceptable imperialist politics. This position of political dissatisfaction simply (but not always openly) echoes the criticism of an earlier generation of feminists who refused the abstractness of human rights: "Abstract rights will authorize the male experience of the world."[28]

A somewhat older criticism of human rights is anthropological in its origins. It denies the possibility of the universalism of human rights and argues that universalistic claims not only disregard local conditions and traditions but also impose a Western way of life on non-Western societies.[29] For example, some argue that Western private property is alien to most places in Africa, where collective property prevails; private property would not only destroy these idyllic relationships but would generate oppression in these sublime communities, which naturally know no gender discrimination. (What is missing in these vitriolic fables is that, contrary to what some shortsighted World Bank bureaucrats once claimed, the constitutional guarantee of private property does not require the privatization of collective property; famously, constitutional protection does not entail access to property.)

Authoritarian rulers and nationalist leaders happily echo these arguments. Without universalism, the local is king, and circumstances can justify an array of oppressive policies for the greater future good in the

---

[27] C. Schmitt, *The Concept of the Political* (University of Chicago Press, 1996), p. 54.

[28] C. A. MacKinnon, "Feminism, Marxism, Method, and the State: An Agenda for Theory," in K.T. Bartlett and R. Kennedy (eds.), *Feminist Legal Theory: Readings in Law and Gender* (Westview Press, 1991), p. 195. Interestingly, Edmund Burke, a thinker antithetic to feminism, disliked human rights for their abstractness.

[29] A. A. An-Na'im, "Decolonizing Human Rights: An Urgent Plea for Rebuttal," Lecture at Oxford University. YouTube (July 20, 2017), www.youtube.com/watch?v=yveTevoQplM. While most drafters of the Universal Declaration were committed to Western values, the Declaration did not take a position on the source(s) of human rights (except in the desire to avoid the barbarism of the immediate past). J. Maritain, "Introduction," in *Human Rights: Comments and Interpretations; A Symposium Edited by UNESCO* (UNESCO, 1948); J. Maritain, *Man and the State* (University of Chicago Press, 1951), p. 77.

name of consent.[30] Once again, we arrive at popular endorsements advocated by populist and authoritarian leaders and a growing number of their citizens.

Furthermore, public acceptance of human rights in the past decades (especially where personal experience of oppression and barbarity had faded or did not exist) was bolstered by the economic performance of regimes claiming to respect human rights: as fundamental constitutional rights formed part of the political arrangement in successful democracies, they were embraced as part of an effective and attractive political system. This was a performance-based legitimacy, a legitimacy by association. The mantra asserted that Western-type rights-respecting regimes would bring welfare: liberation and wellbeing go hand in hand. This was certainly the hope in Eastern Europe in 1989. However, the lack of satisfactory economic results following the transition to a market economy in many new democracies explains how this disappointment extended to a belief that rights were seemingly useless. Once the socioeconomic performance of the state becomes unconvincing, especially in terms of individual benefits, respect for human rights shares the consequences of this disappointment. Beyond the negative experiences contradicting the utilitarian, development-based assumption, an even stronger intellectual challenge has arisen with the success of China. Here, even economic liberties remain limited, while others do not even exist, and yet the country has seen mass-scale improvement of living conditions without freedom and democracy.

6.4 Substantive Changes in Human Rights and Ensuing Difficulties

The catalog of fundamental and human rights has grown longer since 1789,[31] with socioeconomic rights being the great addition of the last century. The expanding list and scope of rights resulted in rights inflation. Quite often, the new "rights" do not represent individual entitlements and reflect new expectations vis-à-vis the state. This changed conceptual basis contributes to the intellectual delegitimation of human rights.

---

[30] N. Le, "Are Human Rights Universal or Culturally Relative?," *Peace Review*, 28:2 (2016), pp. 203–11.
[31] In 1787, more than fifty rights could be found in American state constitutions. Many were not incorporated into the Bill of Rights and were deleted from state constitutions.

The UN Universal Declaration of Human Rights was silent on the foundations of human rights, but it was expressly concerned about past brutality. With time, constitutional courts increasingly concluded that fundamental rights are based on the equal dignity of all human beings. Critics labeled this individualist-liberal, but accepted it as a foundation, even in the Vienna Declaration and Programme of Action (1993), which at the same time codified a new approach to human rights. Centering human rights in dignity is a catch-all concept. A more substantive understanding of dignity has also justified socioeconomic rights: people living below a certain standard cannot have a dignified life, and dignified life becomes the standard for government services. Dignity seemed attractive as a common foundation because it conformed with Western values (see Christian and Kantian traditions). Unfortunately, this has not been the case with all other cultures, which do not know the term. However, the reference to dignity has not been particularly problematic as long as this obscure notion entitled all human beings to be worthy of equal respect by the state.

With the emergence of the substantive concept of dignity, human rights gradually morphed into social justice issues. The grammar of rights changed. The new, social rights–inspired aspirations expected the state to perform and provide services in line with the dictates of rights, as if state power was always decent, responsive, and nonoppressive. Rights were expected to do the work of democratic decision-making. Human rights here serve as a justification and battle cry for social movements. Rights mean obligations and policies to provide state services. The traditional approach, which was concerned with the rights of the *autonomous individual*, became neglected, as if it were irrelevant.

6.4.1 From Vulnerability to Security

The conceptual change in human rights relates to the language of victimhood and *vulnerability* (and victim status as a form of vulnerability). It is not the dire need of all, nor their autonomy or dignity as such, but a specific vulnerability that necessitates special human rights to satisfy the special needs of the vulnerable position. This logic alters the justification for traditional rights, too: prisoners deserve protection due to their vulnerable position and not because inhumane treatment is an unacceptable affront to humanity. In an alternative version: the treatment of prisoners will be considered inhuman *because* they are vulnerable. The anthropological shift from a self-conscious, autonomous person with a reasonable life path to the vulnerability of an individual naked body is fundamental.

According to the vulnerability theory, an ever increasing number of groups in society are particularly vulnerable, and it is the need for enhancing their capacities to undo such vulnerability that necessitates human rights.[32] Given the majority's lack of interest in the particular suffering of special groups, the emphasis on vulnerability is an understandable and efficient mobilizing strategy. Victimhood became a useful competitive argument in a politically predetermined environment.[33]

Still, there is little room for freedom of religion or speech here, as these freedoms are not matters of vulnerability, except for minority religious groups. Grounding free speech in the vulnerability of the speaker would yield a completely different arrangement compared to that of the First Amendment. It would claim that speech is to be protected because the speaker is weak against the oppressive state. (*A contrario*, a government official is not entitled to the same level of protection.) In reality, the vulnerability argument works *against* free speech, in favor of the listeners and their vulnerability, and in particular in favor of "vulnerable audiences." A lot of important speech is offensive, and offensive speech is particularly effective speech – therefore, it will be less and less protected.

Victimhood dictates partially similar conclusions: "[T]he Rights of Man turned out to be the rights of the rightless .... They appeared more and more as the rights of the victims, the rights of those who were unable to enact any rights or even any claim in their name."[34] In the new approach, the rights of women, sexual minorities, children, disabled people, and other (persecuted or simply disadvantaged) groups like

---

[32] For an example of vulnerability-based human rights theory, see A. A. An-Na'im, "The Politics of Religion and Morality of Globalization," in M. Juergensmeyer (ed.), *Religion and Global Civil Society* (Oxford University Press, 2005), p. 39.

Many claims by members of vulnerable (or marginalized) groups are legitimate and reasonable: from a liberal perspective, the problem is that universal rights were not extended to them. Alternatively, the rights were applied equally, but certain special difficulties in the enjoyment of the right were not taken into consideration. Where there is a right to elect representatives, the physical accessibility of the voting booth can be an issue, albeit this is an equality issue to be decided on reasonable grounds and is not an absolute right pertaining to disability as a rights generator.

[33] *See* T. A. Jacoby, "A Theory of Victimhood: Politics, Conflict and the Construction of Victim-based Identity," *Millennium: Journal of International Studies*, 43:2 (2014), pp. 511–30.

[34] J. Ranciére, "Who Is the Subject of the Rights of Man?," *The South Atlantic Quarterly*, 103:2–3 (2004), p. 298.

refugees are the human rights. Yes, it is the presumed incapacity that becomes the very right: rights are a matter of (underprivileged) *status*.

The Vienna Declaration illustrates the shift from autonomy to status, thus from liberty to identity. Its Programme of Action concerns providing special groups with equal access to the same right by eliminating specific group-related obstacles. This fits into the old paradigm. The Declaration singled out these groups in view of their challenges. Prima facie, thus far this represents solely a robust, inclusive understanding of existing human rights: if there is a right to receive information, the hearing impaired must have access to news via sign language during television broadcasts. The special concern means only how to enable vulnerable members of society to enjoy rights like all others do. But at a certain point this problem-oriented approach turns into *specific* rights (e.g. of women, disabled people, etc.), as if these rights were different from other rights that pertain to both sexes, apply to men only, or, as in some theories, serve male domination.[35]

The vulnerability thesis contains many sources, including critical race theory, certain feminist theories, and other academic approaches. According to Martha Fineman: "Vulnerability is typically associated with victimhood, deprivation, dependency, or pathology." In her influential and sophisticated scholarship, vulnerability is elevated to *the* human condition, the fundamental category of human existence. On this anthropological foundation she refutes the world view of political liberalism, which served as the foundation of constitutionalism and classic human rights legitimation, with a "liberal legal subject" as the ideal citizen: "this subject is an autonomous, independent and fully-functioning adult, who inhabits a world defined by individual, not societal responsibility, where state intervention or regulation is perceived as a violation of his liberty."[36]

The role or duty of the state is to generate legal policies that increase resilience to vulnerability, first and foremost, by creating genuine, substantive (and not only formal) equality. In Fineman's admittedly

---

[35] See, for example, Catherine MacKinnon's criticism of freedom of expression: C. MacKinnon, *Only Words* (Harvard University Press, 1996), p. 49.

[36] As found in a 2015 blog entry: M. A. Fineman, "Fineman on Vulnerability and Law," New Legal Realism (blog, November 30, 2015), www.newlegalrealism.org/2015/11/30/fine man-on-vulnerability-and-law/. In her more recent writing, Fineman seems to realize that the vulnerability approach entails defenselessness and dependence and that this limits the possibility of action for the vulnerable, forcing them into the straitjacket of victimhood. See further M. A. Fineman, "Vulnerability and Inevitable Inequality," *Oslo Law Review*, 4:3 (2017), pp. 133–49.

antiliberal theory, the role of the state implies an affirmative obligation "to actively structure conditions for equality."[37] Like in the case of Moyn, here too the universal human rights of all are transformed into a social (socialist) policy for specific groups.

The twists and turns in the cult of vulnerability relate to a major historical event: military imperialism, and Carlyle and Nietzsche (for other reasons), cultivated violent heroes; these cults were cults of violence. After the experience of two world wars, and with the unmasking of violent imperial oppression, naked force and brute violence became less attractive (although not necessarily in the playful world of popular culture – see especially movies and video games). Moving away from the cult of force reminds us of the victory of the powerless in Christianity, so detested by Nietzsche, where the victims took their revenge and transformed their frailty into a moral argument. Of course, this change was linked to the political success of well-organized movements in the political sphere, where fringe votes were needed in the absence of clear majorities and where reference to force resonated in the nefarious consciousness of those who benefited from the injustices of their predecessors and ancestors. Once the moral fabric of globally influential, affluent societies became porous and self-doubting, the fundamental assumptions and self-confidence of liberal (i.e. liberty-oriented) human rights lost its grip. (The affinities with populism, where the authentic and powerless people is the victim of the elite, is more than obvious.)

Two consequences of this shift are relevant for this study of the intellectual origins of the human rights backlash. First, the cult of vulnerability directly conflicts with the culture and ethos underlying human rights as understood in the Universal Declaration and the Kantian tradition. The individualist liberty offered by the classic concept of human rights assumes people of equal dignity and endowed with a faculty of reason. Dignity follows from the sheer fact of being born human, but even in this antimeritocratic perspective, human beings are masters of their fate, and rights exist to enable (to some extent at least) the realization of this fact. Vulnerability exempts individuals from the responsibility for their own fate. From the human rights perspective, a hidden paradigm shift has occurred: the individual who was worthy of equal respect simply for being human (and no more than that minimum)

---

[37] M. A. Fineman, "The Vulnerable Subject: Anchoring Equality in the Human Condition," *Yale Journal of Law & Feminism*, 20 (2008), p. 21. Other feminists are less state-centered: Judith Butler does not trust the state or "governability."

is replaced by a vulnerable victim or victim in waiting. Autonomy vis-à-vis the state is replaced with dependence on the state.

Second, the new force of the victimhood-based argument turns human and constitutionalized rights into competitive claims of neglect and disregard: whomever is more vulnerable shall receive (more) rights protection. Victimhood is a sure sign of injustice, and the interest in injustice replaces rights. The argument that religious people and religion itself are the victims of secularist legislation does not only mobilize Evangelicals but has been able to shape the understanding of freedom of religion in the United States.

The shift toward vulnerability carries practical consequences, as vulnerability dictates very different choices compared to classic human rights. From the demands of the Enlightenment to the Universal Declaration, human rights have enabled personal individual autonomy. They serve autonomous beings. The classic rights were necessary against nearly unlimited government power. Where government power is unlimited, society without rights may descend into barbarism and slavery. This consideration is now replaced by a positive program of social justice that seeks to counter vulnerability. Hence individual rights become irrelevant; they can be granted for instrumental purposes, namely, to force the state to fulfill its mission to counter vulnerability. This gives birth to a cult of the state that provides security to all bodily vulnerable subjects.

Vulnerability creates a new hierarchy of rights. Illegal occupants (squatters) with children jump the queue for social housing to the detriment of lawful applicants.[38] Vulnerability prevails over merit and liberty rights. The centuries-old right to cross-examine witnesses is sidelined to protect children and women victims, as a matter of victim rights. While understandably victims should not be compelled to testify where this would re-ignite their trauma (hence victims' interests do matter), it does not follow that a person should be convicted where the sole or decisive piece of evidence is not assessed before a judge and not cross-examined by the accused.

The underlying interest here again is to provide security, a demand that is elevated to a right. Everyone is vulnerable, and all of us are prone to accident and illness. As consumers, we may buy unsafe food or purchase a car with faulty brakes. These days we all are considered (are

---

[38] *Government of the Republic of South Africa and Others* v. *Grootboom and Others* [2000] ZACC 19; 2001 (1) SA 46; 2000 (11) BCLR 1169.

considering ourselves) victims of potential terror attacks, and we all can fall victim to fake news (whose maiden name was disinformation). The logic of the security fixation leads to demands – a right! – for a "safe space." People insist on freedom from harassment (which is increasingly understood as being sheltered from *troubling ideas*).

The social desire for security is understandable. But once the paradigm is based on vulnerability, security becomes a right, and a decisive one. The security scare justifies a police state in the name of an alleged human right to live in security, a right that tends to absorb all other rights. This right to security has little to do with the "right to security of person" recognized in Article 3 of the Universal Declaration. That security meant protection against state coercion, such as arbitrary detention and imprisonment; in other words, protection *against* state arbitrariness.

Security measures help dominant powers to avoid criticism and accountability. It is in the name of security (sometimes called harmony in Singapore) that governments exercise control over their political and intellectual opponents. The rights of defense and the conditions of lawful detention move from fundamental rights to obstacles to the rights of victims and the administration of justice. After a while, this is not seen as rights curtailment. Thanks to the norm-transformative power of the factual (i.e. the power of what happens over what is prescribed), foundational assumptions about rights are brought in line with what the majority (or a vocal minority) does or wishes to happen.

6.4.2   The Cult of the Local

Human rights are defined in international law as universal, pertaining to all. Yet this does not mean that there are no important cultural disagreements on fundamental human conditions. There is a universal right to life, but societies differ on the meaning, beginnings, or borders of life. Where there is a fundamental agreement, like equal respect or liberty for all, local considerations cannot prevail: slavery was culturally accepted either as a fact of life or on racial grounds, but this always ran contrary to the idea of equal liberty for all. Its absence and tangible impossibility do not challenge the retrospective truth of this idea.[39] A principle can be right (morally true) even if it is impractical.

---

[39] In ancient Greece, "life proceeded on the basis of slavery and left no space, effectively, for the question of its justice to be raised.... [In Greece] considerations of justice and injustice were immobilised by the demands of what was seen as social and economic necessity." B. Williams, *Shame and Necessity* (University of California Press, 1993), p. 124.

Nevertheless, anti-imperialist rights criticism and postcolonial studies continue to argue that universal human rights disrespect local traditions, values and circumstances and in general destroy diversity. (Note that diversity, a fact, is elevated into a value without further explanation.) While many of these critics claim to be radical or revolutionary, the criticism itself fits into a trend that was established by Edmund Burke. This should not surprise us: the cult of the local is deeply conservative. It is also often deeply insensitive, for example, when female genital mutilation is defended in the name of local cultural traditions. The same inhuman perspective is behind the position that advocates restrictions on women, claiming that such restrictions (notably "living in modesty" or serving the family) merely support the culturally determined expression of female dignity.

In a further complication, this position is often bolstered by a localist understanding of freedom of religion: restrictions on women are justified as religious dictates and therefore protected by religious freedom rights. Religions often encompass traditional concepts of purity to the detriment of those groups these religions consider "impure" – women in particular – and sacred religious texts often codify patriarchal supremacy. For this reason freedom of religion remains in a tense juxtaposition with the Enlightenment, a major source of modern human rights. The conflict surrounding women entering the Sabarimala shrine in India's Kerala state on grounds of impurity effectively illustrates this point.[40]

6.5   Inflation, Overreach, Abuse

6.5.1   Inflation and Overextension

The list of human rights grows, with new claims based on justifications and applicability that fundamentally differ from those applied to the classic rights. Some debate whether such additions strengthen the credibility of human rights (as they respond to everyday needs of the general public) or render human rights impractical and less credible (because of their partial, political, and ad hoc nature). Rights proliferation runs the risk of turning human rights into something banal (inflation). Losing their steering capacity pits more and more rights against each other,

---

[40] "Sabarimala: Women Who Defied Temple Mobs 'Have No Fear,'" BBC News (January 4, 2019), www.bbc.com/news/world-asia-india-46764721.

resulting in an increasing number of legal conflicts, decided in an unprincipled and therefore delegitimating manner.[41]

Beyond the problem of the proliferation and inflation of human rights, legitimacy suffers from overextension (i.e. "excessive" application), when most or too many social problems are transformed ultimately into human rights issues (a phenomenon that is used by illiberal leaders to delegitimize human rights and rights defenders). The difficulties of human rights, including the loss of political incontestability and steering power, are partly due to the very logic of past successes. Because human rights were so attractive, many social complaints or grievances were formulated in human rights terms, and to the extent these efforts were successful, they were included into the international catalog, resulting in rights inflation. This had delegitimating effects, for example, when animal rights (originating in the respectable demand that animals be treated without cruelty and with decency) were argued as human rights.

Understandably, activists of all sorts formulated claims and grievances in human rights terms with excessive zeal. Once a group grievance can be framed as a rights claim, it loses its partial or partisan nature, thanks to the neutral (universal, nonpartial) language of rights. The neutral language can hide special interests and stop conversation. Special claims can be successfully spun against traditional human rights. See, for example, the argument that bakers selling a cake exercise their rights of artistic freedom, and their artwork (the cake) could be seen as celebrating gay marriage, against the artist-baker's conscience.[42]

---

[41] "In its devalued state, the currency of human rights is actually more likely to buy cover and legitimacy for dictatorships than purchase protection against the abuse of citizens by such states. And thereby the process of rights inflation actually undermines the core values of liberty and the rule of law that should underpin the concept of human rights." J. Mchangama and G. Verdirame, "The Danger of Human Rights Proliferation. When Defending Liberty, Less Is More," *Foreign Affairs* (July 24, 2013). Cranston warned against such inflation (M. Cranston, *What Are Human Rights?*, [Bodley Head, 1973]) and insisted that only extremely important issues should be treated as human rights. The problem is that for a given group, an interest can be particularly important, while not particularly relevant for the average, or abstract, individual.

[42] *Masterpiece Cakeshop* v. *Colorado Civil Rights Commission*, 584 US ___ (2018); "At its most general level, the cake at issue in Mr. Phillips's case was just a mixture of flour and eggs; at its most specific level, it was a cake celebrating the same-sex wedding of Mr. Craig and Mr. Mullins." J. Gorsuch, concurring. *Masterpiece Cakeshop* is, like the *Ladele* case in the ECtHR (*Eweida and Others* v. *the United Kingdom*, ECtHR, App. nos. 48420/10, 59842/10, 51671/10 and 36516/10, Judgment of 15 January 2013), a paradigmatic instance of narcissistic aggrandizement of minor personal grievances and idiosyncrasies; a trivialization and banalization of conscience.

With rights inflation, rights conflicts grow increasingly common. Groups rallying in the name of human rights compete and conflict with other interest groups also mobilizing under the human rights banner. Presenting anything as a right diminishes the power of the idea of rights. Real and imaginary overextension hurts the credibility of human rights. With rights inflation, rights are easily brought into culture wars, which makes them partisan and even trivial. The extension of human rights increases surreal expectations that cannot be satisfied; expectations bring frustration, and frustration breads disillusionment.

The most common accusation of overextension comes from countries whose human rights records are routinely criticized by international actors, particularly NGOs. Human rights violators find refuge in the argument of human rights overreach, claiming that such criticism derives from foreign conspiracies, used as a tool to destabilize them. Very often this is expressed in the best traditions of Soviet propaganda:

> [Malaysian Prime Minister] Najib Razak said Islam and its followers are now being tested by new threats under the guise of humanism, secularism, liberalism and human rights. He said this mindset appeared to be becoming a new form of religion which was fast expanding locally and abroad.
>
> They call it human rightism, where the core beliefs are based on humanism and secularism as well as liberalism.
>
> "It's deviationist in that it glorifies the desires of man alone and rejects any value system that encompasses religious norms and etiquettes. They do this on the premise of championing human rights," he said.[43]

6.5.2   "Human Rightism"

Delegitimation has descended to such a degree that human rights protection is ridiculed as an "ism," suggesting a dogmatic ideology, a matter of excessive imagination with zealous believers, like communism. This contempt is summarized by the French term *"droit-de-l'hommisme,"* a term most likely invented by the French international law expert Alain Pellet.[44] The rather neutral term acquired a sinister meaning via

---

[43]   J. T. Eberhard. "Malaysian Prime Minister: Islam Being Threatened by 'Human Rightism, Humanism, and Secularism.'" Patheos (May 16, 2014), www.patheos.com/blogs/wwjtd/2014/05/malaysian-prime-minister-islam-being-threatened-by-human-rightism-humanism-and-secularism/.

[44]   A. Pellet, "La Mise en œuvre des Normes Relatives aux Droits de L'homme," in H. Thierry and E. Decaux (eds.), *Droit International et Droits de L'homme – La Pratique Juridique Française dans le Domaine de la Protection Internationale des Droits de L'homme* (Monchrestien, 1990), p. 126.

a statement by Hubert Védrine, minister of foreign affairs in one of the French socialist governments. In 2007, Védrine stated that *droit-de-l'hommisme* is just posturing; it is used only because we are unable to intervene, including militarily. It has no impact on the Russian, Chinese, and Arab world.[45]

6.6   Direct Attacks

Thus far, this chapter has addressed the various intellectual mechanisms that led to the demise of the legitimacy of human rights without directly challenging it. However, the number of direct intellectual attacks is also on the rise. This includes the patent denial of the existence of human rights. Marx always took a negative approach to human rights, and many Marxists maintain that it remains a plain, bourgeois ideology that reinforces class oppression. Other Marxist and communitarians have criticized human rights as pure individualist egotism and claimed that such individualism is sociological nonsense. From the perspective of antiliberalism and antiglobalization, the French philosopher Alain Badiou summarizes the most radical contemporary rejection of human rights as a tool of oppression. Human rights are "the rights of the powerful to carve up states, to put in power... corrupt valets who will hand over the totality of the country's resources to... the powerful for nothing."[46] Furthermore, a nihilist critique of law, which considers the RoL an illusion or disguised form of the domination of special interests, refutes the legitimacy of human rights law. Here, the attack concerns the use of legal forms, while the revolutionary arguments still rely on human rights claims. This deprives human rights of institutional support.

For communitarians and populists who prefer a strong state (as only a strong state can serve the "genuine" people), human rights are an affront to democratic popular will. Supporters of sovereignty reject constitutional and international courts and the inherent legitimacy of human rights. In a telling twist on the reclaimed power of sovereignty, in

---

[45] R. Werly, "Hubert Védrine Le «droit de l'hommisme», posture de repli," Le Temps (May 24, 2007) www.letemps.ch/opinions/hubert-vedrine-droit-lhommisme-posture-repli. Védrine made this remark on the occasion of the nomination of his successor, Bernard Kouchner, a leader (and co-founder) of Médecins Sans Frontières, to the Ministry of Foreign Affairs.

[46] A. Badiou, *The Rebirth of History* (Verso, 2012), p. 5. *See* further Z. Manfredi, "Recent Histories and Uncertain Futures: Contemporary Critiques of International Human Rights and Humanitarianism," *Qui Parle*, 22:1 (2013), pp. 3–32.

response to such pressure the ECtHR declared that restrictions of fundamental rights adopted by a national legislature in a proper procedure are
presumed not to violate human rights.[47] This is the exact opposite of the
original understanding of human rights, which is based on the conviction
that it is impermissible to turn the sovereignty of the state against the
supremacy of human rights law.

6.7   Fundamental Rights and Illiberalism

The liberal and conservative press, as well as human rights defenders, are
inclined to describe the emerging illiberal regimes as autocracies that
violate human rights.[48] However, the relation of populist illiberalism to
fundamental rights is more complex. In fact, the lists of fundamental
rights in the Venezuelan, Bolivian, and Ecuadorian populist constitutions
were innovative as well as inclusive for many previously excluded groups;
they also "constitutionalized" international human rights law, making
human rights treaties and international case law directly applicable.[49]
The Turkish constitutional amendments of 2010 provided for efficient
rights protection, while the fundamental rights chapter of the HFL elicits
only minor objections.

In a way, these constitutions did not dare to take the position of
established authoritarian constitutional regimes, like Singapore, where
according to the Constitution the citizenry prefers "harmony" to disrup-
tive rights. In the early days of regime building, when their constitutions
were drafted, these not-yet self-confident new regimes felt that they had
to demonstrate they were good citizens of the international community.

---

[47] *Animal Defenders International* v. *the United Kingdom,* ECtHR, App. no. 48876/08,
Judgment of 22 April 2013, paras. 108–9.
[48] "Established autocrats and their admirers continued their disregard for basic rights."
K. Roth, "World's Autocrats Face Rising Resistance," Human Rights Watch Keynote
(2019), www.hrw.org/world-report/2019/keynote/autocrats-face-rising-resistance. This
is perhaps true of Turkey's Erdoğan, the Philippines' Duterte, or Maduro in Venezuela,
but most illiberal democracies have not (yet?) reached the despotic oppressive stage. The
sins listed by Roth with regard to EU illiberal democracies are not typical fundamental
rights violations affecting the citizenry at large. This is what Roth held against these
regimes: "Kaczyński . . . intended to limit reproductive rights. Italy's interior minister . . .
Matteo Salvini, closed ports to refugees and migrants, scuttled efforts to save migrants'
lives at sea, and stoked anti-immigrant sentiment."
[49] The Constitution of Venezuela states that international human rights treaties shall "have
constitutional rank" (Article 23). (See also a comparable amendment in Turkey in 2010.)
The reality might have been different from day one.

In contrast, in Singapore, where the authoritarian potential of illiberal democracy is clear, the demands of government authority and stability render constitutionally sanctioned rights meaningless. As Article 14 of the Singapore Constitution [Freedom of speech, assembly and association] states:

> Parliament may by law impose –
>
> (a) on the rights conferred by clause (1)(a), such restrictions as it considers necessary or expedient in the interest of the security of Singapore or any part thereof, friendly relations with other countries, public order or morality.[50]

Compared to this generality, the grounds for rights limitation in the language of the HFL remain fairly liberal, notwithstanding collective dignitarian restrictions,[51] as a general clause requires that rights limitations must be proportionate to their legitimate goal.

Thus far, the illiberal member states of the EU have been reluctant to move in the direction of Singapore. Not even the most thorough and critical liberal review of the HFL could find specific points on which to object in 2011. (Later amendments did indicate a nationalistic and conservative hierarchy of rights and interests.) The original objections to the new Constitution were based on a disagreement over world views:

> In sum, the concept of law of the Fundamental Law reflects the intention of the Hungarian state not to remain neutral as regards the life and ideologies of its citizens. Furthermore, it seeks to restrict citizens' rights which undermines the value of these entitlements. This restrictive approach to rights presents a conception which is hardly defensible in a modern society based on the plurality of forms of life.[52]

---

[50] The Constituent Assembly restored the police's powers to make arrests on their own authority and "judges were granted the power to hold suspects detained on suspicion for six days." "Venezuela" in *World Report 2001*, Human Rights Watch, 2001. www.hrw.org /legacy/wr2k1/americas/venezuela.html.

[51] Article VIII HFL states: "(4) The right to freedom of expression may not be exercised with the aim of violating the human dignity of others. (5) The right to freedom of expression may not be exercised with the aim of violating the dignity of the Hungarian nation or of any national, ethnic, racial or religious community."

[52] Z. Fleck, G. Gadó, and G. Halmai et al., *Opinion on the Fundamental Law of Hungary* (June 2011), p. 16. The Venice Commission expected only "more precise indications . . . in line with the international human rights instruments." See Venice Commission Opinion no. 621/2011 on the new Constitution of Hungary, Venice, June 20, 2011, para 148.

This early criticism captured what happened well: the state was abandoning neutrality. Again, this was not a direct fundamental restriction of rights.

In its journey toward potentially despotic rule, and at least during the early stages of the journey, the illiberal constitutional state still subscribes to human rights, albeit with reservations and readiness to disregard them in a circumscribed way whenever deemed necessary for the consolidation of power. The legitimacy of human rights is not challenged, but it is not necessarily understood as the right of all humans (e.g. migrants).[53]

Formal respect for human rights is surprising given the populist aversion to any form of dissent (whether in parliament or by civil society), and also the presentation of human rights in populist rhetoric as cosmopolitan, elitist, and contrary to common sense. It is paradoxical because the regime is illiberal by its own proud admission and generates regime legitimacy by catering to nationalist sentiments and rural traditions. The regime and its legal and political order are legitimate in the eyes of a popular majority precisely for being illiberal, reflecting an authoritarian, partly premodern popular identity that is rather common in Eastern Europe or rural Turkey. And yet no ruler of a European illiberal regime, not even autocrats, would deny the relevance of human rights. That would be too revolutionary. As Andrew Janos has argued, liberal hegemony places a "web of constraints" on nondemocratic governments that seek to maintain international respectability and viability.[54] They denounce only what they consider "excessive" in human rights, and consider as "excessive" anything that does not respect local cultural traditions (e.g. gay rights and same-sex marriage). The HPM has stated this position eloquently: "the really fatal disease threatening Europe is more of an intellectual nature. A common cause lies at the root of the troubles: Europe does not acknowledge its own identity. Today the European spirit and its people believe in superficial and secondary things: in human rights, progress, openness, new kinds of family and tolerance. These are nice things, but are in fact only secondary, because they are merely derivative. Yes, Europe today believes in secondary things, but does not believe in the source of those things. It does not believe in Christianity, it does not believe in common sense, it

---

[53] Even in the United States, where free speech was endorsed unconditionally, the general public has always been ready to support speech restrictions on grounds of content or in view of the speakers.

[54] A. Janos, *East Central Europe in the Modern World: The Politics of Borderlands from Pre- to Postcommunism* (Stanford University Press, 2000), pp. 97–99.

does not believe in military virtues, and it does not believe in national pride."[55] In Orbán's view, Europe's problem is the loss of its belief in the values these things originate from: Christianity, common sense, military vigor, and national pride.

The secondary status of fundamental human rights relates to the populist exaltation of people's sovereignty. Majority will as the embodiment of the nation's existential interest is entitled to overrule the foreign, doctrinal dictates of human rights. In many respects, this ideology corresponds to the antielitist criticism of human rights that is common in anticolonialist literature. To quote the HPM once again: "In Europe there's a tendency to use foreign policy as a vehicle to export value systems and to prove the West's moral superiority in terms of human rights, democracy and humanism."[56] This nicely echoes Putin, who argues that certain countries – the United States and its NATO allies – violate "international law and state sovereignty" under the banner of universal human rights.[57]

However, in illiberal EU member states, the conflict with "international forces" does not extend to denying such rights; rather, it is limited to *deceitful reinterpretation*, relying on the ambiguities of the current system, pitting rights against rights and inventing new grounds for limitation. Such reinterpretation changes the meaning of existing rights, grants new powers to traditional grounds for limitation.[58] In the

---

[55] V. Orbán, "Prime Minister Viktor Orbán's speech at the 26th Congress of the Fidesz – Hungarian Civic Union, December 13, 2015," Prime Minister's Office Website (December 17, 2015), https://2015-2019.kormany.hu/en/the-prime-minister/the-prime-minister-s-speeches/prime-minister-viktor-orban-s-speech-at-the-26th-congress-of-the-fidesz-hungarian-civic-union.

This position echoes Lee's 1992 speech on "Democracy, Human Rights and the Realities." M. Barr, *Cultural Politics and Asian Values: The Tepid War* (Routledge, 2002), p. 36. "Whilst democracy and human rights are worthwhile ideas, we should be clear that the real objective is good government. That should be the test for ODA [official development assistance]. Is this a good government that deserves ODA? Is it honest and effective? Does it look after its people?" "Speech by Mr. Lee Kuan Yew, Senior Minister of Singapore at the Create 21 Asahi Forum" (speech, November 20, 1992, Tokyo), www.nas.gov.sg/archivesonline/data/pdfdoc/lky19921120.pdf, pp. 18–19.

[56] "Interview [on May 1] with Prime Minister Viktor Orbán in the Italian newspaper La Stampa," Prime Minister's Office Website (May 1, 2019), https://2015-2019.kormany.hu/en/the-prime-minister/the-prime-minister-s-speeches/interview-with-prime-minister-viktor-orban-in-the-italian-newspaper-la-stampa. In the same interview the HPM declared that "a spiritual community is shared" with President Trump.

[57] W. Partlett. "Vladimir Putin and the Law," Brookings Institute (February 28, 2012), www.brookings.edu/opinions/vladimir-putin-and-the-law/

[58] See the improper use of various restriction grounds in Chapter 7.

familiar manner of cheating by law, it subverts the concept of the state's *positive obligation* to promote rights to instead promote the causes of the government, its values, and the interests of organizations allied with it. For example, according to the Hungarian government, the Geneva Refugee Convention (1951) prescribes that refugee status should be requested solely in the first safe country in which the seeker arrives. In public discourse, this translates into illiberal language, sending the message that foreigners are not welcome in Hungary.[59] Human rights are not rejected but rather *reinterpreted* in an illiberal way for the purposes of the regime. They are not fundamental rights that pertain to all humans. The only rights that count are those which are taken for granted in the way of life of the "authentic people."

Exceptionally, rights are reinterpreted to send a message of ideological commitment to the regime's conservative, authoritarian supporters. One can see this in the context of the institutional protection of marriage, which illiberal regimes constitutionally define as a union between a man and a woman or similarly codify at the statutory level.[60] However, given the lack of consensus in Europe, the ECtHR does not consider barriers to marriage for all a discriminatory violation of equality.[61] The international system, as exemplified by the ECtHR, has moved toward disregarding universalism due to growing respect for national tradition – a respect that reflects current trends in most European countries.

Instead of abandoning the human rights language, illiberal regimes sometimes hijack it to serve their conservative, traditionalist and religious agenda. This is the case with reproductive rights, where greater weight has been given to the rights of the unborn (as a matter of right to life). Rights protection can also be used to restrict fundamental rights, for example, when enhanced personality rights protection aims to silence critical free speech.[62] Contrary to authoritarian systems, the PLD only

---

[59] Interestingly, the legal practice differs somewhat from the antirefugee rights rhetoric; in contemporary Hungary, should a refugee successfully overcome the administrative and physical barriers that were created by the authorities, the application would be evaluated more or less in conformity with EU law (while continuing to detain the applicant). In 2017, more than 1,000 people were granted protected status in Hungary, but only 60 in 2019.

[60] Similar attempts failed in a Romanian referendum, and the country tried to resist the recognition of foreign same-sex marriage.

[61] *Ilias and Ahmed* v. *Hungary*, ECtHR, App. no. 47287/15, Judgment of 21 November 2019. The CJEU took the opposite conclusion.

[62] In 2019, the Hungarian government submitted a bill that envisioned granting state organs the right to petition the HCC should their fundamental rights be violated. The measure was justified by the need to protect individual rights against the power of global

sparingly restricts fundamental rights. It prefers to use rights for its own purposes. This entails a lot of manipulation of the scope and application, all within the grand scheme of legal cheating.

Government propaganda concocts a fundamental right to security to the detriment of privacy rights, more or less along lines familiar in most Western democracies. The main difference between resilient and illiberal democracies is the absence of any credible threat in many countries. In this imagination it is "our traditional/Christian way of life" that is threatened. This line is then used to justify disregarding refugee rights as well as some fundamental liberties following the dictates of xenophobic, government-generated fear.[63] The right to security is not an invention of illiberal regimes (see Section 6.4.1 above): it is a manifestation of the inherent illiberalism and authoritarianism of constitutional regimes. The illiberal regime is ready to transgress fundamental rights standards in its paranoid self-defense. Quite tellingly, three months after PiS came to power, the 1990 Act on Police (a major first step in the transition to democracy) was amended allowing "any data to be stored that is deemed to be 'significant for the security of the state' and 'significant for the defensive capabilities of the state.'"[64] In Hungary, terrorism scares, surveillance fetishism and continued, nontransparent legal amendments have increasingly resulted in unchecked surveillance.[65]

The consequences of the selective use of the state duty (positive obligation) to promote rights can been seen with regard to freedom of religion and church autonomy. The inherent authoritarianism in freedom of religion (protection of the undomesticated authoritarianism in

corporations. Here comes the spin: in case an ordinary court would find against a state organ, the standing would allow an appeal to the more trustworthy HCC. For example, if the state organ is required to disclose public information, it could appeal on grounds of a violation of fair trial. The amendment was withdrawn, at least temporarily.

[63] The antialien, antimigrant policies are embedded in social racism that is common in former communist countries. Eastern European governments condone such popular attitudes in order to maintain their harmonious relationship with their electoral base. The ambiguous relationship of the government to xenophobia is a major challenge for human rights given the lack of effective nondiscrimination social policies.

[64] There is only ex post judicial control for data collection. "It is questionable whether the court will be able to properly evaluate the presented materials . . . . The act does not contain provisions on informing ex post anyone whose data has been collected by the police about any proceedings initiated against them." E. Łętowska and A. Wiewiórowska Domagalska, "A 'Food' Change in the Polish Constitutional Tribunal?," *Osteuropa Recht*, 1 (2016), p. 80.

[65] See *Szabó and Vissy* v. *Hungary*, ECtHR, App. no. 37138/14, Judgment of 12 January 2016. The provisions that enable the disproportionate use of surveillance were never amended.

many religions) has been unleashed by the right-wing illiberal regimes of Europe. In Hungary, churches that are loyal to power and represent a certain national identity are protected according to a concept of positive state obligations (state promotion of rights). To the extent freedom of religion means supporting the autonomy of traditional and conservative churches, there appears to be a marked increase in religious freedom in the form of generous state subsidies and exemptions – coupled with discrimination or even persecution of nontraditional religious organizations.[66] Such an endorsement, which moves closer to entanglement, has a negative impact on other civil liberties since conservative churches dictate government positions that undermine women's rights[67] and gender equality. Significantly, in defense of the rule of law (!), the Bulgarian Constitutional Court declared that ratification of the Istanbul Convention (Council of Europe Convention on preventing and combating violence against women and domestic violence) would be contrary to the Bulgarian constitutional identity ("Bulgarian legal tradition") because the Constitution defines marriage as a union between a man and a woman in the biological sense.[68] To prove that the Istanbul Convention is contrary to the RoL, the Bulgarian Constitutional Court argued that "despite its undoubtedly positive sides, the [Istanbul] Convention is internally incoherent and this contradiction creates a second layer in it," shifting its meaning beyond its declared aims – protection of women from violence. The point of contention is the concept of "gender" (and "gender identity," mentioned once in Article 4.3). "In the Convention's flawed, unofficial translation, the Bulgarian

---

[66] See, for Hungary: *Magyar Keresztény Mennonita Egyház and Others* v. *Hungary*, ECtHR, App nos. 70945/11, 23611/12, 26998/12 et al., Judgment of 8 April 2014. Technically, the discrimination violation was not separately discussed, as it was absorbed into the violation of freedom of religion.

It is likely that the very generous support for mainstream churches is more a conservative gesture and a reasonable investment in political backing and does not express a popular attitude. Only 28 percent of Hungarians believe that the government should support religious values and beliefs (Poland: 25 percent; Germany: 40 percent). *Eastern and Western Europeans Differ on Importance of Religion, Views of Minorities, and Key Social Issues*, Pew Research Center (October 29, 2018).

[67] The record is ambiguous here, too. In Poland, the first prime minister of the PiS government in 2015 was a woman; currently, the President of the Constitutional Tribunal, the First President of the Supreme Court, and the Marshal of the Senate are women. On the imposition of illiberal, discriminatory policies within religious organizations, affecting millions of people, see Chapter 1.

[68] Ruling 13 (Bulgarian Constitutional Court, 27 July 2018), www.constcourt.bg/bg/Acts/ GetHtmlContent/f278a156-9d25-412d-a064-6ffd6f997310. The Government of Hungary also rejected ratification due to "gender," without further explanation.

word for "sex" [пол] is used for "gender" as well, making it indistinguishable from "sex." Just once, in Article 4.3, is "gender" translated as "social sex" [социален пол] to distinguish it from "sex" as ground for nondiscrimination in the Convention's application, triggering speculations that a "third sex" [трети пол], alongside biological sexes, is introduced there."[69]

The protection of freedom of religion may culminate in the total abuse of the positive obligation to protect: in Russia, the protection of religious sentiments has resulted in the criminal convictions of atheists and others who attacked the political regime by vehemently criticizing its religious supporters.[70] At the same time, so-called "extremist" religions and "religious extremists" have been persecuted under antiterror amendments (the so-called Yarovaya amendments of 2016). At the further end of religious discrimination we can find governmental raids on Baptist, Jehovah Witnesses, and Islamic congregations, the incarceration of religious leaders, and severe punishment for criticism of the Russian government for the invasion of Crimea, deemed "extremist speech."

A fundamental tenet of the prevailing illiberal human rights doctrine is that the individual is a rights holder, due to membership in the national community. As Judge Pokol, a Fidesz-nominated judge, has stated: "in the exercise of his rights, beyond his self-realization, the survival of his community, his nation has to be safeguarded."[71]

Community here means a *Schicksalgemeinschaft*, a blood relations–based, tribal national community with partly imagined, carefully selected and falsified conservative values, myths, and symbols of a re-imagined history. What seems to be part of an illiberal assortment of human rights (e.g. traditional family values and a lack of reproductive freedom) flows from the national identitarian dream of right-wing

---

[69] R. Smilova, "Promoting 'Gender Ideology': Constitutional Court of Bulgaria Declares Istanbul Convention Unconstitutional," OxHRH (August 22, 2018) http://ohrh.law.ox.ac.uk/promoting-gender-ideology-constitutional-court-of-bulgaria-declares-istanbul-convention-unconstitutional. The Bulgarian Constitutional Court replaced gender as "socially constructed roles" as defined in the Istanbul Convention with individual choice of social roles.

[70] In Russia, where members of Pussy Riot were convicted for "hooliganism motivated by religious hatred," the ECtHR found a violation of Article 10 (*Mariya Alekhina and Others v. Russia*, ECtHR, App. no. 38004/12, Judgment of 17 July 2018). Such discrimination is not unheard of in stable democracies (see the Austrian attitude to Jehovah's Witnesses). For the roots of an authoritarian protection of religious sensitivities see *Otto-Preminger-Institute v. Austria*, ECtHR, App. no. 13470/87, Judgment of 20 September 1995.

[71] 1/2013 (I. 7) AB hat, para. 89.

populism.[72] So-called traditions set the standard for proper conduct ("a Hungarian would never do this or that"); rural traditions are presented as "natural" and opposed to artificial, oversophisticated rights and values (i.e. the rationality, generality, and abstractedness of the Enlightenment). In this perspective, human rights cannot be but alien impositions: our proud traditions provide better protection, without the showy foreign nonsense.

Emphasizing membership in the national community (a consolation to populist sentiment) adds greater weight to its public interests, to the detriment of the individualistic and unconditional nature of human and constitutional rights. Rights (particularly freedom of speech) without responsibility have no place in this equation.[73] Illiberalism repeats with pleasure the unfortunate liberal formula, according to which fundamental (human) rights are not absolute.[74] Reminiscent of communist dogma, although probably inspired by Catholic social doctrine, rights are conditioned on corresponding duties. The HPM claimed that the HFL reflected the wish of the great majority of Hungarians who opted for a balance between rights and duties. Freedom exists but is balanced with the welfare of the community.[75]

The authorities of illiberal EU member states do not rely on the systemic violation of fundamental rights, at least for now;[76] plebiscitarian

---

[72] On the return to traditional values to the detriment of human rights see R. Horvath, "The Reinvention of 'Traditional Values': Nataliya Narochnitskaya and Russia's Assault on Universal Human Rights," *Europe-Asia Studies*, 68:5 (2016), pp. 868–92.

[73] Jean-Paul Costa, a former President of the ECtHR, stated that "liberty gives rise to responsibilities." *Enhorn* v. *Sweden*, ECtHR, App. no. 56529/00, Judgment of 25 January 2005 (concurring).

[74] Here, too, they can rely on a rather illiberal concept of constitutional democracies. The ECHR emphasizes that freedom of expression "carries with it duties and responsibilities," a clause that is absent with regard to other rights in Article 10(2). The ECtHR has insisted that journalist responsibilities go beyond professional ethics. *Pentikäinen* v. *Finland*, ECtHR, App. no. 11882/10, Judgment of 20 October 2015.

[75] Viktor Orbán on July 5, 2013, quoted after G. Halmai, "The rise and fall of Constitutionalism in Hungary," in P. Blokker (ed.), *Constitutional Acceleration within the European Union and Beyond* (Taylor and Francis, 2017), p. 219. According to the HFL Preamble, "individual freedom can only be complete in cooperation with others." The Venice Commission noted "a shift of emphasis from the obligations of the state toward the individual citizens to the obligations of the citizens toward the community." Venice Commission Opinion no. 621/2011 on the new Constitution of Hungary, Venice, June 20, 2011, para. 57.

[76] At least this was the case at the time of the submission of this manuscript (September 2020). Since that date the situation has rather rapidly deteriorated. Very often the rights restrictions were boarderline. Unlike the CJEU, the ECtHR Grand Chamber found no violation in the Hungarian treatment of refugees.

domination is based on cheating the RoL (see Chapters 2 and 7) and systemically restricting conditions for the free exercise of rights. The monopoly of power is obtained by *creating dependencies* and removing social and institutional autonomy, not by direct oppression of the individual. It is control over public institutions that is crucial for building illiberal democracy; curtailing individual fundamental rights is not.

Furthermore, in an illiberal democracy the restriction of human rights is hardly ever extralegal. The regime is eager to provide legal grounds for its interventions, as it is via legal rules that it can tell friends and foes apart. Recall that progovernment speech and assembly are always welcome. The need to violate fundamental rights, if such a violation occurs, indicates that the plebiscitarian democracy failed to deliver and is in a freefall toward despotism; in illiberal democracies, as long as they remain illiberal democracies, state actors do not need to rely on direct violations of human rights as state policy, even if in some cases, these possibilities materialize in sporadic but frightening ways. However, important changes at the statutory level already enable additional, formally authorized, far-reaching restrictions of fundamental rights, primarily for future use, but with an immediate chilling effect and threatening free exercise of certain rights.

Even in Russia, Turkey, and for a long time Venezuela, the regimes insisted on legal formalities when it came to such violations. These formalities turned into the harassment of politically "inconvenient" people (see the frequent accusations of pedophilia in Russia and the use of extended pretrial detention, where the procedure itself is the punishment).[77]

The rigid application of formal rules (be they prohibitions or authorizations) that does not consider the aim of the provision, and therefore cheats the law, is a favorite tool of oppression.[78] The governments of the illiberal member states of the EU may "coexist indefinitely with meaningful democratic institutions." Provided that incumbent governments "avoid egregious (and well-publicized) rights abuses" these kind of contradictions are manageable. "Using various forms of 'legal'

---

[77] Russia, Turkey, and Venezuela have already crossed most red lines; it is not only the selective application of ambiguous provisions but the substantive criminalization and legal authorization of unlimited control and harassment of citizens that prevails.

[78] During the COVID-19 emergency, assemblies were banned in Hungary. A small number of opposition activists and MPs on bicycles and in cars used bells and horns to protest. As the participants were moving in traffic, it was hard to argue that this amounted to prohibited assembly. The demonstrators were immediately fined by the police (present in strong numbers) for using "warning signals" without necessity, thereby disturbing road safety.

persecution, governments may limit opposition challenges without provoking massive protest or international repudiation."[79]

The level of rights constraints and violations varies among illiberal
democracies. The more despotic the regime, the more inclined it is to
discipline rights – and rightsholders by violent means. This is not an
unpopular venture and resonates well with the "common sense" of
"ordinary citizens," a favorite point of reference in antielitist populism.
In Venezuela, even under Chavez, and in Turkey, even before the putsch,
there were serious and large-scale violations of human rights. Once the
values of universal human rights are used to criticize the regime, and the
practice of freedom becomes embarrassing for the exercise of power,
antipathy toward common or universal standards clearly emerges.
Official propaganda will paint such criticism as part of a universal elite
conspiracy against the nation or a doctrinaire position that cannot
understand national realities and the people's genuine wishes.

In East Central European illiberal democracies, visible violations of
individual rights occur primarily to overcome accidental resistance to the
regime, partly stemming from the illiberal ideological commitments of
the ruling party (more in Poland than in Hungary). Hungary adopted
a series of measures to restrict the rights of trade unions and rendered
strikes nearly impossible in the public sector, not by banning them, but
by setting fuzzy conditions that cannot be satisfied because the conditions depend on government discretion.[80] Foreign or foreign-associated
NGOs that provide protection to causes that aggravate the government
are not shut down (that would be the authoritarian solution): they are
harassed by tax inspectors and burdened with special taxes. Other
restrictive measures range from the duty to register, declare and publish
which NGOs directly or indirectly receive support from abroad (as in
Hungary)[81] to the total prohibition of foreign funding (as in
Venezuela).[82] All these measures indicate a growing illiberalism drifting
toward authoritarian rule. However, in many respects, these measures

---

[79] S. Levitsky and L. A. Way, *Competitive Authoritarianism. Hybrid Regimes after the Cold War* (Cambridge University Press, 2010), p. 59 (stated with respect to contemporary authoritarian regimes).

[80] The law failed to provide a clear definition of essential services, and the courts deny the right to strike where the government insists on the essential service clause. For further examples of this type of cheating, see Chapter 8.

[81] Act LXXVI of 2017. The CJEU found it to be discriminatory and unjustified. Case C-78/18, *Commission v. Hungary* [2020] EU:C:2020:476.

[82] The Law for the Defense of Political Sovereignty and National Self-Determination, Asamblea Nacional No. 960 (*Ley de Defensa de la Soberanía Política*

reflect an international trend, where increasingly illiberal states become the trend setters. The boundaries are shifting.[83] What was once considered a peculiarity of oppressive illiberalism and demagogy has been normalized by governments that are not usually classified as illiberal regimes.[84]

Illiberalism and the perpetuation of illiberal power necessitate restrictions on speech, assembly, and association as well as demand regulation of moral behavior (reproductive rights, sexuality, etc.), harsh retributive punishment, and support for the privileged ethnic, racial and/or religious group identity. But contrary to classic authoritarianism, these restrictions are applied within the grammar of fundamental rights, and RoL techniques can be used to their detriment. In Russia, the refusal to allow Jehovah's Witnesses to register was not an arbitrary decision of the lawmaker but a judicial ruling based on evidence. The law only required that, as a precondition for the national-level recognition of a religious organization, its believers not engage in illegal activities. This appears relatively neutral, even reasonable, even if not motivated by a deep commitment to freedom of religion. Under the law already in force, local registration for Jehovah's Witnesses had been denied, and the Witnesses could not register their places of worship (which was a matter for local authorities, as there was no national recognition). Once the believers congregated without authorization, this was considered

---

y *Autodeterminación Nacional*, IAZG/VCB/DJPP, 2010). See J. Corrales, "Autocratic Legalism in Venezuela," *Journal of Democracy*, 26:2 (2015), pp. 37–51.

[83] M. Glasius, J. Schalk, M. De Lange, "Illiberal Norm Diffusion: How Do Governments Learn to Restrict Nongovernmental Organizations?," *International Studies Quarterly*, 64:2 (2020), pp. 453–468.

[84] On February 4, 2020, the Greek Parliament enacted a law providing for a "Greek and Foreign NGO Members Registry" for all NGOs working on migration and social inclusion, their employees, and their partners (!). According to the Ministerial Decision implementing the law: "The Ministry may at its discretion reject the registration of an individual applicant in the NGO Members Registry following an assessment of the legal requirements, in combination with 'elements pertaining to the personality and activities of that applicant.'" *Risk of Repression, New Rules on Civil Society Supporting Refugees and Migrants in Greece*, Refugee Support Aegean, RSA Comments (May 2020), p. 3.

For other examples of rights restrictive legislation with crossfertilization between illiberal and nominally liberal EU member states, see the criminalization of the "facilitation" of illegal migration in an overbroad and unclear manner, and without exempting humanitarian aid and advocacy, in Hungary and France. Venice Commission Opinion no. 919/2018, on the Provisions of the so-called "Stop Soros" Draft Legislative Package Which Directly Affect NGOs, Venice, June 25, 2018. The remaining (important) difference is that France, under public pressure, added some sensible exceptions to the authoritarian law.

illegal, just like their missionary activity, which could not have been authorized by their religious organization, as it was not operative under local law. They therefore must have been missionaries without the formal recognition of a religious organization because the religious organization could not be registered. Once the believers' misdemeanors consisting in religious exercise were collected and presented in front of the Supreme Court in the church recognition case, there was enough "objective" evidence from throughout the country to consider Jehovah's Witnesses as constant law-breakers. That was a formally perfect "objective" ground, in the best tradition of Joseph Heller's *Catch 22*, to happily conclude that with repeated law-breaking the Witnesses must be an extremist religion.[85]

The overall public attitude toward fundamental human rights remains one of indifference. The general public is not confronted with restrictions that would infringe on their rights or disturb their way of life, certainly not for the majority that counts as the people. NGOs may be inconvenienced, but the negative impacts on civil society does not bother the "authentic" people; NGOs are not civil society, "only" its protector. Though there may be limits to academic freedom, this does not directly burden students, not to speak of the general population, even if the quality of education suffers. Other general restrictions concern invisible, unpopular minorities (prisoners, refugees, and the homeless) and may be met with public support.

The shrinking of private autonomy and classic freedom primarily originates in *structural* changes (the centralization of state power, precluding autonomous institutions, including the media; and cultural hegemony). While limitations on access to information are popular among illiberal regimes, criminal charges are seldom pressed against journalists, and there is no censorship; neither is there persecution or employment discrimination on grounds of religious convictions. What matters is the structural erosion of rights: people are free to speak and write (although workplace sanctions cannot be ruled out), but there are fewer and fewer platforms to communicate critical opinions, or facts, and the government only selectively provides access to information (not allowing opposition or independent media to attend governmental press conferences, etc.).

---

[85] "Russian Authorities Move to Ban Jehovah's Witnesses as Religious Extremists," Radio Free Europe/Radio Liberty (March 16, 2017), www.rferl.org/a/russia-jehovah-witnesses-extremist-organization-/28374043.html.

O. Sibireva, *Freedom of Conscience in Russia: Restrictions and Challenges in 2017* (SOVA Center for Information and Analysis, 2018).

In illiberal EU member states, freedom is restricted primarily by institutional change. The restrictions on rights are structural. The state has thus gradually limited the possibility of an individual's free mental choices. The government takes control over the spheres of communication and the manufacture of ideas. In the media sector, the illiberal government exercises de facto control of decisive influence; although on paper various media outlets are free, they are free to serve the government (see Chapters 2 and 3). In Hungary, the government nationalized and centralized all former municipal schools (in the name of standardizing quality in public education), then transferred the management of select (better) public schools to specific religious denominations to enhance freedom of religion, even where there was no public demand for such schools. Parents can to send their children to the school of their choice (denominational or state, except in smaller towns where there is only one high school), but the state schools offer less attractive conditions. The justification was again based on rights: satisfying the right to parental choice in education. In 2020, the government took a further step towards the authoritarian educational model of the prewar and communist times and limited the choice of school textbooks to two governmentally approved sets, both reflecting a strongly biased nationalist history curriculum.

Likewise, academic freedom was curtailed through institutional change. In 2019, the public research institutes that operated under the umbrella of the autonomous Hungarian Academy of Sciences were transferred to an officially "autonomous" management entity under the decisive influence of the government. One cannot claim that this arrangement excludes academic freedom (of the researchers); researchers are free to follow their professional choices, but the state ownership and funding structure has far-reaching consequences for the research choices. Opinion is also free, and journalists with press not controlled by the government can follow their professional standards. The "only" problem is the disproportionately low number of mass media not under the government's spell.[86] Individual voting rights are not affected, but the electoral system and the fairness of electoral competition have been structurally altered to favor the incumbent party.

---

[86] Comparable trends were already noticeable one or two decades earlier in Russia and Turkey (see Chapter 1). Poland is somewhat exceptional as a good number of broadcasters are owned by multinationals who are less interested in government perks and so far have not been subject to direct threats. (There is discussion about restrictive legislation or nationalization.)

As a consequence, society is less free but without the formal restriction of individual freedoms. A kind of "bourgeois" freedom is still available: the freedom to make and spend money (unless this conflicts with oligarchic interests), and the freedom to cultivate the garden of a private life.[87] The princely art of maintaining Caesaristic power consists in sustaining a sufficiently large number of citizens in the resulting happy state of stupor. Illiberalism in power prefers the collective, and officially dislikes individualism, but at the same time accepts a *consumerist* concept of privacy and personal bodily freedom:[88] "Wellness is a daily, active pursuit."[89] The illiberal power does not insist on directly interfering in private life, although it indirectly promotes a traditional role model for women and firmly endorses traditional family at the symbolic level.[90]

In Hannah Arendt's description of tyranny, political isolation – the impossibility of influencing the political sphere, while the private sphere [work, family, etc.] remains intact – is crucial.[91] The illiberal dual state maintains a dual system of rights protection. If only for pragmatic reasons, the illiberal regime greatly satisfies the expectations of a minimal liberalism, à la Benjamin Constant, where "the private sphere is the proper arena in which to pursue the fullness of human development."[92] And yet here comes an illiberal twist: The boundaries of the private sphere are drawn by the illiberal state, with little room or opportunity to contest the step-up. Structural obstacles turn opinions on public affairs into issues of private conversation. At the same time, the most intimate choices about private and family life become issues of very public (and very hostile) identity politics. There is individual freedom

---

[87] According to *The Economist*, this was Putin's original deal: freedom, "as long as they stayed out of politics." "Russia's leading business paper is being gagged," *The Economist* (May 7, 2020), www.economist.com/europe/2020/05/07/russias-leading-business-paper-is-being-gagged.

[88] Consumerist privacy here refers to the favorite values of the millennial generation (technology, pop culture, tolerance, clothing, etc. – if we believe somewhat outdated data from 2010). *Millennials. A Portrait of Generation Next*, Pew Research Center (February, 2010); Millennial Americans are less committed to democracy than earlier generations (which means in most respects, *less* liberal generations). R. Stefan Foa and Y. Mounk, "The Democratic Disconnect," *Journal of Democracy*, 27: 3 (2016), pp. 5–17.

[89] "Millennials," Goldman Sachs, www.goldmansachs.com/insights/archive/millennials.

[90] The plebiscitarian leader readily accepts popular values and tries to change them carefully: Kaczyński did not push ahead with an absolute ban on abortion when he ran into mass demonstrations; Fidesz did not change abortion regulations.

[91] H. Arendt, *The Origins of Totalitarianism* (Meridian Books, 1958), p. 474.

[92] G. A. O'Donnell, "Horizontal Accountability in New Democracies," *Journal of Democracy*, 9:3 (1998), p. 112.

here, but without independence; and what kind of freedom is one that slaves enjoy? For citizens, the system protecting rights, and freedom in general, increasingly resembles the condition of a slave serving a benevolent master.[93] The master hardly ever uses coercive means – but is the slave free solely on the assurance that they are untied from the leash if they behave properly?

A second aspect of the structural restriction of fundamental rights concerns the protection of declared rights. Here again institutional changes lie at the source of weakening rights protection.[94] The demise of human rights is facilitated by the deterioration of protection mechanisms, especially independent institutions, a process that results from the regime's need to concentrate unlimited and unchecked power in the leader's hands (see Chapters 1 and 4). Where the independence of the judiciary and the impartiality and integrity of the public administration cannot be taken for granted, rights protection will be at risk. Access to courts is made more difficult (by increasing costs) and attacks on judicial independence undermine effective rights protection, although both in Hungary and Poland many ordinary courts continue to provide remedy in individual cases.[95]

In addition, uncertain laws provide the foundation for future crackdowns, generating fear and confusion and burdening the practical, though not yet unavailable, remedies. Most often, the increasing repressiveness remains unnoticed as it stems from a facially neutral reform or practice: for example, where remand by a second instance court does not trigger the end of pretrial detention or where the law does not set reasonable limits to absolute length of such custody. Such changes remain below the radar of rights sensitivity, although these shifts may radically change what fair trial means. The real deterioration may indeed occur at this level, without formal changes in the written law, through increasingly servile or bureaucratic reinterpretation. For example, access

---

[93] P. Petit, *Republicanism: A Theory of Freedom and Government* (Oxford University Press, 1997), p. 23.

[94] Again, there is some ambiguity here. Since 2012, individual constitutional complaints are allowed in Hungary, and in that context, the HCC does arrive at individual rights protective rulings, at least from time to time.

[95] Even after five years of continuous governmental attacks on the judiciary, in July 2020 a regional administrative court found a local ordinance declaring a village an LGBT ideology–free zone to be unconstitutional for being discriminatory. "Kolejna uchwała 'anty-LGBT' uchylona przez sąd. 'To pojęcie odnosi się do ludzi,'" Polsat News (July 15, 2020), www.polsatnews.pl/wiadomosc/2020-07-15/kolejna-uchwala-anty-lgbt-uchylona-przez-sad-to-pojecie-odnosi-sie-do-ludzi.

to information will be more difficult where the interpreter of the law reclassifies information on the use of public funds as a business secret, or (as in Hungary) an official, unclassified document will be classified as a preparatory document for an official decision that cannot be disclosed. Indeed, remarkably, even without substantive changes to the freedom of information law (a right endorsed by the HFL) the government could invent countless obstacles that transformed this right into an empty shell, in order to hide corrupt transactions between public authorities and beneficiaries of the regime. While all this may be a rights issue, it is also about democracy: the government avoids accountability by excluding transparency.

The trends are not unequivocal. Not even restrictive laws result in oppressive practice. In Poland, notwithstanding restrictions on the freedom of demonstration and related oppressive police behavior, "in the majority of cases judges, public prosecutors and attorneys treated the parties respectfully and the proceedings were conducted in a fair and professional manner."[96] But "[i]t is not obvious why a judiciary cordoned off from political accountability would protect rights, and if it did, which minorities and which rights the judiciary would protect. On the other hand, to the extent that judges would take on this protective role because they are politically accountable in some way, it becomes unclear what the judiciary adds to majoritarian politics."[97]

While in some politically and ideologically sensitive areas preparatory steps to legalize rights-restrictive practices have been taken, in other areas that are not seen as threatening the survival of the political regime, human rights may even progress.[98] Consider a Hungarian development: the new criminal procedure code (Act x c of 2017) provides more defense protection than ever before. Prisoners' rights have also improved, at least formally, having the right to compensation for inhuman treatment in prison. New prison blocks were built to reduce overcrowding. (To what

[96] Polish Helsinki Foundation for Human Rights, *Polish Courts Mostly "Fair and Professional" in Handling Freedom of Assembly Cases – Report*, Liberties (November 28, 2019), www.liberties.eu/en/news/freedom-of-assembly-before-polish-courts-hfhrs-case-monitoring-report/18373.

[97] G. Helmke and F. Rosenbluth, "Regimes and the Rule of Law: Judicial Independence in Comparative Perspective," *Annual Review of Political Science*, 12 (2009), p. 346.

[98] Sometimes such progress (not the first time in the history of human rights) originates from privileges granted to influential social groups. Lawyers hate being intercepted and have good reasons to be concerned. They may receive special guarantees: lawyer–client privileges are observed in most surveillance regimes, and such privileges are granted in illiberal regimes, too. The regime can be proud: the RoL is respected.

extent the latter gives reason for celebration from a human rights perspective is a different and paradoxical matter; the improvements quickly fell victim to one of the government's fear and hate campaigns.)

Perhaps concluding that in the absence of asylum seekers the grind mill of "we need the government to protect us against the enemy" was running out of feed, in the early days of 2020 Fidesz turned against prisoners and their lawyers and foreign- (Soros-)sponsored rights defenders. Beneficiaries of the government-created scheme then became compensation-money-suckers, not worthy of a penny of scarce public resources when they serve their well-merited prison terms. A new law suspended the enforcement of court-ordered compensation for time spent in inhumane conditions. This legislative denial of the execution of judgments is probably the first open frontal attack on an identifiable, uncontested element of the rule of law, namely that final judgments are to be executed.[99] Other instances of gross disregard, like judicial retirement or denial of severance, had a façade of legal justification, in the form of some fake legal reason. Here, it was only a sense of social justice (generated by a hate campaign) that justified the disregard of the rule of law.

At the same time, clearly frightening changes do not materialize, or at least not immediately (but the chilling effect is still there). Article U of the HFL, an elaborate condemnation of communism and its collaborators, did not result in anticommunist purges. While the Seventh Amendment of the HFL stated that "[t]he exercise of the freedom of expression and assembly cannot entail the invasion of the private and family lives of others or the trespass of their homes,"[100] promising a serious crackdown on political freedom, prohibitions in the resulting new law on assemblies are still subject to proportionality analysis. According to a leading human rights NGO, the new law is an overall improvement, although the previous system, where the police may apply a prior prohibition subject to expedited judicial review, still remains in place. There were and are legal loopholes for the authorities to hinder demonstrations – if they so wish, but they will not do so until an important interest of the power is at stake (too many critics of the government would like to demonstrate). So far

---

[99] The tantrum necessitated another act of cheating: European Arrest Warrant transfers receive a diplomatic assurance that the transferees will be placed in the newly built facilities, providing the EU the opportunity not to take action.

[100] Another new constitutional measure, reflecting the concept of order of an authoritarian (law and order) majority, concerns the prohibition (and additional criminalization) of inhabiting public spaces. This is directed against the homeless, but little actual action followed the law, as courts were not partners to the police action.

judicial practice has not particularly supported police zeal.[101] Likewise in
Poland, a 2016 amendment to the Law on Assembly granted the government some advantage by giving priority to so-called cyclical demonstrations (i.e. recurrent demonstrations on historically important days). In
locations used for cyclical demonstrations by the government or the
church, there can be no other (counter)-demonstrations within a 100-
meter radius. While this authoritarian hierarchy[102] is a content-based
discrimination and unlikely to stand the test of proportionality outside
the chambers of the PCT, it does not rule out the expression of opinions
in a relevant time and place, notwithstanding the disadvantage this poses.
What really matters is the behavior of the authorities, including the
police, in case of a politically unwelcome protest. In fact, there remains
a vibrant culture of expressing dissent by demonstration but participants
at counter-demonstrations are often interrogated and police brutality is
increasing.[103]

---

[101] The 2018 amendments to the HFL initially envisioned the creation of a new administrative
court system filled with handpicked judges, but at least for the time being, the government
has withdrawn the bill.

[102] The PCT found that the reference to national values in the Preamble of the Polish
Constitution creates a legitimate aim.

[103] W. Sadurski, *Poland's Constitutional Breakdown* (Oxford University Press, 2019), p. 153.
Sadurski reports that counterdemonstrations to cyclical demonstrations are banned at
the last minute, a practice that renders judicial review impractical.

7

Profiting from the Rule of Law

In times when the law was clear, the law was distorted, and when that was not possible, it was broken.

Gustav III[1]

7.1 The Ambiguity of the Rule of Law

Critics often dismiss illiberal democracies and developing countries for their lack of RoL.[2] When the respective accused governments search for defense, they turn to indeterminacy. Responding to both domestic and international criticism, they claim that "there is no way to judge us. You just try to impose your problematic concept on us. By the way, we do respect the law. And by the way, you, critics don't live up to the standards you try to impose on us."

Alas, they may have a point.

The RoL is a conceptual tool in search of its own concept. As scholarship acknowledges, "the rule of law is an essentially contested concept."[3] The scholars and politicians who discuss it mostly reproduce their cultural presuppositions or institutional ideals and fantasies. The World Bank or the EU, and other organizations as well as many scholars and politicians, use the RoL to evaluate a country in a morally relevant way – with political consequences and potentially international sanctions. In this exercise, the RoL appears as a set of ideas and practices

---

[1] Gustav III, King of Sweden to the Estates, after his successful coup d'Etat in 1771.
[2] The RoL serves both business interests and political evaluation, as in the cases of EU accession, investment security, or international developmental aid (see the Washington conditionalities).
[3] J. Waldron, "Is the Rule of Law an Essentially Contested Concept (in Florida)?," *Law and Philosophy*, 21:2 (2002), p. 151.
   Dicey believed the same: "words ... full of vagueness and ambiguity." A. V. Dicey, *Introduction to the Study of the Law of the Constitution* (Palgrave Macmillan, 1959), p. 187.

limiting government arbitrariness and aggrandizement. However, its legal criteria hardly translate into moral judgment. This is the exact problem of the RoL review when applied to illiberal democracies: the actual violations do not add up to a legally meaningful, RoL-conforming finding that moral consideration would demand: namely, that these regimes do not observe RoL.

Notwithstanding the conceptual disagreements, specific structures enable law to bind authority and the arbitrariness of authorities, at least in "normal" circumstances. "Normal" here means that the players are sufficiently committed to follow the rules, at least in the absence of unforeseen, extraordinary pressure. By most accounts, these structures contain a few indispensable elements: they must be "general, promulgated, non-retroactive, clear, coherent, requiring the possible and constant through time," and there must be a "congruence between official action and declared rule."[4] There is practical concordance on these matters, but the RoL is more than a formal structure of the law or a system of government of men through law. It is an ideology with normative impact: the shared modes of acting and thinking are supposed to have a tempering effect. This, however, does not occur in illiberal democracies: given their lack of a belief in anything other than mundane material interests and the calculus of power, the instrumentalism common among such rulers undermines this moral tempering.

The legal system under the RoL binds authority. Problematically, however, this same authority, which is supposed to be limited, creates and applies the law. The RoL requires that the ruled and ruler be subject to the same law. "It just happens" in illiberal democracy that this same law favors the ruler. Here is where illiberal democracies depart from constitutional democracies. Of course, bending the law occurs often in the latter, but this is not systematic, and even if it were, there are effective (legal) means of correction. If such correction fails this is sufficiently known, demonstrated, and condemned, and once legal self-correction fails, democracy may provide it by electing rulers more committed to the RoL. That is not the case in illiberal democracies, where for purposes of power aggrandizement the authorities will twist legal structures, including application of the law. This does not mean that laws will fail to protect expectations nor that results cannot be foreseeable, but that they enable bias and favoritism, in violation of equality and reasonableness. For Rousseau, the object of laws should always be general; hence the

---

[4] R. G. Manrique, "Autonomy and the Rule of Law," *Ratio Juris*, 20:2 (2007), p. 280.

prohibition on naming individuals.[5] A patronage-based system needs to disregard that requirement.

How can these leaders guarantee indispensable favoritism in abstract and general legal terms? The laws will not serve their manifest goals, which are otherwise legitimate but irrelevant, or will correspond to legitimate goals only nominally. Instead of their declared goals, the law will serve illegitimate goals, departing from general rules and official statements. Such manipulative use will also undermine the "inner morality"[6] of the law, the good that comes from a minimally well-ordered formal system of commands. The law will lose its power-restrictive force, disrespecting its subjects as equal citizens.

The formally correct structures of the RoL can serve efficient, disciplined arbitrariness.[7] Joseph Raz used the analogy of a sharp knife to describe the RoL. A sharp knife is an excellent knife, but it can be used for various purposes, good and bad.[8] In Singapore, it "has been a key tool effecting the decimation of opposition parties ... the dismantling of independent media ... and the thwarting of an autonomous civil society," as well as sidelining political opposition.[9] While certain characteristics of the RoL are particularly attractive for certain types of abuse, such abuse, even if socially and politically regular, and certainly common in illiberal democracies, is not the "fault" of the RoL. The inherent problem of the RoL is different, not just a matter of a dark or bright side.[10] The RoL bears an inherent readiness to endorse its own abuse. It contains elements that limit its own applicability for good: respecting these internal limitations (perfectly reasonable per se) becomes the source of

---

[5] J.-J. Rousseau, *The Social Contract & Discourses* (J.M. Dent & Sons, 1920), chap. II.6.

[6] L. L. Fuller, *The Morality of Law* (Yale University Press, 1964), pp. 38–39; D. Dyzenhaus, *The Constitution of Law: Legality in a Time of Emergency* (Cambridge University Press, 2006), p. 147.

[7] U. Mattei and L. Nader, *Plunder: When the Rule of Law is Illegal* (Wiley-Blackwell, 2008). Mattei and Nader provide examples where RoL rhetoric is "used as a cover, camouflage, or as a propaganda when engaging in lawless or criminal operations." Ibid., p. 4. Contrary to "plunder," where the RoL is used against the powerless, illiberal democracies deploy the RoL as a defensive tool, but when necessary can turn it against adversaries.

[8] J. Raz, *The Authority of Law* (Clarendon Press, 1979), p. 225.

[9] J. Rajah, *Authoritarian Rule of Law: Legislation, Discourse and Legitimacy in Singapore* (Cambridge University Press, 2012), p. 46. See further T. Moustafa, "Law and Courts in Authoritarian Regimes," *Annual Review of Law and Social Science*, 10:1 (2014), p. 281. Moustafa refers, in the context of Egypt, to the judicial control of political activities (including special courts, often constitutionally prohibited in illiberal democracies) and to media control. Once again, showing the inherent weakness of the RoL, judges can protect government interests merely by applying the existing biased law.

[10] Mattei and Nader, *Plunder*, p. 5.

abusive application, which precludes the reduction of state arbitrariness and injustice. In too many instances, the law cannot render justice because it sets conditions to its own application (e.g. a statute of limitations).

At a different level, the RoL is understood as a principle (generating, or consisting of, a set of standards). It becomes meaningful when its institutional and cultural guarantees are taken seriously. When authorities act in accordance with the law (legality), they should act with integrity. Arguably, an RoL system (even if limited to its formal elements) adds moral legitimacy to the system (the state) that relies upon it (and, even if indirectly, to individual autonomy or collective welfare). Hart believed that "[T]hough the most odious laws may be justly applied, we have, in the bare notion of applying a general rule of law, the germ at least of justice."[11] Others would question the morality of a system that treats slaves equally badly. Anyway, the strictly legal concepts of the RoL do not rule out oppression, even if oppression is not formally arbitrary.[12] Yet social and political commitment to the RoL can prevent the legal system from becoming an instrument of predictable oppression.

This chapter considers the changes in the structure of the law that will occur when the law is determined by the needs of PLD, and the extent to which legal structures serving plebiscitarian illiberalism may reduce arbitrary power and therefore become compatible with the RoL.

7.1.1   What Is the Rule of Law Good For?

Historically, institutions and processes related to the RoL served basic business and personal interests: the hope was that clear, foreseeable, and neutral rules, along with independent courts (independent from state interference and private bribery), could guarantee security. Max Weber referred also to a political dimension, namely the *legitimacy* of political rule: he claimed that in the German Empire legality was a sufficient criterion of legitimacy.[13] He also emphasized the advantages of the RoL for governing: the Prince will be able to control distant civil servants.

---

[11] H. L. A. Hart, *The Concept of Law* (Oxford University Press, 1994), p. 213.

[12] See M. Tushnet, "Authoritarian Constitutionalism," *Cornell Law Review*, 100 (2015), pp. 391–462.

[13] Beyond political legitimacy, legality is important for law observance (i.e. acceptance of legal prescriptions, irrespective of sanctions). In this respect, the acceptance of law as legitimate is intimately related to the RoL's coordinating function. The legitimacy-based acceptance of the law makes social coordination feasible.

In modern societies, such legitimacy can come from respecting the RoL (although routinized charisma is a parallel source of legitimacy in illiberal democracies). The RoL is respected not only for its social performance (i.e. the foreseeability provided by its observance); it cannot be fully separated from social expectations and practices of minimal social fairness. Lawyers in countries with a common law tradition have claimed that "respect for the Rule of Law is central to our political and rhetorical traditions, possibly even to our sense of national identity."[14] In Hungary and Poland, the RoL is understood in the German *Rechtsstaat* tradition, and the RoL is not a strong popular expectation. Local academic literature and political rhetoric primarily see the RoL as a situation in which authorities act in accordance with the law.[15] However, if the RoL is to serve legitimation beyond the worlds of legal professionals or political actors, it must provide legitimacy to government in the eyes of the ruled. People expect that certain rights and freedoms pertain to them and these expectations as guaranteed rights give *content* to the RoL. A fundamental, specific expectation is that people are recognized as having entitlements; the RoL has to treat them fairly (of course, the content of this fairness varies according to culture).[16] Where respect, or (more importantly) a socially shared concept of the RoL (at least as specific procedural fairness) is absent, insistence on the RoL may be seen as intruding upon prevailing social values, notwithstanding international agreements.[17] This may well be one of the reasons why illiberal democracies, in their respective countries, can get away with practices that international observers find manifestly outrageous.

Beyond providing legitimacy, the RoL enables social and governmental *cooperation* by lending credibility to public and private promises and expectations. This concern is eminently present in commercial law as noninterference and legal certainty. From the perspective of the ruled, it enables them to plan their life – even in otherwise oppressive regimes.[18]

---

[14] R. H. Fallon, "The Rule of Law as a Concept in Constitutional Discourse," *Columbia Law Review*, 97:1 (1997), p. 3. In Singapore, the RoL is not ideologically neutral but "inextricably ideological," and it is "central to Singapore's conception of nation." Rajah, *Authoritarian Rule of Law*, p. 42.

[15] For a review of the many concepts, see M. Loughlin, *The Rule of Law in European Jurisprudence*, Study 512/2009, Venice Commission, Strasbourg (May 29, 2009).

[16] T. R. Tyler, *Why People Obey the Law* (Yale University Press, 1990).

[17] Populists have been quick to add foreign imposition to their list of grievances whenever observers note specific shortcomings to their favorite solutions.

[18] Even authoritarian regimes may introduce RoL components. Franco's Spain introduced into legislation protection against the abuse of power. J. V. Aldea, "Quelques

The instruments that limit power in the constitutional democracy are also instruments of political coordination and even power generation.[19] Authorities cannot act without legal authorization,[20] yet at the same time, everything that is not prohibited is lawful for the citizen. This can have far-reaching consequences, as exemplified in the Swedish Press Ordinance of 1766, a liberal monument of enlightened despotism:

> §5. What We have thus expressly decreed ... concerning that which shall be deemed to be prohibited in writing and in print no one may in any manner cite or interpret beyond its literal wording, but everything that is not clearly contrary to that is to be regarded as legitimate to write and print.[21]

Ordinary courts in illiberal democracies tend to observe this maxim, but the law's silence does not guarantee a lack of arbitrary discretion in administrative law. For government lawyers what matters is to find gaps in legal prohibitions in order to execute the transactions that enhance government power. The liberal understanding of the RoL as freedom is hardly sustainable in despotic regimes. This was the fate of the RoL as early as the eighteenth century, when despots promised benevolence and to take care of citizens. King Gustav III of Sweden, author of the 1766

---

particularités du détournement de pouvoir en droit administratif espagnol actuel," *International Review of Administrative Sciences*, 26:4 (1960), pp. 364–69. Business–government relations improved (to the benefit of state efficiency and power concentration) when control over Russian business was transferred from the FSB (secret service) to the State Audit, and a law declared the privatization of the 1990s off limits. R. Sakwa, "Putin and the Oligarchs," *New Political Economy*, 13:2 (2008), p. 188.

[19] S. Holmes, "Precommitment and the Paradox of Democracy," in J. Elster and R. Slagstad (eds.), *Constitutionalism and Democracy* (Cambridge University Press, 1988).

[20] For the ambiguous acceptance of this principle, allowing formally justified exceptions on the grounds of discretionary power, see Chapter 8. The principle is quite nebulous in practice. In *Eva Glawischnig-Piesczek v. Facebook Ireland Limited,* the CJEU concluded that the absence of "a territorial limitation ... on the scope of the measures which Member States are entitled to adopt in accordance with that directive" entitles the authorities to impose restrictions globally (i.e. beyond the jurisdiction of the CJEU) because in a different context the preamble of the applicable directive mentions the "global dimension of electronic commerce." Case C-18/18, *Eva Glawischnig-Piesczek v. Facebook Ireland Limited* [2019] EU:C:2019:821.

As an illustration of the shaky grounds of RoL-based adjudication, Directive 2000/31, which was applied in this same case, referred to "any" alleged infringement in some language versions but to "an alleged infringement" in others. The CJEU chose the one that it found convenient for the extension of its power.

[21] *The World's First Freedom of Information Act. Anders Chydenius' Legacy Today* (Anders Chydenius Foundation's Publications 2, 2006), p 12.

Ordinance, completely reversed its essence by "small, barely discernible changes":

> Earlier everything was allowed to be printed if it was not expressly forbidden, but with Gustav III's new law anything that was not expressly allowed to be printed ran a potential risk of being brought to court. The law continued to allow a basic public access to official documents, but all government records were exempted. This did not prevent the king from boasting about the Swedish freedom of print in a draft letter to Voltaire.[22]

7.1.2   What Is the Rule of Law?

For the purposes of analyzing the RoL, it is useful to distinguish between its formal, procedural, and substantive perspectives or conceptions. These are relevant for all legal systems, even if the prevailing local legal culture might not recognize one or another practice as relevant for how it understands the RoL. Notwithstanding growing cross-cultural influence, differences persist: due process remains difficult to sense outside common law, and the European continent traditionally understands the RoL as *Rechtsstaat* or *Etat de droit*. UK law accepts proportionality with reservations; a fair trial means something different in a common law court than it does in an Ecuadorian indigenous court.

Formal conceptions are concerned with the formal qualities of a legal system. Procedural conceptions add the specific way in which the law is applied.[23] Most contemporary accounts contain several desiderata regarding the structure of the legal system and its legitimate procedures, although these are far from settled. For Dicey, the central elements were rather straightforward:

- the supremacy of regular law as opposed to power;
- the equality of all persons before the law; and
- the fact that constitutional law is part of the ordinary law of the land, where ordinary courts deal with rights.[24]

These and other related assumptions are often but not always (and not fully) transcribed into positive law.

---

[22] J. Nordin, "The Swedish Freedom of Print Act of 1776 – Background and Significance," *International Journal of Media and Entertainment Law*, 7:2 (2018), p. 142.

[23] J. Waldron, "The Rule of Law and the Importance of Procedure," in J. Fleming (ed.) *Getting to the Rule of Law* (New York University Press, 2011).

[24] Dicey, *Introduction*.

The substantive understanding does not deny that the rule of law has formal characteristics but goes "further" to argue that "certain rights are based on or derive from the rule of law."[25] There are, then, several substantive conceptions with differing content, some of them equating the RoL with good law. Here, the RoL requires that enacted laws "run the gamut from justice to charity to efficiency."[26] Max Weber believed that material justice destroys formal, rational law – a special problem in illiberalism (see Section 7.2.3 below). Raz has a different concern. If the rule of law must have any meaning, it cannot overlap with a theory of justice or normative political philosophy: "A non-democratic legal system, based on the denial of human rights, on extensive poverty, on racial segregation, sexual inequalities, and religious persecution may, in principle, conform to the requirements of the rule of law better than any of the legal systems of the more enlightened Western democracies .... Conformity to the rule of law also enables the law to serve bad purposes."[27] (In the context of illiberal democracies, it is not so much the bad purpose of a specific legal measure that matters, but its falsehood [where the actual purpose may be bad for the community or individuals].) Conformity to specific RoL principles or rules may serve arbitrariness, and therefore be contrary to the ideal of the RoL. A departure from the ideal of the RoL can be contrary to the value of the RoL and will increase arbitrariness but will still be justified by some other social value (social justice).

The RoL is quintessential to constitutionalism, but it has its inherent shortcomings, which enable its use against its own principles.[28] Adam

---

[25] P. Craig, "Formal and Substantive Conceptions of the Rule of Law: An Analytical Framework," *Public Law* (1997), p. 467. Bingham advances a prominent substantive theory of the RoL in T. Bingham, *The Rule of Law* (Penguin, 2010).

[26] J. Tasioulas, "Rule of Law," in J. Tasioulas (ed.), *The Cambridge Companion to the Philosophy of Law* (Cambridge University Press, 2009), p. 117.

[27] Raz, *The Authority*, p. 211.

[28] This is not to dispute the appropriateness of the RoL as an ideal. An RoL ideal enables and anchors aspirations and provides an ideal dimension to unmask despotism. However, at least the institutional arrangements derived from the ideal, and perhaps even the content of the ideal is open to its own demise, and the legal standards that constitute the pragmatic representation of the ideal are even more capable to undermine the ideal and turn the standards against themselves. Moreover, there is often discrepancy between the pragmatic legal and institutional toolset and the ideal as value. According to Smith, a confusion of the RoL as a constitutional norm, policy instrument, and value "hollowed it out" from a constitutional principle to an expedient policy tool. M. Smith, "Staring into the Abyss: A Crisis of the Rule of Law in the EU," *European Law Journal*, 25:6 (2019), pp. 561–76.

Shinar considers such shortcomings as not internal to the RoL but internal to law resulting from other rules of law. Some of these are created by legislation, others by judicial practice. "Put differently, many jurisdictions that proclaim to abide by the rule of law have devised legal rules that undermine what the rule of law might otherwise command. And ... some rules have been tailored with an eye towards resisting other rules, and there are judicially developed doctrines that acknowledge and even incentivise resistance to otherwise applicable rules of law."[29] As a result the law may not restrain official power. Where control over official action is missing (contrary to the fundamental promise of the RoL), the official will be inclined to act in violation of the RoL, at least vis-a-vis the citizen (though the official will continue to be obedient to his master's command). Shinar mentions rules and doctrines ... such as "standing, political questions, state immunity, suspensions of invalidity, and extensions," arguing that "none of these rules and doctrines were devised so that government could escape its legal obligations. Nevertheless, the argument put forward here is that this is what happens de facto."[30] Shinar is too generous: even democratic governments and their judiciary develop such doctrines to avoid government accountability, or at least to save the judiciary from political embarrassment. The difference between imperfect RoL and the use of the RoL in illiberal democracies is that in the latter, external or internal limitations of the RoL are deliberately and systematically deployed (starting with the limitations on standing at the HCC).

The RoL is about restraining the law (and through law, legal actors) and is a mechanism of self-restraint. This same self-restraint (e.g. being bound to admissible facts), enables legislators, administrators, and judges to serve goals contrary to constitutionalism. Procedures dictated by RoL considerations create closures to legally generated knowledge: the generality of law will rely on abstractions that render it difficult to comprehend. Legal certainty breeds inflexibility, flexibility creates abusable exceptions. Legality will limit the judicial review of legislative intent and in ordinary litigation will set limits to information gathering, accepting only certain judicially canonical sources of information. Legal certainty will become the shelter of villains.[31] The RoL paralyzes

---

[29] A. Shinar, "One Rule to Rule Them all? Rules of Law Against the Rule of Law," *The Theory and Practice of Legislation*, 5:2 (2017), p. 157.

[30] Ibid.

[31] In the so-called Sledgehammer conspiracy case, Turkish generals were arrested and accused of a planned plot. During their pretrial detention, a group of the accused applied

constitutional self-defense. When in November 2015 the Polish Sejm elected judges in superabundance to already-filled positions, the PCT majority, true to its practice and words in applicable norms, declared that it had no competence to deal with the constitutionality of such acts, because in matters concerning itself it did not intend to depart from the pre-existing constitutional interpretation. This was perfectly justified in terms of RoL principles, but it deprived the PCT of a legal means that would have allowed it to protect the constitutionally established system of checks and balances. Restricting the gathering of judicial information may serve the best interest of fairness (see, for example, exclusionary rules), but it forces judges to avert their eyes from the truth. Legalism reduces the complexity of the world into what is legally manageable.[32] This legislative and judicial simplification domesticates the RoL and perpetuates its inherent weaknesses. The RoL remains the captive of its formalism, diminishing public respect of law and courts.

7.1.3 How Far Does the Rule of Law Go?

The modern state (partly because it has assumed an increasing number of administrative functions) has extended the realm of the law and hence the sphere of influence of the RoL.[33] A fundamental political and constitutional assumption in democracies is that the RoL permeates the legal system, but that certain areas of life remain no-go zones for the state.

---

to the ECtHR. By that time it was well known that a confiscated but leaked book had already described the Gulenist infiltration into the Turkish state. Nevertheless, the Court considered that it was not entitled to look into the detentions. It found the claim inadmissible because the matter had been already submitted to the UN Working Group on Arbitrary Detention, a body that was held "similar" to the Court in a previous decision. (Disclosure: the author of this book was member of the Court at that time.) *Hoşgit c. Turquie*, ECtHR, App. no. 6755/12, Judgment of 16 September 2014. After the 2016 military putsch, the Turkish government concluded that the charges against the generals were fabricated by Gulenists and they were set free.

[32] N. Luhmann, *A Sociological Theory of Law*, ed. M. Albrow (Routledge, 1985).

[33] The extension of the administrative state was originally beyond the control of the RoL and legalistic considerations were considered either conservative or at least a burden to administrative efficiency and professional expert knowledge. For example, juvenile justice was deprived of the protections of fair trial in the interest of social rehabilitation. In the last decades, states have been increasingly ready to contract out their activities, which reduces the applicability of RoL concerns. In some instances, judges try to mitigate this loss of control (see *Academic Center of Law and Business* v. *Minister of Finance*, 2605/05 [Israeli High Court of Justice, 19 November 2009]). As indicated below (see the Hungarian National Bank profit transfer case), outsourcing is one of the favorite techniques of circumvention in illiberal democracies.

Private life and private law were thought to be such spheres, at least in nineteenth century liberalism, which took the public–private divide seriously. The RoL not only enables markets but it protects them against democratic majorities.

Another legal no-go zone is a leftover of state authoritarianism. Certain areas of state activity are still not subject to legal regulation and therefore the RoL. Executive privilege (including foreign relations and to some extent national security and non-justiciable political issues) are still exempted from legal control. In many respects, privacy and state secrets (in the areas of *arcanum imperii*) shield state power from the scrutiny and constraints of the RoL. (Constitutionalism here pushes toward some kind of legal supervision with at least minimal RoL guarantees.)

Illiberal democracies may have an interest in escaping the control of the RoL, but strong etatism, centralization, and economic nationalism dictate extension of the legally controlled sphere. Society is colonized through law. But there is a countertrend at work here: once in the firm hands of the leader and his loyalists, it can be advantageous to remove an activity, institution or asset from legal control. In Hungary, the National Bank successfully exempted the use of its sizable profit from public control by transferring it to private foundations (managed by the higher echelon of the bank's management and their relatives). Likewise, education is fully centralized and would be subject to the procedural guarantees of administrative law, but elite schools were transformed into denominational schools where autonomy limits the applicability of general rules.

Overall, managed RoL (like "managed democracy" in Russia) is advantageous to domination in neopatrimonial social systems. Clientelistic transactions are *protected* by elements of the RoL and fundamental rights: the private transactions of the patronage network are shielded by institutions of privacy, official secrets, reputational rules (defamation), freedom of contract, statute of limitations, etc. The law itself can make the sphere of domination impenetrable for law or difficult for it to penetrate: relocating activities into the private sphere exempt these transactions from transparency and accountability.

7.2 Populist Antilegalism

The transformation into illiberal democracy is accompanied by the twisting and turning of the RoL. In the transition period the inherited legal institutions and principles of the RoL are at the crossroad of conflicting approaches. This is due to conflicting aspirations of illiberal rulers and their constituencies. On the one hand populist antielitism and majoritarianism and the interest of power centralization fuels a war on judges and lawyers; at the same time the PLD leader is aware of the usefulness of cushioned coercion. Ruling through the law that has in its baggage the RoL is cheap, quick (or slow when necessary), effective, and allows for setting in place tailor-made privileges for the clients.

The PLD leaders emphasize that the mission of the state is good governance, which requires a substantive concept of the rule of law: the rule of law means that the law serves good goals. How these are achieved is secondary.[34] The consequence can be legal nihilism, which is beautifully expressed when politics is openly raised to be above the law. The Venezuelan TSJ displayed no inhibitions stating this: "law is a normative theory at the service of politics ... and the standards to resolve the conflict between the principles and the provisions have to be compatible with the political project of the Constitution."[35] Or, as the Polish government, disgusted with the judicial "cult of formalism," has stated:

> There is a peculiar bureaucratic corporate culture which has emerged in the Polish administration of justice – leading to a common perception that for some judges the verdicts should be in the first place justified on formal grounds, even if they are not actually fair. This culture stems not only from intricate procedural provisions, but also from the imbalance between powers – namely lack of external incentives to adjudicate in a different way.[36]

Plebiscitarian democracy holds in the highest esteem the will of the people, national sovereignty ("ending foreign yoke"), and social or historical justice.[37] These are not necessarily antithetical to the RoL; the problem is that they are held supreme. When the Polish government introduced a bill that would have added lay members to the appeal courts, the memorandum prepared by President Duda's Administration stated that this measure "will introduce a very important element of social control to cases in which basic elements of the principle of social justice

---

[34] See Chapter 5 on common good constitutionalism.

[35] *Abogados Gustavo Alvarez Arias y otros* case, Sentencia n° 1939 de Tribunal Supremo de Justicia – Sala Constitucional de 18 de diciembre de 2008, quoted in A. R. Brewer-Carías, *Dismantling Democracy in Venezuela. The Chávez Authoritarian Experiment* (Cambridge University Press, 2010), p. 353.

[36] *Executive Summary on the White Paper on the Reform of the Polish Judiciary*, The Chancellery of the Prime Minister of Poland (2018), p. 2.

[37] In Hungary, the Constitutional Court declared a revolution by the RoL, 11/1991 AB hat. pt. III(4) (judgment of March 5, 1991).

may have been breached."[38] In this case, social justice invites extralegal considerations.

Likewise, Latin American populists claim that disregarding legal formalities is necessary to undo discrimination against the poor and the indigenous. When Chávez invited thousands of Cuban physicians to Venezuela to provide health care to the poor, they brought only three years of training and lacked the qualifications to work as doctors under Venezuelan law. Applying the law, the judiciary denied their right to practice.[39] Chávez found the application of the formal criteria unacceptable and sent the Cubans to select villages. Interestingly, however, he did not change the applicable law. A legalistic Caesar would have enacted general laws to eliminate the obstacle to his intent. He could have reduced the general requirement for all or created an extraordinary transitory rule, valid as long as the Cuban mission continued.

Chávez chose the simplest solution: total disregard. He could afford it. There was neither a legal way, nor interest, to challenge what went on in the *barrios*. Supporters of populism demand simple solutions, as it promises a victory for common sense, to the detriment of the law's legitimacy, which originates in complex formalities. "[B]ecause ordinary common sense lacks reflection, its 'self-evident' truths characterize reality 'in inconsistent and unpredictable ways'. This is the majoritarian tyranny: muddled, unruly, readily unmindful of counter-intuitive (textual or institutional) principles."[40]

Populism cherishes an antilegalist popular mindset, which hates the anti–common sense complications of the law. The popular mindset is unhappy with "legal niceties" causing delays in court and protecting malefactors like migrants and "criminals." Populist political movements had enough of court power (with some good reason, given the performance of the judiciary in many countries)[41] and insisted that the rule of

---

[38] Quoted after Venice Commission Opinion No. 904/2017, on the draft Act amending the National Council of Judiciary, on the draft Act amending the act on the Supreme Court, proposed by the President of Poland and on the Act on the organization of ordinary courts, Venice, December 11, 2017, p. 15. Social justice is the battlecry of those political forces (including populists) who find formal legal rationality burdensome.

[39] For the facts see the *Apitz Barbera et al* v. *Venezuela* case, IACtHR, Judgment of August 5, 2008, para. 115.

[40] R. K. Sherwin, "Dialects and Dominance: A Study of Rhetorical Fields in the Law of Confessions," *University of Pennsylvania Law Review*, 136 (1988), pp. 848–49.

[41] When the Venezuelan Judicial Emergency Commission started to fire judges in 1999, it claimed that there were 4,000 complaints against judges over the previous 10 years and

unelected judges must end.[42] This served as strategic justification in attempts to reshape the judiciary to maximize executive power.

In this populist mode, the institutions of the RoL are presented as opponents of popular democracy: for governments, "other institutions – courts and legislatures, for instance – are nuisances . . . . Accountability to such institutions appears as a mere impediment."[43] A number of HCC judges advance a more sophisticated argument: The use of a nonspecific concept of the RoL undermines the RoL. There is no need for a nebulous principle where there is an applicable rule. "In the name of the rule of law, we subordinate to unaccountable and thus arbitrary legal interpretation all the actions of persons, communities, ultimately all the needs, actions and the complete liberty of states. Again, all the needs, all the liberties, all the actions; we allow arbitrary control without any kind of limitations."[44]

Populism's anti-RoL attitude is not simply a matter of legal counter-culture that takes to the extreme the criticism of alleged "government by unelected judges." There is a worldwide growing trend of populist justice: preference in law shall be given to the justice of (alleged) victims. Recall, populism is an expression of resentment, and as such, it fits into a culture of glorified victimhood. Victimhood logic contradicts the fundamentals of the RoL but is increasingly common. Victims shall be judges in their own cases, or the burden of proof should be reversed, so that the evidence of those who claim to be victims is accepted unless the accused can prove their innocence.[45]

---

that people had been waiting in prison for years to be brought to trial. R. Gott, *Hugo Chávez and the Bolivarian Revolution* (Verso, 2000), pp. 180–82.

According to the Prime Minister, the Polish judiciary was held captive by communism, and it was corrupt and incompetent. M. Morawiecki, "Prime Minister Mateusz Morawiecki: Why My Government Is Reforming Poland's Judiciary," *Washington Examiner* (December 13, 2017), www.washingtonexaminer.com/prime-minister-mateusz-morawiecki-why-my-government-is-reforming-polands-judiciary.

[42] This is a standard demand in political constitutionalism.

[43] J. M. Maravell, "The Rule of Law as a Political Weapon," *Working Paper 2001/160* (2001), p. 10 (quoting G. A. O'Donnell, "Delegative Democracy?," *Journal of Democracy*, 5:1 [1995], p. 60).

[44] A. Z. Varga, *From Ideal to Idol? The Concept of the Rule of Law* (Dialóg Campus, 2019), pp. 21–22. Judge Varga of the HCC is a member of the Venice Commission. In his view, "there is no better appropriate device for organising society than the one based on the classical rule of law principles," and this can be restored not with formal but substantive principles, like "*salus populi*" or its Christian (canonical) version: "*salus animarum suprema lex esto.*" Ibid., p. 24.

[45] K. K. Ferzan, "#Believe Women and the Presumption of Innocence: Clarifying the Questions for Law and Life," *Virginia Public Law and Legal Theory Research Paper No. 2020–39* (2000).

All in all, given its populist antecedents, antilegalism is to be expected in illiberal democracy. This is not to say that for the populist certain acts of authority do not count as arbitrary. Arbitrariness will bother the populist for reasons comparable to those that bother those who are concerned about the common law tradition: "If a power-holder failed to give due weight – i.e. respect – to a genuinely respect-worthy thing, the legitimate scope, if any, of his or her power would thereby have been exceeded."[46] The difference between plebiscitarian regimes and constitutional democracy, between authority-bound and democratic equality-respecting cultures, is what counts as a "respect-worthy thing."

7.2.1   The Early Fervor

The anti-legalistic attitudes that carried over from the populist movement stage into the building of illiberal regimes have facilitated disregard for the RoL in the later period of dismantling inherited state structures. The direct expression of the sovereign will of the people "enabled political leaders to circumvent standard institutional channels,"[47] allowing the new Caesar to decide as if he were in an exceptional situation.[48] This was the moment for social justice.

However, the Caesar of plebiscitarian illiberal democracy is not the prince above the law (*legibus soluta*). He is not ready to state that "I, the sovereign, who am outside the law, declare that there is nothing outside the law."[49] ("It is written but *I* say unto you.") He may rely on emergency-like powers, but he does not wish to rule a regime from outside the legal system, if possible. In 2020, Kaczyński refused to use emergency powers even during the COVID-19 pandemic: he wanted elections as soon as possible but was also perhaps considering his personal negative

---

[46] J. Sempill, "Ruler's Sword, Citizen's Shield: The Rule of Law & the Constitution of Power," *Journal of Law & Politics*, 31:1 (2016), pp. 367–68.

[47] F. B. de Lara, "The Pushback Against Populism: Why Ecuador's Referendums Backfired," *Journal of Democracy*, 31:2 (2020), p. 69.

[48] M. Rosenfeld, "Judicial Balancing in Times of Stress: Comparing the American, British, and Israeli Approaches to the War on Terror," *Cardozo Law Review*, 27 (2006), pp. 2079–151.

In a terrorist conviction case, the ECtHR, after declaring that fair-trial rights cannot be diluted, considered the fairness of the trial from the perspective of a nonspecific overall fairness, departing from the existing case law, which relied on factually identifiable shortcomings (the denial of access to a lawyer) and "which call for a separate examination," according to precedents. *Ibrahim and Others v. the United Kingdom*, ECtHR, App. nos. 50541/08, 50571/08 and 50573/08, Judgment of 13 September 2016, para. 252.

[49] G. Agamben, *The Omnibus Homo Sacer* (Stanford University Press, 2017), p. 17.

experience with martial law in communist Poland. (Among those who insisted on the declaration of the state of emergency were important victims of the martial law.) The ruler is less ambitious than Machiavelli's Prince. He is petty: his ambitions are limited to those of a trickster. He is satisfied with ordinary and regular cheating and lying. The trickster Caesar is fully aware of the advantages of the RoL for domination. Once the transition is over, he will quickly revert to a system that claims to meticulously follow the RoL. Illiberal regimes remain within the culture of the RoL, at least within the same vocabulary. To a great extent, law and the RoL remain the prevailing language of power (even if a *vulgata* Latin idiom) and the language of discourse about power.

7.2.2 Duality and Ambiguities in Caesar's Legal System

Why such unexpected endorsement of the RoL that seemingly contradicts the populist playbook? The cronies of governments and their rulers need to protect their positions and assets. They know that transforming the convenient into the legal is cheap and advantageous, as it fully protects corruption and discrimination. But clearly, they do not appreciate the RoL in any deeper sense. They do not see value per se, or virtue, in following the rules of reason and fairness. An instrumentalist has no interest in the inner morality of the law. This "autocratic legalism" favors "the use, abuse, and non-use (in Spanish, *desuso*) of the law in service of the executive branch."[50] Illiberal democracies do not respect the RoL as a value but still prefer to rule by law. "In many states, law has been a very useful vehicle (and at times equally useful camouflage) for authoritarian exercise of power. Where this is so, though rule might be by, it is not of law. Again, it must be stressed, we speak of differences of degree, not categorical distinctions of kind."[51]

In the standard opposition of democracy and the plebiscitarian regime, rule by law is described as the opposite of the RoL, being "personal, irrational, unpredictable."[52] The reality is more ambiguous: illiberal

---

[50] J. Corrales, "Autocratic Legalism in Venezuela," *Journal of Democracy*, 26:2 (2015), p. 38.

[51] M. Krygier, "Rule of Law," in M. Rosenfeld and A. Sajó (eds.), *The Oxford Handbook of Comparative Constitutional Law* (Oxford University Press, 2012), pp. 234–35. Rajah discusses "concealing" the legislation's "rule by law" nature. Rajah, *Authoritarian Rule of Law*, p. 17.

[52] A. Antal, "The 'Rule of Law' under Autocratic Populism" (paper presented at Media freedom and pluralism, and populism in the context of the rule of law, Central European University, Budapest, March 7, 2019), p. 3.

regimes cannot afford not to have rational law. Rule by law entails many of the components of the RoL, even if the goal served differs (e.g. "harmony" in Singapore or "tranquility" in Myanmar). As Waldron argues:

> After all, a demand that the government should rule by law can easily be read as a demand that it should use only legally defined powers. If this makes sense, then we have to concede that the little preposition "by" in "rule by law" is by no means expressive of pure submission to government authority. It makes a strong demand on a government to say that it must actually use law – and therefore legally defined powers – to implement its will.[53]

A regime that relies on rule by law is not interested in the curtailment of the ruler's arbitrariness, though it is often interested in restraining the state. Illiberal democracies maintain a highly ambiguous relationship to the RoL and use the ambiguities of the institution. Government acts are legally authorized, and the authorities follow the rulers' law to the extent possible, although this runs contrary to populist antiformalism and "common sense" veneration. For a number of reasons the leader does not wish to be above the law, and prefers to use the advantages of a compromised and unprincipled RoL (an oxymoron for the theorists of the RoL); instead of simply replacing the law with his naked will ("but I say so"), he will bend the law and set new rules in his favor and in favor of the needs of the regime. Hence the need for constant cheating.

Both the Hungarian and the Venezuelan Constitutions define the state as a state of law (*Estado democrático y social de Derecho*); and likewise the Bolivian Constitution (*Estado Unitario Social de Derecho Plurinacional Comunitario*); in Bolivia, legality is a principle in the administration of justice. There must be a specific advantage in declaring the RoL a directive principle of the regime.[54] The RoL threatens power because it promises to limit the possibilities of the authorities. Accepting limits (even if the regime will continuously challenge and push them further) has regime-specific reasons. Simple arbitrariness does not maximize the leader's power, while an RoL-based legal system improves social coordination (in line with the coordinating advantages of the RoL), and serves the ruler's domination. "[B]y restricting the arbitrary powers of

---

[53] J. Waldron, "Rule by Law: A Much Maligned Preposition," *NYU School of Law, Public Law Research Paper No. 19–19* (2019), p. 20.

[54] G. Helmke and F. Rosenbluth, "Regimes and the Rule of Law: Judicial Independence in Comparative Perspective," *Annual Review of Political Science*, 12:1 (2009), p. 349.

government officials, a liberal constitution can, ... under the right conditions, *increase* the state's capacity to focus on specific problems and mobilise collective resources," not so much for collective purposes, but for the regime's stability.[55] Respecting the RoL benefits regime legitimacy: the smart Caesar, who always keeps in mind that power must be preserved at any cost, realizes that constraints on the state, even on himself, can be enabling and generate credibility.

Of course, there is no intrinsic interest in curtailing the arbitrariness of the administration as a matter of a value per se. Legal norms function as instruments, guiding civil servants according to a central, increasingly autocratic will. The emerging illiberal regimes need servants and rely on a clientele. Servants and clients can be constrained by law to serve, when the interest of domination requires so; the arbitrariness of the authorities is limited, although not for good reason. The RoL may civilize power, but the power of the law will remain a tool of coercion. "A legal order which contains ever so few mandatory and prohibitory norms and ever so many 'freedoms' and 'empowerments' can nonetheless in its practical effects facilitate a quantitative and qualitative increase not only of coercion in general but quite specifically of authoritarian coercion."[56] A formally lawful tax audit can be a most efficient way to teach government critics a lesson. The RoL disciplines enemies as well as friends (clients of the regime) and civil servants.

Operating a system of commands or rules without legitimacy is costly. Illiberal regimes like to present themselves as the RoL states, because even if the RoL is only superficially observed, it will provide legitimacy. Further, the RoL is advantageous in controlling social actors in general, and it is beneficial for the beneficiaries of the regime. "The goal is always to use and abuse the law to protect yourself and your allies."[57] The RoL protects the property of regime supporters, cronies, and the dominant position of the ruling party itself during the next electoral cycle. It makes people believe that possessing assets is legitimate simply because owner-ship is recognized by law.

The "legitimacy of a government might lessen appreciation of injust-ices it commits [especially among beneficiaries like investors in the

[55] S. Holmes, *Passions and Constraint. On the Theory of Liberal Democracy* (University of Chicago Press, 1995), p. xi.

[56] M. Weber, *Economy and Society* (University of California Press, 1968), p. 731.

[57] J. Corrales, "Trump Is Using the Legal System Like an Autocrat," *The New York Times* (March 5, 2020), http://www.nytimes.com/2020/03/05/opinion/autocratic-legalism-trump.html.

concerned countries] ... sufficient injustice might well erode a claim of legitimacy."[58] Illiberal democracies, at least until a certain point in their trajectory, prefer not to commit such "sufficient injustice," at least not to the detriment of too many people. That illiberal regimes accept the principles of the RoL (and observe them at least most of the time in most situations, and pretend to observe them all the time) is less surprising than what one would expect in view of the original populist zest.

Another reason for respecting the RoL façade is that illiberal democracies operate in market economies. During the transition period, property rights were not always protected, and the state interfered in the economy to reward its clients, disregarding the RoL and violating contracts and legitimate expectations. But in the East Central European countries, which are economically dependent members of the EU, one can only envision a temporary suspension of the RoL. Therefore, they have to pretend to play by the rules, and the EU authorities are satisfied with formal observance. It is easy to create the semblance of an independent regulatory agency (e.g. in broadcasting) if the EU is not willing to consider the systematic bias in the decisions of these "independent agencies."[59] The spectacular failure of the EU observing violations of the RoL is a constituent element of the legal cheating occurring in illiberal democracies. While multilevel constitutionalism is increasingly a chimera, multilevel breach of the RoL flourishes.

Once assets have landed in proper hands, property and contracts will be protected with the full force of the law. To a great extent, the market continues to operate according to the needs of certainty and foreseeability. The RoL, or its semblance, also remains important as a matter of international legitimacy. Where international economic and political relations depend on the assumption that parties will respect their commitments, disregarding the RoL threatens all involved, and sanctions are expected.

According to the professional literature on "authoritarian constitutionalism," the advantage of the RoL (courts and constitutions) – that it allows the ruler (or the regime) "to make credible commitments" by

---

[58] M. Krygier, "The Rule of Law and State Legitimacy," in W. Sadurski, M. Sevel, and K. Walton (eds.), *Legitimacy: The State and Beyond* (Oxford University Press, 2019), p. 108.

[59] It goes beyond the present study to what extent the EU tunnel vision is the result of bureaucratic self-blinding, ignorance of political considerations, and bargains. Anyone interested in games of self-blinding should read the monitoring reports of the Commission on the progress of the Bulgarian administration of justice.

increasing the cost of violations – does not apply in authoritarian regimes, because the ruler can alter the constitution (the laws) and the "target audiences know that the rulers can do so."[60] Some of the rulers of illiberal democracies have the same possibility. They can change the terms, including those in the constitution; in the Hungarian case, where changes are easy and handy, such changes are common (at the statutory level as well). Due to its ambivalent commitment to the RoL, the legislator still avoids retroactive, or even retrospective changes (and quite often even the *vacatio legis* is observed). The state tries to disguise its disregard of commitments, using cheating techniques. Only in the early days of the regime building that these commitments were openly disregarded, under the pretext that they were unfair or merely privileges granted by the previous elitist government. This occurred in Hungary regarding pensions (including private pensions), as well as other legitimate expectations. However, the RoL is not very demanding when it comes to legitimate expectations. The state creates the impression that commitments do not (always) matter. Uncertainty is a source of power. For all these reasons, illiberal democracies hide their disregard of the RoL (in particular, the equal treatment requirement) to the extent possible. Consider, for example, how clientelistic networks operate privatized government services, beyond the control of public law, or the private commercial broadcasting outlets that act as a tool of centralized government propaganda, held in the hands of cronies, protected by privacy, reputational rules, contract, and property law.

Is this against the principles of the RoL? Contrary to what some substantive theories claim, namely that unjust law cannot satisfy these principles, a legal system that conforms to the precepts of the RoL can still enable the operation of both good and bad content (good for some is bad for others and vice versa). The RoL may normalize morally reprehensible behavior, for example, when cheating is legalized. Lobbying was a crime in certain US states in the nineteenth century; today, it is a regulated industry.[61] Many countries grant tax amnesties in exchange for a lump

---

[60] Tushnet, "Authoritarian Constitutionalism," pp. 422–23. See further D. S. Law and M. Versteeg, "Constitutional Variation Among Strains of Authoritarianism," in T. Ginsburg and A. Simpser (eds.), *Constitutions in Authoritarian Regimes* (Cambridge University Press, 2014); T. Ginsburg and T. Moustafa, "Introduction: The Functions of Courts in Authoritarian Politics," in T. Ginsburg and T. Moustafa (eds.), *Rule by Law* (Cambridge University Press, 2008).

[61] See also the curious relationship between tobacco industry campaign contributions and voting patterns in the Senate. United States Congress, Senate, Committee on Governmental Affairs, Rept. 105–167, Investigation of Illegal or Improper Activities in

sum payment; monies repatriated from abroad are exempt from investigation.[62] Contrary to most democracies, the normalization of the immoral (e.g. the legalization of self-dealing) does not meet institutional resistance in illiberal democracies. Legalized illicit practices continue, and even form the backbone of patronage-based government, without the blatant violation of legality and the RoL. Law can be observed within the four corners of legality if legislation is able to legalize illicit behavior. Where millions of dollars in subsidies are granted to "friends" on purely discretionary grounds, this is "defining deviancy down."[63]

In conclusion, some form of RoL is indispensable for the illiberal regime and not just for the purposes of domestic and international legitimation. The leader relies on what Cheesman and Waldron consider lower levels (or simply constituents) of the RoL (rule by law) and also on the abuse (and occasional disregard) of the RoL. When it comes to the ruler, the techniques and even principles do not limit his power in a fundamental way, though he tries to impose his will on others within what can be presented as compatible with the RoL (in particular with those elements which invite abuse). The result is that the leader will submit himself at least to (often empty) formalities. Plebiscitarian leaders seem to accept the RoL as part of the power game they play. Or they will at least pretend to accept it. "When PiS violates the Polish Constitution, it does so not on behalf of some revolutionary goals which would trump constitutional provisions, but rather claiming that it does so on the basis of its own interpretation of the Constitution, an interpretation which is as good as, indeed better than, that of the opposition, the Supreme Court, the Ombudsman, numerous scholars, or the Venice Commission."[64] The RoL is both to be observed and systematically disregarded: cheating on the RoL becomes inevitable. The regime, at least in moments of weakness, desperately tries to *hide* its inherent dislike of the ideal behind the RoL. Ultimately, law will not (and cannot) constrain power where power writes the law. But it may constrain those who serve the ruler's ultimate power.

Connection with 1996 Federal Election Campaigns, Final Report, Volume 6 (US Government Printing Office, 1998), p. 8511 et seq.

[62] The "Extraordinary procedure of reliant regularization" was promoted by then-Prime Minister Socrates of Portugal. He personally benefited from the scheme until he was arrested for money laundering, corruption, and tax evasion, after losing the elections.

[63] D. P. Moynihan, "Defining Deviancy Down," *The American Scholar*, 62:1 (1993), pp. 17–30.

[64] W. Sadurski, "How Democracy Dies (in Poland): A Case Study of Anti-Constitutional Populist Backsliding," *Sydney Law School Research Paper No. 18/01* (2018), p. 14.

In using law for consolidating power and controlling the state, the illiberal democracy appears schizophrenic. In certain areas of life, it takes the RoL rather seriously, but the RoL will be disapplied (although through cheating, to preserve a semblance of some kind of formality) where this is needed for domination. Fundamental precepts of procedural RoL can be respected where this does not affect fundamental governmental, party and government-friendly private interests. In some instances, like in Singapore, the RoL operates in a clearly dual legal system:[65] it applies seriously to business law, in areas outside the eminent interest of political power.

In the end, what role does the rule of law play in legitimizing the illiberal state and its ruler? Clearly, it is not irrelevant, as governments work to achieve their, often nefarious, goals through the legal system and in accordance with the rules of the game.

Notwithstanding the advantages of the RoL for winners of the patronage system, they have clear limits in an illiberal democracy. The judiciary's full recognition of RoL principles will challenge the monolithic power of the ruler, and such acts of independence must be immediately neutralized. This happened exemplarily in Singapore, in the instance where judges imported the presumption of innocence into the Constitution. Applying it in a later judgment, the courts consequently ordered an opposition member to be released,[66] though the government immediately "proposed constitutional amendments revoking the court's authority to exercise judicial review in similar cases in the future."[67]

7.2.3   Material (Substantive) vs. Formal Justice

Max Weber considered the rationality of formal law a precondition for an efficient market economy. He expressed great concern about the effects of what he called material (or substantive) justice, where considerations

---

[65] On dual systems where a law-observant administration exists subservient to a system of prerogatives, see E. Fraenkel, *The Dual State: A Contribution to the Theory of Dictatorship* (Oxford University Press, 2018), p. 71; J. Meierhenrich, *The Remnants of the Rechtsstaat: An Ethnography of Nazi Law* (Oxford University Press, 2018). Given that illiberal democracy is the political system of a neopatrimonial regime, a symbiosis of formal and informal normative systems is inevitable (see Chapter 2). Such duality exists also in Russia. M. Popova, "Putin-Style 'Rule of Law' & the Prospects for Change," *Daedalus*, 146:2 (2017), p. 65.

[66] *Chng Suan Tze* v. *Minister of Home Affairs* [1989-1] MLJ 69.

[67] G. Silverstein, "Globalization and the Rule of Law: A Machine That Runs of Itself?," *International Journal of Constitutional Law*, 1:3 (2003), pp. 439–40.

of social justice or other values will undermine the foreseeability of law guaranteed in legal formalism. For Weber, a professional judiciary guaranteed the rationality of the law; judges were to apply the law as if they were "paragraph automats."

The sense of justice often goes against the letter of the law. To the extent laws are held unjust, the judgment and the judge rendering it will become illegitimate. Consider the conflict between creditors and debtors. Creditors would like to see a return on their investments in real terms, while private debtors (to use a current East Central European example) who have to repay foreign currency–denominated debt after the exchange rate has dramatically changed are convinced that they should not bear the loss due to this (for them, unforeseen) development. This position has seemed contrary to the law. The CJEU and some national courts increasingly reinterpret the law in the name of consumer protection, favoring a kind of social justice (i.e. for the consumer/debtor) to the detriment of the formal RoL.[68] This turn toward material justice (be it compatible with the RoL or not) is particularly attractive to populists and plebiscitarian rulers. As Perón masterfully expressed the underlying populist concern:

> I place the spirit of justice above the Judicial Power. Justice, besides being independent, should be efficacious, and it cannot be efficacious if its concepts are not in accordance with public sentiment. Justice must be dynamic, not static, in its doctrines. Otherwise it frustrates decent public expectations and slows down social development, with grave prejudice to the working classes.[69]

Promoting material justice at the expense of formal legality evokes the dangers of revolutionary anti-RoL. When it comes to offering treats to the electorate, the government is ready to disregard elementary rules of contract law; it will protect debtors against banks and consumers against utilities.

The consequences of this populist understanding of existing legal relations manifest after electoral victory. The populists challenge the legitimacy of past political arrangements: contracts with the previous government and legitimate expectations based on statutes enacted under

---

[68] Case C-26/13, *Árpád Kásler, Hajnalka Káslerné Rábai* v. *OTP Jelzálogbank Zrt* [2013] EU:
C:2014:282.
[69] Quoted after T. S. Pappas, *Populism and Liberal Democracy. A Comparative and Theoretical Analysis* (Oxford University Press, 2019), p. 197. For a practical application, see Chapter 8.

them and their predecessors are sometimes declared void for being fraudulent and unjust or at least rescinded with immediate effect. Such attitudes in East Central Europe fit into a restorative (conservative) revolutionary tradition. In other contexts, the revolutionary zeal reflects the morality of a "just society." The 2017 Polish judicial reform was partly justified by considerations of social justice, which reminded the Venice Commission of Soviet lay judges who were supposed to apply revolutionary legal consciousness,[70] the ultimate form of abhorrent material justice of socialist substantive natural law theories.[71]

7.3 Fundamental Precepts of the Rule of Law, and Their (Ab)use in Illiberal Democracies

Some scholars warn that RoL cannot be captured in any "Rule of Law Checklist"[72] of "legal institutions, facilities, principles and procedures," nor be "submerged in some potentially overflowing bundle of moral achievements."[73] However, a few constitutive principles do exist in all legal systems that aspire to be called RoL observant. Among the common elements, the requirements of nonretroactivity, advanced promulgation, internal consistency,[74] and minimal stability are not meaningfully affected in illiberal democracies. In continental Europe, the *Rechtsstaat* tradition requires that officials be legally authorized to act, particularly in applying coercion. Illiberal democracies respect that too.

Legal clarity is occasionally violated in illiberal democracies, at times in areas that are highly sensitive both for the political power and to fundamental rights. Vagueness grants discretionary power that favors the government. Vague laws have censorial effects, and not only in matters of freedom of expression or criminal law. Nonspecific standards of liability have been used against judges in disciplinary and criminal proceedings in Venezuela, Turkey, and Poland. Vagueness enables harassment (as in the case of broadcasting licenses) and muzzling through

---

[70] Venice Commission, Opinion No. 904/2017, on the draft Act amending the National Council of Judiciary, on the draft Act amending the act on the Supreme Court, proposed by the President of Poland and on the Act on the organization of ordinary courts, Venice, December 11, 2017, p. 15.

[71] Weber, *Economy and Society*, p. 874.

[72] For such a list see the Venice Commission. Venice Commission, *Rule of Law Checklist*, Council of Europe (2017).

[73] M. Krygier, "Illiberalism and the Rule of Law," in A. Sajó, R. Uitz, and S. Holmes, *Routledge Handbook of Illiberalism* (Routledge, in press).

[74] This may not be true of the judgments of the TSJ.

the criminalization of expression (offenses to dignity, scaremongering against journalists, etc.).

Vagueness fits into the logic of the patronage system, which requires the allocation of government resources in a way that maximizes domination. For this reason, Hungary leaves an increasing portion of the budget in the general reserve, to be used according to the political needs of the moment, outside of parliamentary control (as the reallocation is left to the cabinet). In addition, the government has nearly unlimited statutorily recognized power to change spending allocations between budget lines. Although fiscal constitutionalism is a known concept in constitutional law,[75] RoL considerations are hardly incorporated into budget and spending law, and illiberal democracies abuse this shortcoming.

Lack of clarity occurs in most RoL-conscious legal systems too (see, for example, "impeachment" for "other high crimes and misdemeanors" in the US Constitution). The lack of procedural hurdles that would mitigate the adverse consequences of the uncertain rule makes illiberal vagueness particularly problematic. Beyond problems with legal clarity, two principles of the RoL are systematically disregarded, not just by sloppiness, but because this serves neopatrimonial domination and the avoidance of political accountability. These are 1) the generality of the law (because the system is based on legalized favoritism) and 2) the requirement that officials adjudicating legal matters do so within the meaning of the laws and the laws governing their activities (honesty and nonarbitrariness in the application of the law).

7.3.1   Generality of the Law and Ad Hominem Laws, and Interpretations Favoring the Powers That Be

The generality of laws satisfies the equality requirement of democracy.[76] Exceptions are granted only when genuine differences or specific circumstances necessitate them. General laws may at times grant such exceptions, but quite often they are left to delegated legislation or the law-enforcing body.[77] Legislation delegates rule-making to the executive, which is supposed to be better situated to consider special circumstances.

---

[75] The term is more often used outside of constitutional law, commonly referring to the most efficient design of the tax system. In constitutional law, it refers to the powers of the executive to counter parliamentary powers in budgetary matters (including spending).

[76] P. Gowder, *The Rule of Law in the Real World* (Cambridge University Press, 2016), p. 5.

[77] The compatibility of delegated legislation with the separation of powers and popular representation is dubious; delegation certainly contributes to executive power grab.

The power to grant exceptions enables the "legalized" concentration of power, undermines equality, and ridicules constitutional accountability, especially if used for political purposes. In Hungary, where in 2019 the opposition assumed control of numerous municipalities, the government invented a series of measures to deprive municipalities of their remaining financial independence. The laws revoking decision-making powers and income (local taxation) were general, disadvantaging government loyalist municipalities too. To help the latter, a second general law authorized the government to declare new investments to be of national interest; in that case, the local tax paid by the new entity would not belong to the municipality, but to the county council, which are all controlled by the government. They will then be able to redistribute the revenue in a "politically expedient" way. New investments will likely be declared in the national interest when they occur in an opposition-controlled village, which will then be deprived of its revenue.[78]

The exceptions granted by general laws, and the general laws of special regimes,[79] are crucial for legalizing privileges and favoritism and hence for neopatrimonial domination, the socioeconomic basis of illiberal democracy. A crucial feature of exceptions in illiberal democracy is that the exception does not relate to its purpose. In 2020, the responsible Hungarian ministry published a call for a cultural subsidy (grant), inviting two named entities: if they satisfy the conditions of the call, they will receive approximately €170,000 each. One of the calls addressed the owner of the most influential progovernment internet portal.[80] The invitee was expected "to produce works of cultural or identity history [or other works] which present faithfully the events of the twentieth century for the general public." The income generated by the sponsored activities should not exceed half of the operational costs. Prima facie, this call conforms to EU law.[81] The political favoritism is authorized within

---

[78] Levitsky and Ziblatt refer to President Trump's attempt to defund "sanctuary cities" and President Chavez's action to take away institutions (like hospitals, etc.) under the control of opposition municipalities. S. Levitsky and D. Ziblatt, *How Democracies Die* (Crown, 2018), p. 182.

[79] Chávez benefited from four enabling acts.

[80] The other beneficiary was a nonfunctioning internet portal owned by a journalist in a leadership position in a government-controlled private media conglomerate (KESMA – see Chapter 8). In one of his articles, the journalist wrote that "liberals, the Nazis of our days, announce a new race theory."

[81] Commission Notice on the notion of State aid as referred to in Article 107(1) of the Treaty on the Functioning of the European Union. 2016/C 262/01 [2016], para. 34. "Taking into account their particular nature, certain activities related to culture . . . may be organised in

general rules. What would count in the world of morals as a kickback, or the illegal financing of progovernmental activities, becomes a state act beyond criticism, thanks to the RoL.

The legislator's strategy creates loopholes and provides for exceptions to increase discretionary power. Such tricks are not unknown in "consolidated" democracies but are not systematically directed at consolidating personal power; moreover, corrective mechanisms are increasingly built into the legal system to enhance the RoL (see increased control over immunities and executive privileges). In an illiberal regime, systemic RoL violations remain uncorrected. The RoL shelters illegality elevated to the norm (see discussion on procurement, below).

Generality runs contrary to privilege, but privilege forms a constituent element in the PLD system of domination. Tailor-made norms, with little respect for fairness, are used to protect government cronies. Berlusconi benefited from at least 38 ad hominem laws during his seventeen years in or close to power.[82] Some of these protected his financial interests (e.g. when legislation and complicit public administration prevented his competitors from establishing competing television channels). Other laws manipulated the rules of the statute of limitations affecting his pending criminal cases. Italian courts and prosecutors tried to block these legislative tricks, and many of these laws were declared unconstitutional. In this respect, the story differs from comparable efforts in illiberal democracies.

Economic favoritism relies on disguised ad hominem regulations and decisions that run contrary to the separation of powers, in the sense that legislation replaces a court of justice or otherwise sanctions an identifiable but unnamed person. The potential for abuse is so great that the US Constitution singles out and prohibits bills of attainder.[83] However, this is not the main concern in East Central European countries. Exceptions entail the nonapplication of sanctions, including nonprosecution (by

a non-commercial way and thus be non-economic in nature. Public funding thereof may therefore not constitute State aid." (Not that the prohibition of state aid [dictated by competition considerations and unrelated to political bias] would not be exempt from exceptions...)

[82] "L'elenco delle leggi ad personam," Liberta e Giustizia (November 9, 2011), http://www.libertaegiustizia.it/2011/11/09/lelenco-delle-leggi-ad-personam.

[83] Personal targeting occurs outside of criminal law too. The Hungarian law on the Kúria (Supreme Court), enacted in conjunction with the HFL, set a condition that the sitting Supreme Court President could not satisfy. See, critically, *Baka* v. *Hungary*, ECtHR, App. no. 20261/12, Judgment of 23 June 2016; D. Kosař and K. Šipulová, "The Strasbourg Court Meets Abusive Constitutionalism: Baka v. Hungary and the Rule of Law," *Hague Journal on the Rule Law*, 10 (2018), pp. 83–110.

setting categories that can be satisfied by the preferred person[s] – see Section 7.3.3). The ad hominem rules (which never name a person, but rather merely apply criteria that can only be satisfied by a single known person) enable the granting of privilege. Where a public competitive tender is used, its objective criteria corresponds to a profile that is satisfied only by the same group of government cronies. Public tenders are legally rigged; technically, this does not even count as an ad hominem preference.

The paradigmatic case of public procurement in Hungary, probably the central element in creating economic power and dependency, illustrates the normalization of disguised ad hominem legislation and normative acts. Hungarian public procurement law must follow EU law. The single market rules cannot be simply set aside, and rules must be followed in disbursing EU transfers, a vital contribution to the national economy. However, special procurement processes shall apply where national or security interests require, a matter left to the national authorities,[84] and public procurement can be dispensed via a tender by invitation. It is just bad luck that Hungary confronts so many security and other special needs! The government knows best what is required for national security; in a separation of powers system, this is subject to limited parliamentary oversight and even less judicial review under RoL considerations. Relying on self-created exceptions is how an inherent vulnerability of the RoL can be abused.

The RoL makes it difficult to prove its own violation. In order to show that the system is not fair, and therefore does not satisfy a substantive concept of the RoL, it is not enough prove that the winners of public procurement processes are always the same. Aren't they not the *best* by objective criteria? After all, they have the best references, including banks, and have won most previous tenders, etc. Moreover, such practical "coincidences" are hardly documented in legally relevant ways, and what happens in other tenders is hardly admissible evidence regarding a specific bid. Moreover, the tender's outcome seems unfair only because it "appears" to systematically favor the government favorite. The tender is immoral, but the above-mentioned facts do not amount to judicially cognizable evidence. Declaring these procurement contracts void will certainly satisfy material justice but only to the detriment of the formal RoL.[85]

---

[84] In the context of broadcast licensing, the Hungarian Media Council may cancel a bid if it finds that "in its judgment the media policy considerations or . . . the goals of the public calls cannot be guaranteed" by continuing the licensing process. No criteria are given.

[85] Of course, under some unconscionability doctrine, the contract can be rescinded in conformity with RoL requirements, but for such a finding specific conditions must be satisfied, which do not seem to exist in this type of systemic, legalized cheating.

The injustice occurs beyond the formalities of law, such as when people are fired for their political views. A careful termination will use legally valid justifications, immaterial and misleading as they might be. The RoL will prevail in Poland or Hungary, as long as the regime is served by sufficiently creative lawyers who can sugarcoat arbitrariness in legal forms. The RoL is inherently open to its own abuse; it is open to cheating.[86] In Palombella's words, "Here cheating means perverting the logic of the system by following the prescriptive rules."[87]

7.3.2 Honesty and the Application of the Law

In the *Rechtsstaat* tradition, state officials and organs act in accordance with their legal authorization. They not only apply and execute the law, they should do so *honestly*, accepting the ordinary or standard meaning of its words. Honesty means that officials base their decisions on relevant facts, or at least, the official shall honestly and reasonably assume that facts exist. Facts shall logically relate to the assumptions of the law.[88] Laws shall be interpreted honestly and professionally (consistently). Courts must construe meaning through a replicable process of reasoning, which remains fairly stable and is consistently applied.[89]

Arbitrary departure from the professionally acceptable meaning (set of meanings) becomes suspect when it follows external, particularly political, influence.[90] Honesty requires that laws and judicial decisions be obeyed by authorities. If this obligation is disregarded, legal norms and legality will make little sense. These are truisms, but it is here that illiberal democracies mobilize RoL-evading practices, eager to resemble the RoL. (In the context of human rights, see Chapter 6.)

Illiberal democracies expect their officials to act in accordance with the law. In principle, the law itself will provide the bias necessary for efficient

---

[86] See Chapter 8. See, critically, G. Palombella, "The Abuse of the Rule of Law," *Hague Journal on the Rule of Law*, 12 (2020), pp. 387–97.

[87] Ibid., p. 391.

[88] For a judicial formulation see *George* v. *Rockett*: "a statutory reference to 'reasonable grounds' for a relevant suspicion, belief or other state of mind, 'require[d] the existence of facts ... sufficient to induce that state of mind in a reasonable person'. The words created an objective test. The focus is on what a reasonable person would think in the circumstances, not the decision-maker's subjective state of mind." High Court of Australia in *George* v. *Rockett* (1990) 170 CLR 104.

[89] M. A. Eisenberg, *The Nature of the Common Law* (Cambridge University Press, 1988), pp. 158–59.

[90] Raz, *The Authority*, p. 213.

domination. But there are too many unexpected situations where applying the law in the spirit of the RoL could backfire. Wherever the interests
of power so require, the law will be construed against logic, or used
arbitrarily, attributing nonsensical meanings to words[91] and disregarding
decisive facts without good reason. Where applying the law unexpectedly
inconveniences the regime, or its premium-class beneficiaries, the system
will try to doctor the inconvenience at the level of execution. The execution will be delayed or avoided.

As the RoL remains a cherished constitutional value, authorities not
only make use of the self-incapacitating possibilities of the RoL but try to
hide dishonesty behind formalism, often simply abusing the RoL.
Sometimes this means extreme pedestrianism, e.g. when the Hungarian
National Electoral Commission rejects requests for popular initiatives:
"Between 2012 and June 5, 2016, 328 questions were submitted to the
[National Electoral Commission] for validation. Only 15 were validated;
313 were rejected. Most of the questions were rejected on grounds of
ambiguity (62%), formal errors (48%), bona fides/proper use (16%) and
competence of the parliament (12%)."[92] An example of pure formalism
would be the HCC's rejection of the overwhelming majority of constitutional complaints for "lack of significant constitutional issue raised,"
without meritorious justification. Again, it is hard to object to this: this
is how respected apex courts work. Such denial of constitutional protection tells us more about the limits of the RoL than the way in which
a constitutional court avoids confrontation.[93] More sophisticated versions of formalism (where the constitutional court actively legitimates

---

[91] As Lord Atkin famously said, "the words indicate an existing something the having of
which can be ascertained, 'If A has a broken ankle' does not mean and cannot mean, 'If
A thinks that he has a broken ankle.'" *Liversidge* v. *Anderson and Another* [1942] AC 207;
[1941] 3 All ER 338.

[92] Z. T. Pállinger, "Direct Democracy in an Increasingly Illiberal Setting: The case of the
Hungarian National Referendum," *Contemporary Politics*, 25:1 (2019), p. 72. Act cii of
2014 imposed a ban on Sunday sales. Civil groups and opposition parties attempted to file
a number of popular initiative proposals to reverse the ban. "A strange race between
supporters and opponents of the ban took place. The supporters of the ban took advantage of the ban on concurring initiatives (Act xxxvi of 2013, para. 38): during the Kúria's
proceedings it was not possible to submit a new question for validation for 90 days. They
started to submit apparently inadmissible proposals thereby blocking the opponent's
initiative. Due to the formalistic practice of the NEC, this approach proved very successful." Ibid., p. 71.

[93] The ECtHR was found to have violated the requirement of justification. *Achabal Puertas*
v. *Spain* (Communication No. 1945/2010, CCPR/C/107/D/1945/2010). SCOTUS denies
cert without giving reasons, but at least there is legal authorization for such total
discretion.

the regime) structure the legal issue in the narrowest way possible to avoid a politically embarrassing judgment.[94]

When formal justifications do not help in the quasi-RoL game, authorities will rely on arbitrary, even nonsensical, interpretations (see Chapter 8). When this also fails, and applying the law runs contrary to the interests of the powerholders, the judgment will be disregarded. Nonexecution of a judgment extirpates all the costly and painful efforts to live by the law.[95] In 2016, the Polish government refused to promulgate PCT judgments (see Chapter 2 on the "Repair Act"), and the Polish authorities refused to follow CJEU indications in the matter of judicial appointments; in particular, the Disciplinary Chamber of the Supreme Court disregarded the CJEU's interim rule that it should not proceed with judicial disciplinary cases.[96]

The Hungarian government is less confrontational. When the CJEU found in 2020 that keeping asylum seekers in border transit zones violates EU law,[97] the detainees were immediately transferred to proper facilities. There was formal compliance. At the same time (true to its tradition of "creative compliance"[98]), Hungary declared that it would no longer accept asylum requests at the border and that such applications could be made at Hungarian embassies only. This kind of execution simply moves the violation of (international) law out of the radar of the legally patrolled world.

---

[94] According to the Hungarian Act on the transposition of the European Arrest Warrant, Hungarian judges must order detention when they receive such warrants and cannot determine what is the most appropriate and least intrusive measure to restrict liberty. The HCC (3025/2014 AB hat. 11. 17) found it sufficiently constitutional that the transposing law efficiently enforces European Arrest Warrants. The HCC was only concerned about whether the words of the EU law were properly translated, and it did not consider whether the requirement for the proportionality of restricting liberty is applicable in surrender situations.

[95] In many countries, nonexecution is simply a phenomenon of state inefficiency. Thousands of monetary awards determined by final judgment (many against the state) are not executed in Ukraine, allegedly for lack of budgetary resources and proper enforcement mechanisms.

[96] For the continued disregard of interim orders in asylum application cases see *M.K. and Others v. Poland*, ECtHR, App. nos. 40503/17, 42902/17 and 43643/17, Judgment of 23 July 2020.

[97] Cases C-924/19 PPU and C-925/19 PPU, *FMS and Others v. Országos Idegenrendészeti Főigazgatóság Dél-alföldi Regionális Igazgatóság and Országos Idegenrendészeti Főigazgatóság* [2020] EU:C:2020:367.

[98] A. Batory, "Defying the Commission: Creative Compliance and Respect for the Rule of Law in the EU," *Public Administration*, 94:3 (2016), pp. 685–99.

7.3.3   Selective Impunity: The Principles of Nullum Crimen, Nulla Poena and Nonretroactivity

The principle that officials shall act only upon authorization by existing, sufficiently clear laws reflects long-established maxims of criminal law and procedure. The maxims of *nullum crimen* and *nulla poena* (and nonretroactivity, which is a generalized formulation of these maxims) have served as foundational guarantees against despotism, which used arbitrary convictions to punish acts of disobedience, inventing the crime or punishment after the act has been committed (see among others the English Star Chamber, abolished in 1641).[99] It remains a hallmark of oppressive regimes that opposition and other unwanted targets (e.g. "non-conformists" like Jehovah's Witnesses in Singapore or Russia) are persecuted on trumped-up charges in disregard of fair trial and on grounds that are either extremely broad or invented during the process.[100]

In contrast to the blatant disregard of the RoL in authoritarian systems, in illiberal regimes the innocent and alleged "enemies" of the regime are not convicted on concocted evidence in kangaroo courts. Illiberal regimes not only respect *nullum crimen* etc., but use these noble principles *not* to reach justice. For example, a very strict application of the rules of procedure or presumption of innocence brings to a halt the administration of justice, at least for government cronies. To the credit of illiberalism, no one is convicted without a pre-existing crime, but some are not convicted even when a criminal provision applies.

The regime relies not on the application of nonexistent law but on the *disapplication* of the law in force. Beyond exception-based favoritism, impunity also lies among the constituent elements of the patronage system. This can be quite "democratic," as in Greece, where mass illegal construction, tax evasion, and pension cheating were tolerated (and

---

[99] Star Chamber is the *par excellence* common law example of arbitrariness. This is ironic, as the Star Chamber was established to promote equality before the law, at a time when it was feared that ordinary common law courts would not be sufficiently courageous or able to hold to account the grands of the country. The specially selected judges were protected by the king and for this reason were able to render justice in secret proceedings where external pressure could not be felt. The Chamber was also an instrument of material justice (in theory), as it intended to punish morally reprehensible conduct irrespective of positive or common law. D. L. Vande Zande, "Coercive Power and the Demise of the Star Chamber," *The American Journal of Legal History*, 50:3 (2008–2010), pp. 326–49.

[100] On the use of legally correct findings in a legally fair process, resulting in the persecution of Jehovah's Witnesses in Russia, see Chapter 6.

sometimes legalized by mass amnesty) so as not to antagonize voters.[101] Because of the ambiguity of the RoL, certain disapplications of the law may be acceptable in an RoL-based system. In many continental systems, the prosecution must press charges when it reasonably suspects a person, while this is not required in the United States. However, once the system of legality is adopted, as in continental Europe, the dictate of the RoL seems obvious.

Amnesty is probably the most common form of impunity used for political purposes.[102] Amnesty means collective favoritism, but it does not directly violate the RoL.[103] It is one of the many remnants of past absolute authority incorporated into the constitution. The statute of limitations is another accepted standard practice that contradicts RoL principles, though ironically is fully supported by it, once applied. RoL considerations precluded holding accountable those who were responsible for communist oppression, including collaborators of the interior secret service. Berlusconi's parliamentary majority shortened the statute of limitations, referring to human rights standards and ECtHR judgments. In France, "over five years, two prime ministers and nearly twenty first-rank politicians were prosecuted. Eventually, in January 1990 the National Assembly enacted a retroactive law that granted amnesty for the prosecuted politician."[104] In East Central Europe, mass-scale presidential pardons and a general amnesty favoring government cronies were used in the Czech Republic[105] and

---

[101] Pappas, *Populism and Liberal Democracy*, p. 208.

[102] Self-amnesty and similar measures are common tools in the hands of antidemocratic regimes. (See Turkey, Constitution of 1982, Provisional Article 15, adopted in a referendum, which granted immunity from prosecution to the 1980 putschist; see also Pinochet for Chile; further Argentina, Brazil, etc.)

[103] In Case C-105/14, *Taricco and Others* [2015] EU:C:2015:555, the CJEU considered the very short statute of limitations period applied to serious fraud affecting the financial interests of the EU. For the Italian Constitutional Court, the extension of the limitation period affecting pending proceedings ran contrary to the principle that a more severe criminal law must not be retroactive (for a contrary position: GFCC, BVerfGE 25, 269 [1969]). The CJEU basically agreed, and the RoL continued to shelter wrongdoers who benefit from the impotence of the administration of justice. Case C-42/17, *M.A.S. and M. B.* [2017] EU:C:2017:936.

[104] J. M. Maravall, "The Rule of Law as a Political Weapon," in J. M. Maravall and A. Przeworski (eds.), *Democracy and the Rule of Law* (Cambridge University Press, 2003), p. 281.

[105] President Klaus "stopped ongoing criminal proceedings that have lasted longer than eight years . . . . This category happens to include several notorious embezzlement and fraud cases that signify the wild post-communist overhaul of the economy in the 1990s, which was spearheaded by Mr Klaus." K. S., "Vaclav Klaus's Controversial Amnesty,"

Romania.[106] The Polish President granted a pardon in a pending case against a former head of the secret services, who was charged under the previous government and who could not be appointed minister given his first-instance conviction.[107] However, the President's politically motivated pardon did not depart from the prevailing, pre-2016 constitutional interpretation, which recognized unfettered presidential power in this context. Here again, the uncertainty of the RoL is palpable. It can be argued that the constitutionally undefined presidential pardon applies to final convictions only, but this is not the prevailing practice in many RoL countries.

As the adage goes, "the laws are applied to the enemies and are interpreted to friends." This is attributed to Italy's liberal Prime Minister, Giovanni Giolitti. In an alternative version, populist President Getulio Vargas of Brazil allegedly said: "for my friends, everything; for my enemies, the law."[108] In this version (also used to describe Putin's rule), friends are above the law; while restrictions on NGOs and related foreign-agent laws indicate the meaning of the phrase "for my enemies, the law." "To be powerful means to have impunity" and "to be subjected to the law is a sign of weakness."[109] In Russia, criminal proceedings and tax inspection have been used to eliminate Putin's potential competitors, and the same techniques of selective application of the law were used at lower levels of power.[110] In many instances, it never became clear to what extent the targets of prosecutorial action were actually criminally liable. There was no need for a final verdict as the extremely harsh procedural measures (asset freeze, pretrial detention) were enough to create irreversible

---

The Economist (January 17, 2013), www.economist.com/eastern-approaches/2013/01/17/vaclav-klauss-controversial-amnesty.

[106] Romania is not a stable populist regime. There has been no charismatic leader who could have established a leader democracy.

[107] KPT 1/17, pending as of February 2020. www.trybunal.gov.pl/sprawy-w-trybunale/omo wienia-wybranych-orzeczen-od-2000-r/art/9740-spor-kompetencyjny-miedzy-prezy dentem-rp-a-sadem-najwyzszym. Highly controversial pardons of political supporters are not unheard of in mature democracies, including pardons in pending cases (see most recently President Trump). Chelsea Manning's sentence was commuted by President Obama, while her case was (and is) still under appeal.

[108] B. D. Taylor, *State Building in Putin's Russia: Policing and Coercion after Communism* (Cambridge University Press, 2011), p. 106.

[109] G. O'Donnell, "Polyarchies and the (Un)rule of law in Latin America," Kellogg Center working paper #254 (1998), p. 9. The dual use of the law is not a specialty of illiberal democracy; it is also deeply rooted in local traditions, as in Latin America.

[110] On the use of "nonpolitical" crimes to eliminate political adversaries, particularly with the help of tax-related proceedings, see Ozan O. Varol, "Stealth Authoritarianism," *Iowa Law Review*, 100 (2015), p. 1707 ff.

situations, transferring assets to the hands of the government and disciplining society.[111] At least in the illiberal democracies of the EU,[112] the Giolitti principle applies: the friends get everything, but through proper legal interpretation.

Centralized control over the prosecution and the police precludes a successful investigation into, and even publicity of, the corrupt activities of patronage beneficiaries. This also serves the interests of the regime, which can hardly afford immorality in its ranks, being virtuous by self-definition. Surprising as it may be, Hungary ranks as one of the least corrupt countries in terms of criminal corruption convictions, due to the total subordination of the prosecution to a former Fidesz loyalist, but also owing to ingenuous legislation that can legalize highly important though "problematic" transactions.[113] In Venezuela, "Mr. Chávez created a system of impunity like no other. His supporters, especially crony capitalists, were allowed to get away with contracts with the state without bids, special access to favorable exchange, protection from tax audits and favorable treatment by the legal system."[114] In other words, here too selective application of the law is based on the nonobservance of a legally relevant fact.

Selective impunity claims are justified by human rights and the RoL: the burden of proof prevents the authorities from prosecuting. The standards of the RoL are turned into shields of the regime. Sometimes the regime also needs a sword (i.e. selective punishment), in order to sustain a sufficient level of fear and obedience. The selective application of the law (bypassing requirements for the generality of the law and the prohibition of discrimination) is used to punish "enemies." For example, opposition parties are defunded after selective review of their finances (without the possibility of judicial review). Kurt Weyland describes the

---

[111] Ibid.

[112] The same applies to Bulgaria and Romania, which are often omitted from the populist family because of their EU complacency.

[113] Following the appointment of a new Prosecutor General in 2010, the number of investigations and charges in politically sensitive corruption cases dropped drastically. "Polt Péter kinevezése óta meredeken zuhan a politikai korrupciós ügyekben indított büntetőeljárások száma," Átlátszó (February 6, 2006), www.atlatszo.hu/2015/02/06/polt-peter-kinevezese-ota-meredeken-zuhan-a-politikai-korrupcios-ugyekben-inditott-bun tetoeljarasok-szama.

[114] J. Corrales, "Trump Is Using the Legal System Like an Autocrat," *The New York Times* (March 5, 2020), www.nytimes.com/2020/03/05/opinion/autocratic-legalism-trump.html. For additional examples see J. Corrales, "Autocratic Legalism."

phenomenon as "discriminatory legalism," which is used to punish critics.[115]

A general relaxation of the standards of the RoL facilitates its use as a sword of the illiberal regime. Changes in the burden of proof and the presumption of innocence, as well as procedural changes like plea bargains or forfeiture during (extremely lengthy) criminal procedures do not originate in illiberal states. Constitutional democracies incorporate interim measures and procedural shortcuts into the RoL, resulting in irreversible harm that "only" increases the bureaucratic zeal of law enforcement. In illiberal democracies, the unbounded coercive power can be used to silence opposition and force business transfers: to freeze all assets of an entrepreneur during multiyear criminal proceedings means that both the company and its owner are ruined even if the case ends in acquittal.

7.3.4   How (If at all) Does the Illiberal Regime Fit into the Rule of Law Paradigm?

The professional literature's recent shift to a substantive understanding of the RoL reflects the dissatisfaction with the inherent futility, oppressiveness, and cruelty of the formal RoL. The case of Singapore, where genuine respect for the RoL is incapable of limiting state power, clearly shows the limits of the RoL in an illiberal democracy.[116] Even judicial independence may turn in favor of the regime: "A court system can enjoy complete formal independence from the executive in terms of appointments, promotions, and discipline and yet face a corporatist form of political control that is equally stifling when practiced within the judiciary."[117] International organizations (the EU, Venice Commission, Organization of American States) consider attacks on judicial independence central to the demise of the RoL in illiberal democracies. Certainly, apex courts are either coopted or pressured, which makes them at least

---

[115] K. Weyland, "Latin America's Authoritarian Drift: The Threat from the Populist Left," *Journal of Democracy*, 24:3 (2013), p. 19.

[116] Rajah, *Authoritarian Rule of Law*, p. 9; G. Rodan, "Westminster in Singapore: Now You See It, Now You Don't," in H. Patapan, J. Wanna, and P. Weller (eds.), *Westminster Legacies: Democracy and Responsible Government in Asia and the Pacific* (University of New South Wales Publishing, 2005), p. 109.

[117] Moustafa, "Law and Courts," p. 290. On judicial independence as ideology of corporate self-interest, see S. Holmes, "Judicial Independence as Ambiguous Reality and Insidious Illusion," in R. Dworkin (ed.), *From Liberal Values to Democratic Transition. Essays in Honor of János Kis* (Central European University Press, 2004), p. 8.

"careful." Deference radiates to the lower courts easily, as they are bound by the precedents of the higher court. Courts can turn from checking to choking other institutions. Nevertheless, "courts are reasonably independent and enforce basic rule-of-law requirements reasonably well. Although judges, especially those on higher courts, are likely to be sensitive to the regime's interests because of the judges' training and the mechanisms of judicial selection and promotion, they rarely take direct instruction from the regime."[118] This should not pose a problem for the regime, as it can change the law whenever necessary.

The RoL becomes oppressive in the inevitable service of majoritarianism; in fact, majoritarianism eminently relies on the RoL, which results in "legal despotism." This was clear already to Tocqueville: "In the United States the omnipotence of the majority, which is favorable to the legal despotism of the legislature, likewise favors the arbitrary authority of the magistrate. The majority has absolute power both to make the laws and to watch over their execution... it considers public officers as its passive agents, and readily confides to them the task of carrying out its designs."[119] The use of the RoL in the current transition to illiberal rule raises the following question: "Is it not inherent to the rule of law that it has disastrous consequences?" Most things have a dark side(s), at least in law. Yet E. P. Thompson famously declared the rule of law to be an "unqualified human good."[120]

In a formal sense, the RoL is concerned with the sustainable structure of a legal system. Arguably, even in these thinner versions there can be no RoL without the authorities explaining their actions. To the extent that the RoL requires specific legal justifications, it contributes to the rationality of the legal and political system. In principle, the duty to explain reduces arbitrariness – in illiberal democracies where the authorities accept the duty of justification, they will be forced to provide fake reasons. Hence the need to cheat (see Chapter 8). In a liberal constitutional democracy, which respects its citizens as free and equal autonomous beings (equal in their freedom) endowed with reason, it is part of the citizens' recognition that the authorities provide a comprehensible (intelligible) justification of legal measures. This is not an inherent feature of the formal RoL, but it does not contradict it: public justification reduces arbitrariness. Mocking the principles that characterize arbitrary

---

[118] Tushnet, "Authoritarian Constitutionalism," p. 451.
[119] A. de Tocqueville, *Democracy in America*, vol. 1, ed. P. Bradley (Vintage, 1990), p. 262.
[120] E. P. Thompson, *Whigs and Hunters: The Origins of the Black Act* (Pantheon Books, 1975), p. 266.

laws denies the respect due to citizens, and it turns illiberal democracy into institutionalized fraud.

Without entering into specifics (where disagreements begin), neither scholars nor governments (including illiberal regimes) would deny that tempering arbitrariness is what makes the RoL quintessential for constitutionalism. According to Martin Krygier, the RoL is not so much about constraining as about tempering "uncontrolled, unpredictable, and/or disrespectful" power.[121] The Hungarian and Polish governments may agree, and their lawyers believe that arbitrariness is indeed controlled in all three aspects if formalities are observed.[122]

At least in Hungary, it is hard to deny that the use of state power is formally controlled, and it is hard to prove that the judiciary cannot exercise control. There are countless examples in which courts ruled against the government, finding some elements of Fidesz legislation unconstitutional. In the many more instances where laws have been upheld as constitution-conforming, this means that the authorities respect the Constitution; the regime is vindicated. After all, one cannot disparage a government that in most cases observes its own legitimate constitution.

Is this legal system unpredictable? Not more than other systems with similar traditions. True, in matters that remain important to political power, legally established exceptions apply; exceptions are all too common, but generality allows exceptions. Formally, the grounds for exceptions fit into standard solutions of the RoL. Exceptions are widely applied in all democracies, or even expressly authorized by EU law. The problem is not unpredictability but *predictable* bias (see Chapter 8 on the abuse of exceptions).

As to Krygier's third element, namely that the arbitrary regime *disrespects* its citizens, illiberal regimes face a serious problem here. The law and its application *cheat*[123] the citizenry. To dupe one's own people is disrespectful. The defense of illiberal regimes would be that they respect the RoL; exceptions are not only necessary given specific situations, but also as a departure from the general rules, in view of consequences and to

---

[121] M. Krygier, "The Rule of Law: Pasts, Presents, and Two Possible Futures," *Annual Review of Law and Social Science*, 12 (2016), pp. 199–229.

[122] Once the regime has been consolidated, a narrowly conceived RoL can be observed, as the examples of Hungary and Singapore demonstrate. In other illiberal democracies the situation remains more fluid, as the leader's power is not yet fully consolidated.

[123] For example, judges are sent into retirement as part of pension reform and the measure serves equality.

the extent they serve good purposes. Where the RoL dictates measures that do not serve good purposes (the "common good"), one shall not be bound by it. At first glance, this argument has its merits. General rules do admit exceptions, and this does not, in principle, violate the RoL.[124]

Further, the illiberal regime's apologist could argue, correctly, that the RoL is a matter of degree and will, and perhaps should, be satisfied to a degree rather than completely. As the RoL consists of several components, important elements can be met with others left unfulfilled, or the shortcomings of one aspect can be countered by other elements of the RoL. This may pose a problem for the legitimacy of the legal system – or not. The picture that emerges reflects this complexity: while important, perhaps decisive, direct attacks on key RoL institutions occur in the illiberal democracies in East Central Europe, they still uphold many elements, especially following the regime's early changes, at the stage of quiet consolidation (and before the descent into despotism). Even where slogans elevate the interests of the nation and material justice above the constitution, the handling of even political issues remains legalistic.

True, forms of the RoL are often (ab)used for purposes contrary to their ideals (foreseeability, respect of legitimate expectations, etc.); however, just like human rights, they are not denied. The RoL bears an inherent readiness to endorse its own abuse: it can serve efficient, disciplined bias. Very often, abuse is merely the realization of what is permissible within the RoL, like exceptions and compromises. What matters is the cumulative effect. The possibilities for excess are pursued regularly in illiberal democracies which, however, also remain interested in observing legality, among other things because it is an efficient protector of power. Legality is a key component of the state ruled by law, the *Rechtsstaat* tradition prevalent in continental Europe. Undeniably, there is a semblance of lawfulness and rule-following in illiberal democracies, in a specific sense of legalism. Judith Shklar defined legalism as a moral attitude and a code of conduct, common to Western countries, related to

---

[124] Consider the exception to the absolute prohibition of retroactivity in criminal law. Following the logic of the Nuremberg trials, Article 7(2) of the ECHR recognizes as lawful the punishment of an act which "was criminal according to the general principles of law recognised by civilised nations," irrespective of the existence of a specific law at the time the act was committed. In other instances, the RoL itself precludes the justice that would follow from general rules. The RoL allows the loss of property by adverse possession: this being an exception to the general rule of property protection by a general rule of exception. The RoL allows pardon and amnesty for serious malefactors, even without generality, where the constitution grants unconditional discretion to the head of state.

rule-following, orderliness, and formalism – and nothing more.[125] This kind of legalism has benefits from the plebiscitarian government's perspective. It is easy enough to rely on superficially following the rules in order to lend some legitimacy to the government's actions: "What the government did was within the letter of law" is a powerful argument. It enables supporters to plausibly deny the government's nefarious intentions. In a tradition of legal positivism, without a culture of fairness, it is not so difficult to (mis)take legality and legalism for the RoL. This cultural tradition expects the law to provide orderly submission and far less protection against the authorities.

It is therefore wrong to assume that the emerging illiberal regimes are based on a radical denial of the RoL. Here lies a dualism, where the RoL is compromised in matters crucial for political power and related economic domination, but much less in everyday life. Legalism and rule by law without principles leads to a pattern where the RoL is simultaneously followed and breached. Of course, this is a special kind of RoL, which necessitates an unusually high number of legal tricks, cheating, and legal indecency. Fake justifications for legislation and in the application of law abound: this is the new normal. The legal system pays a high price. The twisting and turning of the RoL undermines the rationality of the legal system: applications of the law and its changes are not foreseeable by ordinary or legal logic, but by the logic of power (i.e. as a minimum, the outcome must not harm the interests of domination). The law is foreseeable, except that one cannot know where and when the same law will *not* mean the same. However, taken in their isolation, most measures that help the regime, and smack of disrespect of the spirit of the RoL, do fit into a certain RoL logic. Where a sufficient majority can change laws democratically and in accordance with the constitution (either neutral in the liberal sense or reflecting specific value preferences), the Fullerian or Razian expectations of the RoL can remain observed. This inconvenient conclusion is not incompatible with the historical experience with the RoL. It has always been a status quo doctrine, a tool of social and political coordination benefiting the state, although at the same time, it remains a less painful form of oppression and discipline than more unconstrained forms of rule. As the use of law in illiberal democracy described in Chapter 8 indicates, notwithstanding numerous abuses and disregard of specific RoL standards, it is not only such disregard (cheating) that makes the RoL specific in illiberal democracies. This is an odd use of the

---

[125] J. N. Shklar, *Legalism: Law, Morals, and Political Trials* (Harvard University Press, 1964).

RoL, one that disregards its *ideal*. According to Gianluigi Palombella "[t]he Rule of law ideal requires institutional settings that actually depend on time and context, but they must have in common coherence with the normative objective that the ideal evokes. ... [T]his ideal concerns the law [and more specifically] the adequacy of legal institutions to prevent the law from turning itself into a sheer tool of domination."[126] The legal tricks that characterize the cheating originate from the institutional inadequacy created in the illiberal transformation.

Political science or moral philosophy analysis may convincingly conclude that the regime does everything to perpetuate the power of the ruling party and uses law to undermine constitutionalism,[127] but in the absence of ex ante criteria, it would hardly be compatible with the RoL to consider Hungary or Poland as countries that violate the RoL in the legal sense.[128] And yet, the way law is (ab)used in these countries does something fundamentally wrong to the ideal of the RoL, including the normative power of the very ideal.

E. P. Thompson, the Marxist historian, famously praised the RoL for "the imposing of effective inhibitions upon power and the defense of the citizen from power's all-intrusive claims."[129] The rulers of illiberal democracies, at least in formative years of their regimes, do not impose "all-intrusive claims"; they do allow the citizenry to live as they would like, as long as this does not represent a danger to the rulers. Yet no one

---

[126] G. Palombella, "The Rule of Law as an Institutional Ideal," in L. Morlino and G. Palombella (eds.), *Rule of Law and Democracy* (Brill, 2010), p. 2.

[127] An amendment to the HFL prohibited reliance on precedents created under the old Constitution, as these precedents contained a number of restrictions on what a supermajority could do constitutionally. While the aim and consequence was detrimental to constitutionalism, the constituent maintained the power to insist on the exclusive applicability of the Constitution. The constitutional declaration of discontinuity is not implausible, especially in a revolutionary constitutional refoundation.

Such restrictions would satisfy academic critics of judicial review. See J. Waldron, "The Core of the Case Against Judicial Review," *Yale Law Journal*, 115 (2005), p. 1346; R. Bellamy, *Political Constitutionalism: A Republican Defense of the Constitutionality of Democracy* (Cambridge University Press, 2007); M. Kumm, "Institutionalising Socratic Contestation: The Rationalist Human Rights Paradigm, Legitimate Authority and the Point of Judicial Review," *European Journal of Legal Studies*, 1:2 (2007), pp. 1973–2937.

[128] In 2018, the EU Parliament provided a list of violations indicating a clear risk of a serious breach of the RoL requirement of the Treaty on European Union (see the resolution passed on the Sargentini Report). In some of the more egregious cases, Hungary formally complied with a judicial finding of violation, and the Commission or other international bodies were satisfied with the remedy. But the application of Article 2 of the Treaty is a matter of international law and remains a political decision.

[129] Thompson, *Whigs*, p. 266.

can be sure that the law has really imposed effective inhibitions on power. The RoL exists in so far as certain "*manières d'agir et de penser*" are shared within groups of people, and there is no evidence that such mentality prevails, is attractive, or even exists.[130] The constant cheating and tinkering with the law indicates a lack of respect and commitment.

The PLD rulers and their legal servants disregard the purpose of the RoL, namely reducing the arbitrariness of power. Unfortunately, in a practical sense, the RoL cannot catch unfaithfulness, which enables its destruction within its own forms.

[130] G. Poggi, *Forms of Power* (Polity Press, 2001), pp. 58–59.

8

Cheating

The Legal Secret of Illiberal Democracy

8.1 The Moral and Cognitive Problem of Cheating

> Perfect truth was not of determining importance in the exposition of Gold's theory: he felt mutinously that he had as much right to falsehood, bias and distortion in *his* memoirs of Kissinger, as Kissinger did in his memoirs of Kissinger.
>
> Joseph Heller[1]

"There are two ways in which injustice may be done, either through force or through deceit; and deceit seems to belong to a little fox, force to a lion. Both of them seem alien to a human being; but deceit deserves a greater hatred."[2] Notwithstanding deceit's bad reputation, however, Machiavelli (in his revolutionary disdain of his contemporaries' chivalry) held that the wise commander should "never attempt to win by force" what he "was able to win by fraud."[3]

Indeed, despite the moral depravity of deceit, ruling by cheating is all too common. As Bolívar stated in his Angostura address: "We have been ruled more by deceit than by force, and we have been degraded more by vice than by superstition."[4] For many leaders, cheating with the law, and on the law, is not a moral problem, and this is particularly true of populist rulers: they break the laws that they believe should not exist. This suits the mood of a post-truth world. If truth is not possible there can be no lies, and cheating and corruption become ordinary morals. Vaclav Havel described communism as a system where citizens live in lies. He hoped that one day they would step out of "living with the lie" and that would be

---

[1] J. Heller, *Good as Gold* (Corgi Books, 1980), p. 365.
[2] M. T. Cicero, *On Duties (De Officiis)* (Harvard University Press, 1913), p. 41.
[3] Quoted in J. B. Bell and B. Whaley, *Cheating and Deception* (Transaction Books, 2009), p. 37.
[4] Message to the Congress of Angostura, December 18, 1819 in S. Bolivar, *Selected Writings of Bolivar*, compiled by V. Lecuna, ed. H. A. Bierck, Jr. (Colonial Press, 1951), vol. 1, p. 211.

the end of communism.[5] We are "living in lies" again. The lies of the government go beyond law; they permeate politics and culture. The arbitrary regime that rules by cheating disrespects its citizens and makes them complicit in its deceit.[6] Regardless, they are treated as dupes to be manipulated. The government claims that it observes the RoL when it only rules by law; it boasts of democracy when it offers only plebiscitarian acclamation and not common decision developed through discourse.

This book has presented manipulations with the law and of the law as constitutive elements of a potentially self-perpetuating political system (a regime) that claims to satisfy the formal requirements of a constitutional democracy. Plebiscitarian leader democracies are of a populist stamp and are ruled by cheating (and by all the progeny of the concealment of truth in order to mislead: lying, deceit, fraud, spin, tricks, etc.). Illiberal democracy manipulates what and who the people is; it twists and bends the law to resemble a system that faithfully observes the constitution and the RoL; it cheats to enable the favoritism that it needs to dominate in a patronage system and perpetuate its power. A constitutional democracy cannot thrive amidst constant misinformation that deprives its citizens of the facts and honest norms needed for rational discourse.[7] A legal system that claims to empower people when it only caters to their bias and prejudice becomes a cheater: it will deprive people of their rational capacity for democracy, and at the same time, will increase its own legitimacy fraudulently, by making deceived people and innocent bystanders believe that the system is democratic, constitutional, etc.

8.1.1   Defining Cheating

In order to verify the hypothesis that illiberal democracies cheat the constitutional order, one must firstly examine what is meant by "cheating," and secondly, how this term, which refers to everyday interactions, can be used in a legal context.

---

[5] "Living within the lie can constitute the system only if it is universal . . . everyone who steps out of line denies it in principle and threatens it in its entirety." V. Havel, "The Power of the Powerless," in J. Vladislav (ed.), *Vaclav Havel: Living in Truth* (Faber & Faber, 1986), pp. 55–56.

[6] The politically unconnected businessperson will participate in a public procurement tender, deliberately presenting a losing offer, only to become one of the subcontractors of the winner.

[7] On President Trump's systematic use of lies and its devastating consequences for democracy, see S. Levitsky and D. Ziblatt, *How Democracies Die* (Crown, 2018), p. 198 et seq.

"Lying" is the willful misrepresentation of facts to others, while "deceit" is a truthful but deliberately misleading representation (that successfully deceives them), which may be valid or not. A "misrepresentation" may generate behavior detrimental to the deceived (tricked into doing something, etc.); and/or benefit the cheater, who would not have otherwise obtained the advantage. Some misrepresentations may not harm others, but the fraudster gains an advantage where a misrepresentation makes someone believe the cheater possesses a certain quality.

"Fraud" is misrepresenting a fact with the intent to gain advantage to the detriment of the person to whom the misrepresentation was addressed. Lying and fraud overlap: people who commit the crime of fraud (e.g. selling a stolen car as their own) will not only lie about the car's legal status but also will pretend that they fulfill the legal duty to tell the truth.

"Cheating" is pretending to observe a rule in order to depart from it, most often reaping undeserved benefits from the cheated persons or from the "system"; "in violating a rule that others follow, and thereby breaching an obligation to restrict his liberty in a manner agreed, the cheater gains an unfair advantage."[8] In the act of cheating, the cheater (mis) represents himself as conforming with the norms. Cheating sometimes entails other falsities, but it does not necessarily require making a false statement. Using an extra ace under my sleeve in a card game enables me to show four aces in my hand. The four aces are there, but I have breached the underlying assumptions of the game. Players assume that all of them follow the (same) rules of the game, which is based on a shared norm. (The borders of the meaning of cheating remain somewhat fluid here: my act can be considered a lie about my rule observance – but I had not said anything about the *honesty* of my conduct, and we often must play with people whom we know are not honest, trustworthy, etc.). The process of playing generates a continuous assumption among my playmates that I play honestly. This assumption reflects an implicit agreement that all players play by the book. If my outraged partners call my bluff, they will call me a cheater, because for them the rule breaking, the manipulative act, is what matters, and not my moral character, the lack of honesty.

Referring to Green, Gianluigi Palombella offers a different understanding of cheating. In his view, "cheating implies a violation of

---

[8] S. P. Green, *Lying, Cheating, and Stealing: A Moral Theory of White-Collar Crime* (Oxford University Press, 2007), p. 55. See further M. S. Quinn, "Practice-Defining Rules," *Ethics*, 86:1 (1975), pp. 76–86.

regulative (prescriptive) rules in order to keep oneself within the game itself: the structural sense of the game is valued, and so is its purpose and the objective, for example, of winning a football match (Maradona scores by handling the ball into the net)."[9] *Mutatis mutandis*, illiberal (alleged) "RoL," might well be based on using some rules of the game: the "regulative" rules are followed, and yet the players are cheating. This is really subverting the case, in so far as the players are playing by the rules [of] a different game: by following the regulative rules (say, of legalism, the "law of rules"), the players are pretending to stand by the constitutive rules of that very practice called the RoL. At the same time, they are inverting or overthrowing the teleology of the game.[10]

In the present discussion, cheating in law both violates the prescriptive rules (especially by using inadequate prescriptive rules, or even creating new ones) and disregards the common assumptions about (or underlying) the game. The cheater does not value the game's purpose. For the cheater, playing poker (the fun of it) is irrelevant; acquiring money is what matters. He will argue that this is a much more important value than enjoying a foolish game. (Returning to national purity is a higher value than observing formal law.)

To continue with Palombella's football analogy, consider the example of a controversial offside goal. Today, the matter can be determined with certainty via VAR.[11] Let's assume that VAR shows that there is an offside situation. The player offside did not cheat, though they did violate the rules. The referee is mistaken in honestly believing that there was no offside. If the referee has a duty to check VAR and continues to deny the visible offside, the referee would be cheating in allowing the goal. It is also possible that the rules leave the option to consult VAR or not to the referee's discretion. The referee's refusal to check the video may be an honest but legitimate mistake or an act of cheating depending on the person's knowledge and intention. (This resembles cheating in law, a quasi-privilege of those who officially apply or create it.) Cheating in illiberal democracies may go beyond what the referee can do: the sovereign state may claim with authority that VAR shall simply not apply, because it is unreliable or breaks continuity in the game or departs from the sport's

---

[9] G. Palombella, "The Abuse of the Rule of Law," *Hague Journal on the Rule of Law*, 12 (2020), p. 391. Palombella refers to Green, *Lying*.

[10] Palombella, "The Abuse," p. 391.

[11] The video assistant referee (VAR) is an assistant referee in association football who reviews decisions made by the main referee with the use of video footage and a headset for communication.

traditions. Using these deceiving arguments, the authorities will prohibit "VAR" (i.e. deny judicial review). Sovereignty has its limits: prohibiting the use of VAR will exclude the country's teams from international competitions. In that case they will allow the use of VAR, leaving full discretion to the referee in its use, and will carefully select the referee, at least for important games, most likely by exercising decisive control over the league and the referees' association.

Cheating can occur with and without deceit. When reading a procurement call for proposals, everyone in the interested Hungarian business community knows that the neutral and objective criteria refer to solely one or another company, and no one is deceived by the formally neutral criteria of the procurement law or the call for proposals. Only citizen bystanders are misled, believing that there is value for money in this system – in the whole legal system.[12]

What makes cheating morally reprehensible (wrong)? Is the moral wrong found in the intent or the consequences? Is the intent of the false communication to mislead, deceive, defraud enough for condemnation, or does harming the addressee or audience make it wrong? Is intent to harm necessary for moral condemnation? Or is it the unfair advantage obtained or intended to be obtained that makes cheating morally reprehensible? Perhaps these two considerations overlap, at least to some extent.[13] Following R. Ross, Carson indicates a third possibility beyond intent and consequences. He states "that all lies are *prima facie* wrong because they are instances of promise-breaking; it is *prima facie* wrong to lie because to lie is to break an implicit promise to tell the truth that one makes whenever one uses language to make statements."[14]

8.1.2 The Meaning of Cheating in Law

According to the Hungarian proverb, "a lying man will be caught sooner than a limping dog." ("The path of a liar is short" would be the Swahili equivalent.) But that is not so obvious when it comes to illiberal democracies and their legal systems. These systems pretend to satisfy the

---

[12] In fact, there is enough public information for people to know that they were cheated and their public money embezzled. The problem is that they do not want to know, and this is to some extent rational as they cannot do much about it, as the matter is "legal." This is how the regime is sustained.

[13] Green, *Lying*.

[14] T. L. Carson, *Lying and Deception: Theory and Practice* (Oxford University Press, 2010), p. 24.

requirements of the RoL by following specific legal requirements and/or precepts of the RoL, but disregarding the relevant standard or principles.

The concepts of various misrepresentations are not easily transferable to legal cheating or chicanery in law-making and application.[15] The first difficulty originates in the law's normative nature. A legal norm is not quite like a fact and it cannot be misrepresented like one. It is a command with a meaning that can be reproduced with different levels of accuracy. But this reproduction (interpretation) is a creative act. The meaning of commands cannot be conceived as something fixed; it is less determined and concrete compared to a fact (and "facts" are much less certain than assumed). But one can still cheat in determining the meaning of the command.

A further difficulty originates in the law's inherent, constitutive uncertainty. A command may have more than one legitimate meaning. As a useful illustration, consider the problem of legal misrepresentation within three common contexts of legal activity:

- legislation as a representation of the constitution and (quite differently) the normative reflection of social and political reality and will in it;
- implementation of laws in the form of regulations and administrative acts (e.g. a zoning ordinance); and
- interpretation of norms within individual cases, primarily as a matter of judicial interpretation (including interpreting the constitution in the context of the constitutionality of a norm or even individual judgment).

The specificity of the (mis)representation question here replaces correspondence to facts with faithfulness to a norm, although when it comes to facts in law, cheating often occurs as well. Facts can be disregarded or misconstrued, resulting in a legal lie.

Given the uncertainty of the applicable law (particularly the constitution), it is less obvious where cheating begins. The constitutional system is more than the text of the constitution; it consists of conventions and assumptions about decency, and behind them, the constitution's presupposed spirit (which may however be pure imagination in the hands [dreams] of the constitutional scholar – see Chapter 5). Conventions

---

[15] Cheating in the form of fraud is an important consideration of the law, with clear legal definitions when it comes to individuals. However, this approach does not offer sufficient guidance for evaluating an entire legal system or even for determining at which point the behavior of legal actors becomes a matter of cheating.

are notoriously open to change, as they depend exclusively on the existence of shared beliefs among select actors. It is enough for one party to decide not to follow a convention (a traditionally followed pattern of behavior). Departing from the shared beliefs may be a legitimate act by those in charge of making and interpreting law, even if it counts as betrayal in the eyes of loyalists. Or, perhaps, the belief was never really shared at all.

Notwithstanding these difficulties, one can identify legal cheating: it is pretending to be faithful while violating underlying principles. It is not a defiant departure.

To prove legal cheating remains a challenging task. Law is uncertain and offers different visions and distortions of reality. "[T]he Constitution is not a static document whose meaning on every detail is fixed for all time ... the practices that were in place at the time any particular guarantee was enacted into the Constitution do not necessarily fix forever the meaning of that guarantee."[16] This is not to agree with Owen Fiss, who claims that "there are any number of possible meanings, that interpretation consists of choosing one of those meanings, and that in this selection process the judge will inevitably express his own values," or that "[a]ll law is masked power."[17] There is difference in the plausibility of "those meanings" and one of the professionally important values for judges is to restrict the desire of expressing one's own values.

Many instances of legal cheating, including those related to the exercise of power in illiberal democracies, do not involve the relationship between facts and representation, although legislation may deliberately misrepresent reality. Legislation often relies on political lies about real legislative intent (see Section 8.2.1 on legislative intent analysis). For example, the legislator cheats when denying poverty and instead grants child support only in the form of a tax credit, while those who truly need assistance, those with children in need, will not benefit from the scheme.

Law-making is a legitimate act of will: the law is not determined fully by the constitution, giving the legislator much freedom; a statute can legitimately leave discretion for regulation and individual administrative acts, granting freedom to the decision maker. Establishing what is right and wrong, or what is the wish or interest of the majority, is a construction of a fluid reality, and not a definitive reconstruction of *a* reality. Volition may prevail over facts without misrepresentation.

---

[16] *Marsh* v. *Chambers*, 463 US 783 (1983), p. 816 (J. Brennan, dissenting).
[17] O. M. Fiss, "Objectivity and Interpretation," *Stanford Law Review*, 34 (1982), pp. 740–41.

A statute that prohibits the death penalty may be contrary to majority opinion (a kind of misrepresentation, even if based on a political lie), but it will not be a moral misrepresentation.

Legislation is not a game of poker; the legislator as a player has far more freedom to dictate the rules of the game. He may choose to play chess, instead of poker, or even invent a new game. But the question of faithfulness remains relevant: which games are permitted or not is determined by the constitution and its underlying principles, conventions, etc. Courts and interpretations compete; different meanings are attributed to the same legal concept or a single event (facts, acceptable facts, and "facts" as construed by authority), and it is not obvious which interpretation will be fake. It very much depends on the chosen frame of interpretation, where competing frames are equally legitimate or at least acceptably relevant. Many of these competing interpretations of facts and norms are legitimate possibilities within a certain range, and even beyond this range when another set of acceptable principles (a new paradigm) is brought in. Relying on one or another interpretation (including that of the constitution by the legislator) is not abuse, cheating, or a mistake, even if opponents call it that. The correctness of a presentation, the "truth" of one or another conclusion, depends on normative choice, and although the choice itself may be based on a misrepresentation or lie, it is to a greater extent merely a matter of authorized discretion.[18] A legitimate constitutional conclusion only presupposes the use of pre-existing methods and assumptions, relying on acceptable and transparent reasoning processes. It follows that similarly conflicting but valid legal conclusions are perfectly normal.

Moreover, constitutions are written as "incomplete contracts."[19] "Both contracts and constitutions rely to a certain extent on background principles and understandings not specified in the text. These can include the parties' expectations of proper behavior, unwritten norms and understandings, or other legal documents that are seen as having normative force and are relevant to the terms of the deal."[20] Part of the

---

[18] When in 2019 Prime Minister Boris Johnson advised the Queen of the prorogation of Parliament, he was not cheating as far as the applicable conventions were concerned. Many lawyers and courts shared the view he represented, even if, ex post, the UK Supreme Court concluded that this understanding was mistaken.

[19] O. E. Williamson, *The Economic Institutions of Capitalism: Firms, Markets, Relational Contracting* (Free Press, 1985).

[20] T. Ginsburg, "Constitutions as Contract, Constitutions as Charter," in D. J. Galligan and M. Versteeg (eds.), *Social and Political Foundations of Constitutions* (Cambridge

constitutional structure is unwritten and thus a matter of uncertain practices and background assumptions (see Chapter 7.3.2), another source of reasonable disagreement. To depart from constitutional custom can result in confrontation, but in the absence of a clear norm, it is not cheating.[21] "Showdowns occur when the location of constitutional authority for making an important policy decision is ambiguous or contested, and multiple political agents (branches, parties, sections, governments) have a strong interest in establishing that the authority lies with them."[22] Incursions into the competence of another branch occur often. These are "normal" constitutional conflicts and do not raise serious issues of legal cheating. To use an example from the early days of the American Republic, in the debate concerning the power of Congress to establish a national bank, the parties could rely on legitimate arguments in an unsettled situation. The outcome influenced abstract power relations (state versus federation) but did not result in the power aggrandizement of a specific political actor (person).

To assume a fixed, predetermined meaning to a constitutional text can be a mistake. There are instances where the constituent did *not* intend to clarify certain matters, finding it necessary to leave them undecided. But in most situations, both in illiberal and constitutional democracies, there is a zone of accepted interpretations and meanings, which are accepted, among other reasons, because they were reached honestly, in accordance with certain established and respected methods. These methods determine which questions should be addressed "through the accepted techniques of legal reasoning . . . [and] each side exploits the indeterminacy of the materials and the flexibility of technique to argue that its solution is simply law application."[23] Consider the situation of the PiS government

---

University Press, 2013), p. 197; J. E. Finn, *Constitutions in Crisis: Political Violence and the Rule of Law* (Oxford University Press, 1991), p. 24.

[21] The first two Presidents of the United States delivered the State of Union address in person before a joint session of Congress. This seemed to establish a tradition, until President Jefferson found it contrary to the *republican* tradition (as the British monarch delivered such an address in person to Parliament), and this principled approach became the tradition corresponding to the republican spirit of the US Constitution – until President Wilson did the opposite – and that became the norm until this day. Where is the spirit? What is it in this case? (See also the tacit convention that no President shall run for a third term – until Roosevelt did.)

[22] E. Posner and A. Vermeule, "Constitutional Showdowns," *University of Pennsylvania Law Review*, 156 (2008), p. 1002.

[23] D. Kennedy, "Authoritarian Constitutionalism in Liberal Democracies," in H. A. García and G. Frankenberg, *Authoritarian Constitutionalism*, p. 163.

in Poland, which is regularly accused of violating the Polish Constitution. The Polish authorities, in the tradition of other arbitrary regimes, invent for themselves a new power that hampers the functioning of the existing constitutional institutions, especially when the results do not favor the government. This is what happened in 2016, in the fatally decisive case of the nonpromulgation of PCT decisions, enabling the incapacitation of the PCT (see Chapter 2).[24] But in other instances, for example when the Polish parliamentary majority uses the shortcomings, loopholes, and open texture of the Constitution, the matter is not a straightforward falsification. Consider here the PiS-enacted law on the composition of the new Judicial Council (see Chapter 2). This law was not contrary to the sloppy provision of the Constitution, as the PCT rightly concluded. But it was held contrary to judicial independence by the CJEU. Judicial independence is an undisputed principle of the Polish Constitution, recognized by the PCT, even in its latest incarnation. The Judicial Council Act went against the spirit of the Constitution, as it used newly created removal powers to diminish the independence of the judiciary by submitting judicial appointments to the total control of a political branch. The PCT's finding of constitutionality was a matter of cheating: it disregarded the unwritten but uncontested constitutional principle. Disregarding the applicable principle violates the underlying rules of the game: it is cheating.

At the level of applying the law, misrepresentation may involve correspondence between norms, or between norms and their application. Once again, it is a mistake to treat an apparently applicable norm as if it were a fact and assume that is has a single meaning. But even within a range of meanings, some interpretations will still be mistaken, misrepresenting the norm as unruly, erroneous, or unfaithful to some core or "normalized" meaning(s) (a meaning that was already attributed authoritatively). Such disregard will amount to cheating where the interpretation pretends to correspond to a theory of interpretation, or where it chooses

---

[24] The January 2020 election of Luis Parra to President of the Venezuelan National Assembly was an undisputable violation of the Constitution of Venezuela. Parra was proclaimed Assembly President without a quorum, and in the absence of the sitting President, Juan Guaidó, who was being forcibly restrained by the armed forces. In May 2020, the TSJ found this parliamentary coup constitutional. "Sala Constitucional Del TSJ Ratifica A Luis Parra Como Presidente de la Asamblea," Noticias TSJ (May 26, 2020), www.tsj.gob.ve/-/sala-constitucional-del-tsj-ratifica-a-luis-parra-como-presi dente-de-la-asamblea-nacional. The Constitutional Chamber found all the procedural steps to be appropriate; it did not consider the lack of a quorum or Guaidó's absence (partly due to how the problem was framed, as required by the *amparo*).

a precedent that no one believes to be applicable given the established sphere of its application.

While the normative nature of legal reasoning sets limits to the cheating analogy, cheating can be identified in legal reasoning: when a regulator or judge applies meaning to a term that does not exist in the recognized, referenced source. This occurs eminently when such manipulation helps the government to win the case. Recall the card player who shows four aces, bringing the fourth one from under the sleeve; the player never had four aces in accordance with the rules. Or consider the Supreme Court of Nicaragua in 2009, when it declared the Constitution unconstitutional, stating that the presidential term limit set in the original text violated the unconditional equality of all citizens (among them the President) in their passive electoral right. The Court invented an absolute human right for sitting presidents to remain eligible,[25] certainly a gross falsity given the text of the Constitution, the canons of interpretation, and a view of constitutionalism that prohibits the perpetuation of power. The idea that an original constitution is unconstitutional is cheating as it undermines the basic assumption of the game, namely that the game is played according to the constitution and the supreme court is called to uphold it.

Carson offers an effective example of deceit that can be considered in the discussion of a legal system. You are selling a car that is overheating, and when asked, you say that you had no problem with it on a very hot day in the desert; though you were in the desert four years ago and the car is overheating now. Your statement is true but deceitful.[26] Where elections are free but the monopoly over broadcasting has created insurmountable obstacles to the opposition to make its voice heard, the characterization of the electoral system as fair is deceitful. When the law introduces a ban on political advertising during the electoral period, claiming that all parties have the right to participate in debates broadcast for free, that ban is a cheat: the prohibition guarantees a hidden advantage to the governing party. The ban's claim is only true in a limited context: free access to broadcasting debates certainly satisfies fairness, it

---

[25] Case No. 602–09, in the *Amparo Writ Ortega et al.* v. *the Supreme Electoral Council of the Republic of Nicaragua*. Sentencia [S.] No. 504, de las 5:00 p.m., 19 Oct. 2009, Corte Suprema de Justicia; "Nicaragua: Supreme Court Decision Permitting President, Others to Seek Reelection," Library of Congress (December 18, 2009), http://www.loc.gov/law/foreign-news/article/nicaragua-supreme-court-decision-permitting-president-others-to-seek-reelection.

[26] Carson, *Lying*, pp. 15–16.

is even advantageous to parties with few resources, but the regulation disregards the full picture, in particular that the incumbent, powerful party has other resources through which it can reach the public at all other times.

Hungarian public procurement offers a second illustration. Public calls for proposals often set objective criteria that can be satisfied by one company only ("five years of experience building suspension bridges over a river with the characteristics of the Danube"). It is hard to say what exactly is misrepresented, but the award of the contract results from cheating. If only one company can satisfy the criteria, there appear to be no problems; simply this is the reality of the market. But in illiberal democracies criteria are determined with the future winner in mind. The authorities cheat on the normative assumption of equality among economic actors (recognized as a principle of public procurement).[27]

Again, however, in applying the notion of cheating in a legal context (both for those who make the law and those who apply it), one must admit that the interpreter, and even more so the lawmaker (endorsed by popular will and legislative authority), maintain a certain legitimate power to determine the very object they represent. When the car seller provides deceptive information about their car overheating, they have no power to determine what overheating is, as this is clearly defined: a red light appears on the dashboard. But the regulator who defines when this red light comes on has considerable discretion in implementing a law that requires road safety or roadworthiness.

As mentioned, cheating is a breach of an implicit promise of truth-telling, including telling the truth about faithfulness to norms and metanorms (e.g. rules of interpretation). A statute, administrative decision or judgment will breach a promise of truthfulness when these legal acts directly (purposefully) serve a goal that differs from the declared legitimate purpose. Cheating results from the discrepancy from the promised principle, or from denying the existence of an applicable one. This is a fundamental breach of trust in a democracy, which assumes that rulers govern *for* the people and that citizens can trust their institutions in their legitimate political and other choices. The rigged procurement rules are also deceitful for breaking the promise of truth: the public procurement system promised fairness and equality not only to competitors, but to the general public, who therefore expected that the authorities would spend public funds efficiently and in the public interest. (In reality, such competitors are simply nonexistent. They

---

[27] Art 2(2) of Act CXLIII of 2015.

may not exist, because they were excluded via selective competition law sanctions or are just afraid to compete.)

To quote Carson once more: "Those who have fiduciary duties to others have extensive positive duties to provide information to others – they must do more than refrain from lying and deception."[28] Likewise, illiberal democracies fail to uphold the constitutional promise that the government will truthfully inform the public about public affairs,[29] with serious consequences for legal legitimacy. (As mentioned repeatedly, other grounds of legitimacy will instead sustain the regime.)

A regime that cheats in its use of the law breaches a promise of "truth" or the authenticity that the underlying norms of the game will be observed. The constitution, with its entrenchment rules, promises a strong commitment to certain rules of the political game. But once again, we encounter difficulties when we try to determine cheating should the constitution be changed. Constitutions do not promise immutability (except in eternity clauses). At what point does a change in the constitution become a cheat on the constitution? What happens if the changed constitution promises and enables illiberal solutions and principles? Consider the standard Latin American constitutional promise made during the transition to democracy, namely that presidents shall serve a single term. This rule reflected the foundational experience with dictatorship. After some time, sitting presidents proposed to change the rule. If the constitution is amended, the president can run again. Is this a breach of the constitutional promise? After all, the constitution is an entrenched promise, but there is no constitutional promise that the constitution cannot be changed. Term limits are not unamendable. What if the prohibitive provision is changed in a proper procedure? Does abolishing the term limit breach an underlying promise? If this underlying promise aims to prevent the perpetuation of any one individual's rule, changing it will be cheating, in particular (as is normally the case) where the initiative serves the sitting president.

8.2 Abuse as a Constant of (Constitutional) Law: Limiting Techniques

Legal theories seek to explain the virtues of existing arrangements or criticize the state and its courts for failing to satisfy the demands of virtue

---

[28] Carson, *Lying*, p. 198.

[29] "[T]he correct explanation of why liars are blameworthy includes the liar's imposing [an epistemic] risk on the audience." S. F. Krauss, "Lying, Risk and Accuracy," *Analysis*, 77:4 (2017), p. 727.

as the critics see it. Consequently, legal scholarship and constitutional (or political) theory show little interest in the problem of constitutional cheating,[30] although abuse of rights and law is common in constitutional democracies. It is a feature of the legal system that law abuses law,[31] and legal authorities cheat with regularity. In ancient Rome when reasons to delay a vote on land reform had run out, the remainder of the year was declared a "sacred period in which no assemblies could be held or votes taken."[32] The law is so malleable, and in so many respects, that it nearly invites abuse. Abuse, especially the abuse of rights, does not explicitly violate the law but remains illicit. Those who cheat the law are careful to cover their backs. "A skillful legal craftsman can usually reach the desired result without directly overruling established cases or obviously making new law."[33] Constitutional cheating, which disrespects the fundamental assumptions of the constitution to generate false legitimacy, is destructive to the very constitutional order. An intuition of Justice Scalia indicates the gravity of the problem: "Government by unexpressed intent is ... tyrannical."[34] He compares this "to posting of edicts high up in the pillars, so that they could not easily be read," a clear example of cheating (pretending the law is publicly accessible by hampering it).

The need to protect the Constitution against covert violations deriving from legislation was obvious at the dawn of constitutional review: "Should Congress, in the execution of its powers, adopt measures which are prohibited by the constitution; or should Congress, under

---

[30] Legal theory is interested in the context of contracts (promise, trust, fraud). Law has its mechanisms of self-defense, especially in private and administrative law, and in various doctrines of the abuse of power, the abuse of law and the abuse of rights. The abuse of rights occurs when the right is used differently from its content. See A. Sajó (ed.), *Abuse: The Dark Side of Fundamental Rights* (Eleven International, 2006). In the classic French doctrine of *detournement de pouvoir*, the use of public power shall relate to the specific function of the administration. It is hard to prove such violations in French administrative law. N. P.-G. Leclerc, *Droit Administratif: Sources, Moyens, Contrôles* (Editions Bréal, 2007), p. 243.

[31] Characteristically, the Declaration of Independence is a list of grievances, describing the systematic legal abuse of the birthrights of the colonists, committed by the Crown.

[32] E. J. Watts, *Mortal Republic. How Rome Fell into Tyranny* (Basic Books, 2018), p. 204.

[33] W. F. Murphy, *Elements of Judicial Strategy* (University of Chicago Press, 1964), pp. 22 and 30.

[34] A. Scalia, "Common-Law Courts in a Civil-Law System: The Role of United States Federal Courts in Interpreting the Constitution and Laws," in A. Guttman (ed.), *A Matter of Interpretation: Federal Courts and the Law* (Princeton University Press, 1997), p. 17. Scalia provided arguments *against* judicial involvement in intent analysis: in his view, this would result in judicial arbitrariness. The personal intent of the legislator does not count; the judge deals with the objectified intent (meaning) of the text.

the pretext of executing its powers, pass laws for the accomplishment of objects not entrusted to the government; it would become the painful duty of this tribunal, should a case requiring such a decision come before it, to say that such an act was not the law of the land."[35] This looks like a declaration of faith: the Court shall fight against cheating (understood as "under the pretext") in legislation. A careful reading of the text indicates that this role is limited. Primarily, it lacks competence (related to a specific American constitutional problem, namely the enumerated powers of federal legislation). Transgressing competence is a serious and common problem, but it does not encompass cheating on substantive matters (where the law is enacted within the competence of the law-making body, but it does not serve the constitutional goal).

What prevents constitutional cheating (and resulting arbitrariness) from prevailing in a constitutional democracy is moral and cultural restraint among constitutional actors, resulting from the restrictions and conventions that decent politicians, administrators, and lawyers accept without second thoughts or under the pressure of morally sensitive public opinion. Moreover, there are institutional mechanisms of constitutional and subconstitutional supervision that patrol the abuse and other misapplications of the law. (These are the first to disappear in illiberal democracies.)

Fraudulent aggrandizement of one or another branch of power is a constant, constitutionally troubling phenomenon. This was one of Madison's nightmares.[36] The authority (branch of power) uses a pretext to gain power through its inappropriate application. The beneficiary (the cheater or another political or private actor) hopes to make his lie or trick prevail, and assumes that the power grab will enable him to control the new status quo, precluding meaningful corrections. When *Marbury* v. *Madison* was pending in SCOTUS, Congress passed the Judiciary Act of 1802. This "general" reform cancelled the 1802 August court term, clearly aiming to prevent the possibility of judgments favoring the federalist cause. This Act satisfies the criteria of legal cheating: it relies on an existing constitutional power (regulation of the federal judiciary), and under the guise of a legitimate constitutional goal, uses it to its advantage for an identifiable partisan political purpose, departing

---

[35] *McCulloch* v. *Maryland*, 17 US 316 (1819).
[36] A. Hamilton, J. Madison, and J. Jay, *The Federalist Papers*. *No.10* (Mentor Book, 1961). The other nightmare was populist democracy: a rule of passion and "a rage for paper money, for abolition of debts, for an equal division of property."

from a constitutional principle (namely noninterference into the activities of the judicial branch, especially a pending case).

Gradual extensions of competence and jurisdiction, resulting in power aggrandizement, often rely on subtle cheating where the use of legal tricks intends to hide the likely unconstitutional change. This is one of the favorite techniques used by US presidents to extend control over agencies that were created by, and accountable to, Congress. Peter Strauss explains how a technical shift amounts to illegality by stealth: "The Federal Register Act does not mention the President. Performing its essentially ministerial responsibilities has not been assigned to the President and then delegated by him to the Government Printing Office. President Clinton's executive order thus conferred on himself what no statute has created: the right in effect to require his countersignature on agency rulemaking. By statute, the authority to adopt rules is placed in the agency head, not the President; this assertion, in effect that White House approval was also required, crossed the line from consultation to control."[37] Note that it was the President granting himself a power; this is a typical move in illiberal regimes, except where, as in Hungary, there is no reason to cheat by stealth: the Parliament will vote for whatever the leader needs.

8.2.1 Objective Difficulty of Identification

Constitutional (apex) courts are called upon to protect the constitution against all forms of abuse. However, when it comes to legislative cheating on the constitution (i.e. when the majority pretends that they serve a constitutional goal), judges are often incapacitated from identifying the hidden departure from the constitution and its underlying values and conventions. This is the consequence of judicial competence rules and self-imposed idleness (deference), two fundamental judicial virtues in the eyes of many commentators.

Deference grants the benefit of the doubt to the honesty of legislative intent and the appropriateness of its means. Outside the sphere of fundamental rights, SCOTUS remains satisfied with "facially legitimate and bona fide" reasons that justify administrative action. In a 2018 travel (entry) ban case, even in the presence of presidential statements

---

[37] P. L. Strauss, "The Trump Administration and the Rule of Law," *Revue Française D'administration Publique*, 170 (2019), p. 437. The technique of nonpromulgation reflects the one used in Poland in 2016 in the PCT decisions.

indicating anti-Muslim animus, for SCOTUS the declared intent did not matter. A phalanx of legal cheating techniques was mobilized: "ignoring the facts, misconstruing our legal precedent, and turning a blind eye to the pain and suffering the Proclamation inflicts upon countless families and individuals."[38] Even where SCOTUS itself admitted that it deals with institutionalized cheating and fraud in partisan gerrymandering it refused to intervene, even though it admitted this endangers democracy and electoral fairness. Closing its eyes, it hid behind the political question doctrine,[39] although it has been able to set standards for districting in racial gerrymandering cases, and lower courts have provided judicially manageable standards in the very cases in front of the Court.

Courts are reluctant to examine legislative cheating in any substantive sense:[40] they accept the declared goal of legislation (or even invent a legitimate one) and will endorse the assertion that the goal serves a constitutional purpose, or at least is not constitutionally prohibited. A "declaration of the legislative findings deemed to support and justify the action" is enough to find constitutionality: "revealing the rationale of the legislation" is sufficient "unless, in the light of the facts made known or generally assumed, it is of such a character as to preclude the assumption that it rests upon some rational basis within the knowledge and experience of the legislators."[41]

The reluctance to review the legislator's genuine intent, or to admit the possibility that the administration might be cheating, also holds true in English and German administrative law. English administrative law considers a decision irrational if it is "so outrageous in its defiance of logic or of accepted moral standards that no sensible person who had applied his mind to the question could have arrived at it."[42]

---

[38] *Rucho v. Common Cause* 588 US ___ (2019).

[39] In the best tradition of populism, and without the shame or hypocrisy that remains prevalent in Budapest, the North Carolina legislator in charge of developing a districting plan submitted it with the following honest justification: "I think electing Republicans is better than electing Democrats. So I drew this map to help foster what I think is better for the country."

[40] Courts are more active in the scrutiny of competence: was the lawmaking (rulemaking) authority entitled to legislate? To let this kind of cheating go unnoticed is less likely.

[41] *United States v. Carolene Products Co.*, 304 US 144 (1938) at 152.

[42] *Associated Provincial Picture Houses Ltd. v. Wednesbury Corporation* [1948] 1 KB 22 (Wednesbury unreasonableness). German law includes a requirement of suitability (*Geegnetheit*), but this only means that "a particular measure must be theoretically capable of contributing to achieving its aim." G. Nolte, "General Principles of German and European Administrative Law: A Comparison in Historical Perspective," *The Modern Law Review*, 57:2 (1994), p. 191.

This reluctance to investigate the truthfulness of underlying justifications is grounded in good, or at least reasonable, judicial considerations
(such as difficulties with evidence that would satisfy procedural fairness,
separation of powers, and politicization). But it comes at a price: the
discrepancy between the norm (or its application) and the underlying
presuppositions (e.g. genuine constitutional or legislative intent) is simply not considered. In *Vékony v. Hungary* (the Hungarian tobacco license
case – see Chapter 3.1), the ECtHR refused to entertain the applicant's
argument that the government's claim was false (i.e. that the measure
protects public health). The Court found it sufficient that limiting the sale
of tobacco to tobacco sale points *could have* served the protection of
health. The Court was even less interested in the allegation of partisan
financial interest.

In principle, no fatal obstacle could stop a constitutional court from
applying more intensive forms of review. However, the ordinary reconstruction of legislative intent and purpose does not concern the sincerity
of goals. Legal interpretation addresses the meaning and application of
a legal text, and legislative intent exists only as a necessary abstraction to
create the impression that interpretation reflects an objective and pre-
existing meaning. "Legislative intent" is an oxymoron as there is no
simple intention, only a majority vote.[43] Ordinary legislative intent
analysis does not search for a hidden purpose in order to reveal impermissible uses of the law. The judge assumes the legitimacy of whatever
intent is discovered.

It can be argued, however, that constitutional review fundamentally
differs from standard statutory interpretation and the more the political
system is dictatorial, the more appropriate the political motive analysis
should be.

The constitutional review of legislation entails the review of the constitutional purpose of a piece of legislation, but this is a review of the
legitimacy of the declared or conceivable purpose and not of its
authenticity.[44] Substantive purpose review may, however, apply where
the law restricts fundamental rights, especially in matters of speech,
religion, and racial discrimination, but the consideration of underlying
legislative intent is rare.[45] "This does not mean that one must uncritically

---

[43] K. A. Shepsle, "Congress Is a 'They,' Not an 'It': Legislative Intent as Oxymoron,"
International Review of Law and Economics, 12:2 (1992), p. 239.
[44] *R. v. Safarzadeh-Markhali*, 2016 SCC 14 (CanLII), [2016] 1 SCR 180, para. 36.
[45] For a review of legislative animus see, for example, *Church of the Lukumi Babalu Aye, Inc.*
v. Hialeah, 508 US 520 (1993) (which considers statements made during legislative

accept the legislature's stated purpose at face value: a reasonable person in the claimant's position would not accept the exclusion of women from the workplace based merely on the legislature's assertion that this is for women's 'own good.'"[46]

Of course, intent analysis is intuitively attractive as it fits into a spontaneously developed tradition of private law, which has generated principles (good faith) and rules against the abuse of rights and even of power. In the Roman law[47] doctrine of *aemulatio*, the exercise of a right with the sole intention of causing annoyance is abusive, illicit, and nonenforceable. Notwithstanding a common moral indignation, these doctrines of abuse are hardly transposable to legislative abuse and cheating.[48] The legislator has constitutionally endowed power to follow its own caprice, except when it collides with a specific constitutional prohibition or right.

The determination of actual legislative (or judicial) intent is difficult when the decision is taken by a collective body whose members hold divergent views and intentions. (The matter is simpler in illiberal democracies where the parliamentary majority has only one will: to conform to the wishes of the leader.) But courts refer to cognitive difficulties even in matters of executive action, where in some instances the case concerns the actual behavior of the executive (a person) and not the fictitious intent of a legislative body. The general rule in US administrative law opposes inquiries into "the mental processes of administrative decisionmakers,"[49] but exceptionally it will consider the quality of the justification for rulemaking.[50] In the UK, in *Miller(2)*, the plaintiffs questioned the motive of the Prime Minister when he suggested the prorogation of Parliament to the Queen, but the UK Supreme Court

---

process). Equal protection is violated where the discriminatory legislative measure "seems inexplicable by anything but animus toward the class it affects; it lacks a rational relationship to legitimate state interests." *Romer* v. *Evans*, 517 US 620, 632 (1996).

[46] *Gosselin* v. *Québec (Attorney General)*, 2002 SCC 84 (CanLII), [2002] 4 SCR 429, para. 27.

[47] It is debated to what extent these concerns were reflected in Roman law before Justinian. See U. Breccia, "L'abuso del Diritto," in *Diritto privato 1997*, vol. iii (Cedam, 1998).

[48] Some countries, as well as the EU, recognize remedy in torts for damage caused by unconstitutional legislation.

[49] *Citizens to Preserve Overton Park, Inc.* v. *Volpe*, 401 US 402 (1971) at 420. The courts' role is to assess only whether the decision was "based on a consideration of the relevant factors and whether there has been a clear error of judgment" at 416.

[50] In *Department of Commerce* v. *New York*, 588 US ___ (2019) (the Census case), SCOTUS was ready to notice the disconnect between the decision made and the explanation given but did not directly challenge the honesty of the ex post and very occasional justification provided by the administration.

was reluctant to enter into intention analysis: "We are not concerned with the Prime Minister's *motive* in doing what he did. We are concerned with whether there was a reason for him to do it."[51]

Judicial reluctance to investigate the truthfulness of underlying justifications relates to the constitutional function of courts and epistemological limitations. Legislation and the legislative branch are protected by the constitutional myth that they express supreme popular will. Further, as a rule, apex courts deal with a single case or statutory provision.[52] In this isolated analysis, it is difficult to identify systemic cheating. However, finding even a single incident of legal cheating is difficult, because in the absence of a smoking gun (e.g. a clear admission of an improper or constitutionally impermissible purpose), the finding will look speculative and contrary to evidence-based RoL.

Stanley Fish has argued that "the difference between reaching political conclusions and beginning with political intentions is that if you are doing the second you are not really doing a job of legal work."[53] Once a court embarks on the review of the intent of legislation, it leaves the world of legal activities and thereby risks its own legitimacy. It will open itself to accusations of politicking. Beyond the respectable reasons for avoiding intent analysis (the search for objective meaning, difficulties of cognition and proof of intent, and deference to legislation), a fundamental objection is that the judicial function is simply incompatible with being political. An essential assumption of constitutional review and legal analysis holds similarly. This is understandable given that the legitimacy of judicial review comes from the exclusion of the political.

However, intent review and systemic analysis of cheating are possible,[54] and happen, even if rarely. There can be judicially cognizable evidence of illegal or impermissible legislative purposes,[55] and the

---

[51] *R (on the application of Miller) (Appellant)* v. *The Prime Minister (Respondent)* [2019] UKSC 41. para. 58.

[52] There are important exceptions where the apex court comprehensively reviews a whole set of interrelated laws and regulations governing a whole area of life. See, for example, the Columbian Constitutional Court, reviewing health care, Decision T-760 of 2008.

[53] S. Fish, "On Legal Autonomy," *Mercer Law Review*, 44 (1993), p. 738.

[54] An "unconstitutional state of affairs" exists when actions or omissions, as structural problems, result in a repeated and continuous violation of rights, affecting a large group of people and requiring the intervention of multiple state actors. D. Bilchitz, "Constitutionalism, the Global South, and Economic Justice," in D. Bonilla (ed.), *Constitutionalism of the Global South: The Activist Tribunals of India, South Africa, and Colombia* (Cambridge University Press, 2013), pp. 65–66.

[55] The draft Bill that served as the basis of the law that created the tobacco distribution monopoly in Hungary was prepared on the computer of a distributor who happened

assumption of legislative honesty may prove to be unsubstantiated or even wrong. After many years of hesitation, the ECtHR devised a doctrine that called for reviewing the discrepancy between declared and genuine legislative purposes:

> [A] restriction [of a Convention right] can be compatible with the substantive Convention provision which authorizes it because it pursues an aim permissible under that provision, but still infringe Article 18 because it was chiefly meant for another purpose that is not prescribed by the Convention; in other words, if that other purpose was predominant. . . . Which purpose is predominant in a given case depends on all the circumstances. In assessing that point, the Court will have regard to the nature and degree of reprehensibility of the alleged ulterior purpose, and bear in mind that the Convention was designed to maintain and promote the ideals and values of a democratic society governed by the rule of law.[56]

The standard may be useful where the issue concerns a restriction of fundamental rights and where the grounds to limit rights is established in the constitution. However, the tricks used in illiberal democracies typically do not concern such scenarios.

The CJEU also dared to venture into a kind of political/constitutional intent review in response to a crucial power-grabbing act by the Polish government, to the detriment of judicial independence. In this case, it contrasted the official justification of the forced judicial retirement scheme (judicial reform, consolidation of the pension system) with the political and constitutional aims of the government (namely the disregard of irremovability for ideological reasons). Here, the declared goal's lack of authenticity was not based on specific personal intent. The CJEU doubted that the judicial retirement age reform served its declared aims and could not rule out that

---

to be an acquaintance of the responsible minister. The "typist" became the concessionary monopolist; the annual profit of the concessionary was roughly three times the license fee. G. Kovács, "Óriási Dohányt Szakított Lázár János Ismerőse az Állami Monopóliummal," Hvg.hu (June 20, 2019), www.hvg.hu/kkv/20190620_Oriasi_dohanyt_szakitott_Lazar_Janos_dohanyos_baratja_az_allami_monopoliummal.

[56] *Merabishvili v. Georgia*, ECtHR, App. no. 72508/13, Judgment of 28 November 2017, paras. 303 and 307. The standard (a breakthrough) is criticized as restrictive because only a "predominant" purpose is considered abusive, and the requirement of "predominance" can render the standard meaningless. Further, it is not clear to what extent the standard applies to legislation. Even if it is formulated broadly, it was developed and applied exclusively in the context of the application of the law. The ECtHR has a very strong presumption regarding legislative honesty. *Animal Defenders v. the United Kingdom*, ECtHR, App. no. 48876/08, Judgment of 22 April 2013.

it was made "with the aim of side-lining a certain group of judges of that court."[57]

8.3   Cheating in Illiberal Democracy

The natural inclination to cheat in legal regulation is particularly strong in Caesaristic regimes. Benjamin Constant has singled out the importance of imposture, duplicity, and perfidy[58] in regimes of "usurpation." Andrew Arato considers duplicity to be a general feature of contemporary illiberal democracies where "Napoleonic usurpation makes extensive use of liberty, law and modern political institutions."[59] Duplicity characterizes illiberal regimes whose constitutions promise the RoL and fundamental rights, only to render this promise empty by allowing exceptions to general rules and restrictions of rights. The system is managed with measures that create "a significant discordance between appearance and reality by concealing under the mask of law."[60]

The need for cheating in law relates first and foremost to the need for legitimacy: by successfully hiding the illegality (even at the price of a moral scandal or error in logic), the maker or applicant of the law signals commitment to the normative system.

Cheating through law (abuse of power) complicates the work of constitutional bodies tasked with control and accountability functions (superior courts, etc.) (and thereby reduces potential conflicts with the powers that be). In illiberal democracies, there are additional reasons to cheat (which is how cheating becomes systemic). A ruler or legal actor who openly violates the rules sends a message to all subjects, which may trigger coordinated action (including, exceptionally, coordinated general social resistance). In uncertain cases of cheating (including misleading justifications), the message is not clear, and the chances of coordinated opposition activity diminish.[61]

---

[57] Case C-192/18, *European Commission (11)* v. *Republic of Poland* [2019] EU:C:2019:924. The Court therefore had no choice but to conclude that the Polish authorities did not pursue a legitimate objective.

[58] B. Constant, *Constant: Political Writings*, ed. B. Fontana (Cambridge University Press, 1988), p. 65. Imposture was characteristic of the rule of Napoleon, the quintessential plebiscitarian leader before democracy.

[59] A. Arato, "Conceptual History of Dictatorship (and its Rivals)," in E. Peruzotti and M. Plot (eds.), *Critical Theory and Democracy. Civil Society, Dictatorship, and Constitutionalism in Andrew Arato's Democratic Theory* (Routledge, 2013), p. 237.

[60] O. O. Varol, "Stealth Authoritarianism," *Iowa Law Review*, 100 (2015), p. 1685.

[61] M. Tushnet, "Authoritarian Constitutionalism," *Cornell Law Review*, 100 (2015), p. 430.

Illiberal democracies use the laws and institutions of constitutional democracy in a systematically inauthentic way, indifferent to the assumptions of constitutionalism. Varol called this state of affairs "stealth authoritarianism": "legal mechanisms that exist in regimes with favorable democratic credentials are used for anti-democratic ends."[62] For Varol and other connoisseurs, the specificity of "authoritarian stealth" lies in its direction, that it moves toward some kind of authoritarianism. It is certainly true that illiberal democracies shift from constitutionalism (to the extent that they were ever constitutionalists), but the direction is uncertain, even if the increase in centralized unchecked power is clear. Varol and his followers are more interested in abuse by stealth than in cheating, more in regime transformation than in its management: in stealth the measures are legitimate but serve the masked transformation of the legal and political system into something authoritarian (not in its openly violent and illegal version, but still resulting in an erosion of democracy). These are important, even crucial, tricks in the making of the illiberal regime; however, cheating is more about the regime's regular, normal functioning, how the ordinary use and meaning of law is denaturalized.

Professor Brewer-Carias may have been the first to address the issue of illiberal (populist) constitutional cheating. As one of the few non-Chavezista members of the Venezuelan Constituent Assembly, he had a head-start in observing the making of what he called constitutional "fraud." The Venezuelan constituent process started in 1999 with a fraudulent interpretation of the Constitution. Endless constitutional transition followed. The distorted interpretations of the constitution "in many cases ... legitimize and support the progressive building of the authoritarian state ... through 'constitutional mutations.'" The words remain the same, but they receive a different meaning.[63]

The TSJ's Constitutional Chamber, being an ardent supporter of Chávez, has provided the judicial definition of "constitutional fraud": it occurs when democratic principles are destroyed "through the process of making changes within existing institutions while appearing to respect constitutional procedures and forms." This is to be distinguished from the "falsification of the constitution," when "constitutional norms are

---

[62] Varol, "Stealth Authoritarianism," p. 1684.

[63] A. R. Brewer-Carías, *Dismantling Democracy in Venezuela. The Chávez Authoritarian Experiment* (Cambridge University Press, 2010), p. 241 Corrales also refers to the centrality of cheating on the law (abuse and non-use) in Venezuela. J. Corrales, "Autocratic Legalism in Venezuela," *Journal of Democracy*, 26:2 (2015), p. 38.

given an interpretation and a sense different from those that they actually possess."[64] The latter departure may fall under the competence of courts, but the "demasking" of "fraud" is not as straightforward as the TSJ, itself a leading falsifier, claims in the above-cited case.

8.3.1   Techniques of Legal Cheating

In order to serve the PLD, the legislative branch and the judiciary engage in professionally indefensible gimmicks. The unfaithfulness to the principles of the RoL and constitutionalism and the narrowness in interpretation disclose the importance of cheating with law as a central legal and social technique of illiberal democracy. The following incomplete laundry list (together with the abuses of the RoL) presents some key techniques of legal cheating.

Circumvention

Circumvention of the law in illiberal democracy is not just a clever avoidance of the law. It involves a workaround, "a way of dealing with a problem or making something work despite the problem, without completely solving it."[65] Beyond avoidance of the merits of the case, primarily on procedural grounds[66] and for the greater glory of the RoL, legal circumvention emerges from regulatory loopholes that are created, not always innocuously, by the regulator. Tax loopholes are the most obvious example; these are used all over the world, sometimes under the venerable heading of tax planning. Loopholes and other circumvention opportunities are quintessential in illiberal democracies, enabling the swift operation of favoritism. In Hungary, Act LIII of 2006 already created the category of "outstanding national economic interest" to facilitate the implementation of public projects. (The law was enacted under a socialist government, not immune to cronyism.) According to the Act as currently amended, the government has the power to exempt

---

[64] Decision No. 74 (January 25, 2006) quoted in Brewer-Carías, *Dismantling Democracy*, p. 222.

[65] *Cambridge English Dictionary Online*, s.v. "workaround," https://dictionary.cambridge.org /dictionary/english/workaround.

[66] This is a very common practice in mature constitutional systems even with a reputation of judicial activism. In 1956, two years after *Brown* v. *Board of Education* 347 US 483 (1954), SCOTUS "dismissed an appeal in a case in which Virginia nullified a[n interracial] marriage … on procedural grounds that I make bold to say are wholly without basis in the law." H. Wechsler, "Toward Neutral Principles of Constitutional Law," *Harvard Law Review*, 73:1 (1959), p. 34.

certain companies and activities from the general rules of granting permits. (A similar regime was established to create exemptions for public procurement. For the role of exceptions, see Chapter 7.3.1.) The government has unfettered power to determine who can be the privileged. Once classified as "outstanding national economic interest," the circumvention begins: general rules of issuing permits do not apply. The "outstanding" status has many advantages in addition to fast-tracking permitting: there is no oversight. Public data on public spending that benefits an "outstanding" venture can become "classified information" to protect the outstanding national economic interest. Without transparent information, there can be no efficient democratic control. Note, however, that the illiberal regime insists on its own self-presentation as a country of RoL. Modern oppressive regimes insist on being RoL countries. The apartheid government of South Africa went very far in this respect, paying the same price illiberal democracies do: the South African judiciary was forced to cheat to prove that the regime respects the RoL.[67] In the same spirit of bypassing proudly declared rights and values, the Hungarian government does not challenge the idea that public data should be accessible and transparent. It simply repeals the laws on access to public information or creates statutory exceptions.

The introduction of temporary (procedural) measures represents another technique of circumvention by exceptionalism. Article 256 of the Venezuelan Constitution describes the process and conditions for removing TSJ judges, with standard safeguards. In 2004, a law introduced the possibility of suspending justices pending an impeachment vote; another invention allowed the nullification of their appointments on vague grounds (the "public attitude [of the judge] . . . undermines the majesty or prestige of the Supreme Court"). This was an ad hoc law, written for the removal of specific judges considered dangerous to power. (It was kept in force as a general possibility in case of other rebellions.)[68]

---

[67] In apartheid South Africa "at issue was whether a detainee was entitled to a statement of reasons for his detention when the emergency regulations under which he was detained said that the detaining officer has the power to detain when he 'has reason to believe' that someone 'intends to commit an offence. . .'. Hefer CJ went out of his way to find arguments which led to a conclusion that the legislature did not intend that a court should have authority to demand that the detaining officer show reasons that could reasonably justify his belief." D. Dyzenhaus, "Law as Justification: Etienne Mureinik's Conception of Legal Culture," *South African Journal on Human Rights*, 14:1 (1998), p. 20.

[68] *A Decade under Chavez*, Human Rights Watch, www.hrw.org/reports/2008/venezuela0908/3.htm#_ftnref128. See also the 2004 law purging the TSJ, in Chapter 2, with further examples.

The TSJ held that adding new possibilities to the exclusive constitutional procedure of judicial removal is not unconstitutional as such measures do not amount to removal, although the judges are unseated for good by a constitutionally unauthorized body.

Doctored Meanings; Arbitrary Application of the Rules of Legal Construction

Illiberal democracies use legal notions in a denaturalized or arbitrary way. They exploit the ambiguity of familiar terms and introduce new definitions or legal terms (classifications) that trigger a different set of applicable norms, without changing the law itself. Such shifts enable circumvention, with serious consequences for the treatment of rights holders.

The lack of clear rules offers great opportunities for less discernible cheating, as in the case of institutional conventions. In the absence of specific rules, existing practices are generally held applicable. For example, without a rule on counting abstentions for determining a quorum in a decision-making body, the established practice becomes decisive. However, in the regime of chicanery, where the outcome under the pre-existing practice would not be to the liking of the powers that be, the standard reaction is to deny the existence of the practice.[69] To argue that the practice rule exists but does not apply is the emergency solution.

Changing the meanings of legal terms helps the future despot to maintain appearances. Consider freedom of assembly. Definitions of assembly in implementing statutes generally address only the number of participants, modalities of advanced notification, or grounds to deny permits. In the illiberal state, the meaning of "assembly" is transformed, for example, when the right to assembly does not entail the right to demonstrate on national holidays or at historically relevant places (especially where an entire city center carries such relevance). Or consider the potentially different meanings of the term "detention." A person in detention is entitled to certain protections. The illiberal regime does not deny these but will provide a new, narrow understanding of what it means to be detained. Of course, similar shifts also occur in RoL-observing systems, and illiberal democracies merely use such authoritarian potential. The ECtHR once followed a set of considerations for

---

[69] In Mark Tushnet's terminology this is "constitutional hardball": the government relies on practices that are not constitutionally prohibited but which violate existing constitutional conventions. Tushnet, "Authoritarian Constitutionalism."

defining the deprivation of liberty, accounting for the "type" and "manner of implementation" of the measure in question and regarding the specific context and circumstances surrounding different types of restriction (other than the paradigm of confinement in a cell). Notwithstanding these considerations (allegedly in application of them), it ruled that seven hours of kettling (containment of passersby within a police cordon during a violent demonstration) in a central London square did not amount to deprivation of liberty or detention.[70]

An infamous example of disregarding the ordinary and even legal meaning of "detention" occurred in the context of asylum seekers caught in transit zones at the Hungarian border. These zones are surrounded by barbed wire, with no right to exit from them. The choice of an implausible meaning over an ordinary one contradicts the standard maxim of interpretation, namely that such departure is legitimate only "[w]here the plain language of the statute would lead to 'patently absurd consequences,' that 'Congress could not possibly have intended.'"[71] For the Hungarian authorities, the transit zones were not a place of detention, as the asylum applicant could always return to Serbia, a third safe country according to Hungarian law. However, returning would mean the automatic cancellation of the asylum request. The Chamber of the ECtHR ruled that this was detention without legal basis (for the Hungarian authorities, this was not detention and thus there was no need to regulate it). The Grand Chamber overruled the Chamber, declaring that presence in the transit zone was "voluntary."[72]

The reinterpretation of meanings may occur through the reinterpretation of unwritten canons of interpretation. This is of a somewhat Putinesque inspiration: there is no truth, only competing narratives; grab the most convenient for the occasion. It also fits into the tradition of the populist strategy that brought the leader into power. Populism intends to change speech norms.

All this is reminiscent of Orwell's newspeak (without the ambition to transform the mind), but it is even closer to Lewis Carrol's Humpty

---

[70] *Austin and Others* v. *the United Kingdom*, ECtHR (GCh), App. nos. 39692/09, 40713/09, and 41008/09, Judgment of 15 March 2012.

[71] *Public Citizen* v. *Department of Justice*, 491 US 440 at 470 (1989), J. Kennedy (concurring).

[72] *Ilias and Ahmed* v. *Hungary*, ECtHR (GCh) App. no. 47287/15, Judgment of 21 November 2019. However, the CJEU concluded that the transit zone counts as detention. Cases C-924/19 PPU and C-925/19 PPU, *FMS and Others* v. *Országos Idegenrendészeti Főigazgatóság Dél-alföldi Regionális Igazgatóság and Országos Idegenrendészeti Főigazgatóság* [2020] EU:C:2020:367.

Dumpty, as quoted by Lord Atkin dissenting in *Liversidge* v. *Anderson and Another*: "The words have only one meaning. . . . I know of only one authority which might justify the suggested method of construction: 'When I use a word,' Humpty Dumpty said in rather a scornful tone, 'it means just what I choose it to mean, neither more nor less.' 'The question is,' said Alice, 'whether you can make words mean so many different things.' 'The question is,' said Humpty Dumpty, 'which is to be master – that's all.'"[73] When the President of the Hungarian National Bank intends to use its profit for purposes unrelated to its mandate he declares that this is not public money – and this is enough, as he is the master.

In some instances, meanings remain the same but facts are interpreted to apply a term with a different meaning. For example, "asylum seeker" is replaced with "migrant," or illegal entrant, which fundamentally alters the living conditions of, and the regime applicable, to refugees, and undermines the application of the Geneva Refugee Convention, etc. Definitional changes regularly occur in the legal world; the trick here is that the authorities claim that they continue to observe international refugee law, while the protected refugee ceases to exist by administrative and legislative fiat.

Fallacies, Faulty Syllogisms, Non Sequiturs

Cheaters seem to have no shame when it comes to relying on fallacies[74] and non sequiturs, and they are not deterred by evident mistakes in elementary logic. The same shamelessness applies to the use of (knowingly) false factual assumptions, including the denial of obvious facts, as if a predilection for the absurd in judicial interpretation were at work here. Previous chapters have raised numerous examples that indicate how far the authorities can go in disregarding the dictates of ordinary reason, hiding behind a withered fig leaf of legality.

A company close to the Hungarian government applied for a permit to operate a temporary quarry in a nature reserve. The competent authority admitted that there should be no activity of this sort in the protected zone

---

[73] Lord Atkin (dissenting) in *Liversidge* v. *Anderson and Another* [1942] AC 207; [1941] 3 All ER 338, a case where the RoL was only formally respected, at best.

[74] "The fallacies that attract the attention of logicians are those that are faulty, but not obviously flawed – 'arguments which, although incorrect, are psychologically persuasive' or those 'that may seem to be correct, but that prove, upon examination, not to be so.'" K. W. Saunders, "Informal Fallacies in Legal Argumentation," *South Carolina Law Review*, 44 (1992–1993), p. 344, quoting I. M. Copi and C. Cohen, *Introduction to Logic* (Macmillan, 1990), p. 95.

but concluded with a fully speculative assumption that it would not cause serious harm (a consideration not mentioned in the law) and thus authorized the activity.

Other common fallacious techniques include setting impossible conditions (in violation of the RoL maxim "*ad impossibilia nemo tenetur*") and circular reasoning,[75] where each statement depends on the other to be true. The two fallacies often go hand in hand. In 2016, the PiS-controlled Polish Sejm passed the "Repair Act," which paralyzed the activities of the PCT by setting unfeasible procedural requirements (see Chapter 2). The Act was applied with immediate effect. The government claimed that the PCT should apply the procedural rules of the Act when it reviewed its very constitutionality, as the Act was already in force when the Tribunal considered it. This would have required, among other things, a special majority for finding a violation, which was not possible at the time given the way the Sejm had elected judges. The Sejm obviously knew of this impossibility it has created. "To assess the constitutionality of the Act in accordance with the rules as outlined in the Act itself – a trap likened by one legal expert to 'a snake eating its own tail.' The Tribunal responded in a ruling issued on March 9, 2016 that the object of review cannot simultaneously provide the basis for the review itself if the constitution is to retain its supremacy over statutes issued by parliament."[76]

A special form of setting impossible conditions occurs when the condition depends on the government. The Hungarian law on churches (Act CCVI of 2011) created different categories (classes) of religious organizations. One "objective" condition for admission into the most privileged category was "an agreement with the state on cooperation for the realization of collective goals." This "objective" criterion depends on the government, which can arrange, or not, such an agreement.[77]

---

[75] See also the KESMA case (below).

[76] C. Davies, "Hostile Takeover: How Law and Justice Captured Poland's Courts," Freedom House, www.freedomhouse.org/report/special-reports/hostile-takeover-how-law-and-justice-captured-poland-s-courts#_edn17.

In PCT case K 47/15, the problem with the "Repair Act" was that it was to be reviewed by the full composition, which required a quorum of thirteen judges, when only the twelve lawfully elected judges were allowed to sit. "However, since one act of law cannot be at the same time the basis and the subject of control, the Tribunal decided to adjudicate the case in the full panel existing at the moment, i.e. by twelve judges." E. Łętowska and A. Wiewiórowska Domagalska, "A 'Good' Change in the Polish Constitutional Tribunal?," *Osteuropa Recht*, 62:1 (2016), pp. 87–88. The Act was declared unconstitutional, among other reasons, for paralyzing the functioning of the PCT.

[77] See Chapter 6. Once the conditions are met, the final recognition is left to discretionary parliamentary resolution without judicial review. The law was found to be contrary to the

Consider also the case of Central European University (CEU) in
Hungary, an American university accredited in the United States. The
university operated in Budapest and was recognized by the Hungarian
Act of Higher Education as a private university (together with denominational universities). However, it was founded and funded by George
Soros, whom Fidesz government propaganda had elevated to public
enemy number one.[78] Law x x v of 2017, adopted in an urgent legislative
procedure, introduced a new operational requirement for university
certification: foreign-registered universities can operate only with an
agreement between the respective governments. The Hungarian government first claimed that an interstate agreement must be concluded with
the US federal government. This was impossible, as there is no federal
competence under the US Constitution in such educational matters.
After a period of uncertainty, the Hungarian government's representative
prepared an agreement with authorities from the State of New York, but
the Hungarian government, without explanation, never signed it. Even
assuming that a government can set ex-post, retrospective conditions, it
is easy to call the bluff: the government sets an objective condition (the
international agreement), but its fulfillment depends on the very same
government. The original condition should read: "if the government so
wishes." The snake granted himself the power to decide if there is a tail at
all.[79] CEU ceased to operate in Hungary.

Self-blinding and Falsification of Facts, Norms and Terms; Error in Inference

A statute may institutionalize cheating by excluding relevant facts from
consideration in official decision-making; a court can cheat by finding an
application or evidence inadmissible or irrelevant or by declaring a fact

HFL (6/2013 (iii. 1) AB hat. (HCC)) and the ECtHR. The unconstitutional provision has
not been changed thus far.

[78] See Opinion of Advocate General Kokott in Case C-66/18, *European Commission
v. Hungary* [2020] EU:C:2020:172. The author of this book is a CEU employee.

[79] The infringement procedure was initiated for violation of the General Agreement on
Trade in Services (GATS), the freedom to provide services as well as academic freedom.
The political attack behind the allegedly neutral rule remains invisible for law.
Interestingly, it was the Hungarian government that raised the issue of political bias: it
took the view "that the Commission brought infringement proceedings for purely political reasons, in breach of its duty of impartiality. The proceedings are, it is contended,
solely in the interests of the CEU in Budapest." Opinion of the Advocate General, para. 80.
The Advocate General believed that the infringement procedure was not about CEU, as it
concerned a general provision. See Ibid.

nonexistent with a specific (impermissible) outcome in mind.[80] When the HFL entered into force, the new law on the successor body of the Supreme Court terminated the mandate of the Vice-President of the Supreme Court. The Vice-President's mandate was defined by the Constitution: he was elected for six years. The HCC had previously adopted a position that institutional reorganization cannot justify terminating a position in a constitutional institution. Such termination, according to the HCC in its earlier incarnation, would be contrary to both the RoL and the protection of institutional autonomy. This time (i.e. during Fidesz times), the HCC found that the termination was appropriate due to important changes in the functions of the Supreme Court, including new functions of its Vice-President. To prove the importance of this change: while the Vice-President's role was mentioned only twice in the old law, it was now mentioned in relation to thirteen specific functions, mostly in the context of receiving reports from other courts. The new law also mentioned that the Vice-President was authorized to chair certain precedent-setting sessions of the Kúria. In the past, says the HCC, these functions could not have been considered, as this type of decision did not exist. (The fact is, the Supreme Court had similar adjudicatory functions.) "It cannot be ruled out that the new functions necessitate a person of different orientation." This was followed by a mysterious Freudian slip: "In view of these changes the relationship of trust is of increased importance, as expressed in the past constitutional and present statutory rules." In other words, if there is no trust, the judge cannot continue in his position. The removal of the judiciary's second in command, or the implications for judicial institutional independence, was not even mentioned, as dissenters were quick to point out.[81]

Disregarding relevant facts is common. In Hungary, the National Bank could channel its profit to private charitable foundations under the implausible theory that such profit loses its public nature when transferred to a private fund. The fund's board is appointed by the Bank as founder; practically, the money will be used for whatever "public purpose" the directors wish. All this was considered permissible because the law was silent on such use of public money (how could one foresee it?). The matter was treated as an issue of private law because the case concerned a private foundation regulated by the Civil Code. In private

---

[80] Rules of procedure (in observation of the RoL) are particularly helpful to avoid the inconvenience of taking a position in politically sensitive cases. See, for example, *Gündüz* v. *Turkey*, ECtHR, App. no. 35071/97, Judgment of 14 June 2004.

[81] 3076/2013 (III. 27) AB hat. (HCC).

law, very liberally, the prevailing principle dictates that what is not prohibited is permitted. The issue's public law origin was disregarded, and the entire case was framed in a government-friendly way by closing judicial eyes to the public law issue, namely that this was public money.[82]

Once the relevant facts were ignored, legal formalism (so dear to the heart of Max Weber because of the resulting legal rationality) turned into a travesty of rationality. Nonsensical justification via formalism is a lawyer's favorite in this game; it makes jurists feel comfortably professional, and even smart and creative, for figuring out the implausible.

Playing with Time

Time is the highest court. The passing of time perpetuates the status quo, something the clients of the law know too well, but judges and principled scholars, the people of eternal justice, tend to forget. In a judicialized world, only the executive seems to have learned that in most legal systems, legal proceedings last long enough to implement a litigated program with irreversible consequences. This is one of the self-defeating effects of the RoL, which requires the exhaustion of remedies, and limits the grounds for interim relief. Act C X X V I I of 2003 on "Excise Taxes and Special Rules for Commercial Products Subject to Excise Taxes," one of the first laws of the new Fidesz government in August 2010, exempted excise duty on 50 liters of home-distilled *pálinka* (fruit brandy), in clear violation of the applicable EU law. For a few years, the plainly illegal practice could continue, increasing the popularity and credibility of the government, at no cost other than the costs of the CJEU procedure. It took four years for the CJEU to end this practice,[83] an outcome the government considered scandalous. Viewing its 2010 law an act of liberation, the government instead continued its war for the national drink and the protection of Hungarians.[84]

---

[82] See further *Vékony* v. *Hungary*, ECtHR, App. no. 65681/13, Judgment of 13 January 2015; 3194/2014 (V I I. 15) AB hat. (HCC). In this case, tobacco sales licenses were revoked to provide the opportunity to grant new lucrative licenses for a select number of people "close" to Fidesz politicians. A similar technique was used to create a gambling casino monopoly. The HCC found the original revocation of the gaming machine licenses, a laudable measure in the fight against compulsive gambling, a public health concern. See 20/2014 (V I. 30) AB hat. (HCC).

[83] Case C-115/13, *Commission* v. *Hungary* [2014] EU:C:2014:253.

[84] "Minister Defiant After EU Court Says Hungary Must Tax Homemade Spirits," Budapest Beacon (April 12, 2014), http://www.budapestbeacon.com/minister-defiant-after-eu-court-says-hungary-must-tax-homemade-spirits.

Even where courts are willing to apply temporary injunctions against government action (e.g. in the United States), with proper twists the government can successfully execute its plans, like with the 2018 Muslim travel ban case.[85] As Professor Yoo has stated, where a president "knew that his scheme lacked legal authority, he could get away with it for the length of his presidency. And, moreover, even if courts declared the permit illegal, his successor would have to keep enforcing the program for another year or two."[86] Such acts may be contrary to the purpose of a law or the constitution (although see the broad margins of permissible constitutional disagreement); however, until they are found unconstitutional with final authority (or, to some extent, in a democratic decision), their illegality will prevail, as planned.[87]

Authorities control the timing of decisions, even where there are tight deadlines.[88] A late finding of unconstitutionality (like an acquittal after an executed death sentence) cannot reverse the social changes enabled by the unconstitutional situation – see the Hungarian judicial retirement case.

The power of delay should never be underestimated. Administrators continue with illegal practices, or fail to carry out measures in disregard of final judgments, until a situation becomes irreversible. Apex courts can allow the destruction of the constitution and constitutional order by simply delaying the day of judgment in politically sensitive cases.

In the CEU case, the HCC suspended proceedings, claiming that it had to wait for the CJEU ruling on the EU aspects of the case, although it had never before considered this a necessity, and the matter in front of the HCC concerned the domestic constitution.

[85] *Department of Homeland Security* v. *Regents of the University of California*, 591 US ___ (2020). The public statements of the President, signaling his intent, were not held relevant.

[86] J. Yoo, "How the Supreme Court's DACA Decision Harms the Constitution, the Presidency, Congress, and the Country?," *National Review* (June 22, 2020), www.natio nalreview.com/2020/06/how-the-supreme-courts-daca-decision-harms-the-constitu tion-the-presidency-congress-and-the-country.

[87] For a debate on this matter in the context of the US Deferred Action for Childhood Arrivals Act (DACA). J. Borger, "White House Calls in Torture Memo Lawyer to Explore Ruling by Decree," *The Guardian* (July 21, 2020), p. 23.

[88] *Trump* v. *Hawaii*, 585 U.S. ___ (2018) (the Muslim entry ban case). Following a restraining order, the administration convinced the court to suspend it for ninety days, citing a need to establish adequate standards to prevent infiltration by foreign terrorists. With similar, per se reasonable, requests the administration bought time and managed to prevent Muslims from the concerned countries from entering the United States.

Applying Wrong [but Convenient] Standards

The judicial reinterpretation of precedents and definitions established in judicial practice is a regular legal phenomenon that is considered legitimate as long as it follows its own rules. How constitutional courts cheat by unprincipled disregard of precedents to support the government is best explained using the example of an important Turkish judgment. Two judges of the TCC were arrested the day after the July 15, 2016 military putsch. Ordinarily, TCC judges can be arrested by a justice of the peace only in *flagrante delicto*. On July 20, 2016, the government declared a state of emergency. On this basis, Legislative Decree no. 667, published in the Official Gazette on July 23, 2016, authorized the Constitutional Court to dismiss any members who were considered to belong, be affiliated with, or be linked to terrorist organizations. On August 4, 2016, the TCC judges dismissed their fellow members. "In reaching that decision it noted, on the basis of Article 3 of Legislative Decree no. 667, that 'information from the social environment' and the 'common opinion emerging over time' among members of the Constitutional Court suggested that the applicant [the dismissed judge] had links to the organisation in question, making him no longer fit to practise."[89] Here, the TCC applied the emergency decree without discussing the constitutionality of its declaration. It is true that Article 137(2) of the Constitution states that "during the state of emergency, the Council of Ministers, meeting under the chairpersonship of the President of the Republic, may issue decree-laws on matters necessitated by the state of emergency." However, according to precedent, the TCC regularly reviewed declarations of emergency. This practice was abandoned abruptly in this case and without explanation.

What is striking is the denaturalization of the ordinary, established meaning of legal concepts (e.g. the judges' arrest disregarded the Turkish law's existing, clear definition of *flagrante delicto*, which provides the sole ground for detention).[90] Most importantly, the TCC replaced evidence with "information from the social environment" about the "illegal membership" of its fellow judges. The evidence consisted of "common opinion emerging over time": this runs clearly against the fundamental rule of evidence-based decision-making, an essential principle of the RoL.

---

[89] T.C. Anayasa Mahkemesi, 2016/6E. ve 2016/12K cited in *Alparslan Altan* v. *Turkey*, ECtHR, App. no. 12778/17, Judgment of 16 April 2019, para. 23.

[90] The ECtHR was very firm in condemning this gimmick: "the principle of legal certainty may be compromised if domestic courts introduce exceptions in their case-law which run counter to the wording of the applicable statutory provisions." *Alparslan Altan* v. *Turkey*, ECtHR, App. no. 12778/17, Judgment of 16 April 2019, para. 111.

"Common opinion" pertains to socialist and medieval legal traditions, where socialist legal consciousness, or an irrational belief in supernatural forces, determined the fate of the accused.[91]

In Hungary, in 2018, the owners of a considerable number of national media outlets "decided," all on the same day, to donate their media assets to the Central European Press and Media Foundation (KESMA), a private entity.[92] Both the donors and the board members of KESMA were government cronies.[93] KESMA became the owner of 457 media outlets, controlling 37 percent of the commercial advertising market, in addition to its already considerable holdings (which it gained from other "magnanimous donations" by Fidesz clients). In principle, such concentration is subject to review by the Competition Authority.[94] However, Article 24/A of the Competition Act[95] authorizes the government "in the public interest, in particular to preserve jobs and to assure the security of supply, [to] declare a concentration of undertakings to be of strategic importance at the national level."[96] Concentrations of strategic

---

[91] See T. Olcay, "Firing Bench-mates: The Human Rights and Rule of Law Implications of the Turkish Constitutional Court's Dismissal of Its Two Members: Decision of 4 August 2016, E. 2016/6 (Miscellaneous file), K. 2016/12," *European Constitutional Law Review*, 13:3 (2017), pp. 568–81.

[92] According to the Articles of Association of the not-for-profit foundation: "We believe that, making a joint commitment to our national and Christian values . . . we see our task as creating . . . solutions which will serve the responsible provision of information to our nation . . . our goal is to strengthen Hungarian print media and to establish structural cooperation between other media (TV, radio, online), which in the long term will assure preservation of the culture of the traditional Hungarian print media."

The idea that the future despot needs a friendly progovernment media conglomerate has a long history: already Perón created a progovernment media holding. R. D. Crassweller, *Perón and the Enigmas of Argentina* (W. W. Norton, 1987), p. 200.

[93] Note that for Heinz-Christian Strache, Vice-Chancellor of Austria, the Hungarian media practice served as an inspiration for his infamous dealings. He resigned in 2019 after a video was released where he expressed willingness to grant business advantages in exchange for positive news coverage of his far-right populist party.

[94] The concentration review would have been (at least in principle) a sensitive issue as the National Media and Infocommunications Authority earlier refused a Ringier-Springer European-level merger, until Ringier sold its stake in *Népszabadság*, Hungary's most important opposition daily, to an Austrian with good contacts with Fidesz. Six years later, the paper was shut down on the grounds that it produced loses. K. Simon and T. Rácz. "The Shutdown of Népszabadság: Orbán Comes One Step Closer to Complete Media Dominance," Heinrich-Böll-Stiftung (October 17, 2016), www.boell.de/en/2016/10/17/shutdown-nepszabadsag-orban-comes-one-step-closer-complete-media-dominance.

[95] Act LVII of 1996 on the Prohibition of Unfair and Restrictive Market Practices.

[96] The Hungarian terminology used here is "of nation-strategy interest" (nemzetstratégiai jelentőségű). Nation-strategy is a word originally referring to a strategy dealing with Hungarians outside of Hungarian territory.

importance are exempt from reporting to the Competition Authority; thus, there was no need to review the effects on media pluralism and no need to consider the opinion of the National Media and Infocommunications Authority, which is in charge of protecting media pluralism.

The HCC found that the governmental declaration of "strategic importance" was constitutional as media pluralism remains protected.[97] Article IX (2) of the HFL provides that "Hungary shall recognise and protect the freedom and diversity of the press, and shall ensure the conditions for free dissemination of information necessary for the formation of democratic public opinion." According to HCC case law (22/1999 (VI. 30) AB hat.),[98] which it quoted in this case, safeguarding external pluralism is necessary to provide impartial information. The point of departure for the Court was that this case did not concern a fundamental constitutional right, where stringent proportionality applies, as the complaint did not refer to an individual right but diversity (for all). In other words, the Court used a RoL principle, namely, to be bound by the complaint, to disregard the RoL.[99]

The HCC emphasized that petitioner opposition parties did not refer to any circumstances from which it would reasonably follow that the freedom and diversity of the press, and the conditions of free information and orientation necessary for the formation of democratic public opinion, would not be ensured in Hungary. The Court concluded that it was called upon to compare two constitutional values: on the one hand, the national interest, which requires the nation-strategy exemption, and on the other hand, media pluralism ("diversity"). On the one hand, economic interest (protection of nation-strategy interest) is elevated to a constitutional value, although the HFL does not mention public interest as such, which means that an extremely broad implicit constitutional value (which restricts other, expressed values) is created without textual reference. On the other hand, media pluralism was demoted to the rank of an ordinary constitutional value, although the HFL imposes on the state certain duties to protect a particular fundamental right.

The problem was that the HCC had to find a public interest that can be confronted with the principle of pluralism and related rights justifying the restriction. Where no constitutional value can be found, it will be

---

[97] 11/313/2019 AB hat. (June 23, 2020).

[98] However, the quoted HCC judgments pertained to broadcasting and not printed press.

[99] However, the case law allows consideration of issues directly related to the petition.

invented. The government decree provided a nice example of circularity in its justification of the exemption as being in the public interest. The decree simply declared "the concentration to be of nation-strategy interest in the public interest." The Court considered the nation-strategy exemption to be an act of economic policy, where the government has broad discretion that is not subject to constitutional review, as it is rather a matter of political accountability. Nevertheless, "There can be reasonable grounds, related to the specificities of the media market that in a given market segment a more concentrated media activity is occurring." In this case, "Concentration is [must have been] the public interest." Where the government finds a public interest, there must be one; and if the government refers to public interest, that means that "it has reasons" (sic, para. 63). This follows from the standard canon of interpretation: in the interpretation of norms, it shall be assumed that the norms (i.e. the government providing the norm) serve "a purpose that corresponds to common sense and the public good, are moral and economic [sic]."[100] This is crucial: this fundamental assumption keeps the legal house of cards in place. This is how RoL assumptions destroy the RoL.

For the HCC, there is public interest in "concentration" (an illicit situation in other circumstances) and media pluralism is not endangered, although, according to the HCC, the Media Authority could not exercise its powers. Not a problem: The Court, relying on circular reasoning, found that there are "other" means to protect pluralism, like constitutional review. For the Court, the elimination of control by the body that is called upon to "safeguard" pluralism does not "directly" affect "the fundamental right." (Here suddenly a fundamental right appears.[101]) Without further explanation, the Court concludes that the subjective aspect of the right is not affected either. Of course, as the Court admits, where a single entity controls at least one-third of the printed press, and an overwhelming majority of the local press, the fundamental right to receive information is restricted. Again, this is not a problem, as the core of the issue, namely that the KESMA foundation is de facto controlled by the government and the ruling party, is deliberately left out of the analysis, although the Court itself quoted its own case law (22/1999 AB hat.) in that direction. By construing the case as one of balancing two competing constitutional values, and closing its eyes to the

---

[100] This is perfectly acceptable under the traditional English reasonableness test, except that it would not leave out the consideration of rights.

[101] Media pluralism is often considered to be only an "objective of constitutional value." See 86–210 DC du 29 juillet 1986, French Constitutional Council. The French Constitution of 1958 is silent on the matter.

consequences, the HCC applied the wrong standard in a cheating manner. There is freedom of expression for all, but voice is left only to the government. This is somehow reminiscent of the universal freedom of the press that the Bolsheviks granted in 1918, except that newsprint was available only to the communist propaganda papers.

Inventing Competence and Applying Nonexistent Law

It is a fundamental assumption of the *Rechtsstaat* that authorities act according to accessible laws, especially where official conduct affects citizens. The illiberal state pretends to satisfy *Rechtsstaat* conditions by concocting pseudo-grounds for state action in a tricky manner. If this is insufficient, the authorities are ready for outright falsification, including shameless denial of existing legal and moral norms, or the occurrence of a specific event and the invention of an alternative legal reality.

Norms are not only denied: they can be invented to serve political power (e.g. to create competence). The Hungarian government invented the institution of national consultation (e.g. surveys on specific questions sent to all households) to prove the popular legitimacy of various planned measures and policies. This institution is unknown in statute books, and there is no rule governing such expensive manipulation of public opinion. True, the responses do not have legally binding consequences. In Russia, an all-Russian vote was invented for approval of the 2020 constitutional amendments. Article 135 of the Russian Constitution knows no such institution. In consequence, the standard rules of referendum do not apply, including those that would otherwise require public discussion (access to media), while government propaganda is considered mere information.

In the 2015 PCT appointments saga, following the election of judges by the outgoing Sejm, the President (elected on the PiS ticket) refused to make himself available for their swearing-in (claiming himself the power to determine who is and is not a properly elected judge). Because they had not taken the oath, the PiS majority claimed that the elected judges could not be considered judges, inventing a convenient rule.

Manipulating the Rules During Decision-Making in Favor of the Decision Maker

In 2012, the Romanian Parliament initiated the impeachment of an increasingly unpopular President.[102] In order to block all possible

---

[102] To enact legislation that changes the outcome of a pending case (in particular, where one of the parties is the state) is considered a violation of the RoL and the separation of

institutions that could have hindered this effort, it replaced the Ombudsperson (the only authority who could challenge ex ante Parliament acts) as well as the Speakers of the two Houses (who would have served, one after the other, as President *pro tempore* should the President be removed).

As Vlad Perju stated in this context, the Romanian Parliament made "a mockery of the dignity of legislation when short-circuiting processes of deliberation in Parliament; when immunizing Executive Ordinances via the takeover of the Ombudsman's office; by establishing ready-to-use extra-constitutionalism mechanisms, such as Executive Ordinances that mirrored the substance of statutes pending before the Constitutional Court, in order to bypass the decisions of the Court."[103] The President asked his supporters to boycott the referendum. It was very likely that these deliberate abstentions, together with those who never vote, would have prevented his dismissal, because the referendum would have failed to reach the necessary quorum (participation of 50 percent of the electorate). Therefore, the day before the Romanian Parliament called for the President's dismissal, the Referendum Act was amended,[104] abolishing the threshold rule. The Parliament set a twenty-four-hour deadline for a Constitutional Court advisory opinion on the meaning of the constitutional provision ("grave act against the constitution") that was used as the legal basis for the impeachment. Departing from some its precedents, the Court rendered a contradictory decision within twenty-four hours. However, while the decision found the impeachment initiative highly problematic constitutionally, it failed to state that the referendum was unconstitutional operationally. The referendum was thus held, and the majority voted against the President. In the meantime, the Constitutional Court, sensing European pressure, changed its course midway, and in

---

powers (interference into judicial independence). *Stran Greek Refineries and Stratis Andreadis v. Greece*, ECtHR, App. no. 13427/87, Judgment of 9 December 1994. The RoL was violated, even if "in the instant case the appearances of justice were preserved." Para. 49.

[103] V. Perju, "The Romanian Double Executive and the 2012 Constitutional Crisis," *International Journal of Constitutional Law*, 13:1 (2015), p. 270. "The judges found that the resolutions subject to judicial review are 'individual,' rather than 'normative,' acts and, as such, fall outside their powers of review." Ibid., p. 266.

[104] Likewise, in Poland, the modalities of the electoral law were changed amidst preparations for an imminent presidential election. The COVID-19 crisis resulted in a fictitious "election": the modalities were changed, and the Sejm deliberately created a situation where no one could cast a vote. The modalities of the new law, applicable to the postponed vote, favored the incumbent.

clear violation of its earlier case law, declared that the Constitution requires a double majority in the referendum (which was not achieved). Under EU pressure, the Prime Minister decided not to openly challenge the Constitutional Court and the President was reinstated.[105]

Judgments without Bite

Constitutional and other courts may find that a violation has occurred without providing a proper remedy. Bark without bite was the strategy of the HCC majority before its total overhaul: at times it found that an unconstitutional rule remains applicable in pending cases, as in the dismissal without cause of civil servants.[106] In other instances it failed to determine the proper remedy to be applied in the law that Parliament enacted (see judicial retirement case; likewise the CJEU in the same case).

Purely Formal Execution of Judgments

In 1988, four dissidents were detained under Singapore's Internal Security Act; when the country's highest court ruled that the government failed to follow statutory procedures and that the dissidents must be released, the ruling was obeyed. However, once released, they were immediately rearrested. "This time, however, the government followed the statutory procedures to the letter."[107] Likewise in 2020, Osman Kavala, a Turkish human rights activist, was rearrested upon his release, after the ECtHR declared his detention contrary to the ECHR.[108] Such behavior is called "symbolic and creative compliance." This may "occur when an addressee pretends to align its behavior with the prescribed rule or changes its behavior in superficial ways that leave the addressee's

---

[105] One argument in the debate was that an Opinion of the Venice Commission claimed that referendum quorum is against the RoL. Of the votes cast, 85 percent were for dismissal.

[106] The HCC was acting lawfully, and in compliance with the RoL, as the law granted it the discretionary power to maintain unconstitutional norms in force for the sake of legal certainty. (This is another paradoxical contradiction of the RoL.) Similar rules exist in Germany, and SCOTUS found (in the DACA case, precisely as this is being written) that an illegal rule cannot be simply rescinded without the procedural guarantees of administrative procedure. *Department of Homeland Security* v. *Regents of the University of California*, 591 US ___ (2020).

[107] G. Silverstein, "Singapore's Constitutionalism: A Model, But of What Sort?," *Cornell Law Review*, 100 (2015), p. 15.

[108] In the 2004 Belmarsh case, the House of Lords declared that the indefinite detention of suspected terrorists without trial is contrary to the ECHR. *A* v. *Secretary of State for the Home Department (No 2)* [2005] UKHL 71. The suspects were subjected to renewed detention on different legal grounds. See also the execution of the CJEU judgment in the Hungarian judicial retirement case (Chapter 2).

original objective intact. [I]n the former the addressee puts legislative change in the books which, however, is never put into action, while in the latter the addressee accepts measures that, in their totality, render enforcement action inconsequential."[109]

In the world of legal cheating, the formal execution of a judgment may amount to blunt nonexecution; the government will be shamelessly disrespectful in order to send a message to the public that it does not care about the visibility of its lawlessness. The message is that it can afford the calling of its bluff. In other instances, it continues to play "catch me if you can" to demonstrate to its supporters that it doesn't forsake its promises to restore justice even in face of judicial resistance.[110]

Of course, once cheating in execution and implementation remains unpunished and thus normalized, governments will feel encouraged to go (even) further. In 2020, the Hungarian Parliament suspended the enforcement of judicial awards to prisoners who had suffered inhuman treatment due to prison overcrowding.[111] The reason given for legislative intervention in the execution of these judgments was that the awards solely support agents of George Soros and the lawyers who benefit from the "prison business." Around the same time, directly challenging the CJEU, the Polish Disciplinary Chamber of the Supreme Court continued disciplinary proceedings against certain judges, notwithstanding the findings of the Supreme Court and the CJEU that the Chamber was not properly constituted.[112]

Inventing Alternative Theories of Interpretation

In many instances, disregarding precedents and elementary rules of evidence is insufficient to coat government goals with a glaze of legality. Where the unconstitutionality of an act is uncontestable in light of

---

[109] A. Batory, "Defying the Commission: Creative Compliance and Respect for the Rule of Law in the EU," *Public Administration*, 94:3 (2016), p. 689.

[110] In the 98 percent severance tax case (see Chapter 2), notwithstanding the judgments of the HCC and ECtHR, the Hungarian Parliament continued to reenact the tax (reducing it to 75 percent). It was abolished only in 2018, exempting the outgoing ministers of Fidesz, who lost their portfolios in government reshuffling.

[111] The compensation scheme was based on a recently approved Act of Parliament that was adopted to execute the ECtHR judgments.

[112] The PCT Disciplinary Chamber disregarded the injunction but continued to play in accordance with the rules; it did not waive the immunity of the judge charged, providing another example of dancing around the RoL. A beneficial reading of the event is that the Chamber acted in accordance with the RoL but within the wrong constitutional frame. A. Rettman, "Poland 'crossed rubicon' against EU court injunction," EUobserver (June 10, 2020), www.euobserver.com/justice/148609.

precedents, courts may develop alternative constitutional theories. Because the National Assembly under the impulsive Chávez often had to enact laws that were obviously contrary to the letter of the Bolivarian Constitution, the Venezuelan TSJ had to be creative in order to uphold them. In some cases, it relied on a populist concept of popular power, an idea the Bolivarian Constitution actually endorsed. This theory may not provide sufficient grounds to reinterpret the text of the Constitution, but it can be a popularly convincing justification for disregarding the otherwise applicable specific constitutional provisions. The reference to people's power was not an outlandish, irrelevant, or bogus theory, even if disregarding the constitution in the name of the people is hardly compatible with constitutionalism. Applying standard interpretations and alternative constitutional values to nonstandard conclusions can legitimize different constitutional meanings.[113]

The Bolivarian Constitution (Article 67) states that "the financing of political associations with Government funds will not be allowed." In 2007 Chávez attempted, unsuccessfully, to rewrite this provision via referendum, providing an exception for the public funding of parties. After the referendum's failure, the TSJ daringly ruled that the government may finance "electoral activities."[114] It claimed that the prohibition applies to internal expenses but not campaign expenditures during electoral periods. This interpretation runs contrary to a strict (nonstructural) reading of Article 67. However, one could argue, as the TSJ did, that the solution follows from the *"reserva legal,"* as "the Constitution requires legislation to regulate elections and this applies in the context of political pluralism as an essential element of the rational participative democracy."[115] The Court considered public financing of electoral campaigns necessary to avoid excessive private influence, in accordance with the prevailing view in Europe (quoted extensively in the decision). Outside of its context, the TSJ position does not represent constitutional

---

[113] Constructivist international relations scholars, at least, find that norm contestation is not "normatively undesirable." J. Wolff and L. Zimmermann, "Between Banyans and Battle Scenes: Liberal Norms, Contestation, and the Limits of Critique," *Review of International Studies*, 42:03 (2016), p. 515; A. Wiener, *Contestation and Constitution of Norms in Global International Relations* (Cambridge University Press, 2018). Radical constitutional reinterpretation favoring governmental activities hardly represents desirable norm contestation: the plausible (mostly pre-existing) interpretation is simply disregarded and left unrefuted in the service of power perpetuation.

[114] Decision No. 780 (May 8, 2008).

[115] Quoted in A. R. Brewer-Carías, "El Juez Constitucional Como Constituyente : El Case Del Financiamento de las Campanas Electorales Partidos Politicos en Venezuela," *Revista De Derecho Publico de Venezuela*, 117 (2009), p. 115.

usurpation. However, once the context forms part of the interpretation, what seemed defensible in democratic theory, becomes politically motivated cheating, intended to support the presidential party in elections. (Of course, the judgment emphasized that public campaign funding cannot be partisan...)[116]

8.3.2 Cheating as a System

Legal cheating is not a PLD specialty. It exists in liberal democracies as well, but in illiberal democracies, the entire constitutional and legal system is increasingly and deliberately deceptive, and the mechanisms of correction cannot suitably address the problem – or cease to exist. The trick of the regime is exactly this: it relies on the inherent contradictions and shortcomings of the RoL, or alternatively, as in Latin American PLDs, employs an alternative constitutional reference. The claim is that genuine popular power enables unorthodox solutions for the greater good of the real people.

European PLDs import authoritarian leftovers in a strategic, mala fide, way from Western democracies that are "beyond-criticism." They rely on "the fallacy of composition," which assumes "that if the components of an aggregate... have a certain property, the aggregate... must also have that property."[117] True, there survive too many authoritarian leftovers in constitutional democracies that do not undermine democracy in their original country, but in the collection of illiberal democracies, the cumulative effect becomes lethal to constitutional democracy. "Each step, legal in itself, might undermine liberal democracy a little bit more."[118] Difference of degree turns into difference of kind. The result is the Frankenstate,[119] an entire system of illiberal fakes. However, this is not ordinary arbitrariness, which would deprive the regime of the blessings of

---

[116] The procedural history of the case supports the above conclusion: the case originated in an abstract interpretation request presented by two parties associated with Chávez following the unsuccessful referendum.

[117] A. Vermeule, *The System of the Constitution* (Oxford University Press, 2011), p. 9.

[118] D. A. Strauss, "Law and the Slow-Motion Emergency," in C. R. Sunstein (ed.), *Can it Happen Here?: Authoritarianism in America* (Harper Collins, 2018), pp. 365–66; Tushnet, "Authoritarian Constitutionalism," pp. 409–10; R. Uitz, "Can You Tell When an Illiberal Democracy is in the Making? An Appeal to Comparative Constitutional Law Scholarship From Hungary," *International Journal of Constitutional Law*, 13:1 (2015), pp. 279–300.

[119] K. L. Scheppele, "The Rule of Law and the Frankenstate: Why Governance Checklists Do Not Work," *Governance*, 26:4 (2013), pp. 559–62.

the RoL; such cheating is not the illiberal unconstitutionality described in Fraenkel's *Dual State*, where the "law as applied has no relation to the stated law."[120]

Increasingly, democracies are led by leaders who think that the law exists only to be circumvented.[121] Democratic governments tend to replace accountability with the semblance of responsive government, turning spin doctors into key players in communications, where governance is replaced with rhetoric about governing. Spin-doctored democracy has reached new levels of fraud in illiberal democracies. In these regimes, too many government actions, including laws, are merely spin operations. The spin pretends that the government actions are "normal in a constitutional democracy" and/or conform with international law. Government actions regularly depart from their declared, constitutionally or even morally acceptable, goals. But note: the admitted, articulated goals do not differ from what is acceptable in any constitutional democracy. In the currently prevailing deferentialism (aka legal defeatism), the standard assumption is that the purpose of the law must be taken at face value and the people's choice is correct (as there is no higher standard).

Constitutional cheaters refer to constitutional purposes and intent, which disguises impermissible goals, effects, or means. This relates, at least partly, to the desire to look "constitutional," or RoL observant. The domestic and international public has little interest in doubting the authoritative statements of the law and its servants or is too shortsighted to do so. After all, what can one object to regarding illiberal democracies? In matters of restricting rights, liberal constitutions solely require a sufficiently weighty public interest, and what the RoL requires is that the public administration be properly authorized to act. One cannot expect the judiciary to undo the illiberal regime's web of cheating, even if the judiciary was not handpicked and trained to be subservient to the regime. Judicial deferentialism and legal complicity (together with complicity in business and public morality) hide the regime's fundamental secret, namely that the measure serves private political interests, although the disguise of its real intentions, the respect for formalities, is often shamelessly superficial.

The success of the "patent legal falsity" of illiberal regimes originates in "willful ignorance."[122] The contemporary problem is that democracies

---

[120] M. Tushnet, "The Possibility of Illiberal Constitutionalism," *Florida Law Review*, 69:6 (2017), p. 1773.

[121] President Duterte, known for his open contempt of the law, is somewhat exceptional.

[122] As demonstrated by Justice Harlan in *Plessy* v. *Ferguson*, 163 US 537 (1896) at 557 (dissenting).

operate in a world of heightened manipulation (fake news) that makes it less likely that cheating in law will be unmasked. Even if it is, there are no legal consequences. Intellectual and moral revisionism makes legal (and underlying political) cheating hardly a matter of outrage. Cheating is not even a matter of concern: it is beyond the radar, increasingly unnoticed. So it goes. A lack of constitutional honesty and morality matters little in a cynical world, which questions the very possibility of truth, and moral truth in particular, and where being economical with the truth is a sign of power. Where politicians of a mature democracy can shamelessly and publicly claim that electoral districting is about maximizing seats for the party, irrespective of actual majorities and equal voting power (as in North Carolina, without any legal action by SCOTUS), one can hardly claim any sense in value-based standards. Where there are no standards, there can be no cheating, no moral violation. In fact, the rules of the game are changing: in order to have four aces at all times, everyone in power will try to keep four extra aces up their sleeves. They still claim to play poker, but this is not *that* game, if a game at all.

8.4 The Consequences of Cheating

The constitutional regime of illiberal democracy is a regime of cheating. At times close to the inventiveness of Orwell, it calls itself a constitutional system of checks and balances, where in reality separation of powers serves only one-man rule. Law speaks of democracy and the people but caters to plebiscitarian leaders, with massive and constant manipulation and exploitation of state resources. It promises equality but provides privileges to a coterie of loyalist clients around the leader. It claims to respect freedom of expression, and refrains from punishing those who insult the government, but the remaining critical voices will not be heard in the noise of government brainwashing machines spreading propaganda "in the service of the nation and its authentic people."

In many respects, the illiberal regime reached near perfection via counterfeit. Legal cheating is hardly identifiable with the ordinary means of law (at least in the hands of domesticated lawyers and judges). Counterfeiters can proudly sell their products as legal. But they are modest. This is one reason for their success. "The very ideological use

---

Duncan Kennedy doubts that the patent legal falsity "must be product of bad faith." Kennedy, *Authoritarian Constitutionalism*, p. 163.

of law involved not cheating *all* of the people *all* of the time, for the ideology must be believed, and 'the essential condition for the effectiveness of law, in its function as ideology, is that it should [. . .] actually seem to be just.'"[123] Illiberal democracy knows how to behave itself, and contrary to communism or even contemporary Russia, it cheats only to the extent necessary. Formally, citizen rights are visibly respected, at least to a sufficient extent. This is how the consequences of constitutional chicanery differ from the minimalist legalism of authoritarian or totalitarian rule.

Law remains *the* prevailing language of power[124] (even if a *vulgata*), and the RoL serves as the reference point in the discourse on power. Nationalism and identitarianism are key to public mobilization, and provide a *source* of plebiscitarian support for power, but the rulers of illiberal democracies insist on legal legitimacy (perhaps they have more control over obedient law than over capricious multitudes).

A system based on cheating and lies can be efficient for the survival of the regime but at considerable price:[125] "why would you not try to evade taxation since the fiscal authorities will most likely not punish your evasion; or not make a practice of fraudulently collecting a pension; or not even decide to illegally build

---

[123] M. Krygier, "The Rule of Law and State Legitimacy," in W. Sadurski, M. Sevel and K. Walton (eds.), *Legitimacy: The State and Beyond* (Oxford University Press, 2019), p. 118. The internal quote comes from E. P. A. Thompson, *Whigs and Hunters: The Origins of the Black Act* (Pantheon Books, 1975). In a part omitted from the quote, Thompson requires one additional thing: the law "should display an independence from gross manipulation." This element is the least satisfied in illiberal democracies, but the standard is *display*, and not an actual lack of manipulation, a sort of cheating. Once again, this is constitutional chicanery, which is difficult to capture in RoL terms. See A. Sajó and R. Uitz, *The Constitution of Freedom* (Oxford University Press, 2017), p. 4.

[124] In political propaganda nationalism and a specific understanding of the public interest (the idea of "good change" in PiS propaganda) prevail. "These words of good change have infected our everyday language and our thinking . . . . It is easier than the language of democracy. It has made us lazy: instead of providing us with information and then making us judge this information, it provides us with information that has already been judged." Michal Rusinek, interview in C. Turp-Balazs, "Doubleplusungood: How the language of 'good change' is taking over Poland," Emerging Europe, www.emerging-europe.com/after-hours/doubleplusungood-how-the-language-of-good-change-is-taking-over-poland.

[125] The centralized power is capable of countering some of the inefficiencies. The Hungarian tax authorities introduced online invoicing, and the VAT gap has continuously declined. *Study and Reports on the VAT Gap in the EU-28 Member States: 2018 Final Report*, Center for Social and Economic Research [Warsaw] and Institute for Advanced Studies [IEB] (September 11, 2018), p. 39.

a home on public land in the knowledge that the government will eventually legalize it for a small fee."[126] What Hale (quoted above) noted with respect to Russia applies to most illiberal regimes (Singapore excepted): where official cheating is the norm rather than the rare exception, it will be accepted even if people abhor corruption. "And when they expect virtually everyone to practice corruption and nepotism and believe that they cannot rely on others to obey or enforce the law, then they face very strong incentives to engage in the very same practices themselves if they want to get anything done – even good things."[127] In Hungary, cheating is tolerated socially, as being "ingenious."[128] Such tolerance enjoys a long tradition in Hungary as well as in a number of other less robust democracies. Historically, in order to survive in an oppressive regime, norm-breaking was essential; the hero of folktales was a smart, dirt-poor country boy who won over the local lord with tricks and cheating. In Hungary, "trickiness" is a sign of cleverness. It is accepted as a norm, part of the survival strategy of ordinary citizens.

The morality (or better: lack thereof) of officials will become that of subjects. Moreover, there is a generalized loss of trust both in authorities and in fellow citizens.[129] Faith in the possibilities for rational discourse disappears in the fake contrast between friend and enemy. This means the end of substantive democracy, as there is no democracy without reason-based deliberation. This is what regimes of usurpation achieve: the authorities will "have to strive to banish all logic from the spirit" of citizens. "All words would lose their meaning."[130]

Public morality, like that of the officials, will become cynical, although the regime will flourish in the hypocrisy it enforces through its institutions: "this hypocrisy will prove still more corrupting since no-one will believe in it. It is not only when they confuse and deceive people that the

---

[126] T. S. Pappas, *Populism and Liberal Democracy: A Comparative and Theoretical Analysis* (Oxford University Press, 2019), p. 206.

[127] H. E. Hale, "Russian Patronal Politics Beyond Putin," *Daedalus* 146:2 (2017), p. 35.

[128] According to a 2019 Eurobarometer survey, corruption is accepted in Hungary more than in any other EU member state, though 80 percent consider that high-level corruption is not pursued sufficiently. Polish people remain far more sensitive to corruption. *Special Eurobarometar 502, "Corruption" Report*, European Union (2020).

[129] Sadurski attributes this loss of trust to the destruction of civilized discourse by populism. W. Sadurski, *Poland's Constitutional Breakdown* (Oxford University Press, 2019), p. 7.

[130] Constant, *Political Writings*, p. 66.

lies of authority are harmful: they are no less so when they do not deceive them in the least."[131]

Unsurprisingly, ruling by cheating is socially accepted in PLD. On the road to despotism, Hannah Arendt warns, "totalitarian movements conjure up a lying world of consistency which is more adequate to the needs of the human mind than reality itself; in which, through sheer imagination, uprooted masses can feel at home and are spared the never-ending shocks which real life and real experiences deal to human beings and their expectations."[132]

A political system based on an intermingling of lies, deceit, and misrepresentation cannot be authentic, but paradoxically, it is the inauthenticity, the respect of law and democracy in their breach, that renders it efficient in the sense of stability. The institutions fall in line first, but after a while, a growing number of citizens accept the lies and become accomplices[133] of the regime; some of them cynical, others enthusiastic. Even if the cheating is obvious, and the statements of the government or the decisions of the authorities are fake (e.g. regarding the legality of a procurement that results inevitably in the victory of the same people), public reaction may not change.[134] The logic of illiberalism and the attachment to cheating will drive even unwilling leaders to be less and less modest in their autocracy, and yet the same minority will keep the leader in power democratically, even after he became despotic.

Despotism exists by the verdict of our souls and by the consent of the citizens who accept it as their own regime and love it as their mirror image. A selective, blurred and segmented despotism is still only despotism.

---

[131] Ibid.

[132] H. Arendt, *The Origins of Totalitarianism* (Houghton Mifflin, 1994), pp. 352–53.

[133] In the imaginary community "the members of the audience are turned into accomplices of the regime." G. Frankenberg, "Authoritarian Constitutionalism: Coming to Terms with Modernity's Nightmares" in García and Frankenberg, *Authoritarian Constitutionalism*, p. 25.

[134] Even if people acknowledge that the information is incorrect, their feelings toward the source of the misinformation can remain unchanged. B. Swire-Thompson, U. K. H. Ecker, S. Lewandowsky, and A. J. Berinsky, "They Might Be a Liar But They're My Liar: Source Evaluation and the Prevalence of Misinformation," *Political Psychology*, 41:1 (2020), pp. 21–34.; B. Nyhan, E. Porter, J Reifleret, et al., "Taking Fact-Checks Literally but not Seriously? The Effects of Journalistic Fact-Checking on Factual Beliefs and Candidate Favorability," *Political Behavior*, 42 (2019), pp. 939–60.

Where tyranny exists
that tyranny exists
not only in the barrel of the gun
not only in the cells of a prison

. . . .

in tyranny's domain
you are the link in the chain,
you stink of him through and through,
the tyranny IS you . . .[135]

---

[135] G. Illyés, "A Sentence About Tyranny," trans. G. Szirtes, in G. Gömöri and G. Szirtes (eds.), *The Colonnade of Teeth: Modern Hungarian Poetry* (Bloodaxe, 1996), pp. 31–36.

INDEX

Printed in the USA
CPSIA information can be obtained
at www.ICGtesting.com
LVHW021222221023
761808LV00004B/594